Exploring Omnichannel Retailing

Wojciech Piotrowicz • Richard Cuthbertson
Editors

Exploring Omnichannel Retailing

Common Expectations and Diverse Realities

 Springer

Editors
Wojciech Piotrowicz
Supply Chain Management and Social
Responsibility, Department of Marketing
Hanken School of Economics
Helsinki, Finland

Oxford Institute of Retail Management
Saïd Business School, University of
Oxford
Oxford, UK

Richard Cuthbertson
Oxford Institute of Retail Management
Saïd Business School, University of Oxford
Oxford, UK

ISBN 978-3-319-98272-4   ISBN 978-3-319-98273-1   (eBook)
https://doi.org/10.1007/978-3-319-98273-1

Library of Congress Control Number: 2018961137

This Springer imprint is published by the registered company Springer Nature Switzerland AG
The registered company address is: Gewerbestrasse 11, 6330 Cham, Switzerland

Preface

This book considers the current state of omnichannel development in retailing from a range of perspectives, markets, and sectors. The coverage reflects the diversity of retailing. Markets covered include Finland, India, Italy, Malaysia, Poland, Turkey, the UK, and the USA, with sectors from grocery to fashion to pharmaceuticals. The chapters discuss strategic issues, such as strategy implementation and channel integration, as well as operational and technological issues, such as product delivery and mobile apps. Such diverse realities suggest different approaches to omnichannel development, with different resulting solutions, and yet there are many common expectations. Consumers, retailers, and suppliers all over the world expect online markets to be fully integrated with physical channels, with faster delivery and higher service levels than ever before. The challenge of meeting such expectations is huge—hence the need for this book.

This book resulted from discussions at the annual Oxford Institute of Retail Management conference at the University of Oxford.

Following a general introduction to omnichannel development, we have deliberately allowed the contributing chapters to cover a broad range of subjects to reflect the wide disruptive impact of these new developments. Moreover, each contributing chapter has focused in depth on a few topics of interest. These diverse perspectives are then all brought together in the final chapter, which analyses the common expectations, synthesises the diverse realities, and so leads to the creation of a framework that practitioners may use in their decision-making today and academics in their future research.

Many thanks to all of those who have contributed to make this happen.

Helsinki, Finland
Oxford, UK
June 2018

Wojciech Piotrowicz
Richard Cuthbertson

Contents

Editors and Contributors

About the Editors

Wojciech Piotrowicz (PhD Brunel, MA Gdańsk, PGDipLATHE Oxon) is Associate Professor in Sustainable Supply Chains and Social Responsibility at Hanken School of Economics and HUMLOG Institute, Helsinki, Finland. In addition, he was elected as International Research Fellow at the University of Oxford, Saïd Business School and is a member of the Wolfson College. His research is related to information systems, logistics, supply chain management, performance measurement, and evaluation, with a focus on transitional countries and retail contexts. Wojciech has considerable experience as member of large international research projects within both the public and private sectors, working with organizations such as Intel, BAE Systems, the European Commission, and Polish government. He is recipient of Outstanding and Highly Commended paper awards from Emerald Literati Network for Excellence.

Richard Cuthbertson is a Senior Research Fellow and Research Director at the Oxford Institute of Retail Management at Saïd Business School, University of Oxford and *Vice-Principal of Green Templeton College, University of Oxford*. His research interest lies in understanding and assessing the challenges of the increasingly digital world on retail, particularly through technology innovation and the use of customer data. His work is international in scope, in particular looking at how retail practice and policy are developing in countries like India and China, and he regularly acts as a consultant to retailers and governments. He is author of over 100 published articles and has worked with many companies, including Tesco, Sainsbury's, P&G, Casino, T-Mobile, BP, Abbey, IBM, KPMG, and BCG. Richard is a Board Member of the Charity Retail Association. He was awarded the Emerald Literati Network Award for Excellence (twice) and the Pegasus Prize for eBusiness Future Insights (2006).

Contributors

Sutapa Aditya Long Island University, New York, NY, USA

Shahriar Akter University of Wollongong, Wollongong, NSW, Australia

Bethan Alexander Fashion Business School, London College of Fashion, University of the Arts, London, UK

Mohua Banerjee International Management Institute Kolkata, Kolkata, West Bengal, India

Francesca Bonetti School of Materials, University of Manchester, Manchester, UK

Marta Blazquez Cano School of Materials, University of Manchester, Manchester, UK

Lanlan Cao NEOMA Business School, Mont-Saint-Aignan, France

Richard Cuthbertson Oxford Institute of Retail Management, Saïd Business School, University of Oxford, Oxford, UK

Ida D'Attoma Department of Statistical Sciences, University of Bologna, Bologna, Italy

Juan Carlos Gázquez-Abad Faculty of Business and Economics, Department of Economics and Business, Agrifood Campus of International Excellence ceiA3, University of Almería, Almería, Spain

Işık Özge Yumurtacı Hüseyinoğlu Department of Logistics Management, Faculty of Business, Izmir University of Economics, Izmir, Turkey

Muhammad Ismail Hossain University of Dhaka, Dhaka, Bangladesh

Husnayati Hussin Faculty of Information and Communications Technology, International Islamic University Malaysia, Selangor, Malaysia

Marco Ieva Department of Economics and Management, University of Parma, Parma, Italy

Erne Suzila Kassim Faculty of Business Management, Centre for Applied Management Studies, Universiti Teknologi MARA, Shah Alam, Malaysia

Uraiporn Kattiyapornpong University of Wollongong, Wollongong, NSW, Australia

Anthony Kent Nottingham Trent University, Nottingham, UK

Steven Lu University of Sydney, Camperdown, NSW, Australia

Patsy Perry School of Materials, University of Manchester, Manchester, UK

Jana Pieriegud Department of Transport, Warsaw School of Economics, Warsaw, Poland

Wojciech Piotrowicz Supply Chain Management and Social Responsibility, Department of Marketing, Hanken School of Economics, Helsinki, Finland

Oxford Institute of Retail Management, Saïd Business School, University of Oxford, Oxford, UK

Olli Rusanen Department of Marketing, School of Business, Aalto University, Aalto, Finland

Tasnim M. Taufique Hossain University of Wollongong, Wollongong, NSW, Australia

Cristina Ziliani Department of Economics and Management, University of Parma, Parma, Italy

List of Abbreviations

APAC	Asia Pacific (region)
App	(Mobile) Application
AR	Augmented reality
B2B	Business to business
B2C	Business to consumer
BLE	Bluetooth low energy
BRIC	Brazil, Russia, India, China
C2C	Customer to customer
CA	Cluster analysis
CAGR	Compound annual growth rate
CEO	Chief executive officer
CnC	Click and collect
CRM	Customer relationship management
DBMS	Database management system
DTP	Direct to pharmacy
E-Commerce	Electronic commerce
EU	European Union
FC	Fulfilment centre
FB	Facebook
FDI	Foreign direct investments
FMCG	Fast moving consumer goods
GM	General merchandise
GMV	Gross merchandise value
GPS	Global Positioning System
GTIN	Global Trade Item Number
ICR	Interactive voice response
ICT	Information and communications technology
ID	Identity document
IG	Instagram
IP	Intellectual property
IIT	Interactivity technology

IT	Information technology, information technologies
LED	Light-emitting diode
MCA	Multi-correspondence analysis
m-Commerce	Mobile commerce
MMS	Multimedia message
mPOS	Mobile point of sale
NCR	National Capital Region (in India)
NFC	Near field communication
NGO	Non-governmental organisations
OCR	Omnichannel retailing
OTC	Over the counter (medicines)
PC	Personal computer
PESTEL	Political, Economic, Social, Technological, Environmental, Legal
POM	Prescription-only medicines
POS	Point of sale
PSA	Personal shopping assistant (device)
RBV	Resource-based view
R&D	Research and development
RFID	Radio-frequency identification
ROI	Return on investment
RQ	Research question
SA	Subgroup analysis
SCA	Sustainable competitive advantage
SERVQUAL	Service quality (model)
SKU	Stock Keeping Units
SM	Social media
SMS	Short text message
SNS	Social networking sites
SWOT	Strengths, weaknesses, opportunities, and threats
TAM	Technology acceptance model
TPB	Theory of planned behaviour
UK	United Kingdom
URL	Uniform Resource Locator
US	United States of America
USD	US Dollar
VR	Virtual reality
VRIN	Valuable, rare, inimitable, and non-substitutable (resources)
WAP	Wireless application protocol

Exploring Omnichannel Retailing: Common Expectations and Diverse Reality

Wojciech Piotrowicz and Richard Cuthbertson

Abstract This introductory chapter provides a brief overview of the current academic literature focused on omnichannel retailing. However, its main purpose is to introduce the chapters included in this book. This book includes, in addition to the introduction, eleven chapters. Chapter coverage reflects the diversity of retailing, with papers from Europe, North America, and Asia. Different retail sectors and product groups are analysed, including fashion, grocery, and pharmaceuticals. The chapters consider top-level, strategic issues, such as strategy implementation and channel integration, as well as operational and technological aspects, such as the use of mobile phones in store and channel fulfilment. Such a variety highlights that we can expect the creation of many different models and solutions rather than one model of omnichannel retailing, all based on the use of technology and channel integration, but adjusted to a specific country, culture, market place, customer segment, and/or product characteristics. This chapter maps the other chapters against the main research themes and gives a short overview of the content of each chapter in the book.

1 Introduction

Omnichannel retailing is just retailing in a new context. It is an emerging phenomenon. This is reflected in the academic literature, which aims to capture the development occurring in the commercial world, tries to foresee future developments, and attempts to make sense of the concept and its components. This book covers a diversity of approaches, as it includes field studies at a company level, conceptual

W. Piotrowicz (✉)
Supply Chain Management and Social Responsibility, Department of Marketing,
Hanken School of Economics, Helsinki, Finland

Oxford Institute of Retail Management, Saïd Business School, University of Oxford, Oxford, UK
e-mail: Wojciech.Piotrowicz@hanken.fi

R. Cuthbertson
Oxford Institute of Retail Management, Saïd Business School, University of Oxford, Oxford, UK

© Springer Nature Switzerland AG 2019
W. Piotrowicz, R. Cuthbertson (eds.), *Exploring Omnichannel Retailing*,
https://doi.org/10.1007/978-3-319-98273-1_1

1

work informed by practice and secondary data, as well as theoretical developments driven by the existing literature. Practical studies are considered at the country, sector, and organisational levels. The country coverage is wide, with studies investigating omnichannel practice in markets as diverse as India, Poland, Finland, Turkey, Malaysia, the United States, and the United Kingdom. These studies indicate that while there are differences in the level of modernisation of the retail sector across the world, many market segments are utilising similar technologies and communication channels. This should not be surprising as customers increasingly are utilising globally available technologies regardless of location. Mobile solutions and social media are growing in popularity in all markets.

However, while some practices may be similar, the concept is relatively new, and so there is still a need to define the meaning of omnichannel. What comes under this heading? This issue was considered earlier by Picot-Coupey et al. (2016) who compared omni- with multi- and cross-channel retailing concepts, concluding that omnichannel retailing is a holistic approach, where strategy takes account of all channels as customer touch points, which potentially allows for a seamless customer journey (Picot-Coupey et al. 2016). Similarly Beck and Rygl (2015) categorised retail via different channels distinguishing eight retail categories that reflect different retail developments of integration between company and customer, within omni- with multi- and cross-channel retailing. Categories that differentiate retail models are determined by who triggers and who controls the interactions in the channels and processes as well as the level of such interactions (Beck and Rygl 2015). Changes in retail settings are influencing the whole retail landscape: the nature of exchange, actors, and the retail offer (Hagberg et al. 2016), creating a new environment where companies and customers are increasingly intertwined. This chapter considers the key issues in such an emerging environment. Firstly, the literature focussing on the topic of an omnichannel retail strategy is reviewed. This chapter then presents the main chapters included in the book, separating them into appropriate categories to enable the reader to pick and choose their particular focus. For example, there are strategy related studies, country reviews, and research focused on specific omnichannel issues, such as questions surrounding technology, quality, and product delivery.

2   Reality, Limitations in Implementation of Omnichannel Retailing

While the promise, or expectation, to deliver a seamless customer experience is a key message in omnichannel retailing (Piotrowicz and Cuthbertson 2014; Verhoef et al. 2015) to deliver such a promise is far from easy. As Piotrowicz and Cuthbertson (2014) indicate that there are challenges in channel integration, the impact of mobile technologies and social media, the changing role of traditional stores, diverse customer groups, trade-offs between privacy and personalisation, and the need to redesign, or even build from scratch, the whole supply chain. However, the first problem is to define and implement an initial omnichannel strategy. As noted by Picot-Coupey et al. (2016) to implement a new omnichannel strategy there is a need to go through a transition period, which covers changes in organisation, culture, management, marketing, and resource utilisation. Picot-Coupey et al. (2016) suggest that such changes should be followed by modifying the marketing mix, information systems, and Customer Relationship Management (CRM). A study by Hansen and Sia (2015) indicated that omnichannel strategy implementation required a global alignment of the brand, enhanced e-commerce support for business partners, and complementing the store experience with in store digital innovations, such as apps and e-commerce platforms. However, there is no single "best" way to create new omnichannel processes and networks. As Hübner et al. (2016) indicated to redesign the last mile delivery and fulfilment in grocery retailing, a variety of factors have to be considered, such as the existing network of stores and warehouses, country specific issues, customer behaviour, the level of automation, and legal requirements, among other factors. At the same time, such new logistic networks should allow flexibility and integration across all channels (Peltola et al. 2015).

This book aims to consider this wide variety of issues (Table 1). Starting from the ways in which an omnichannel strategy can be implemented, to what functions have to be changed to deliver the promised seamless customer experience in practice, how the future of retailing might look, and how different approaches to the implementation of an omnichannel strategy differs between countries, sectors, and product groups. The importance of logistics and fulfilment is also illustrated.

3 Chapters in This Book

The order of the chapters that follow begins mainly focused on strategy, followed by a number of country studies, then diving down into the detail of specific functions, technologies and sectors. However, in practice the chapters all consider the main theme, and so also touch on different points related to omnichannel development, as it is impossible to discuss only a single element of the omnichannel without reference to other areas. All the elements of omnichannel implementation, from strategy to operations, from market to products, from technologies to customers, are interlinked and coexist in both the physical and online worlds. Thus, in investigating an aspect of omnichannel development, it is inevitable that many components and actors will be considered. In addition, many differences between countries and retail sectors are considered at various levels of analysis (Table 2).

Table 1 Mapping chapters and main themes

Chapter	Strategy	Channel integration	Supply Chain	Store, product and service characteristics	Customer expectations and communication	Technologies
Rusanen (2018)	X				X	
Cao (2018)	X	X				
Akter et al. (2018)		X		X		
Yumurtacı Hüseyinoğlu (2018)	X	X	X			X
Banerjee (2018)	X	X	X		X	
Pieriegud (2018)	X	X		X		
Perry et al. (2018)				X	X	X
Alexander and Cano (2018)				X		X
Ziliani et al. (2018)		X			X	
Kassim and Hussin (2018)	X	X	X		X	X
Piotrowicz and Cuthbertson (2018a, b)	X		X	X		

Table 2 Book chapters, country coverage, sector, level of analysis and data sources

Chapter	Country	Sector	Level of analysis	Methodology, data
Rusanen (2018)	Finland, United Kingdom	Retail	Country, sector, company	Focus groups
Cao (2018)	US	Retail	Country, large retailers	Secondary data
Akter et al. (2018)	International	Retail	NA	Secondary data
Yumurtacı Hüseyinoğlu (2018)	Turkey	Grocery retail	Company	Focus groups
Banerjee (2018)	India	Retail	Country	Secondary data
Pieriegud (2018)	Poland	Pharmaceuticals	Country, pharma	Secondary data
Perry et al. (2018)	International	Fashion	Store, technology	Secondary data
Alexander and Cano (2018)	UK	Fashion	Company	Interviews
Ziliani et al. (2018)	Italy	Retail	Customer	Experiment
Kassim and Hussin (2018)	Malaysia	Events related	Company	Interviews, observations
Piotrowicz and Cuthbertson (2018a, b)	United Kingdom	Grocery retail	Sub-sector of retail, large companies	Secondary data

3.1　Crafting and Implementing Omnichannel Strategy

The second chapter of this book is focused on the key issue of omnichannel strategy. Rusanen (2018) discusses the sources of competitive advantage as well as barriers to strategy implementation. At the same time the author is comparing the omnichannel related narratives with reality. The chapter analyses omnichannel retailing beyond just organisational, or even supply chain levels of analysis. The resulting framework proposed views omnichannel developments from the differing perspectives of the wider society, consumers, industry experts, company management, and all employees. This work, developed after series of expert workshops, contributes to our understanding of omnichannel in a wider context.

Implementation of the omnichannel strategy is also covered by Cao (2018). Data from 91 US retailers are used to look at how they are approaching channel integration and the various stages involved in such a process. The creation of an omnichannel takes time and several stages are identified, starting from the silo mode, to multi-channel with a minimal level of integration between channels, then the level of integration increases, and the final stage is full integration, the omnichannel. Omnichannel development does need to be a revolutionary approach, but an evolution where the company is moving step by step, gradually changing its operations.

3.2 Country Level Studies

The three chapters that follow are investigating at the country level. These chapters cover developments in very different markets, including Turkey, India, and Poland.

The chapter by Yumurtacı Hüseyinoğlu (2018) considers omnichannel strategy from a practical angle, analysing the leading Turkish grocery retailer. The author indicates that channel integration is driven by changes in the industry as well as shopping habits, which in turn create the need for higher productivity in logistics and supply chain processes. As the decision to implement omnichannel is made, the change in strategy results in changes in operations, which is not surprising, but hard to implement in practice. This work applied focus group interviews to gather empirical data.

India, one of the largest markets in the world in terms of population, is analysed by Banerjee (2018). This chapter analyses the development of the Indian market, where it is possible to observe the emergence of omnichannel. However, as the country is dominated by small, unorganized retailers, omnichannel development faces many barriers and challenges, such as lack of infrastructure, and insufficient use of technology by retailers among others. Despite such challenges the leading retailers are moving from a multi- to an omnichannel environment. This includes the transition of traditional retail to the online space, as well as the move of online companies towards the traditional retail sector, by increasing offline presence. This development is supported by changes in supply chain and logistics.

Another chapter focused at the country level, but looking at a highly regulated sector, pharmaceuticals, is written by Pieriegud (2018). The author analyses the development of the Polish pharma market, looking at the failed approach to create multi-channel sales of drugs. This is an interesting case, as such failures are not widely reported even though they provide valuable lessons. In this chapter both prescription and over the counter medicines are analysed. The different channels used to communicate with customers as well as those for transactional purposes are considered.

3.3 Omnichannel and Service Quality

Omnichannel developments are not only about the delivery of products, as the lines between channels, services, and products become blurred. There is a need to explore the meaning of service quality. Thus, the chapter by Akter et al. (2018) looks at the quality of in-store, digital, and integration processes, proposing an analytical frame-work that covers the key elements, such as channel service configuration and integrated interactions. Integrated interactions are composed of content and context consistency, while channel service configuration includes channel choice, transparency, and the appropriateness of the configuration chosen.

3.4 Communication with Customers, Print vs Online

Communication is a key aspect of an omnichannel strategy. Ziliani et al. (2018) look at the role of a traditional communication tool, the flyer, analysing the impact of these traditional, paper-based, printed formats, against online flyers, which are reaching customers both directly and by a new type of intermediary, the "flyer aggregators". Empirical work indicates that 80% of Italian customers respond equally to print and online in term of purchase behaviour, while the remaining 20% are more responsive to printed than online versions of the flyers. However, at the same time online flyers have many advantages such as cost, ease of update and distribution compared to paper versions.

3.5 Technologies in Omnichannel

Alexander and Cano (2018) focus their research on the technologies used, or that are emerging, in the context of a physical store. Physical stores, especially in fashion retailing, are expected to continue to be around in some form, though most likely in a different form compared to those known today. Changes include the use of a whole range of technologies that change customer experiences, integrate channels, and influence customer service.

Omnichannel is integrating all communication channels between the retailer and customer. Mobile technologies play a critical role as they are blurring the line between in-store and online shopping. Perry et al. (2018) covers this topic in relation to the use of mobile technologies by customers while in the physical, traditional, store. Mobile technologies includes not just phones but also smartphones and tablets as they are used by customers. Applications include QR codes, RFID tags, devices used by shop staff, iBeacons, and many more. While mobile technologies are challenging the traditional retail environment in many ways, they also create opportunities to integrate the brand experience across online and physical retail spaces.

3.6 Delivery and Fulfilment in Omnichannel

Malaysia is another country from Asia analysed in this book. This chapter (Kassim and Hussin 2018) focuses on a company where service and on demand production are critical elements of the offer. At the same time, the chapter provides a good illustration to show that omnichannel is not restricted to the retailing of physical products. This case discusses how a company that is providing goods and services related to events (marriage ceremonies) is utilising multiple channels of communication, not only through web pages and traditional flyers, but also through social media and mobile applications. This chapter points to the need to design omnichannel in line with local settings, such as customer needs, culture, and traditions.

The final chapter focuses on last mile logistics in the context of British grocery retailing (Piotrowicz and Cuthbertson 2018a, b). The authors analyse different fulfilment models: home delivery, Click and Collect, and automated collection points. However, the main theme of the chapter is to look at how the delivery model is linked to the company strategy, customers, infrastructure, and other factors that have to be taken for consideration when the fulfilment processes are designed and executed. The last mile framework for omnichannel retailing is proposed as a tool for delivery mode selection.

4 Conclusions

Based on the literature, and the chapters included in this book, it is possible to recognise that there is some discrepancy between the promises of omnichannel retailing and the idealistic view of omnichannel development as perceived as a single business model that is going to determine the future of all retailing.

We can see that omnichannel development is not uniform across the world with some markets and sectors ahead while others are trying to replicate the emerging model. Instead, omnichannel development is developing for different customer groups with distinct solutions adjusted to the local needs. This is particularly visible when contrasting emerging markets with more developed ones. Omnichannel retailing is growing in both countries, but with different customer demographics and cultural expectations, which differ not only between countries, but also within them. Differences between product characteristics also may determine the use of an omnichannel approach at each of the customer/retailer stages of interaction, from communication via different channels, such as the use of social media, up to the delivery or collection of the product or service. The type of the product, range, price, and composition of the service delivery all add complexity. The attitude to the product, such as buying fashion goods or items for a marriage ceremony or grocery products, is clearly different, and thus the whole process may looks different. Regulations and public policy, such as in case of the pharmaceutical market, alongside culture, the level of logistics and IT infrastructure available, the level of retail modernisation, and other contextual factors are clearly influencing omnichannel development.

All this variety of examples and analysis leaves an open question: are we eventually aiming for one dominant omnichannel model, or more likely for many omnichannel models, in the plural form. So, while there may be similar technologies, similar logistics solutions, product categories, or even similar customer groups, are we are creating solutions adjusted to such variables? Or will each brand aim to create its unique version of omnichannel retailing? Will such a model be unified across the world? Or adjusted to local settings?

At this stage we, both academics and practitioners, are unable to fully answer such questions. However, this book is a step towards increasing our understanding of omnichannel retailing as an emerging phenomenon and stresses both the similarities and differences in a wide variety of approaches to omnichannel implementation.

References

Akter, S., Hossain, M. I., Lu, S., Aditya, S., Hossain, T. M. T., & Kattiyapornpong, U. (2018). Does service quality perception in omnichannel retailing matter? A systematic review and agenda for future research. In W. Piotrowicz & W. Cuthbertson (Eds.), *Exploring the reality of omnichannel retailing: Theory and practice*. Cham: Springer.

Alexander, A., & Cano, M. B. (2018). Futurising the physical store in the omnichannel retail environment. In W. Piotrowicz & W. Cuthbertson (Eds.), *Exploring the reality of omnichannel retailing: Theory and practice*. Cham: Springer.

Banerjee, M. (2018). Development of omnichannel in India – Retail landscape, drivers and challenges. In W. Piotrowicz & W. Cuthbertson (Eds.), *Exploring the reality of omnichannel retailing: Theory and practice*. Cham: Springer.

Beck, N., & Rygl, D. (2015). Categorization of multiple channel retailing in multi-, cross-, and omni-channel retailing for retailers and retailing. *Journal of Retailing and Consumer Services, 27*, 170–178.

Cao, L. (2018). Implementation of omnichannel strategy in the US retail – Evolutionary approach. In W. Piotrowicz & W. Cuthbertson (Eds.), *Exploring the reality of omnichannel retailing: Theory and practice*. Cham: Springer.

Hagberg, J., Sundstrom, M., & Egels-Zandén, N. (2016). The digitalization of retailing: An exploratory framework. *International Journal of Retail & Distribution Management, 44*(7), 694–712.

Hansen, R., & Sia, S. K. (2015). Hummel's digital transformation toward omnichannel retailing: Key lessons learned. *MIS Quarterly Executive, 14*(2), 51–66.

Hübner, A., Kuhn, H., & Wollenburg, J. (2016). Last mile fulfilment and distribution in omnichannel grocery retailing: A strategic planning framework. *International Journal of Retail & Distribution Management, 44*(3), 228–247.

Kassim, E., & Hussin, H. (2018). A framework for omnichannel differentiation strategy. Integrating the information delivery and product fulfilment requirements. In W. Piotrowicz & W. Cuthbertson (Eds.), *Exploring the reality of omnichannel retailing: Theory and practice*. Cham: Springer.

Perry, P., Kent, A., & Bonetti, F. (2018). The use of mobile technologies in physical stores: The case of fashion retailing. In W. Piotrowicz & W. Cuthbertson (Eds.), *Exploring the reality of omnichannel retailing: Theory and practice*. Cham: Springer.

Peltola, S., Vainio, H., & Nieminen, M. (2015). Key factors in developing omnichannel customer experience with Finnish retailers. In *International Conference on HCI in Business* (pp. 335–346). Cham: Springer.

Picot-Coupey, K., Huré, E., & Piveteau, L. (2016). Channel design to enrich customers' shopping experiences: Synchronizing clicks with bricks in an omnichannel perspective – The direct optic case. *International Journal of Retail & Distribution Management, 44*(3), 336–368.

Pieriegud, J. (2018). The development of digital distribution channels in Poland's retail pharmaceutical market. In W. Piotrowicz & W. Cuthbertson (Eds.), *Exploring the reality of omnichannel retailing: Theory and practice*. Cham: Springer.

Piotrowicz, W., & Cuthbertson, R. (2014). Introduction to the special issue information technology in retail: Toward omnichannel retailing. *International Journal of Electronic Commerce, 18*(4), 5–16.

Piotrowicz, W., & Cuthbertson, R. (2018a). Exploring omnichannel retailing: Common expectations and diverse reality. In W. Piotrowicz & W. Cuthbertson (Eds.), *Exploring the reality of omnichannel retailing: Theory and practice*. Cham: Springer.

Piotrowicz, W., & Cuthbertson, R. (2018b). Last mile framework for omnichannel retailing. Delivery from the customer perspective. In W. Piotrowicz & W. Cuthbertson (Eds.), *Exploring the reality of omnichannel retailing: Theory and practice*. Cham: Springer.

Rusanen, O. (2018). Crafting an omnichannel strategy: Identifying sources of competitive advantage and implementation barriers. In W. Piotrowicz & W. Cuthbertson (Eds.), *Exploring the reality of omnichannel retailing: Theory and practice*. Cham: Springer.

Verhoef, P. C., Kannan, P. K., & Inman, J. J. (2015). From multi-channel retailing to omnichannel retailing: Introduction to the special issue on multi-channel retailing. *Journal of Retailing, 91*(2), 174–181.

Yumurtacı Hüseyinoğlu, I. Ö. (2018). Drivers for channel integration and omnichannel strategy: Evidence from the leading grocery retailer in Turkey. In W. Piotrowicz & W. Cuthbertson (Eds.), *Exploring the reality of omnichannel retailing: Theory and practice*. Cham: Springer.

Ziliani, C., Ieva, M., Gázquez-Abad, J. C., & D'Attoma, I. (2018). Retail promotional communication: The comparative effectiveness of print versus online. In W. Piotrowicz & W. Cuthbertson (Eds.), *Exploring the reality of omnichannel retailing: Theory and practice*. Cham: Springer.

Wojciech Piotrowicz (PhD Brunel, MA Gdańsk, PGDipLATHE Oxon) is Associate Professor in Sustainable Supply Chains and Social Responsibility, at Hanken School of Economics and HUMLOG Insitute, Helsinki, Finland. In addition he is an as International Research Fellow at the University of Oxford, Saïd Business School and is a member of Wolfson College. His research is related to information systems, logistics, supply chain management, performance measurement and evaluation, with a focus on transitional countries and retail contexts. Wojciech has considerable experience as a member of large international research projects within both the public and private sectors, working with organisations such as Intel, BAE Systems, the European Commission and the Polish government. He is a recipient of Outstanding and Highly Commended paper awards from the Emerald Literati Network for Excellence.

Richard Cuthbertson is a Senior Research Fellow and Research Director at the Oxford Institute of Retail Management at Saïd Business School, University of Oxford and *Vice-Principal of Green Templeton College, Oxford*. His research interest lies in understanding and assessing the challenges of an increasingly digital world on retail, particularly through technology innovation and the use of customer data. His work is international in scope, in particular looking at how retail practice and policy are developing in countries like India and China, and he regularly acts as a consultant to retailers and governments. He is author of over 100 published articles and has worked with many companies, including Tesco, Sainsbury's, P&G, Casino, T-Mobile, BP, Abbey, IBM, KPMG and BCG. Richard is an ex-Board member of the Charity Retail Association. He was awarded the Emerald Literati Network Award for Excellence (twice) and the Pegasus Prize for eBusiness Future Insights (2006).

Crafting an Omnichannel Strategy: Identifying Sources of Competitive Advantage and Implementation Barriers

Olli Rusanen

Abstract Omnichannel retailing (OCR) is an emerging concept with an emphasis on channel integration for providing seamless customer experiences across various channels. Scholars have studied omnichannel consumption extensively, but there is a need for research on the sources of competitiveness and the potential implementation barriers associated with omnichannel strategies. The purpose of this chapter is to broaden the applicability of omnichannel retailing from a narrow marketing base to take into account societal context (public policy), competitive factors (strategy), and intra-organizational structure (management). I will identify new research areas for academics and issues relating to the strategic management of omnichannel retailing for practitioners.

Two workshops were organized for a mixture of academics, retail managers, and consultants. Five OCR-related topic areas emerged from these workshops: (1) societal context, (2) established research regarding omnichannel consumption, (3) internal omnichannel resources as a driver of sustainable competitive advantage, (4) unique features of an omnichannel strategy as a driver of a differentiated market position, and (5) structural implementation barriers of an omnichannel strategy. These areas were further specified through a problematization-based literature review. The results are summarized in a model: the omnichannel strategy triangle.

1 Introduction

Omnichannel retailing (OCR) has emerged as a core concept for retailers because it has the potential for field-transforming change (Rigby 2011; Verhoef et al. 2015; Grewal et al. 2017). Two workshops were arranged for a mixture of academics and practitioners regarding the management of omnichannel retailing and the retail sector's role in society. The participants confirmed the key results in previous omnichannel literature: ongoing technological advancements are transforming the

O. Rusanen (✉)
Department of Marketing, School of Business, Aalto University, Helsinki, Finland
e-mail: olli.rusanen@aalto.fi

© Springer Nature Switzerland AG 2019
W. Piotrowicz, R. Cuthbertson (eds.), *Exploring Omnichannel Retailing*,
https://doi.org/10.1007/978-3-319-98273-1_2

retail sector and retailers need to integrate both emerging digital and existing physical channels in order to provide a seamless customer experience across all channels (Rigby 2011; Piotrowicz and Cuthbertson 2014). However, some participants expressed frustration at omnichannel scholarship, since it does not adequately provide guidance on how to achieve channel integration in practice. The managerial problem of omnichannel retailing is that it crosses over traditional organizational functions and creates implementation barriers due to a 'silo mentality' (Piotrowicz and Cuthbertson 2014, p. 8). There is also the problem of idiosyncratic unique features of a strategy, which has the potential to create a competitive advantage over rivals but which has not been studied in the field of OCR (Porter 1996). Furthermore, it is unclear how emerging resources, such as customer data, can be leveraged in a valuable but hard-to-imitate manner (Barney 1991; Sirmon et al. 2007). The objective of this chapter is to broaden the applicability of omnichannel retailing to take into account the broader societal context and to include aspects of strategic management: the competitive advantages of omnichannel retailing, and implementation barriers associated with omnichannel strategy.

I pursue this objective via a problematization-based literature review of omnichannel retailing using strategic management as a lens. Problematization has the potential to lead to influential theories because it refers to challenging core, often implicit, assumptions about existing theory (Alvesson and Sandberg 2011). While gap-spotting seeks to extend the existing theory base, problematization thrives on identifying new continents in a sea of knowledge (Sandberg and Alvesson 2011). Strategic management of OCR is the new continent, full of riches and awaiting adventurous explorers. For academics, this chapter categorizes new research areas in strategic management in OCR and generates questions for future research. For managers, this chapter identifies key features of OCR as a source of competitiveness but also major implementation barriers that can thwart such a strategy. For public policy, this chapter places omnichannel retailing into the larger societal context and identifies challenges that the retail sector is facing due to the emergence of OCR. I consider two research topics on omnichannel strategy: (1) competitive advantage and (2) implementation barriers.

Firstly, omnichannel retailing is claimed to be a source of competitive advantage that is completely transforming the retail industry (Rigby 2011; Bell et al. 2014; Herhausen et al. 2015; Verhoef et al. 2015). This logic is rooted in the digital revolution in retail that is driving omnichannel consumption where customers expect a seamless consumption experience across the digital and the physical channels (Verhoef et al. 2015; Grewal et al. 2017; Ross et al. 2017). However, competitive advantage is created through unique activities that can promote differentiation. If a certain action is identical to all, it is an industry-transforming best practice. No best practice can be a source of sustainable competitive advantage (SCA) as competitiveness relies on unique activities (Porter 1996). A strategy can only be a source of SCA if only a few retailers adopt it or if it is adopted in different ways by different retailers (Porter and Siggelkow 2008). There is an open question:

RQ1 What are the sources of sustainable competitive advantage for an omnichannel strategy?

This question is pursued by examining internal factors (the resource-based view) and external factors (industrial organization) because they form two major explanatory models of SCA in strategic management (Hoskisson et al. 1999).

Secondly, channel integration requires coordination, which can encounter powerful implementation barriers. One option is to adopt omnichannel as a centralized top-down initiative, but this approach can have unintended consequences because it disrupts internal power relations by intervening in functional autonomy. This is a potential source of internal zero-sum games, gatekeeping, and other sources of structural inertia. Strategy process scholars have emphasized the role of middle management in championing novel initiatives (Burgelman 1983), emergence as a pattern of smaller initiatives (Mintzberg 1978; Mintzberg and McHugh 1985), and strategy discourse (Mantere 2005; Mantere and Vaara 2008). These streams of literature point to implementation barriers for centralized and planning-oriented omnichannel strategies. There is an open question:

RQ2 What intra-organizational implementation barriers exist for an omnichannel strategy?

In this chapter, I will challenge that even if, ex ante, there is a positive prospect for headquarters' value added, if everyone pursues this goal in an identical fashion, this prospect ceases to be valuable ex post. Further, even if one were to design a unique omnichannel strategy that cannot be replicated by rivals, its implementation is challenging due to structural complexities and other sources of intra-organizational inertia associated with channel integration. These observations are summarized in a model: the omnichannel strategy triangle.

This chapter is structured as follows: (1) The next section defines key constructs. (2) The Methodology section explains how the model was crafted: identification, specification, research quality, and limitations. (3) The Analysis section identifies five retail problems for OCR based on two workshops. These areas are examined and specified using a problematization-based literature review. (4) Synthesis presents a holistic model that summarizes the results: the omnichannel strategy triangle. (5) The Conclusions explains the contribution which broadens the applicability of omnichannel retailing to take into account the broader context and strategic aspects. I also present new research areas for academics and discuss the applicability of the model for practitioners.

2 Constructs and Definitions

This chapter explains key constructs and their definitions to ensure construct clarity (Suddaby 2010).

Channel Integration is defined as *"the degree to which different channels interact with each other"*. Physical channels can promote knowledge of digital channels (offline-online integration), or digital channels can promote knowledge of physical channels (online-offline integration) (Herhausen et al. 2015, pp. 310–311). Channel integration has three elements: channel stage, type, and agents (Saghiri et al. 2017). A of multiple channel integration is variability of the delivered customer experience: only integrated channels can provide a seamless customer experience. In order to achieve such an objective, successful channel integration requires functional coordination and supply chain redesign (Piotrowicz and Cuthbertson 2014). Conversely, non-integrated channels are characterized by a silo mentality, functional separation, incomplete support by operational resources, and variability in the delivered customer experience for each channel.

Industrial Organization is an external theory regarding the profitability of a firm. In this approach, industry structure drives conduct (strategy), which jointly determines performance. This paradigm states that firm profitability is based on its position in the competitive landscape, and each position is protected by mobility barriers (Porter 1981). Competitive advantage is created for firms that occupy a profitable position while other positions face fierce competition. Superior profits can be sustained if mobility barriers are high, since firms are not completely free to move from one position to another (McGee and Thomas 1986).

Omnichannel Retailing (OCR) extends the concept of multichannel retailing with a broader channel focus and scope, especially to include emerging digital channels. OCR is defined through its management as *"the synergetic management of the numerous available channels and customer touchpoints, in such a way that the customer experience across channels and the performance over channels is optimized"* (Verhoef et al. 2015, p. 176). This definition is holistic (performance across all channels), and it emphasizes cross-channel management (integration). Omnichannel retailing is a complex adaptive system that has several aspects that are related to each other (Saghiri et al. 2017). These aspects are utilized for identifying and specifying a strategy foundation for OCR.

Problematization-Based Literature Review Gap-spotting is the prominent way of constructing research questions from the existing literature. It refers to reviewing the existing literature, categorizing the contributions and identifying gaps of knowledge, or unresearched areas. This approach shares the norms and assumptions of existing theory (Sandberg and Alvesson 2011). In contrast, problematization methodology seeks to generate research questions by systematically challenging taken-for-granted assumptions or finding new ways of thinking about a particular phenomenon. Problematization is thus defined as an *"endeavour to know how and to what extent it might be possible to think differently, instead of what is already known"* in order to *"disrupt the reproduction and continuation of an institutionalized line of reasoning"* (Sandberg and Alvesson 2011, p. 32).

Resource-Based View (RBV) is an intra-firm theory about profitability. It assumes that firms have imperfectly mobile and heterogeneous resources. If a resource satisfies the VRIN conditions (valuable, rare, imperfectly imitable, non-substitutable), it is a source of **sustainable competitive advantage (SCA)** (Barney 1991).

Strategy Process studies strategic management as an embedded and contextualized activity with several levels of analysis, as temporally evolving phenomenon, utilizing a holistic explanation model, and focusing on explaining the outcomes of the process (Pettigrew 1992). Major themes are the formulation and implementation of strategies and the process of strategic change (Van de Ven 1992). Rather than viewing strategy as a fixed plan and an activity of planning, Mintzberg (1978, p. 935) defines realized strategy as a *"pattern in a stream of decisions"*. Strategy process has problematized whether strategies are realized as planned: strategies can also emerge as bottom-up processes.

3   Methodology

This purpose of this research is to broaden the applicability of omnichannel retailing to include the broader societal context and aspects of strategic management. These areas are summarized in a model that contains five analytical areas about different aspects of omnichannel retailing. This chapter explains its development process: (1) identification of five retail problems in two expert workshops, (2) specification of content using a problematization-oriented review, and (3) validation of the whole model by consideration of the research quality and limitations.

Phase 1: Identification of Unexplored Topics and Determining Retail Problems About Omnichannel Retailing Based on Two Expert Workshops Previously, omnichannel-related empirical research has utilized expert workshops for improving practical relevance of an abstract and theoretical area (Piotrowicz and Cuthbertson 2014). A group-based research setting enables participants to share different views, interact and engage in dialogue. Group interaction can encourage participants to discuss problem areas and engage in social interaction that would not arise in interviews (Warr 2005). Participatory groups, where all participants (including the researcher) have an active role in informal discussion about an open topic, enable addressing views that have not been served by established research or addressing views that have not been heard (Wilkinson 1998). In particular, group-based data collection enables participants to connect an abstract strategic concept (OCR) to other related areas (societal context, intra-organizational and competitive aspects) and to discuss struggles related to pursuing such an objective. In this way, for participants, the group-based approach enables the sharing of views and learning about a concept but also discussion about experiences in problem areas. As part of a retail-related research project,[1] such a group-based approach was adopted, and two workshops were arranged in Finland during 2015–2016. Both workshops had 23 participants (17 organizations): academia, the public sector (ministry and public funding agency), retail experts (business press, general retail consultancy, digital consultancy, and retail association), and the retail sector (physical retailer, digital retailer, and shopping centre operator). The workshops were arranged to steer research activities and to identify managerially relevant but un-researched areas in retail digitalization in general and omnichannel retailing in particular. There were two open themes that required further enquiry: society and retail, and omnichannel retailing.

The first **workshop focused on public policy.** The retail sector is an innovative and economically important sector, but it was excluded from governmental texts as a viable source of growth (Cuthbertson et al. 2016). This perceived exclusion as a spearhead sector motivated the public policy workshop where participants discussed the role of retailing in Finnish society and identified potential research themes for the ongoing project. In order to encourage participation, at this point no validation was completed of the feasibility of the topics. The participants identified 14 areas of retail-related risks versus opportunities and generated 37 emerging themes for academia, practitioners, and the public sector. The results were published as a Tekes policy brief (Cuthbertson et al. 2016) and are used for identifying the societal context for OCR.

The second workshop focused specifically on omnichannel retailing. For academics, the objective was to identify unexplored but managerially relevant research areas about retail digitalization and omnichannel retailing. For practitioners, the objective was to provide an overview of the omnichannel literature, share and discuss practitioners' views, and learn more about an abstract and emerging concept—omnichannel retailing. The workshop also considered differences between the UK and Finnish retail sectors. The second workshop had an influential role in identifying three analytical approaches for the strategic management of omnichannel strategies: internal and external sources of competitiveness and strategy implementation.

Phase 2: Specification and Determining the Content of the Model Based on a Problematization-Oriented Literature Review After the two workshops, I had a crude model with five retail problem areas and two research questions; the model was missing detailed content. I decided to pursue these questions via a problematization-based literature review. Literature reviews are often conducted for gap-spotting. This means that the reviewer examines a particular set of literature, categorizes it, and then identifies unexplored areas, i.e. gaps in knowledge. An

---

[1]The project (2015–2018) is called Red Queen Effect: Strategies for an Innovative Landscape. The researchers are from Aalto University, the University of Jyväskylä, and the University of Oxford. The funding organizations are Citycon Oyj (shopping centre operator), S Group (co-operative retailer), Solita Oy (digitalization consultancy), Tieto Oyj (digitalization consultancy) and Tekes (public research funding agency).

alternative approach is to examine deep, often implicit, assumptions about a particular set of literature and then consider alternative research directions where these assumptions are relaxed. Such a problematization-based approach is recommended for identifying new research topics and for generating interesting research questions. The problematization approach challenges an institutionalized way of approaching a particular topic (Sandberg and Alvesson 2011).

In fact, the workshop participants had already problematized omnichannel retailing due to its narrow marketing focus, which did not fully consider the societal context, competitive strategy, or implementation barriers. In the literature review, I identified six problematizations (Table 1). Relaxation of these problematizations led to strategic management as a lens for considering the OCR literature. Even with the decision to limit the enquiry to strategic management, the scope is nevertheless broad. Two research areas were selected using an overview of strategy schools (Hoskisson et al. 1999): the resource-based view examines internal conditions of competitiveness, and industrial organization examines external conditions of competitive advantage. Research question 1 is explored using these two schools. Research question 2 is explored by examining strategy process theories, since it has contributed to the strategy implementation literature (Van de Ven 1992; Mintzberg 1994).

Phase 3: Validation of a Holistic Model and Consideration of Research Quality and Limitations In the finalization of the model, parsimony is emphasized—each element of the model is scrutinized and all border-line alternatives are eliminated from the model. Despite this emphasis, the model covers societal discussion, marketing-based omnichannel academia, and three schools of strategy thought. The expense of such a broad scope is that only seminal publications of the theories can be examined and detailed exploration of each individual topic is left for future research. The following actions were taken to ensure trustworthiness (Lincoln and Guba 1985).

- Credibility through member checks (Shenton 2004). The first version of the model was presented and discussed with academics and retail experts in the second workshop. This led to subsequent revision and cross-examination of omnichannel retailing using three theories of strategic management.
- Transferability was enhanced by involving members from various organization types and different positions associated with the retail field.
- Dependability is ensured by using overlapping methods (Shenton 2004): two workshops and a review.
- Confirmability is a limitation for problematization-based approaches.

There are two main limitations in this research. Firstly, the problematization approach has limited confirmability. Problematization is used for generating interesting research questions (Sandberg and Alvesson 2011), but generally novel research designs arrive at the expense of methodological rigour (de Villiers and Dumay 2014). In gap-spotting, the researcher can draw from established methods and a clearly defined gap. But in a problematization-based approach, the scope is much wider and the research has an explorative nature. Whereas gap-spotting is based on explaining and categorizing existing research, problematization emphasizes the logical deduction of the researcher. Each cited reference requires logical questioning of core assumptions by the researcher, which may create problems with confirmability (Shenton 2004). Bearing this limitation in mind, problematization is used because it has potential for a paradigm shift or for uncovering truly novel research avenues (Alvesson and Sandberg 2011). The whole point is that these topics need to be further examined through rigorous research. Secondly, the model is contextualized on the Finnish and the UK retail sector due to its origins in two project workshops. Further, it is possible that there are additional relevant topics about omnichannel retailing that did not arise in the workshops or strategy-oriented literature review. Due to the extensive scope, additional research is needed to ensure comprehensiveness.

4 Analysis: Five Retail Problems Concerning Omnichannel Retailing

The objective of this research is to broaden the applicability of omnichannel retailing to take into account the broader societal context and to include aspects of strategic management. Two workshops are utilized for identifying five retail problem areas in omnichannel retailing. This is followed by an examination of each problem and a specification of content for an analytical area using a problematization-based literature review. This section presents the results: (1) workshop-based identification of five retail problems and (2) a problematization-based literature review used for specifying content in each problem area.

Identification of Five Retail Problems in Omnichannel Retailing Based on the Workshops The first public policy workshop identified 37 emerging themes in the retail sector. The participants highlighted several different retail-related areas: collaboration between retail and public sector; retail citizenship, participation in societal concerns; regulatory investment barriers and asymmetric competitive landscape; retail globalization, servitization and digitalization; polarization of work, concern toward low-skill work, a need for highly specialized professionals, educational development; data-based businesses vs. privacy; and active experimentation culture (Cuthbertson et al. 2016). The first workshop was influential in the identification of contextualization and integration problems (see the bullet points below): omnichannel retailing is considered in a context of broader societal changes. Furthermore, omnichannel theorization should be broadened to include several stakeholders: society, consumers, industry experts, middle- and top management, and employees.

In the second workshop, core results of omnichannel retailing (Neslin and Shankar 2009; Rigby 2011; Piotrowicz and Cuthbertson 2014; Verhoef et al. 2015) were presented to a group of retail professionals. This was followed by an informal discussion and a sharing of experiences. An important theme that emerged was how the organization structure affects the viability of omnichannel strategies. It was noted that retail digitalization has moved at a slower pace in Finland than in the UK, for example in the adoption rate of self-service checkouts or online retailing. While there are differences in macro-economic factors and consumption behaviour, two factors arose to explain the differences: some participants were sceptical whether omnichannel retailing could be a source of competitive advantage, and retailers had encountered internal resistance in the adoption of digital initiatives. The participants expressed a need for more strategy-oriented research and a focus on implementation barriers in OCR. This led to formulating research questions 1 and 2 to consider these themes. The second workshop was influential in identifying strategic management issues in omnichannel retailing: resource management, competitiveness, and coordination problems.

A Problematization-Based Literature Review Is Used for Specifying Content After the workshop, I had identified five retail problems in omnichannel retailing. This observation expands the notion of omnichannel retailing from a narrow integration problem to include problems in contextualization, resource management, competitiveness and coordination. These retail problems were further examined and specified using a problematization-based literature review. I examined omnichannel retailing through the lens of selected theories of strategic management, based on relevance to the identified retail problems. The five retail, primary stakeholder (in brackets), and selected theories are identified:

1. Contextualization problem (society): public policy workshop and sector-related literature (Cuthbertson et al. 2016; Treadgold and Reynolds 2016)
2. Integration problem (consumer): omnichannel retailing workshop and problematization of omnichannel retailing (Alvesson and Sandberg 2011; Verhoef et al. 2015)
3. Resource management problem (industry expert): the resource-based view (Barney 1991)
4. Competitiveness problem (management): industrial organization (Porter 1981)
5. Coordination problem (employee): strategy process (Van de Ven 1992; Mintzberg 1994)

The notion of five retail-related problem areas means that omnichannel retailing is not just about channel integration. Successful omnichannel strategy is portrayed as a matter of addressing five problems simultaneously. Any of these five areas can cause problems for an omnichannel strategy. The next five sections examine and specify each retail problem using a problematization-based literature review.

4.1 Contextualization Problem: Societal Contribution

This section examines the societal context of omnichannel retailing. Strategy involves multiple levels and functions in organizations, and it both affects and draws from a broader context within a sector and the society (Pettigrew 1992).

Effective strategy work requires an understanding of the development of the competitive landscape but also the consideration of societal changes. Contextualization can explain anomalies, it is required to ensure both internal and external validity, and it is needed for developing applicability to practitioners (Johns 2017).

Societal implications and the context of omnichannel retailing are mainly based on the results of a public policy workshop (Cuthbertson et al. 2016). The nature of competition is a major societal problem: omnichannel retailing can increase rivalry in a competitive landscape (Treadgold and Reynolds 2016), or it can result in market concentration and non-competitive pockets (Porter 1981, 2008)—and this will have an impact on all stakeholders, especially employees (Ton 2014). Regarding the societal context, three categories emerged in the workshops (Cuthbertson et al. 2016) that are relevant for omnichannel retailing: globalization, intangible value drivers, and the changing nature of work. These aspects require three retail activities: adaptation to an increasingly global and digital competitive landscape, redefining the value proposition to take advantage of intangible resources, and participation in a socially responsible manner.

Globalization of omnichannel retailing is a catalyst for an increasingly global competitive landscape within each part of the retail value chain (Treadgold and Reynolds 2016). Omnichannel scholars have used global firms, such as Walmart, Amazon and Apple, as a source of inspiration (Brynjolfsson et al. 2013; Weill and Woerner 2015). Major global retailers possess a sufficient resource base to achieve channel integration and to utilize state-of-the-art technological solutions on a large scale. In contrast, at the national level, smaller retail markets have observed a high degree of retail market concentration (for example, see the Finnish case by Björkroth et al. 2012). There are large policy questions about market entry barriers and competitive legislation that protects consumers from oligopolistic competition, both local and global. Society has to consider how to promote the overall welfare of consumers by ensuring that the retail landscape remains competitive, where omnichannel strategies trigger competitive actions by rivals and leads to industry-wide competency development. Ideally, this leads to increased product and service availability, enhanced quality and lower prices. This process is known as red queen competition (Barnett and Hansen 1996).

Intangible Value Drivers occupy a central part in omnichannel theorizing due to retail digitalization (Rigby 2011; Herhausen et al. 2015; Weill and Woerner 2015; Treadgold and Reynolds 2016; Grewal et al. 2017). Mobile solutions in particular are a 'critical enabler of these changes' (Brynjolfsson et al. 2013, p. 24). Customer data creates privacy concerns but also opportunities for commercialization (Kiron et al. 2014a, b). The emergence of intangible resources also reflects supply chain redesign, the changing value of physical spaces, and the utilization of social media (Piotrowicz and Cuthbertson 2014). Valuable business solutions often bundle digital applications with intangible services. This blend of intangibility and globalization has intra-organizational (structural) implications, as retailers are adapting to this disruption of the operating environment. For public policy, several governmental practices are designed in a physical or material context. For example, zoning, construction, and planning legislation is under pressure due to the changing role of physical places in an increasingly digital world. Taxation has been arranged in a physical store setting, and the competitive intensity of competitive legislation has been calculated from physical stores' catchment areas. Furthermore, interesting collaborative initiatives exist between retailers, NGOs and the public sector, such as the provision of public services (library, health care) in a shopping centre environment. Such public-sector services are a channel type that can increase consumer flow to stores.

Changing Nature of Work and the polarization of employees' working conditions is a global megatrend. Retail digitalization requires highly specialized knowledge and technological know-how. This can create recruitment challenges for retailers, but it also highlights the role of educational institutions in providing access to trained employees. Retail has traditionally had an important societal role because of its significant demand for low-skill workers. However, automation and process engineering have the potential to drive down uneducated workers' salaries or the employment rate. There is potential for societal problems in part-time work, fixed-term contracts, low wages and poor working conditions. On the other hand, there are retailers who explicitly invest in employee training and motivation in order to realize cost advantages (Ton 2014). The boundaries of different job titles and between various retail sector operators are blurring. Even low-skill retail work requires the ability to perform in a context of increasing task variability.

4.2 Integration Problem: Crafting a Seamless Customer Experience

This section examines omnichannel consumption and problematizes the established OCR literature. Since the objective is to problematize, this chapter does not provide a detailed account of omnichannel retailing; there are already high-quality reviews and special issues on the topic (see Neslin and Shankar 2009; Piotrowicz and Cuthbertson 2014; Verhoef et al. 2015; Saghiri et al. 2017). This section has two parts: (1) examining the core concepts of omnichannel retailing for consumers; (2) problematizing key elements that form the basis for strategy-related theorization in the next three sections (problems in resource management, competitiveness, and coordination).

Firstly, omnichannel consumption is driven by a quest for a seamless consumer experience, utilization of modern retail technology, and the holistic management of channel integration. An omnichannel consumer seeks a seamless customer experience across all channels (Rigby 2011). Digital solutions provide more information for consumers by enabling price comparisons and online word-of-mouth in social media (Piotrowicz and Cuthbertson 2014). Customers have access to increased price transparency and social features such as reviews and feedback. On the other hand, retailers have more information about their customers and are able to personalize offerings (Bradlow et al. 2017). In particular, mobile and in-store technologies have been pointed out as ongoing areas of interest for retailers (Piotrowicz and Cuthbertson 2014). These developments are major opportunities for retailers to create new sources of value for customers.

Omnichannel retailing represents a paradigm shift that takes an explicitly holistic approach (cf. Pettigrew 1992) by emphasizing the integration problem in order to provide a seamless customer experience (Piotrowicz and Cuthbertson 2014; Saghiri et al. 2017). This paradigm shift does not mean that multichannel scholars would have argued for non-integrated channel management or would have recommended variability in different channel experiences. In fact, channel integration is included as part of multichannel retailing (Neslin and Shankar 2009). The difference between multichannel and omnichannel is in emphasis, where channel integration is foregrounded and discussed explicitly in the context of digitalization. Atomistic channel management has the risk that potential integration benefits are not realized (Verhoef et al. 2015). If each channel provides value for a customer, an integrated omnichannel strategy provides more than the sum of its parts. Successful integration thus has the premise of providing headquarters' positive value added, which is also a classic strategy problem (Rumelt et al. 1994). The main retail activities are acquiring (Sirmon et al. 2007) appropriate channels, both digital and physical, and crafting (Mintzberg 1987) a holistic, seamless customer experience that creates added value for both the firm and the customer.

Problematization of Omnichannel Retailing is based on a review of selected articles. A challenge in this approach is that many assumptions are influential but implicit or in the background. I will examine each assumption by focusing on articles where the assumption is particularly visible. There are four potential assumption categories for problematization: (1) in-house assumptions are shared assumptions in a given field, which are accepted as unproblematic; (2) root metaphor assumptions are broader images or influential metaphors; (3) paradigmatic assumptions are ontological, epistemological or methodological approaches common for a certain period of scholarly thought; and (4) ideology assumptions are political, moral or gender-related positions in a field (Alvesson and Sandberg 2011). Table 1 contains the list of assumptions, their classification and problematization. It is noteworthy that many of these assumptions are reasonable for particular research because of academic convention. For example, marketing researchers focus exclusively on consumers. It is crucial to problematize these assumptions in order to address areas of neglect in the strategic management of omnichannel retailing.

Channel Integration as a Pure Marketing Phenomenon The participants in the two workshops highlighted the social context, competitive advantage, and implementation barriers associated with OCR as areas of interest (Cuthbertson et al. 2016). Channel integration implies management challenges in achieving integration and highlights a need for digitalized resources and competencies (Rigby 2011). This is a difficult task to achieve. As Piotrowicz and Cuthbertson (2014) show, retail man-

Table 1 Problematized assumptions for model construction

Assumption	Type (implicit/explicit)	Explanation	Problematization	Implications	Major stakeholder
Channel integration as a pure marketing phenomenon	Ideology assumption (im)	Digitalization and mobile technologies enable new forms of consumption to be studied	Emerging omnichannel offering and channel integration has societal, competitive and intra-organizational implications	Contextualization of society and use of strategy as a lens	Society, expert, management and employee
Amazon halo	Root metaphor (ex)	Idealization of global born-digital retailers and the risk of a halo effect. OCR treated as a set of homogenous resources.	Asymmetric adaptation of born-digital and an established physical retail chain	Asymmetric options due to a heterogeneous resource base and positional or structural implementation barriers	Industry expert, management and employee
Adapt-or-die	Root metaphor (ex)	Omnichannel as a sector-wide isomorphic disruption. Retailers face a choice between adapt to omnichannel retailing or perish	Best practice cannot be a source of SCA	Industrial organization: unique omnichannel strategy as a source of differentiation	Management
Effortless integration	In-house assumption (ex)	Objective is to provide a seamless customer experience across digital and physical channels	Channel integration creates a need for functional coordination and requires bundling of strategic resources that are imperfectly mobile	Bundling and leveraging of immobile core resources for SCA. Coordination problem as an implementation barrier	Industry expert and employee
Omnichannel as a plan	In-house assumption (im)	Omnichannel as an officially stated strategic plan	Autonomous omnichannel initiatives	Organization culture and strategy discourse that promotes organization-wide participation	Employee
CEO-driven omnichannel strategy	In-house assumption (im)	Omnichannel as a top-down initiative	Emergent initiatives and decentralized omnichannel strategies	Implementation barriers and emergent strategy	Employee

agers need to redesign the supply chain, redefine existing physical space, and understand diverse and changing customer needs by using customer data analytics. Channel integration needs to take into account other organizational functions and aspects such as intra-organizational resources (logistics, IT systems, customer data). In this sense, channel integration should not be viewed as a purely marketing phenomenon because it has managerial implications in related fields.

Amazon Halo *"One of the biggest challenges for brick and mortar retailers is finding a strategy to compete with online-only sellers such as Amazon"* (Zeng et al. 2016, p. 22). Indeed, several scholars have used modern digital retailers as illustrative examples for theoretical motivation (Rigby 2011; Brynjolfsson et al. 2013; Herhausen et al. 2015; Verhoef et al. 2015). Human beings have a tendency to generalize isolated observations about success. If someone is excellent in one thing, he or she is often perceived to be excellent also in other unrelated things. The reverse case has also been observed for low performance. This phenomenon is called the halo effect. As a consequence, a firm with high performance is seen as doing everything in a superior fashion, while a firm with bad performance is perceived to get everything wrong (Rosenzweig 2007). Thus, caution is needed when studying success cases due to this polarization associated with the halo effect. The Amazon metaphor is also problematic because it implies a two-way street for omnichannel. Born-digital platforms represent a substantially different business design than most omnichannel retailers. They are competitive substitutes, but they are part of different strategic groups and face asymmetric competitive options (Weill and Woerner 2015). The retail landscape can be divided into four generic strategic groups, based on information (offline versus online) and fulfilment (pickup versus delivery) choices (Bell et al. 2014). The most likely explanation for these asymmetries is that many traditional physical retailers are not adopting Amazon-like digital strategies because such initiatives are not profitable for them, or that there can be implementation barriers that prevent adoption. While noting that several born-digital retailers are doing excellent business, it is a different thing for an established retail chain to add a digital channel than for a digital Internet retailer to add a physical channel. Nor does it automatically mean that established retailers must add a digital channel; it remains useful to consider single-channel strategies. It is likely that there are substantial asymmetries both in evaluated performance and the ability to implement omnichannel strategies.

Adapt-or-Die Metaphor The march of omnichannel is driven by the premise of a digital revolution in the retail sector (Brynjolfsson et al. 2013; Bell et al. 2014). The core argument is that digital logic represents an isomorphic shift in the retail sector where traditional retailers face an adapt-or-die situation. Retailers need a reality check, since new technologies are developing rapidly. OCR can be compared with the revolution of telecommunications: *"the phone system was dead and had to be rebuilt from scratch"* and that retailers *"need the same start-over mentality"* (Rigby 2011, p. 69). The adapt-or-die metaphor is closely associated with the Amazon halo, since an omnichannel strategy is often represented as the only available option for retailers. However, this leaves the question of uniqueness completely open. In fact, adapt does not automatically mean replicate. One can also react to this disruption by choosing a novel path. A sustainable competitive advantage is built on unique features that are sources of differentiation (Porter 1996). OCR is relevant for all retailers because it changes the competitive landscape. But that does not mean that everyone has to adopt it or even should adopt it in a similar way. The competitive landscape is differentiated into distinct market segments. An interesting research topic is the minimal omnichannel approach, i.e. boundary conditions, regarding the viability of single-channel or mostly physical strategies. European hard discounters (Aldi, Lidl) are potential case studies for this purpose.

Effortless Integration Channel integration requires a redesign of the logistics system, physical space, and the use of data to understand diverse customer require-ments (Piotrowicz and Cuthbertson 2014). Retailers could become more agile, but previous experiences with the dot-com bubble, sunk costs, low performance of investments in in-store technologies, financial metrics and incentive structure, and established culture are preventing retailers from adopting omnichannel strategies (Rigby 2011). In addition to these two articles, omnichannel scholarship is surpris-ingly silent about the structural factors associated with channel integration. For example, integration is defined as delivered interaction of channel stages, types, and agents where implementation is seen as a specific realized offering across channels (Saghiri et al. 2017). I am arguing that implementation barriers and asymmetries are paramount topics for organization studies regarding omnichannel retailing. Many retailers are organized as separate functions, which creates a coor-dination problem for these different isolated units. Channel integration has implica-tions for the co-management of omnichannel resources, and it is shaped by implementation barriers.

CEO-Driven and Planning-Oriented Omnichannel Strategy Since omnichannel retailing requires integration or coordination, it is tempting to define it solely as a top-management responsibility. For example, Neslin and Shankar (2009) provide game-theoretical evidence that coordinated structure dominates uncoordinated struc-ture in an omnichannel context. But this contradicts the results of Alonso et al. (2008), who have shown via game theory that in specific circumstances a decentralized organization can outperform centralized solutions, even when coordi-nation is required. And process scholars have emphasized that large realized strat-egies are often the result of a series of smaller, uncoordinated initiatives (Mintzberg 1978). Change can be induced by an official top-management plan, but it can also be driven by initiatives falling outside an official conception of strategy, i.e. an auton-omous strategy (Burgelman 1983). These streams of literature point to middle management as a crucial source of innovation and show that major plans often are not realized as planned (Mantere 2005; Mintzberg 1994). One should be cautious of conceptualizing omnichannel as a major centralized top-down plan. In contrast, since so many retailers are pursuing an omnichannel strategy, there is an interesting opportunity for scholars to study omnichannel emergence, autonomous initiatives, and middle management participation, and the strategy discourse that promotes or impedes such initiatives.

4.3   Resource Management Problem: Internal Sources of Sustainable Competitive Advantage

This section examines the resources of an omnichannel strategy and their management process. This is achieved by utilizing the resource-based view that examines internal sources of sustainable competitive advantage (Barney 1991). This section is divided into three parts: (1) Omnichannel resources and conditions of sustainable competitive advantage (SCA); (2) bundling a channel mix with operational resources such as logistics and IT systems; and (3) customer data analytics leveraging external opportunities to enhance the value of omnichannel resources.

Firstly, omnichannel retailing involves the management of several different types of resources. The construct of a resource is defined broadly. Resource is anything that can be considered as a strength or a weakness; for example, scale is a resource (Wernerfelt 1984). Firm resources are assets, processes, special attributes, information and knowledge (Barney 1991) that are owned or controlled by the firm (Amit and Schoemaker 1993). Thus, omnichannel resources are all assets, channels, organizational functions, and knowledge that potentially have an effect on the performance of an omnichannel strategy. Channel resources include channel types such as physical stores, in-store technologies, Internet channels, mobile solutions, and visibility in social media, but also specific choices about channel stages and agents (Piotrowicz and Cuthbertson 2014; Saghiri et al. 2017). In addition to channel resources, there are resources that are not visible to customers but are required for ensuring the daily performance of each channel. I call these operational resources. In particular, OCR involves redesigning the supply chain (Piotrowicz and Cuthbertson 2014) and a digital strategy (Ross et al. 2017) for IT systems. In addition, customer data is an important resource type (Kiron et al. 2014a, b). Resource management of OCR involves the holistic integration of all omnichannel resources: channel mix, operational resources (logistics, IT systems), and customer data analytics.

The resource-based view assumes that firms have heterogeneous resources that are imperfectly mobile (Barney 1991). This starting point addresses the two previously problematized assumptions (Table 1) about the Amazon halo (homogeneous resources) and effortless integration (mobile resources). This means that different retailers compete with an asymmetric set of resources and imitating a competitor's resource portfolio is time-consuming. They draw from a distinct set of competencies, and an omnichannel strategy should take such asymmetries into account. Retailers have created a heterogeneous resource base by distinct investments in fixed assets (e.g. physical stores, logistics and IT systems) and intangible, knowledge-based assets (e.g. brand, look and feel, product portfolio, digital channels, loyalty programs, and data analytics). Digitalization and globalization are making the competitive landscape more turbulent, complex and unpredictable (Rigby 2011; Weill and Woerner 2015; Treadgold and Reynolds 2016). Empirical research has shown that knowledge-based resources perform in an uncertain and changing environment, while physical assets perform in a stable environment (Miller and Shamsie 1996). For physical retail chains, omnichannel retailing does not merely imply the inclusion of digital channels into a channel mix. Omnichannel can be understood as a transition towards an increasingly knowledge-oriented and non-physical resource portfolio due to the global and rapidly digitalizing competitive landscape. The use of these resources requires specialized technological knowledge, which makes industry experts (middle managers, internal analysts, and external consultants) important stakeholders in all stages of the resource management process.

If a single resource is valuable, rare, inimitable, and non-substitutable (VRIN conditions), it is a source of sustainable competitive advantage (Barney 1991). Some omnichannel resources are not valuable when isolated in a stand-alone fashion. For example, customer data can be collected, but mere possession of data does not make it valuable. Current omnichannel literature does not explain conditions of sustainable competitive advantage (SCA) because it does not address the imitability or rarity of new digital channels. Competitors can easily introduce digital channels, which have made the Internet retailing landscape more competitive. It is unlikely that the mere acquisition of an individual channel could fulfil the VRIN conditions.

Omnichannel retailers face a resource management problem: structuring (acquiring) a channel portfolio, bundling channels with operational resources (logistics and IT systems) to form omnichannel capabilities, and leveraging these capabilities by using data analytics to exploit external opportunities (Sirmon et al. 2007). In fact, channel integration could be understood as a holistic bundling of channel mix and operational resources. Imitation of a functioning resource management process is more difficult than imitation of a single channel resource. Thus, when studying internal sources of SCA, one should examine VRIN conditions in all aspects of the resource-management process. This extends the analysis from an acquiring activity to cover the activities of bundling and leveraging.

Secondly, channel integration can be examined as a resource-bundling activity. Bundling channels with operations is a complex and difficult task that requires cooperation from several organizational functions. Valuable resource bundles are more likely to enjoy SCA than single resources because imitating bundles requires structuring a set of resources and private tacit knowledge of their co-management across organizational functions (Peteraf 1993). Omnichannel retailers thus face a task of crafting a unique bundle containing both physical and knowledge-based resources that fulfil the VRIN conditions.

The retail sector contains several interesting cases about successful bundling. One of the biggest growth cases in corporate history is the rise of Walmart, which simultaneously built a store network, invested in complementary distribution centres, a truck fleet, cross-docking, supplier relations, and IT systems to achieve an integrated bundle that maximizes economies of scale and efficiency (Stalk et al. 1992). In online grocery retailing, Tesco has utilized its existing store network for home deliveries. In this bundling solution, a store has a dual role—as a physical channel and a distribution location for home deliveries (Fernie et al. 2010). Retailers pursuing an omnichannel strategy face similar resource management problems, but in an increasingly digital environment.

Interestingly, the existing OCR literature has identified bundling as an important activity, but it is considered mostly in terms of bundling channels with each other.

OCR is conceptualized as the bundling of the channel stage, the channel type and the channel agent (Saghiri et al. 2017). All of these dimensions are visible to the customer. Bundling can be viewed more broadly to include operational resources. Physical retail chains often need to bundle newly acquired digital channels with existing channels and support them with internal IT systems and logistics.

Thirdly, customer data is a leveraging resource. Customer data analytics can be conceptualized as a leveraging activity. This emerging theme is increasingly gaining attention (George et al. 2014; Kiron et al. 2014a, b; Ross et al. 2017; Grewal et al. 2017). Big data capture involves sales and inventory data (ERP systems), loyalty cards, online data, profile information, mobile and location-based data (Bradlow et al. 2017). Some organizations are able to utilize customer data, while others have a massive database with limited follow-up that would create value for the firm or for its customers (Kiron et al. 2014b). Properly managed analytics can enhance the value of a resource bundle due to the ability to exploit external opportunities. This is known as leveraging (Sirmon et al. 2007). Most retail organizations have data, but the challenge is how to leverage or monetize this data.

Customer data is only valuable because it can be used for leveraging external opportunities (Sirmon et al. 2007). Customer data has no value of its own, but it can make other resources and bundles more valuable if properly leveraged. Customer data can have a negative value due to concerns about data protection, customer privacy, and unethical conduct (Bradlow et al. 2017). Data leaks can have a devastating and long-lasting effect on a corporate brand. Furthermore, Kiron et al. (2014b) argue that 34% of firms are currently not using their data effectively, i.e. the value of data is virtually zero. In such instances, retailers are harvesting data, but they lack practices for utilizing the data effectively. The value of customer data is undetermined; it can be negative, zero or positive, depending on how the leveraging activity is organized in practice.

Customer data is an imperfectly mobile and heterogeneous resource. Customer data is imperfectly mobile due to legislative limitations in sharing data and because firms have taken strong measures to protect their customer data. Data protection and privacy discussions have also created powerful non-governmental organizations (NGOs) that promote the mobility barriers of data resources (Bradlow et al. 2017). Customer data is a heterogeneous resource, as firms cater to different segments. In highly concentrated markets, only a few firms have a comprehensive customer database, which makes such data rare by definition. In addition to size and concentration, specialized activities increase the rarity of customer data. If a firm is highly specialized and serves a highly specialized segment, it can have access to customer behaviour that its rivals do not have. In contrast, medium-sized firms in homogeneous markets, catering to common customer needs, generate the kind of customer data that is in possession of rivals. Customer data is most likely to be a source of SCA for large omnichannel retailers or small highly specialized retailers.

Customer data is characterized by causal ambiguity. One can see three levels of analysis: certain, uncertain, and ambiguous. While an uncertain situation involves decision under risk, a decision can be ambiguous if the decision-maker cannot reasonably estimate the probabilities. Causal ambiguity implies a situation where the source of competitive advantage and resource value are not known (Peteraf 1993). Causal ambiguity makes imitation difficult because competitors are uncertain whether or not a resource is valuable (Lippman and Rumelt 1982). The causally ambiguous nature of data has created a situation in the retail sector where different organizations treat customer data in substantially different ways and make different choices in terms of the scale of investments (Kiron et al. 2014a, b). Causally ambiguous customer data is a two-sided sword. It is unclear how one can maximize the value of customer data and how one can specifically leverage it. Furthermore, causal ambiguity can create inter-organizational conflicts and lead to decision biases because different stakeholders hold different propositions on how customer data should be utilized and what are the sources of competitive advantage (Amit and Schoemaker 1993). On the other hand, organizations that are able to utilize customer data effectively are likely to enjoy a sustained advantage due to imitation barriers created by causal ambiguity. Ambiguous data implies that value is determined through trial-and-error, and it requires an organizational culture that tolerates failure and promotes experimentation.

Customer data may be highly fungible, and have low opportunity costs. Highly fungible resources can be applied in several different contexts with various applications. The utilization of a resource with a low opportunity cost does not reduce its applicability in other contexts. Examples of resources with high fungibility and low opportunity costs are computer operating systems and brand names (Levinthal and Wu 2010). Therefore, the benefit of customer data is that it can be leveraged in different channels and it can enhance the value of multiple resources through leveraging activities. Furthermore, in principle, customer data can be commoditized and sold in strategic factor markets (Barney 1986), but there are both legal and non-market considerations. The crucial characteristic of customer data is that it is both fungible and has low opportunity cost, so its value may not diminish even when it is applied in a single context. Furthermore, the value of knowledge-intensive assets is enhanced when environmental change is high (Miller and Shamsie 1996). In this sense, data-driven omnichannel strategies offer a way for retailers to respond to a faster pace of environmental change. Retailers can complement their physical resources that require environmental stability with digital resources in order to accommodate to changing consumer behaviour and macro economical fluctuations.

An omnichannel resource management process consists of three interrelated activities: acquiring (digital channels), bundling (integration with operational resources), and leveraging (data analytics). Synchronization of all three activities maximizes the value of the resource portfolio (Sirmon et al. 2007). Acquiring has received disproportionate attention in omnichannel scholarship, but any explanation of internal sources of omnichannel SCA needs to address all three activities simultaneously.

4.4   Competitiveness Problem: External Sources
of Sustainable Competitive Advantage

This section examines external sources of sustainable competitive advantage (SCA) via the lens of the industrial organization (Porter 1981, 2008). An omnichannel retailer should occupy a profitable position within an industry that is not exposed to hyper-competition (Porter 1981). This leads to three important themes: (1) unique competitive actions, (2) competitive asymmetries and (3) idiosyncratic synergies of channel integration.

Firstly, competitive advantage is built on unique activities (Porter 1996). The previously problematized adapt-or-die metaphor (Table 1) treats OCR as a disruption that completely redistributes the revenue streams. In this line of reasoning, everyone must adopt an omnichannel strategy or perish, which reduces OCR to a mere best practice. For example, the only long-term strategy for pure brick and mortar retailers is to *"move toward being dual-channel retailers"*, and when this is accomplished, to adopt data systems and integrate channels (Brynjolfsson et al. 2013, p. 25). There are two general arguments about improved profits through a digital strategy: increased revenue or decreased costs. Omnichannel retailing is essentially a claim about improving top-line revenue through an improved customer experience (Rigby 2011; Cao and Li 2015; Table 1 by Saghiri et al. 2017), while digital-driven cost savings are created from automation, logistics innovations, and economies of scale. However, digital strategies often focus exclusively on operational efficiency but neglect difficult-to-imitate opportunities for customer engagement or technology-driven digital solutions (Ross et al. 2017). While being important, operational efficiency cannot be a source of competitive advantage because everyone can pursue such best practices (Porter 1996). All rivals will utilize digital solutions in the future, but it is unclear how such a strategy can create a unique offering and thus drive a competitive advantage over rivals. An omnichannel strategy therefore has to specify the unique aspects that are not being offered by rivals and are hard to imitate. The unique aspects take into account competitive asymmetries or realized idiosyncratic synergies that are not available to rivals.

Secondly, there are substantial competitive asymmetries between retailers. The retail sector is not a homogeneous space, and the competitive landscape is differentiated: different firms face different options and can draw from heterogeneous competencies. An omnichannel strategy should take into account the retailer's position in the market and establish how technology is used to create unique activities that rivals are not currently pursuing and unable to replicate in the future (Porter 1981; Ross et al. 2017). There are three generic strategies: scale-driven cost leadership, differentiation, and focus (Porter 1980). In the previous section, I examined the rarity of customer data. The overall cost leader is likely to have access to market-covering general data, but rivals are not in possession of similar coverage. A highly focused retailer has access to a unique and highly specialized market segment, increasing the rarity of the data. The challenge for a medium-sized retailer is how to differentiate because differentiation introduces heterogeneity in customer data that rivals are unlikely to possess. Thus, it is crucial for an omnichannel strategy to establish differentiation. This can be achieved by utilizing one or more channels in a way that competitors are not utilizing. This means that instead of trying to offer everything to everyone, an omnichannel strategy should be very careful in selecting a specific market segment or segments for which all channel and subsequent integration choices are tailored. Such an omnichannel differentiation strategy is likely to create a great customer experience for the core segment(s) but intentionally rules out some segments as not central to the business.

The idealization of born-digital retailers neglects asymmetries between different strategic groups. This is particularly important in regards to the Amazon halo (Table 1). The online revolution in retail can be understood as a substitution threat to established physical retail chains (Treadgold and Reynolds 2016). In addition, for analysing rivalry within a strategic group, all firms face competitive pressures by the bargaining power of suppliers and consumers, new entrants, and substitution (Porter 1980, 2008). Existing rivals are experimenting with digital solutions and lowering their operational costs. Retail digitalization lowers market entry barriers because smaller retailers can offer a widened assortment at reasonable costs. For example, smaller retailers do not necessarily need a large space for a large assortment because a physical store can focus on high-volume products while utilizing in-store technologies and online solutions to cover a larger assortment. Large national retail chains are also experimenting with similar solutions, as shown by Sainsbury's acquisition of Argos. Retail digitalization is also altering the bargaining power of suppliers and customers. Consumers are facing an increased ability to choose because of access to quality information from product comparison applications and product review sites. Electronic word of mouth and increased use of social media is transforming customer behaviour (Piotrowicz and Cuthbertson 2014). Online retailing can enable suppliers to engage the customer directly or utilize emerging platforms for online marketplaces. In regards to customer bargaining power, scholars have extensively studied multichannel cannibalization, cross-channel consumer behaviour, showrooming, and webrooming (Verhoef et al. 2015). Omnichannel retailing can then be understood as a phenomenon that has an impact on all of the five forces. It also reconceptualises the online from a mere substitute into a complement (Herhausen et al. 2015). The emergence of online is not just a threat to established physical retailing because all retailers have their own idiosyncratic way of incorporating both physical and digital channels into their channel mix, and leveraging available channel synergies, to provide a seamless and unique customer experience.

Thirdly, channel integration can create idiosyncratic synergies that create cost savings. Firms can be divided into distinct strategic groups. Within a specific group, strategies can look remarkably similar, while between-group strategies can vary considerably. Firms are not free to shift from one group to another because there are considerable mobility barriers that maintain the group structure within the industry (McGee and Thomas 1986). Established physical assets (physical channels, distribution networks) and non-physical knowledge-based resources are distinguishing features for strategic groups but they are also the basis of mobility barriers. For a physical retail chain, an omnichannel strategy is likely to involve a substantial fixed investment in scalable knowledge-based resources. Large retailers can undertake such costs because the investment can be spread across a large sales volume that provides economies of scale. Smaller national retailers encounter more problems in the ability to efficiently cover such costs. Large investments are likely to decrease net margins because the overall sales volume is small. So what is the difference between synergy-driven cost efficiencies and operational efficiency related best practices? The former can be a source of competitive advantage because it is particularly effective in certain strategic groups, namely large multichannel retailers with an established physical store portfolio. The latter is a technological opportunity available to all, and it is pursued in identical fashion by all retailers, i.e. it is merely a best practice (Porter and Siggelkow 2008). In particular, firms pursuing a cost-efficient generic strategy with several channels are likely to encounter synergy benefits due to omnichannel retailing.

In contrast, the costs related to channel expansion have received only a little attention. Hard discounters (a strategic group) in particular have taken a cautious approach to omnichannel retailing. Large investments and operational costs associated with managing several different store concepts and maintaining an extensive online operation for mobile and personal computers—from advertisement to home delivery—can be turned into a source of competitive advantage if omitted. The issue of a minimalistic omnichannel is an open problem. This involves making consistent choices where channel expansion is resisted and related investment costs are bypassed. The savings are further pushed into lower prices. The goal of a minimalistic omnichannel is to build a great single-channel experience in a highly standardized store format with online channels leveraged only to reduce advertising costs. The overall operation of a minimalistic omnichannel looks very different to that of a differentiated national retailer with multiple integrated channels.

To summarize, omnichannel retailing has great potential for several multichannel retailers because there are potential cost savings due to the elimination of overlapping operations, i.e. synergies across different channels. However, an ideal omnichannel strategy has different content for each distinct strategic group in the retail sector (Porter and Siggelkow 2008). Physical retailers encounter a different omnichannel world than do purely digital retailers, and the paths may not converge, even if both pursue an omnichannel strategy. Large actors have room to develop digital solutions internally, while smaller actors may wish to focus on their retail niche and buy required competencies from digital consultancies. For retail management, this requires unique positioning within the competitive landscape (Porter 1996, 2008) and also internal resource orchestration (Sirmon et al. 2011) in order to realize potential synergies and to integrate channels.

4.5   Coordination Problem: Implementation Barriers of an Omnichannel Strategy

The objective of this section is to examine the implementation barriers of an omnichannel strategy. The strategy process is used as a theoretical lens because it considers the implementation of strategic plans (Van de Ven 1992; Pettigrew 1992) and problematizes planning by emphasizing the role of emergent bottom-up initiatives (Mintzberg 1978, 1994). This section is divided into four parts: (1) sources of implementation barriers; (2) functional coordination associated with channel integration; (3) strategy discourse that promotes middle-management participation; and (4) achieving strategic change as a series of small emergent bottom-up initiatives.

Firstly, implementation barriers of omnichannel strategies result from structural inertia. All organizations have external and internal sources of inertia that resist change. External sources of inertia derive from industry conditions. Strong legal mobility barriers, private specialized knowledge, asymmetric information between rivals, and specific legitimacy constraints prevent organizations from changing (Hannan and Freeman 1977). In this light, several institutional barriers such as data privacy acts, labour unions, oligopolies, and contractual arrangements are sources of external inertia that make it harder for retail sector organizations to adapt to technological disruption and changing consumer behaviour. Internal sources of inertia arise from the organizational structure. Organizations with substantial investments in fixed assets, asymmetric internal information, internal politics, and idiosyncratic histories are likely to encounter change barriers (Hannan and Freeman 1977). Large retail chains are naturally inert due to a heavy emphasis on fixed physical assets, such as distribution centres and stores. Retail organizations often have a complex structure and a large number of employees performing various organizational functions. This can create intra-organizational pockets of private information, especially among the top and bottom, where the organization may be steered in multiple and often contradictory directions.

Some retail organizations have pluralistic decision-making structures that are decentralized and have several authority structures. Pluralistic structures are characterized by multiple decision-makers and complex decision-making processes (Denis et al. 2000, 2011). For example, in Finland, the retail chain S Group has historically crafted a dual authority structure, where co-operatives own the headquarters that are responsible for steering the group that includes the co-operatives. Its competitor, K Group, is formed by the cooperation between retail entrepreneurs and the headquarters Kesko, which is an example of a decentralized or networked decision-making structure. Decision-making in pluralistic organizations can lead to indecision, ambiguity in direction of change, and gatekeeping (Denis et al. 2000, 2011).

Retailers face both internal and external inert pressures that resist their attempts to pursue an omnichannel strategy. The current resource base, capabilities, sector position, and intra-organizational culture are powerful asymmetries in a retailer's ability to achieve change. While physical retail chain is often subject to historic growth and investments in physical assets, a digital-born global retailer is subjected to much less inertia. This may be one reason why the omnichannel literature is filled with examples of online retailers (the Amazon halo). Emphasizing examples from born-digital start-ups ignores the implementation problem associated with the omnichannel strategy of established physical multichannel retailers.

Secondly, channel integration requires functional coordination (problematization of effortless integration in Table 1). OCR is a holistic activity that crosses over traditional organizational functions; it penetrates the organization from employee to top management; it promotes specialization requirements and adds decision-making complexity; it changes the competitive landscape; and it has societal implications. The silo mentality has been reported as one obstacle to addressing the coordination problem (Piotrowicz and Cuthbertson 2014). Functional coordination can work against an individual business unit's key performance indicators and thus reduce potential bonuses. Coordination can imply costs to its own business unit while a performance hike is created in a neighbouring business unit.

Functional coordination does not automatically imply centralization. In a game-theoretical model, decentralization outperforms centralization if and only if the need for coordination is small and a bias toward own division is small (Alonso et al. 2008). The former is very interesting, since the birth of the omnichannel literature[2] has highlighted an increased need for channel coordination. In fact, the model of Alonso et al. (2008) can potentially explain why some physical multichannel organizations have a decentralized structure (for example, entrepreneurial networks)—the need for coordination is small in a purely physical multichannel environment. However, in order to achieve synergistic benefits through resource bundling and leveraging across physical and digital channels, the need for coordination becomes crucial. There is also another option when decentralization trumps centralization—if the organization experiences only a little sub-optimization or bias toward its own function (Alonso et al. 2008). This highlights the need to understand intra-organizational culture. Management that encourages participation by systematically rewarding coordination initiatives requires less control than an organization characterized by internal political struggles and sub-optimization.

There is another game-theoretical model that has contradictory results. In the model of Neslin and Shankar (2009), the firm has to coordinate investments in two channels that can experience cannibalization or synergies. They show that through coordination, every firm reaches higher profits in every possible scenario when compared to decentralized investment management. This is in stark contrast to the findings of Alonso et al. (2008), who showed two special cases where decentralization is the dominating strategy. The model of Alonso et al. (2008) focuses on examining the effects of local information held by business unit managers. Neslin and Shankar (2009) assume perfect information across the organization, which also

---

[2]As early as 2006, data integration, channel coordination and resource allocation across channels were identified as key challenges in multichannel retailing (Neslin et al. 2006). Subsequent scholarship has adopted channel integration as the cornerstone of omnichannel retailing (Piotrowicz and Cuthbertson 2014; Verhoef et al. 2015).

leads to the universal recommendation of centralized investment management. If one makes the assumption that store, area, and middle management have specialized local information that is crucial for the success of a strategy, an ideal omnichannel strategy nurtures an informal culture and builds a formal reward scheme in order to take advantage of local information. However, more game-theory modelling is needed for solving the contradictory results in the performance of integration-coordination-(de)centralization.

Thirdly, middle management participation is crucial for championing novel initiatives (Burgelman 1983). Middle management participation (Mantere 2005) and strategy discourse (Mantere and Vaara 2008) are important aspects when considering the implementation of omnichannel strategies. Retail activities involve middle management championing of autonomous bottom-up initiatives and mentoring in order to facilitate an organizational culture that promotes risk-taking and experimentation in technologically oriented initiatives. Channel integration can be understood as a holistic renewal journey which is characterized by a drastic change in organization-wide shared strategic schema. It is an attempt to influence and achieve a widely shared schema of cross-channel collabouration that distinguishes successfully implemented omnichannel strategies from unrealized integration initiatives (Volberda and Lewin 2003). A problem in approaching omnichannel strategy as a CEO-driven top-down plan (Table 1) is that it excludes various forms of participation and ignores the importance of establishing a shared schema while explicitly requiring integration that leads to a need for coordination and participation.

Strategy discourse can encourage or discourage participation (Mantere and Vaara 2008). Omnichannel scholars should examine culturally constructed taken-for-granted assumptions within the omnichannel discourse. Mantere and Vaara (2008) identified three forms of participatory strategy discourse (self-actualization, ditalization, and concretization) and three forms discursive exclusion (mystification, disciplining, and technologization). A problem in omnichannel discourse is that it fulfils all three forms of exclusion: omnichannel is a digital-driven abstract strategy (for example, Rigby 2011; Brynjolfsson et al. 2013) which is represented as a mysterious and technologically oriented solution for the future, and retailers often approach omnichannel solely as a top-management initiative, which is a form of disciplining discourse. The problem of these three forms of omnichannel discourse is that it hinders bottom-up initiatives, participation, and coordination. There is another possible path where a successfully implemented omnichannel strategy proceeds in an emergent fashion, when it is characterized by concrete projects where top management engages in constant dialogue throughout the organization. Omnichannel could provide various forms of self-actualization and reward schemes that would promote organization-wide participation.

Fourthly, strategic change can be realized as a series of small emergent initiatives. The implementation problem in an omnichannel strategy results from an assumption that omnichannel is understood as a plan (Table 1) for channel integration within the physical-digital interface. In a famous critique, Mintzberg (1994) argued for the benefits of strategy emergence, since not all contingencies can be planned. Planning does not guarantee participation. As Mintzberg (1994, p. 109) states, 'The problem is that planning represents a *calculating* style of management, not a *committing* style'. A planning-oriented approach offers a high degree of confidence in a selected course of action while offering only limited tools for reacting to unexpected and non-linear changes. Planning does not ensure the commitment of organizational members to the omnichannel strategy.

Why hasn't everyone been able to pursue an omnichannel strategy, despite its great premise? I have highlighted the crucial role of middle management in championing successful channel integration and as a source of novel initiatives. A successful omnichannel strategy has unique innovations that are idiosyncratic to the organization. An organization that has an entrepreneurial culture that encourages risk-taking, tolerates failure, and favours experimentation is more likely to innovate such unique features. The risk in the strategy is conceptualizing it as a fixed top-down plan, which is unable to adapt to changes in the operating environment and prevents bottom-up innovations (Mintzberg 1994). Thus, a rigid omnichannel plan can lead to various forms of resistance and gatekeeping throughout the organization.

5   Synthesis: The Omnichannel Strategy Triangle

Omnichannel publications paint a picture of the retail sector as a titanic that is about to be hit by an omnichannel iceberg. The retail sector is undergoing a drastic change due to digitalization and changing consumption behaviour (Rigby 2011; Brynjolfsson et al. 2013; Treadgold and Reynolds 2016). This book chapter has examined strategic aspects of omnichannel retailing (OCR) that have been neglected in prior research. This section provides a synthesis (Table 2) for the five identified retail problems, specifies content for each respective analytical level, and presents a holistic model of strategic management for omnichannel retailing: the omnichannel strategy triangle (Fig. 1).

What are the sources of sustainable competitive advantage for an omnichannel strategy? What intra-organizational implementation barriers exist for an omnichannel strategy? I have sought to answer these two interrelated questions by problematizing deep assumptions in the field (Table 1). The relaxation of the problematization has led to the identification and specification of five analytical levels about OCR: society, consumer, industry expert, management and employee. It pools together various concepts to include the societal context (level 1); omnichannel consumption (level 2); strategic aspects of internal resources (level 3); external positions and competitive asymmetries (level 4); and structural implementation barriers (level 5). The three bottom levels are crucial for determining competitive advantage and implementation success of an omnichannel strategy. Table 2 summarizes the results. For each level, I have identified the retail problem, related activities, and the focus areas for management. I have also presented major

Table 2 Key components of the omnichannel strategy triangle, focus areas and research questions

Level: major stakeholder	Theoretical area and information source	Focus areas for retail management	Retail problem: key activities	Major questions for public policy, practitioners and academics
Level 1. Society	Societal context (Pettigrew 1992; Johns 2006): can be read from a newspaper	• Rise of global e-commerce • Intangible value drivers due to technological disruption in retail sector • Changing nature of work • Market concentration and potential welfare loss	Contextualization problem • Redefining • Participating • Adapting	• How can public policy promote red queen competition in omnichannel retailing? • How is digitalization changing resource values in the retail sector? • How is the nature of work changing due to the increased need for technological capabilities? • How can national retailers compete against global retail giants? • How can retailers incorporate services of the public sectors and NGOs into their offering? • How do mainly physical retailers adapt to retail digitalization?
Level 2. Consumer	Omnichannel consumption (Rigby 2011): can be experienced when shopping	• Seamless customer experience • In-store and mobile technologies	Integration problem • Crafting • Acquiring (structuring)	• Does seamless customer experience have a positive value surplus for retail customers, and is this value segmented heterogeneously? • How is customer behaviour changing as a result of technical change? • What channels should a particular retailer acquire as part of its channel mix, and which channel should it not acquire? • What is the effect of channel integration on customer loyalty and brand value?

(continued)

Table 2 (continued)

Level: major stakeholder	Theoretical area and information source	Focus areas for retail management	Retail problem: key activities	Major questions for public policy, practitioners and academics
Level 3. Industry expert	Resource management process (Barney 1991; Sirmon et al. 2007): can be bundled and leveraged	• Bundling channel mix, logistics and IT systems as a unique resource portfolio • Leveraging resource: emerging analytics of customer data	Resource management problem • Bundling • Leveraging	• How can retailers create a VRIN bundle of resources between channel mix, logistics, IT systems and other resources? • How can retailers utilize customer data to leverage external opportunities and enhance the value of adjacent resources? • How can retailers acquire specialized knowledge and take advantage of technological know-how?
Level 4. Management	Industrial organization (Porter 1981, 2008): can be analysed as a longitudinal pattern	• Differentiation through unique omnichannel strategy • Different groups have asymmetric options and capabilities • Matching different activities for integration-related synergies	Competitiveness problem • Positioning • Orchestrating	• What are the unique aspects of successful omnichannel strategies? • How can retailers achieve differentiation through omnichannel strategies? • How can potential synergies of channel integration be utilized? • How can focused (small, specialized) retailers achieve SCA through an omnichannel strategy?

| Level 5. All employees | Strategy process (Mintzberg 1978; Pettigrew 1992; Van de Ven 1992): can be lived with but often taken-for-granted: emergent strategy shaped by formal rules, implicit practices and organizational culture | • Implementation barriers due to zero-sum games, sub-optimization, incentive metrics and silo mentality (culture)
• Coordinating distinct activities
• Mentoring and omnichannel discourse that promotes organization-wide participation
• Middle managers as champions of novel bottom-up initiatives
• Omnichannel strategy as an emergent pattern of small initiatives | Coordination problem
• Championing
• Mentoring | • How can a firm overcome implementation barriers of omnichannel strategies?
• How does organizational structure affect the implementation of strategic change?
• How does informal organization and organization culture affect implementation of omnichannel strategy?
• How can cross-channel coordination be promoted for middle management?
• What role does championing play for enabling bottom-up initiatives?
• Can retailers become omnichannel retailers through the emergence of small initiatives? |

questions for each level and identified a theoretical canvas for addressing these questions.

The contribution of this chapter is to broaden the applicability of omnichannel retailing to take into account the societal context and to include aspects of strategic management. This is achieved by the main model: the omnichannel strategy triangle (Fig. 1). The content of the triangle (what/focus area) represents identified key constructs. These constructs are relevant and have an impact especially for the particular stakeholder for a given level (who/impact). The right-hand side (what/key activity) contains retailers' activities for each level.

The omnichannel strategy triangle model (Fig. 1) is holistic, and the levels are connected to each other. The stakeholder impacts and retail activities are represented by the two arrows. The left declining arrow shows omnichannel retailing as a set of societal changes, technological disruption, and consumption megatrends that require adaptation within the resource base, a competitive position, a formal structure, and a way of working (a culture). This is coupled with the arrow on the right-hand side, which shows key retailer activities for solving specific problems for each level. Middle management championing and top management mentoring is needed for addressing coordination problems and to promote organization-wide participation (level 5). Retail management is concerned about the competitiveness problem, and it can achieve competitive advantage by the orchestration of internal resources and by external positioning within the competitive landscape (level 4). The resource management problem requires bundling the channel mix with operational resources and leveraging customer data (level 3). An organization that can resolve the implemen-

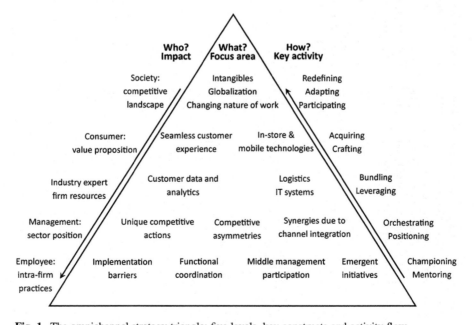

Fig. 1 The omnichannel strategy triangle: five levels, key constructs and activity flow

tation barriers, and address external and internal sources of competitiveness, can credibly pursue an omnichannel strategy and address the integration problem: acquiring new channels and crafting an omnichannel strategy (level 2). Finally, the contextualization problem requires adaptation to societal megatrends, redefining the value proposition, and participating as a responsible corporate citizen (level 1).

6   Conclusions, Implications for Academia and Practice

Digitalization does not imply an end to physical retailing. An omnichannel strategy is about making choices where the core strategic question is in fact, what is not omnichannel? The 20th century marked a period when retail chains built large hypermarkets and department stores that offered an impressive range with low prices for everyone. Recently, such large units have encountered problems due to increased rivalry from various competitors such as hard discounters, but also because of global Internet retailers (Treadgold and Reynolds 2016). Omnichannel retailing can be a solution, but only if it enables the retailer to craft a unique offering. This means that an omnichannel strategy needs to be tailored to the specific market segment to establish a unique market position that is exposed to a lower degree of rivalry. Omnichannel is a holistic approach that emphasizes integration for delivering a seamless customer experience across all channels (Piotrowicz and Cuthbertson 2014). Retail management needs to focus on unique activities (Porter 1996) that omnichannel retailing is delivering because it is these activities that can deliver a sustainable competitive advantage. For the purely physical retail chain, omnichannel resource management consists of acquiring digital resources, bundling them with existing physical channels and operations, and utilizing customer data to exploit external opportunities (Sirmon et al. 2007). These three simultaneous activities help to determine the competitiveness of an omnichannel strategy.

An omnichannel strategy can generate intra-organizational resistance due to its holistic nature and requirements for cooperation, which challenges existing functional logic and its incentive structure. Digital initiatives have an abstract and mystical nature which can discourage participation (Mantere and Vaara 2008). One option for top management is to consider the omnichannel strategy as a series of small risky initiatives and encourage bottom-up solutions. This requires middle management championing and mentoring by top management. The adoption rate of OCR varies across markets. In some markets, the retailers are working on the first steps to overcome implementation barriers. In other markets, such as the UK, there are retailers who have pursued an omnichannel strategy for several years and are now working to turn omnichannel retailing into a source of competitive advantage (Table 1 by Saghiri et al. 2017). The omnichannel strategy triangle (Fig. 1) can be used as a tool for examining omnichannel retailing as a complex construct that penetrates the whole organization, is relevant for several stakeholders and consists of multiple activities. The omnichannel strategy triangle presents new research areas for academics and can be used as a strategy analysis tool for practitioners.

6.1 Implications for Academics

The model opens up potential strategy- and policy-related research avenues (Table 2). This involves specification of four research areas in addition to the existing marketing-based omnichannel scholarship (level 2). These areas are the societal context of omnichannel retailing; management of omnichannel resources; positioning and competitive asymmetries within the sector; and structural aspects of the omnichannel organization. Omnichannel scholarship has utilized quantitative methods extensively (Verhoef et al. 2015) and a similar approach has often been used in studying the resource-based view and the industrial organization (Hoskisson et al. 1999). Qualitative methods provide a complementary approach for examining omnichannel retailing and strategy. The societal context can be studied using expert interviews, focus groups, and workshops (Cuthbertson et al. 2016) and also archive material as sources of data. Studies on competitive advantage (levels 3 and 4) can conduct comparative case studies to distinguish low-performing firms from high-performing firms and to avoid the halo effect (Rosenzweig 2007). Comparative case studies have been used in omnichannel retailing (Saghiri et al. 2017) and in the resource-based view (Miller and Shamsie 1996). Finally, single case studies and discourse analyses (Mantere and Vaara 2008) are useful for studying the role of the organization structure in omnichannel retailing. Extreme cases can be utilized for studying the boundary conditions of omnichannel retailing.

6.2 Implications for Practitioners

The model brings together major relevant themes that should be considered when crafting omnichannel strategies. Omnichannel retailing is a challenging task, but strategy is ultimately about differentiation through unique activities (Porter 1996). For crafting an omnichannel strategy, it is important to define what omnichannel is not and who the retailer chooses not to serve. Retailers can design a unique mix of activities that is based on leveraging customer data for deep understanding of their target segments' needs and to bundle operational resources to realize economies of scale. This conceptualizes omnichannel retailing as a unique strategy that exploits available asymmetries between different retail types and draws from existing competencies in the integration process of new digital channels. Furthermore, many retail organizations are complex (co-operatives, hybrid organizations, network structures and large global retailers), which creates implementation barriers and ambiguity. Middle management has a crucial role in coordination and collaboration for delivering a unique, seamless customer experience by utilizing state-of-the-art technologies across all available channels.

Questions for Discussion and Review

1. Why is contextualization important for strategic management?

2. How are major societal changes affecting omnichannel retailing?
3. Critically evaluate the shared assumptions that academics have about omnichannel retailing?
4. What are the differences between intra-organizational and sector-level explanations of sustainable competitive advantage in omnichannel retailing?
5. What are the critical resources to support an omnichannel strategy?
6. Explain the omnichannel resource management process.
7. Why is omnichannel retailing highlighting the role of technological experts and middle management? How is this related to the polarization of work?
8. Digital initiatives are often justified by cost savings or increased revenue. Explain the differences between the two justifications and when they may be used.
9. Why are omnichannel strategies often seen as best practice, and what should be taken into account when crafting a competitive omnichannel strategy?
10. What are the main obstacles for the implementation of omnichannel strategies?

References

Alonso, R., Dessein, W., & Matouschek, N. (2008). When does coordination require centralization? *American Economic Review, 98*(1), 145–179.

Alvesson, M., & Sandberg, J. (2011). Generating research questions through problematization. *Academy of Management Review, 36*(2), 247–271.

Amit, R., & Schoemaker, P. J. (1993). Strategic assets and organizational rent. *Strategic Management Journal, 14*(1), 33–46.

Barnett, W. P., & Hansen, M. T. (1996). The Red Queen in organizational evolution. *Strategic Management Journal, 17*(S1), 139–157.

Barney, J. B. (1986). Strategic factor markets: Expectations, luck, and business strategy. *Management Science, 32*(10), 1231–1241.

Barney, J. (1991). Firm resources and sustained competitive advantage. *Journal of Management, 17* (1), 99–120.

Bell, D. R., Gallino, S., & Moreno, A. (2014). How to win in an omnichannel world. *MIT Sloan Management Review, 56*(1), 45–53.

Björkroth, T., Frosterus, H., Kajova, M., & Palo, E. (2012). *Kuinka kaupan ostovoima vaikuttaa kaupan ja teollisuuden välisiin suhteisiin?* Kilpailuvirasto.

Bradlow, E. T., Gangwar, M., Kopalle, P., & Voleti, S. (2017). The role of big data and predictive analytics in retailing. *Journal of Retailing; Greenwich, 93*(1), 79–95.

Brynjolfsson, E., Yu Jeffrey, H., & Rahman, M. S. (2013). Competing in the age of omnichannel retailing. *MIT Sloan Management Review, 54*(4), 23–29.

Burgelman, R. A. (1983). A model of the interaction of strategic behavior, corporate context, and the concept of strategy. *The Academy of Management Review, 8*(1), 61–70.

Cao, L., & Li, L. (2015). The impact of cross-channel integration on retailers' sales growth. *Journal of Retailing, 91*(2), 198–216.

Cuthbertson, R., Rusanen, O., Pulkka, L., Paavola, L., Nyrhinen, J., et al. (2016). *Role of retailing in finnish society*. Tekes Policy Brief 9/2016, Ecosystems, spillovers and new policy approaches. Helsinki.

de Villiers, C., & Dumay, J. (2014). Writing an article for a refereed accounting journal. *Pacific Accounting Review, 26*(3), 324–350.

Denis, J.-L., Langley, A., & Pineault, M. (2000). Becoming a leader in a complex organization. *Journal of Management Studies, 37*(8), 1063–1100.

Denis, J.-L., Dompierre, G., Langley, A., & Rouleau, L. (2011). Escalating indecision: Between reification and strategic ambiguity. *Organization Science, 22*(1), 225–244.

Fernie, J., Sparks, L., & McKinnon, A. C. (2010). Retail logistics in the UK: Past, present and future. *International Journal of Retail & Distribution Management, 38*(11/12), 894–914.

George, G., Haas, M. R., & Pentland, A. (2014). Big data and management. *Academy of Management Journal, 57*(2), 321–326.

Grewal, D., Roggeveen, A. L., & Nordfält, J. (2017). The future of retailing. *Journal of Retailing, 93*(1), 1–6.

Hannan, M. T., & Freeman, J. (1977). The population ecology of organizations. *American Journal of Sociology, 82*(5), 929–964.

Herhausen, D., Binder, J., Schoegel, M., & Herrmann, A. (2015). Integrating bricks with clicks: Retailer-level and channel-level outcomes of online–offline channel integration. *Journal of Retailing, 91*(2), 309–325.

Hoskisson, R. E., Hitt, M. A., Wan, W. P., & Yiu, D. (1999). Theory and research in strategic management: Swings of a pendulum. *Journal of Management, 25*(3), 417–456.

Johns, G. (2017). Reflections on the 2016 decade award: Incorporating context in organizational research. *Academy of Management Review, 42*(4), 577–595.

Kiron, D., Prentice, P. K., & Ferguson, R. B. (2014a). Raising the bar with analytics. *MIT Sloan Management Review, 55*(2), 29–33.

Kiron, D., Prentice, P. K., & Ferguson, R. B. (2014b). The analytics mandate. *MIT Sloan Management Review, 55*(4), 1–25.

Levinthal, D. A., & Wu, B. (2010). Opportunity costs and non-scale free capabilities: Profit maximization, corporate scope, and profit margins. *Strategic Management Journal, 31*(7), 780–801.

Lincoln, Y. S., & Guba, E. G. (1985). *Naturalistic inquiry.* London: Sage.

Lippman, S. A., & Rumelt, R. P. (1982). Uncertain imitability: An analysis of interfirm differences in efficiency under competition. *The Bell Journal of Economics, 13*(2), 418–438.

Mantere, S. (2005). Strategic practices as enablers and disablers of championing activity. *Strategic Organization, 3*(2), 157–184.

Mantere, S., & Vaara, E. (2008). On the problem of participation in strategy: A critical discursive perspective. *Organization Science, 19*(2), 341–358.

McGee, J., & Thomas, H. (1986). Strategic groups: Theory, research and taxonomy. *Strategic Management Journal, 7*(2), 141–160.

Miller, D., & Shamsie, J. (1996). The resource-based view of the firm in two environments: The Hollywood film studios from 1936 to 1965. *Academy of Management Journal, 39*(3), 519–543.

Mintzberg, H. (1978). Patterns in strategy formation. *Management Science, 24*(9), 934–948.

Mintzberg, H. (1987). Crafting strategy. *Harvard Business Review, 65*(4), 66–75.

Mintzberg, H. (1994). The fall and rise of strategic planning. *Harvard Business Review, 72*, 107–114.

Mintzberg, H., & McHugh, A. (1985). Strategy formation in an adhocracy. *Administrative Science Quarterly, 30*(2), 160–197.

Neslin, S. A., & Shankar, V. (2009). Key issues in multichannel customer management: Current knowledge and future directions. *Journal of Interactive Marketing, 23*(1), 70–81.

Neslin, S. A., Grewal, D., Leghorn, R., Shankar, V., Teerling, M. L., et al. (2006). Challenges and opportunities in multichannel customer management. *Journal of Service Research, 9*(2), 95–112.

Peteraf, M. A. (1993). The cornerstones of competitive advantage: A resource-based view. *Strategic Management Journal, 14*(3), 179–191.

Pettigrew, A. M. (1992). The character and significance of strategy process research. *Strategic Management Journal, 13*(Winter Special Issue: Fundamental themes in strategy process research), 5–16.

Piotrowicz, W., & Cuthbertson, R. (2014). Introduction to the special issue information technology in retail: Toward omnichannel retailing. *International Journal of Electronic Commerce, 18*(4), 5–16.

Porter, M. E. (1980). *Competitive strategy: Techniques for analyzing industries and competitors.* New York: Free Press.

Porter, M. E. (1981). The contributions of industrial organization to strategic management. *The Academy of Management Review, 6*(4), 609–620.

Porter, M. E. (1996). What is strategy? *Harvard Business Review, 74*(November–December), 61–78.

Porter, M. E. (2008). The five competitive forces that shape strategy. *Harvard Business Review, 86* (1), 78–93.

Porter, M., & Siggelkow, N. (2008). Contextuality within activity systems and sustainability of competitive advantage. *Academy of Management Perspectives, 22*(2), 34–56.

Rigby, D. (2011). The future of shopping. *Harvard Business Review, 89*(12), 64–75.

Rosenzweig, P. (2007). Misunderstanding the nature of company performance: The halo effect and other business delusions. *California Management Review, 49*(4), 6–20.

Ross, J. W., Beath, C. M., & Sebastian, I. M. (2017). How to develop a great digital strategy. *MIT Sloan Management Review, 58*(2), 7–9.

Rumelt, R. P., Schendel, D. E., & Teece, D. J. (1994). *Chapter 1. Fundamental issues in strategy: A research agenda* (pp. 9–47). Boston: Harvard Business Review Press.

Saghiri, S., Wilding, R., Mena, C., & Bourlakis, M. (2017). Toward a three-dimensional framework for omni-channel. *Journal of Business Research, 77*, 53–67.

Sandberg, J., & Alvesson, M. (2011). Ways of constructing research questions: Gap-spotting or problematization? *Organization, 18*(1), 23–44.

Shenton, A. K. (2004). Strategies for ensuring trustworthiness in qualitative research projects. *Education for Information, 22*(2), 63–75.

Sirmon, D. G., Hitt, M. A., & Ireland, R. D. (2007). Managing firm resources in dynamic environments to create value: Looking inside the black box. *Academy of Management Review, 32*(1), 273–292.

Sirmon, D. G., Hitt, M. A., Ireland, R. D., & Gilbert, B. A. (2011). Resource orchestration to create competitive advantage: Breadth, depth, and life cycle effects. *Journal of Management, 37*(5), 1390–1412.

Stalk, G., Evans, P., & Shulman, L. E. (1992). Competing on capabilities: The new rules of corporate strategy. *Harvard Business Review, 70*(2), 54–66.

Suddaby, R. (2010). Editor's comments: Construct clarity in theories of management and organization. *Academy of Management Review, 35*(3), 346–357.

Ton, Z. (2014). *The good jobs strategy: How the smartest companies invest in employees to lower costs and boost profits.* New York: Amazon Publishing.

Treadgold, A. D., & Reynolds, J. (2016). *Navigating the new retail landscape: A guide for business leaders.* Oxford: Oxford University Press.

Van De Ven, A. H. (1992). Suggestions for studying strategy process: A research note. *Strategic Management Journal, 13*(S1), 169–188.

Verhoef, P. C., Kannan, P. K., & Inman, J. J. (2015). From multi-channel retailing to omni-channel retailing: Introduction to the special issue on multi-channel retailing. *Journal of Retailing, 91*(2), 174–181.

Volberda, H. W., & Lewin, A. Y. (2003). Guest editors' introduction: Co-evolutionary dynamics within and between firms: from evolution to co-evolution. *Journal of Management Studies, 40* (8), 2111–2136.

Warr, D. J. (2005). "It was fun. . . but we don't usually talk about these things": Analyzing sociable interaction in focus groups. *Qualitative Inquiry, 11*(2), 200–225.

Weill, P., & Woerner, S. L. (2015). Thriving in an increasingly digital ecosystem. *MIT Sloan Management Review, 56*(4), 27–34.

Wernerfelt, B. (1984). A resource-based view of the firm. *Strategic Management Journal, 5*(2), 171–180.

Wilkinson, S. (1998). Focus group methodology: A review. *International Journal of Social Research Methodology, 1*(3), 181–203.

Zeng, F., Luo, X., Dou, Y., & Zhang, Y. (2016). How to make the most of omnichannel retailing. *Harvard Business Review, 94*(7/8), 22–23.

Olli Rusanen M.Sc. (Tech) is a doctoral student in Aalto University School of Business. His doctoral research examines retail digitalization and the strategic management of intangible resources. He has studied major retail chains the UK, USA, and Finland in order to understand how resource management practices change due to technological change and how firms pursue competitive advantage in an increasingly digital landscape. Olli has also researched strategic management of pluralistic organizations, stigmatization, and how firms restart growth after a period of stagnation. Theoretical areas of interest are strategy-as-practice, strategy process and the resource-based view.

Implementation of Omnichannel Strategy in the US Retail: Evolutionary Approach

Lanlan Cao

Abstract The aim of this chapter is to analyse different stages of omnichannel development and integration. Reports to the New York Stock Exchange, submitted by 91 US retailers are investigated in a comparative analysis. The findings indicate that the creation of an omnichannel retailer and identifies several stages of cross-channel integration strategy. According to the proposed model, the integration starts from a silo mode, when online and traditional are operated separately, through multi-channel with a minimal level of integration between channels, then the level of integration increases (multi-channel, with moderate integration), and the final stage is full integration, the omnichannel. Omnichannel development does need to be a revolutionary approach, but is implemented through an evolutionary approach where the company is moving step by step, gradually changing its operations through integration. Such a model can be used as road map for retailers, when building towards an omnichannel business model.

1 Introduction

The proliferation of sales channels and the ongoing digitalization have dramatically changed the retail landscape in recent years (Verhoef et al. 2015). The search for synergy among retailers' multiple channels in the pursuit of providing a seamless shopping experience to their customers motivates retailers to move from a multi-channel to an omnichannel retailing strategy (Brynjolfsson et al. 2013; Rigby 2011).

Cross-channel integration, as a retailer's chosen way to implement its omnichannel strategy through combining its multiple channels to run together (Cao and Li 2015; Neslin et al. 2006), is therefore attracting increasing attention in the literature (Herhausen et al. 2015; Verhoef 2012; Zhang et al. 2010). Most of the research focuses on issues such as the benefits and costs of integration across channels (Cao and Li 2015; Neslin et al. 2006). Few of these articles deal with

L. Cao (✉)
NEOMA Business School, Mont-Saint-Aignan, France
e-mail: Lanlan.CAO@neoma-bs.fr

© Springer Nature Switzerland AG 2019
W. Piotrowicz, R. Cuthbertson (eds.), *Exploring Omnichannel Retailing*,
https://doi.org/10.1007/978-3-319-98273-1_3

how such integration can be implemented by firms (Hansen and Sia 2015). Zhang et al. (2010) point out that implementation may require organizational changes as well as decisions regarding the retail mix between homogenization and harmonization. Furthermore, studies acknowledge that most retailers develop their cross-channel integration gradually, such that the degree of integration ranges from complete separation to the full coordination of channels (Neslin et al. 2006). As a consequence, the implementation of an omnichannel strategy should be studied from an evolutionary perspective (Cao and Li 2015). Two key research questions are likely to be of interest to both academics and practitioners:

RQ1 What are the different stages of cross-channel integration?

RQ2 And for each stage, how should this integration be implemented?

In addressing these questions, this paper is structured as follows: First, I review the concepts from previous research regarding multi-, omni-, and cross-channel management. In order to provide an analytical framework for my study, I also outline the conceptual foundations for retail business-model innovation. Then, I briefly present my qualitative research design and methodology toward 91 publicly traded US retail firms between 2008 and 2011. Afterwards I go on to report my findings, and then to link them with previous research through my discussions. I conclude the chapter with a summary, managerial implications, and suggestions for further research.

2 Literature Review

I draw my literature review from two dimensions: (1) definition of the concepts: multi-, cross-, and omnichannel management in order to clarify these terms which are often interchangeably used in the literature, and (2) building the linkage between the implementation of an omnichannel strategy and retail business model innovation to provide an analytical framework for my empirical study.

From multi-channel to omnichannel management: retailers' adoption of cross-channel integration approach.

Although the concepts of multi-, cross-, and omnichannel management are used indistinctly in the literature (Beck and Rygl 2015), recent studies have attempted to clarify these terms.

Multi-channel retailing is defined as the set of activities involved in selling merchandise or services to consumers through more than one channel (Levy and Weitz 2009), and omnichannel retailing is perceived to have evolved from this (Brynjolfsson et al. 2013; Piotrowicz and Cuthbertson 2014; Verhoef et al. 2015). In comparison with the multi-channel phase, omnichannel retailing is characterized by several features. First, omnichannel retailing involves more channels: not only interactive channels—including store, online website, direct marketing, mobile channels, and social media—but also customer touchpoints, such as mass-communication channels, including TV, radio, Customer to Customer (C2C) and print (Verhoef et al. 2015). Second, omnichannel retailing has a more customer-centric orientation, with customers moving freely across channels within a single transaction process. The customer journey should be smooth; firms therefore need to provide a seamless, unified customer experience, regardless of the channels used (Kozlenkova et al. 2015; Piotrowicz and Cuthbertson 2014). Third, omnichannel retailing focuses on the brand instead of on retail channels (Piotrowicz and Cuthbertson 2014; Verhoef et al. 2015). It is an integrated multi-channel approach to sales and marketing (Hansen and Sia 2015), demanding firms' synergetic management of the numerous available channels and customer touchpoints (Verhoef et al. 2015). Because the channels are managed together, omnichannel retailing emphasizes customer–brand–channel (rather than simply customer–channel) interactions (Neslin et al. 2014).

Moving from multi-channel to omnichannel management often requires retailers to make significant changes at both strategic and organizational levels (Zhang et al. 2010). Retailers must change nearly every aspect of their businesses, including front-end and back-end operations (Sousa and Voss 2006), supply chain (Piotrowicz and Cuthbertson 2014), and even their organizational structures (Zhang et al. 2010). Chaffey (2010) and Zhang et al. (2010) therefore point out that most retailers need to adopt a maturity model in order to move toward omnichannel retailing. This stage-of-adoption model is discussed in the literature as firms' adoption of cross-channel integration (Berger et al. 2002; Neslin et al. 2006; Yan et al. 2010) from two perspectives: customer- versus firm-centric. Customer-centric perspectives highlight the benefits to consumers (e.g. Gulati and Garino 2000). Firm-centric perspectives instead focus on the benefits for the firm (e.g. Neslin et al. 2006). However, Neslin and Shankar (2009) and Verhoef (2012) point out that neither perspective can fully reveal the firm's expectation of its multichannel retailing strategies alone. Therefore, in the recent study of Cao and Li (2015, p. 200), cross-channel integration is defined as *"the degree to which a firm coordinates the objectives, design, and deployment of its channels to create synergies for the firm and offer particular benefits to its consumers."* This concept creates opportunities for firms to move gradually from a multi-channel to an omnichannel world, from managerial and operational perspectives. Therefore, cross-channel integration can be understood as an approach chosen by retailers to implement an omnichannel strategy.

2.1 Implementation of Omnichannel Strategy: Retail Business-Model Innovation

The discussion in the literature (e.g. Casadesus-Masanell and Ricart 2010; Sorescu et al. 2011) about the similarities and differences between the concepts of strategy and business model seems to indicate a direction in which to analyse the implementation of strategy from a business-model perspective. While the concept of strategy

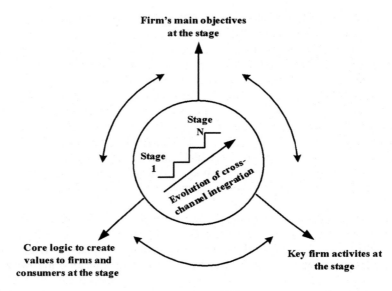

Fig. 1 Analytical framework: three indicators to observe the evolution of cross-channel integration

highlights the organization's goal and position in the marketplace, that of business model focuses on how to implement the, comparatively abstract, strategy by translating it into a more specific interdependent mechanism that guides managers in fine-tuning their actions (Sorescu et al. 2011).

The adoption of a new strategy typically demands the innovation of a business model (Sorescu et al. 2011). Business-model innovation is defined as the "*process of defining a new, or modifying the firm's extant activity system*" (Amit and Zott 2010, p. 2). Sorescu et al. (2011) define retail business-model innovation as a change beyond current practice in one or more elements of a retailing business model (i.e., retailing format, activities, and governance) and their interdependencies, thereby modifying the retailer's organizing logic for value creation and appropriation. These ideas therefore enable us to build the analytical framework of this study, including the dimensions of the firm's objectives, the firm's activities, and the core logic employed to create value for the firm itself and for its consumers. Using this framework (Fig. 1), we can distinguish the different stages of cross-channel development by identifying the firm's different objectives for each stage; we can also observe the firm's key activities and its organization of core logic to create value so that we can understand how it implements cross-channel integration strategy at each stage.

3 Methodology

In this study, I adopted a multi-case inductive-study approach, based on a comparative analysis of 91 US retailers. I explore and highlight, by observing retailers' strategic activities and practices, (1) the evolutionary stages of cross-channel integration that retailers adopt and implement, (2) key objectives that firms aim to achieve at each stage and (3) the mechanisms by which firms argue their strategic choices. The use of multiple case studies allows a replication logic that tends to yield better-grounded theories and more-generalizable results than those from a single case study (Eisenhardt and Graebner 2007). In my research, I followed the procedure recommended by Eisenhardt (1989) and Yin (1994).

3.1 Sample Selection and Justification

The publicly traded retail companies on the New York Stock Exchange were selected because they feature (1) rich diversity in their levels of cross-channel development, (2) substantial competitiveness, and (3) abundant publicly available information.

Given the complexity of describing business-model changes after adopting cross-channel integration strategy, I collected the data from annual reports (Securities and Exchange Commission form 10-K) instead of from self-reported events (Yin 1994). Furthermore, I collected the data on sample firms over a four-year period, from 2008 to 2011. I selected this timeframe because US retailers were, on the whole, moving quickly toward adopting cross-channel integration strategies during this period. The 2012 annual report of the Aberdeen Group indicates that 74% of multi-channel retail operations were characterized by separate channels in 2010, while one year later 50% of leading retailers had moved to align their brand, product offering, and marketing message to offer a uniform customer experience across channels. Longitudinal data collection enabled the examination of each firm's strategic shift over a reasonable period of time, rather than being a simple cross-sectional check. The initial sample comprised 97 publicly traded retail companies on the New York Stock Exchange. Six companies were dropped due to insufficient information being available; this meant that the final sample consisted of 91 retail companies. I outline the main features of the sample firms by Table 1.

3.2 Data Analysis Procedure

I conducted a three-stage data analysis by NVivo 10. First, I read the annual report, paragraph by paragraph, to identify any of the firm's strategic activities that were

Table 1 Overview of the study sample (sample size = 91 retail firms publicly traded retail companies on the New York Stock Exchange)

Sector activity	Drug retailers (retail-sector code 5333): 7.69%
	Food retailers and wholesalers (5337): 6.59%
	Apparel retailers (5371): 29.67%
	Broadline retailers (5373): 5.49%
	Home-improvement retailers (5375): 5.49%
	Specialized consumer services (5377): 16.48%
	Specialty retailers (5379): 28.57%
Size	Average number of physical stores: 3094
Employee	Average number of full employees: 68472

related to multichannel activity or the integration of multichannel development. The objective of this stage was to isolate the relevant data.

Next, I conducted an open coding procedure on the previously isolated data. This stage was conducted by the constant comparative method. Each statement was labeled with in vivo or descriptive codes (Corbin and Strauss 2008). For example, I assigned the label "click and pick up in-store" to this statement: "Generally, US Best Buy online merchandise sales are either picked up at US Best Buy stores or fulfilled directly to customers through our distribution centres." Then, the next unit of data was analysed and compared with the first incident. If similar, it was assigned the same label. If not, it was coded as a different concept. This process continued until all 54 empirical codes were identified. I discussed them with two experts in the field and kept finally only 27 codes, removing the duplicate, ambiguous and inappropriate ones.

Third, I conducted axial coding, where I searched for relationships between and among the subcategories, and theorized and assembled them into categories. I categorized the empirical codes by grouping them into subcategories, based on underlying similarities between them. For instance, the similar empirical codes "click and pick up in-store" and "buy online and return in-store" were grouped under the label "Streamline of consumer order fulfilment" The elements of the scheme eventually emerged based on the firm's choice of distribution channel policy and its objective at each level of integration. For instance, both "Streamline of consumer order fulfilment" and "Integration of consumer information access" shared the same objective of integration to optimize established channels collabouratively, focusing on activities linked to the transaction with consumer. So they were classified as subcategories of the main category Multichannel: moderate integration (stage 3). Furthermore, I highlighted the firms' statements in their annual report by which they argue the reason that they conducted the relevant integration activities. The arguments enabled me to propose the core logic to create values for each stage of multichannel integration. For example, Cabela's argued its activity of "click and pick up in-store" in its 2009 annual report as *Our in-store pick-up program allows customers to order products through our catalogs and Internet site and have them delivered to the retail store of their choice without incurring shipping costs, increasing foot traffic in our stores*". From that, I can propose that one of the core logic to create value for the activity of "click and pick up in-store" is to increase cross-selling and up-selling opportunities. The same analysis was applied for all the firms in the sample.

To ensure the validity of the content, I also provided three experts with a summary report that included the framework and definitions. I examined again the whole axial coding stage according to their feedback. In all 27 empirical codes were grouped into four general categories (four stages of multichannel integration) and eight subcategories (detailed key firm activities at each stage). Table 2 shows the main objectives, key firm activities and core logic to create values for each stage of multichannel integration.

3.3   Research Limitations

This study is not without limitations, which form the basis for an agenda for future research. The first limitation concerns data setting. As with all inductively derived grouping procedures, the classification scheme based on levels of cross-channel integration is a function of the data set used. This research studied the cross-channel integration practices of retailers only in the US. A similar study of retailers in other regions would be interesting, such as in Asia where the development of digital technologies as well as their applications in retail is also dynamic. The second limitation regards the source of data. This research was based mainly on the annual reports published by retailers. From that, we can observe the firms' strategic choices and activities over time. The results of analysing these statements enable us to propose a stage-adoption model regarding cross-channel integration in retail and highlight the firm objectives as well as the apparent logic to create value for each stage of integration. However this is not enough to fully understand the motivations and mechanisms behind these statements. I think complementary in-depth case studies with interviews of retail managers would help in understanding this point.

4   Findings

From 2008 to 2011 the US retail industry was very competitive, with fewer barriers of entry for new businesses, and a proliferation of additional selling channels. The increased competition required retailers to figure out how they could differentiate themselves, and provide the best possible omnichannel experience. I now present how our sample firms implemented their omnichannel strategy. Four stages of implementation of cross-channel integration strategy could be distinguished:

1. Silo mode
2. Minimum integration
3. Moderate integration and,
4. Full integration.

Table 2 Implementation of cross-channel integration strategy: stages, objectives, key activities, and core logic to create values

Stage of implementation	Objectives	Key activities	Core logic to create values both to consumers and firm itself
Multi-channel: silo mode Stage 1	Sell goods or services through more than one channel, but operate these channels independently	Presence in different channels: For example, website, catalogue, kiosk, mobile, social media, and call centre Different retail-mix policy: Different price policies in different channels Different brands in different channels Different assortment policies in different channels Different service in different channels	Avoid channel cannibalization Ensure independence of internet channel to encourage its growth
Multi-channel: minimal integration Stage 2	Optimize established channels collaboratively, focusing on activities linked to marketing communication with consumers	Integrated marketing communication: Consistent use of the same brand in all channels Consistency of marketing message across channels	Create halo effects Leverage the strength of each channel
Multi-channel: moderate integration Stage 3	Optimize established channels collabouratively, focusing on activities linked to consumer transactions	Streamlining of consumer-order fulfilment: Click and pick up in-store Click-to-chat Buy online and return in-store Integration of consumer-information access: Access to online inventory and online orders fulfilled by staff in-store Allowing online consumers to browse the inventory in-store Allowing store staff and consumers to access more and richer information via mobile devices	Improve inventory visibility across channels Increase cross-selling and up-selling
Multi-channel: full integration Stage 4	Optimize established channels collabouratively, focusing on activities linked to consumers' seamless shopping experience	Alignment of fundamentals: Aligned services across channels Aligned promotion across channels	Map customer journey Incorporate customer data and insight into business operation

(continued)

Table 2 (continued)

Stage of implementation	Objectives	Key activities	Core logic to create values both to consumers and firm itself
		Aligned price across channels	Provide tailored products and services
		Aligned loyalty program across channels	
		Aligned assortment across channels	
		Centralization of back-end system:	
		Integration of merchandise-planning systems across channels	
		Integration of logistics across channels	
		Integration of information systems across channels	
		Centralized call-centre service across channels	
		Integration of client database across channels	
		Organization transformation:	
		Sharing knowledge across channels	
		Recruiting talent with double competences in retail and digital commerce	
		Changing organizational structure to adapt to integration of different channels	
		Incentive system linked to both online and offline sales	

Each stage represented a level of collabouration among firms' established channels. Table 2 presents a summary of my categorization, along with the firms' objectives, key activities, and the organization of the apparent logic to create value for themselves and for their consumers that corresponded to each stage.

Stage 1: Multi-channel: Silo Mode

The first stage for retailers (e.g. Walgreen, Home depot, Foot Locker in 2008) was to use more than one channel to sell their products and services, but to operate these channels independently. With the rapid development of internet-based technologies and increasing expectations from consumers, retailers repositioned their businesses from a single-channel to multi-channel model. In my study, most US retailers were motivated to sell products and services through the internet in order to provide their consumers with the value of convenience, so driving traffic to their businesses and boosting sales:

> Our growth strategy is to develop and expand the reach of the Build-A-Bear Workshop brand by opening new stores, investing in value-adding marketing programs including our new virtual world website, buildabearville.com, offering an authentic and unique merchandise assortment and to build our logistical, operational and technology infrastructure to support our growth and improve our efficiencies (Build-A-Bear 2008, p. 5).

Although *presence in different channels (store, website, catalogue, kiosk, mobile, social media, and call centre)* created opportunities for firms, multi-channel retailers faced a number of challenges, especially channel cannibalization which may result if a new channel too closely duplicates the capabilities of existing channels. To reduce the channel conflicts and the risks of negative impacts on the existing business from the failure of operations in new channels, these retailers implemented *different retail-mix policies in different channels* at the first stage of multi-channel retailing. For example, in 2009, Aéropostale used different banners for its store and for its online channel; in 2010, Dick's adjusted its online product assortment to emphasize higher-margin merchandise; in 2008, Best Buy offered more favourable pricing online than offline; and in 2009, J.C. Penney highlighted online exclusive designer brands along with specialized services. At this stage, traditional store-based retailers lacked online business experience. In order to obtain this quickly—and to gain access to online consumers, and to develop distribution infrastructure—some retailers even adopted an external growth strategy via the acquisition of existing online companies. For example, Walgreens advanced its multi-channel strategy by acquiring a leading e-commerce site, Drugstore.com, in 2011. In so doing, it also gained the Beauty.com website, both sites' customer-service and distribution centres, and access to more than 3 million online customers and to 60,000 drug, health, beauty, and skincare products—so expanding their already-strong online offering.

Most retailers intentionally gave a great deal of independence to their internet channels in order to encourage their growth at this early stage of e-commerce development. Dedicated e-commerce teams often focused on dealing with special features of the new business:

> We also provide our customers online shopping at www.AdvanceAutoParts.com and access to over 100,000 parts and accessories. Our new website was launched in October 2009 and is operated by our dedicated e-commerce team (Advance 2009, p. 3)

The silo-based retailers enhanced and improved their multichannel selling capabilities through Internet sites that were supported by new technologies, functionality and fulfilment capacity. To improve the customer shopping experience, some retailers planned to coordinate their activities across channels, providing at least a minimum level of integration.

Stage 2: Multi-channel: Minimum Integration

After the addition of new channels, retailers started to consider integrating the established channels to improve efficiency. The second stage of multi-channel retailing for most of retailers was to *integrate brand and marketing communication across channels*. Using the same brand names across channels, retailers increased consumer awareness of their brands:

> ... through our website, store signage, and media presence, we are creating consumer awareness of the AutoNation brand (AutoNation 2011, p. 4)

Communicating consistent messages across channels increased customers' perception of the association between channels, so leading also to improved brand awareness and greater confidence:

> The program incorporates consistent messaging across a variety of media, and is designed to increase our brand awareness and store traffic and attract more first-time and repeat guests. In addition, our virtual world Web site, buildabearville.com®, promotes brand connection and in-store products and events with branded games, activities and social connectivity features (Build-A-Bear 2010, p. 4)

The valuable and positive brand associations that were formed through the knowledge and/or patronage of one channel could transfer to the other channels through the halo effect:

> In response to an emerging trend of kids' interaction and play increasingly occurring in the online space, in 2007 we updated our virtual world Web site used primarily by children, buildabearville.com®, and we continue to enhance the site. The site is highly complementary to our store experience and positively enhances our core brand values while offering activity options and features that are tied back to in-store events (Build-A-Bear 2010, p. 5)

At this stage, although the different retail-mix policies were still applied in each channel (except brand and marketing communication), retailers were aware of seeking complementary effects by leveraging the strengths of each channel. Taking advantage of having no limit on the space for online channels, they provided an extended range there. For example, Target.com offered a wide assortment of general merchandise, including many items found in its stores, and a complementary assortment, such as more sizes and colours, sold only online. This complementary-assortment arrangement helped retailers to build customer loyalty. Moreover, retailers exploited the unique features of their websites to engage with their consumers. For example, Build-A-Bear Workshop provided a virtual world online to promote the characters and to feature animated "webisodes" of a story for children to view throughout the holiday season. Retailers also used this online platform to provide additional promotional offerings, tips on using products, and new-product information or even after-sales services. Lowe's, a home improvement retailer, allowed customers to upload a video on Lowes.com in case of installation problems, so that experts could diagnose the problem and help find a solution, increasing the level of integration.

Stage 3: Multi-channel: Moderate Integration

After the consolidation of marketing communication across channels, retailers continued experimenting with improving connections between channels. Stage 3 reflects retailers' efforts relating to activities linked with consumer transactions. At this stage, I observed that retailers intended to *streamline consumer-order fulfilment* through collabouration between channels. They redefined their fulfilment strategy to allow customers to shop and return products through any channel. For example, many retailers (e.g. Best Buy, Barnes & Noble, Cabela's, Dick's, GameStop, Macy's, Walmart, and Home Depot) adopted the "click and pick up in-store" model. In 2011, Walgreen introduced "Web Pickup" services at many locations in the Chicago area and San Jose, California, enabling customers to shop online and pick up their orders at a store in as little as an hour.

Some retailers developed further and gave consumers the choice of where to return unsuitable goods—allowing consumers to buy online (or through other channels) and return in-store, or to buy in-store and return online:

> Department stores and Direct generally serve the same type of customers and provide virtually the same mix of merchandise, and department stores accept returns from sales made in stores, via the Internet and through catalogs (J.C. Penney 2009, p. 1)

The operations of "click and pick up in-store" and "buy online and return in-store" enabled retailers to generate store traffic and to create cross-selling and up-selling opportunities. The benefit of this type of channel integration is particularly important for traditionally store-based retailers:

> We offer both on-line shopping with delivery, as well as an in-store pickup option to increase customer traffic. We also utilize the internet as an important customer information resource to drive in-store purchases of our merchandise (hhgregg Inc. 2009, p. 9)

For a greater conversion rate, retailers provided their website visitors with real-time assistance from a contact-centre associate. Website visitors used "click-to-chat" to connect with call-centre staff to gain more services:

> Through our website, which can be accessed through computers, smart phones and other mobile devices, customers can not only purchase products, but can also connect with our associates and with one another to gain product and project knowledge (Home Depot 2011, p. 6)

To cope with the fulfilment strategy in a multichannel setting, retailers integrated customer information access across channels. The visibility of the inventory across channels is essential for retailers to proceed with a cross-channel transaction. Retailers allowed their store staff or in-store shoppers to view the inventory of surrounding stores or of the online facility, and to offer alternatives to customers looking for a product that might be out of stock:

> Store-to-Door enables store associates to sell any item available online to an in-store customer in a single transaction, without placing a phone call. Customers are taking advantage of Store-to-Door by purchasing extended sizes that are not available in-store, as well as finding a certain size or colour that happens to be out-of-stock at the time of their visit (American Eagle 2010, p. 3)

> Our in-store kiosks provide our customers access to our entire inventory assortment, allowing customers to place orders for items that may be out of stock in our retail stores or to purchase items only available on our Internet site (Cabelas 2010, p. 4)

Retailers also allowed their online customers to browse the in-store inventory. Providing store inventory data online reduced the uncertainty of product availability and enabled "buy online and pick up" in stores.

> Online customers can access merchandise no matter where it is located. If we are out of stock of an item at our fulfilment centre, our systems instantly locate whether it is at any of our full-line stores and we can fulfil the online order at the store level (Nordstrom 2010, p. 3).

Retailers were motivated to invest in store-information infrastructure and mobile applications so as to allow store staff and consumers to access more and richer information. The mobile channel, because of its independence from location, was considered as an ideal supplementary channel to the internet channel and physical store and also as a good platform for retailers to coordinate their activities across channels:

> With an upgrade to our store information technology infrastructure, customers and employees have access to more and richer information. Many of our stores incorporate touch screen technology within displays of new and innovative products, so customers can visualize how to enhance their homes or simplify their projects. Additionally, in-store Wi-Fi and barcodes help customers compare shop and access how-to information on their smart phones, allowing them to finish their research and make a purchase decision without leaving the store (Lowes 2011, p. 9)

Increased coordination between channels resulted in a drive towards full omnichannel integration.

Stage 4: Omnichannel: Full Integration

Stage 4 marked a phase of full integration for retailers who had started to make radical and strategic changes by aligning fundamentals and centralizing back-office operations across channels to provide seamless customer experience. In the study, I found retailers could work on three dimensions to satisfy cross-channel consumers and more effectively manage the channels as a whole:

1. aligning fundamentals
2. centralization of back-office operations
3. organization transformation.

Aligning fundamentals (coordination of assortment, service, promotion, price, and loyalty program across channels) enabled retailers to establish and reinforce their brand image, and to create a seamless shopping experience for their consumers by coordinating basic value propositions across channels. Although harmonizing the product assortment across channels was a complex and strategically important decision for retailers, customer expectations drove some retailers to create an integrated operating model to offer the same products to their customers across channels:

> Based on customer feedback, the Company has taken several actions to improve the
> customer shopping experience across all channels, including more closely aligning
> in-store and online promotions and merchandise offerings to improve effectiveness while
> maintaining the capability to address unique customer needs in each channel (J.C. Penney
> 2008, p. 20)

Retailers, which operate at stage 4, did not rigidly operate the alignment of their product assortment across channels; they attempted to find the optimal point in the continuum of the homogenization of offerings in all channels, while considering the strength and restrictions of each channel. For example, since 2009, Target's online shopping site has offered similar merchandise categories to those found in their stores, but excludes food items and household commodities. Since 2010, Christopher & Banks has offered the full range of merchandise carried in-store on its website. Moreover, its online assortment includes an extended range of sizes and lengths.

Although the cost structure associated with each channel was distinct, retailers aligned prices across channels at this stage in order to provide their consumers with the value of transparency:

> Our ASDA® price guarantee program is a great example of that transparency. Our focus on
> the productivity loop helps ensure we drive every day low cost, so we can deliver every day
> low prices across our business (Wal-Mart 2011, p. 3)

Retailers also coordinated their promotion across channels. Barnes & Noble allowed their consumers to redeem in-store the coupons available on its website. Flooring samples of all the products offered by Lumber Liquidators were available in its stores, from its call centre, and on its website.

In order to provide additional value to customers, retailers aligned their loyalty programs across channels, rewarding customers for shopping in-store, online, and/or through other channels. For example, holders of the Barnes & Noble MasterCard (an affinity credit card issued by Barclays Bank Delaware) received an additional 5% rebate for all purchases made in Barnes & Noble stores, B. Dalton bookstores. or at Barnesandnoble.com.

To provide a consistent shopping experience, and to "seal the deal" with cross-channel consumers throughout their purchase process, retailers aligned their services across channels:

> The Company's strategy is to operate each brand's stores, catalogues, and websites as
> integrated businesses and to provide the same personalized service and offer the same
> products to its customers regardless of whether each brand's merchandise is purchased
> through its stores, catalogs, or online (Talbots 2008, p. 7)

Centralizing back-end systems (integration of client database, call-centre, supply chain, information, logistic and merchandising planning system across channels) allowed retailers to streamline the management of operations and to provide a consistent offering to consumers across channels, so potentially gaining a competitive advantage:

Our multi-channel model employs the same merchandising team, distribution centres, customer database, and infrastructure, which we intend to further leverage by building on the strengths of each channel (Cabelas 2008, p. 4)

Integration of the client database allowed retailers to learn more about consumer behaviour, and to have a single consolidated view of customers in order to offer the right product or service to the right customer segment, at the right time, and via the right channel:

We continued to emphasize the integration of stores and online sites at Macy's and at Bloomingdale's. This has helped us to create a 360-degree view of the customer so we can serve her needs across channels, which in turn drives sales in both stores and online (Macy's 2009, p. 1)

The capability to map the consumer journey across channels and to incorporate data into business operations enabled retailers to engage well with their consumers, to improve consumer loyalty, and to create cross-selling opportunities, by providing tailored products and services:

This business model affords us multiple touch points with our customers, which allows us to gather data and communicate with them in person, through our call centre and via the internet...To utilize our extensive customer database to improve customer loyalty, facilitate direct marketing and increase cross-sell opportunities ... (VSI 2011, p. 5)

The call centre enabled consumers to easily access in-depth information and ready-made solutions. Recent call centre technologies have advanced substantially and led to a considerable narrowing of the gap in personalization between the telephone channel and store staff. Therefore, the call centre plays an important role for retailers to provide convenience services in an omnichannel setting. For example, customers may use the Internet for search, the bricks-and-mortar store for purchase, and the call centre for after-sales support. For ensuring consumers' seamless shopping experiences, I observed certain retailers integrate their call centres across channels, for example one call centre supported both online and offline consumers.

We operate a call centre to support both DSW stores and dsw.com to address our customer service needs (DSW 2009, p. 8)

Retailers (e.g. Lowe's, Wal-Mart, Barnes & Noble) significantly invested in integrating the supply chain, information, logistics, and merchandise-planning systems to create synergies across channels and to provide their customers with a more interconnected retail experience:

In 2011 we implemented systems to share information across these channels. These included an upgrade to our store information technology infrastructure, better tools and greater access to information for our contact centre employees, and equipping our on-site selling specialists with tools to help customers visualize a project, provide a real-time quote and tender a sale on site (Lowes 2011, p. 5)

Organizational transformation to adapt to a cross-channel integration strategy seemed the greatest challenge for omnichannel retailers. At the full-integration stage, integration and optimization between online and offline business units presented tremendous organizational challenges. In my study, I found certain retailers (e.g. J.C. Penney, Wal-Mart, Macy's, Lowe's, Walgreen) moving toward a more centralized organizational structure and developing cross-functional teams to reinforce communication across channels:

> In 2010, Walmart consolidated its eCommerce activities around the world in a Global eCommerce Division . . . Our structure also integrates into each operating segment and to each country to ensure we can respond to customers' multi-channel shopping needs (Wal-Mart 2011, p. 12)

To encourage cross-channel coordination, retailers re-examined and revised their current compensation systems, conceiving an incentive system linked to both online and offline sales:

> These Barnes & Noble.com employees participate in an incentive program tied to physical and digital eCommerce sales. The Company believes that the compensation of its management is competitive with that offered by other technology companies" (Barnes & Noble 2011, p. 9)

The implementation of a cross-channel integration strategy demanded talented people who were competent in both traditional and digital commerce. For example, the Barnes & Noble management team was led by managers experienced in both areas; its team employed highly skilled professionals with both media expertise and skills in supply-chain management. This combination ensured a positive customer experience, regardless of the customer's preference for a physical or a digital product.

Sharing knowledge across channels was important for retailers to achieve synergy from their strategic choices on integration. The new investments focused on new technologies, both in-store and online, which improved customers' shopping experience, for example at Macy's. The existing resources and capabilities were leveraged for the business in the new emerging channels, such as at Wal-Mart:

> The factors that drive shopping behaviour—price, assortment, customer experience and trust—are as relevant for e-commerce today as they have always been for our various physical retail formats. What is changing is the technology that enables and shapes the retail transaction . . . We intend to leverage these evolving technologies—and the trust that our customers have in the Walmart brand—to our advantage as we differentiate our business from other online retailers" (Wal-Mart 2011, p. 12)

5 Discussion

The evolution of technology and the proliferation of channels require retailers to change their channel management strategy. The omnichannel strategy provides retailers with an approach of achieving synergy among the retailers' multiple channels and providing a seamless shopping experience to their consumers (Piotrowicz and Cuthbertson 2014; Verhoef et al. 2015). However, to answer the question of how to implement an omnichannel strategy, a small study is insightful

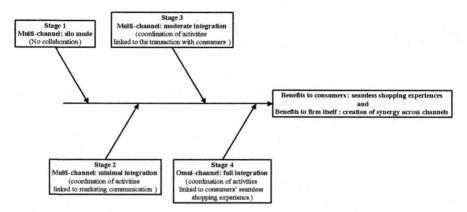

Fig. 2 The roadmap for retailers to move from multi-channel to omnichannel strategy

(Hansen and Sia 2015). This study adopts the perspective of retail business model innovation to build the analytical framework. Based on the comparative analysis of 91 US retailers' transformation experiences from 2008 to 2011, the findings provide insights into how retailers follow a stage-of-adoption model to implement their omnichannel strategy. The whole process is driven by providing benefits to both consumers (in the form of an ultimately seamless shopping experience) and to the firm (as synergy creation across channels). The four stages of implementation involve different levels of collaboration between channels (Fig. 2).

At each stage, firms should focus on the key activities in order to achieve their main objectives through following the special core logic of value creation. At the stage of silo mode, they should focus on adding new channels but operating their channels under different retail-mix policies so as to avoid potential channel canni-balization. The organizational independency of new channels may be necessary to encourage their growth. At the stage of minimum integration, retailers' priority should be to align brands and to integrate marketing communications across channels in order to create halo effects. Although the level of integration is limited, retailers should start to seek complementary effects between channels through leveraging the strengths of each channel. At the stage of moderate integration, they should be able to streamline consumer-order fulfilment and integrate customer-information access. Using multiple channels to realize one transaction with a consumer creates cross- and/or up-selling opportunities for retailers. The visibility of the inventory across channels is therefore essential for retailers at this stage. At the stage of full integration, retailers should engage in radical and strategic changes by aligning fundamentals and centralizing back-office operations across channels to provide a seamless customer experience. Organizational transformation is needed in order to reinforce the capability of mapping the consumer journey across channels and of incorporating the data into the whole business operation. Combining all channels to provide tailored products and services to consumers throughout the purchasing process is critical for retailer–consumer engagement.

Two major theoretical insights emerge from the findings of our study. First, retailers adopt a cross-channel integration strategy and follow a four-stage model of adoption to move from multi-channel to omnichannel retailing. Prior research focusing on the conceptual framework (Chaffey 2010; Neslin et al. 2006; Zhang et al. 2010) has suggested this stage-adoption concept. Neslin et al. (2006) even point out that integration across channels can range from complete separation to full coordination of channels. My findings—based on the comparative analysis of 91 US retailers from 2008 to 2011—extend the literature by revealing more details about this model. I identify four stages in the process of developing cross-channel integration. For each stage, I highlight firms' objectives, key activities, and the organization of the apparent logic in order to create value for themselves and for their consumers.

Second, retailers take both customer- and firm-centric perspectives to develop cross-channel integration. Prior research highlights the benefits either to consumers (e.g. Gulati and Garino 2000) or to the firm (e.g. Neslin et al. 2006) as strategic orientation. Although Neslin and Shankar (2009) and Verhoef (2012) suggest adopting both perspectives to study the phenomena of cross-channel integration, few studies reveal how these two perspectives can work together to drive a firm's development of its omnichannel strategy stage by stage. The adoption of a retail business model innovation perspective in this study enables me to build the linkage between a firm's key activities and value created by the activities both to consumers and the firm at each stage. My research findings reveal that the search for both providing seamless shopping experiences to the consumers and creating synergy across channels to the firm itself drives the retailer to move from multi-channel to omnichannel strategy stage by stage.

6   Conclusions

I conclude this chapter by the summary of my study and the recommendations both for academia and practice. Ten research questions are also suggested for the future research.

In the context of the increasing development of an omnichannel strategy in the retail sector, this study aims to find answers for the question of how to implement an omnichannel strategy from an evolutionary perspective. The literature review for distinguishing the concepts of multi-, omni-, and cross-channel retailing as well as the adoption of a retail business model perspective as the analytical framework build the conceptual foundations of this study. Based on the multiple case studies of 91 publicly traded retailers from 2008 to 2011, the findings of this study suggest a four-stage model (stage 1: silo mode, stage 2: minimal integration, stage 3: moderate integration and stage 4: full integration) for retailers to implement their omnichannel strategy. At each stage, firms should focus on the key activities in order to achieve their main objectives through following a specific core logic of value creation both to consumers and to the firms.

For practitioners, this study provides a roadmap of guidance for retailers who aim to move from multi-channel to omnichannel retailing. For academia, this study suggests the implementation of omnichannel integration is a process of staged development and moving forward in this process is related to retailers' sequential commitment. Even though the search for value both to consumers and to the firm drives a retailer to move forward in the process of cross-channel integration, the sequential commitment allows the firm to adjust its investment plans for each subsequent round. Decision-makers should cautiously judge whether its firm make or withhold further investment, especially considering the fact that the profit return from cross-channel integration is not yet clear (Zhang et al. 2010) and may decline in the short run (Xue et al. 2011). Therefore, the research questions about firms' strategic decisions, resources allocations, metrics and incentives, design, and data management in the context of omnichannel retailing may be revealing.

Moreover, the perspective of retail business-model innovation seems relevant to studying the implementation of omnichannel strategy. Following this perspective, additional research would be interesting, especially studies on the stakeholders involved in creating and delivering a seamless shopping experience for customers, as well as the mechanisms (e.g. contract and incentive systems) that motivate the stakeholders to carry out their roles. These stakeholders include not only retailers and their consumers, but also all the partners in retailers' networks, such as suppliers, service providers (e.g. technological-solution sources and third-party platforms), and even competitors (Sorescu et al. 2011). The research questions around the relationship, engagement and co-creation value between retailers and their partners in the context of omnichannel retailing may also be relevant.

Therefore, I suggest developing research avenues for the implementation of omnichannel strategy in relation to four themes: the retailer, the consumer, the supplier, and service providers (e.g. technological-solution sources and third-party platforms). Some unexplored research questions are proposed in Table 3.

Questions for Discussion and Review

1. Identify and discuss the key differences between multi-channel and omnichannel strategy.
2. What is the roadmap for retailers to move from multi-channel to omnichannel strategy?
3. What are the main objectives, key activities, and core logic to create value at each stage of implementation of an omnichannel strategy?
4. How can retailers reduce channel conflicts between new channels and existing ones?
5. What is the role of mobile technology in the implementation of an omnichannel strategy?
6. How can retailers leverage their store networks to streamline consumer-order fulfilment?

Table 3 Research avenues and unexplored questions

Stakeholders	Areas of interest		Research questions
Retailer	Strategic decisions	RQ-R1	How do industry-level, firm-level, and consumer-level factors influence the firm's escalation of commitment on cross-channel integration?
	Resource allocation	RQ-R2	How should firms spend their limited marketing budgets in the context of omnichannel retailing?
		RQ-R3	How can firms effectively develop their new channels (mobile channels, social channels) to delivering a superior omnichannel shopping experience?
		RQ-R4	How can firms optimize store inventory ordering and allocation policy in the context of omnichannel retailing?
	Metrics and incentives	RQ-R5	How can store staffs be incentivized to provide the customers with omnichannel services?
		RQ-R6	How can store staffs be used as co-creators of omnichannel shopping experience?
		RQ-R7	How should each channel performance be measured throughout the omnichannel shopping journey?
	Data management	RQ-R8	How can firms integrate customer data collected from different channels?
		RQ-R9	How can firms leverage 360° customer data to deliver value for themselves?
Consumer	Relationship	RQ-C1	How can omnichannel strategy create more relevant relationships with individual consumer?
	Engagement	RQ-C2	How do we better measure and enhance omnichannel customer engagement?
Supplier	Co-creation value	RQ-S1	How can retailers maintain and develop partnering relationship with their suppliers relevant to delivering a superior omnichannel shopping experience?
service providers (e.g. technological-solution sources and third-party platforms)	Convergence	RQ-SP1	How will new technologies (social, mobile, cloud and Internet of Thing) and systems affect the implementation of omnichannel strategy?
		RQ-SP2	How can third-party platforms be used to implement omnichannel strategy?
		RQ-SP3	How will augmented reality be integrated into omnichannel strategy?

7. How can retailers homogenize their offerings in all channels, while considering the strength and restrictions of each channel?
8. How does the analysis of the customer journey across channels help retailers increase sales?
9. What is the role of store staff in the implementation of an omnichannel strategy?
10. Does a centralized organizational structure allow a better coordination between channels?

References

Advance Auto Parts Inc. (2009). Form 10-K annual report pursuant to section 13 or 15(d) of the Securities Exchange Act of 1934 for the fiscal year ended January 3 2009.

American Eagle Outfitters Inc. (2010). 10-K annual report pursuant to section 13 or 15(d) of the Securities Exchange Act of 1934 Filed on 03/26/2010.

Amit, R., & Zott, C. (2010). *Business model innovation: Creating value in times of change.*

AutoNation Inc. (2011). Form 10-K annual report pursuant to section 13 or 15(d) of the Securities Exchange Act of 1934 For the fiscal year ended December 31 2011.

Barnes & Noble Inc. (2011). Form 10-K (Annual Report) Filed 06/29/11.

Beck, N., & Rygl, D. (2015). Categorization of multiple channel retailing in multi-, cross-, and omni-channel retailing for retailers and retailing. *Journal of Retailing & Consumer Services, 27,* 170–178. https://doi.org/10.1016/j.jretconser.2015.08.001.

Berger, P. D., Bolton, R. N., Bowman, D., Briggs, E., Kumar, V., Parasuraman, A., & Terry, C. (2002). Marketing actions and the value of customer assets: A framework for customer asset management. *Journal of Service Research, 5*(1), 39.

Brynjolfsson, E., Yu Jeffrey, H. U., & Rahman, M. S. (2013). Competing in the age of omnichannel retailing. *MIT Sloan Management Review, 54*(4), 23–29.

Build a Bear Workshop Inc. (2008). 10-K Annual report pursuant to section 13 and 15(d) Filed on 03/13/2008.

Build a Bear Workshop Inc. (2010). 10-K Annual report pursuant to section 13 and 15(d) Filed on 03/18/2010.

Cabelas Inc. (2008). 10-K Annual report pursuant to section 13 and 15(d) Filed on 02/27/2008.

Cabelas Inc. (2010). 10-K Annual report pursuant to section 13 and 15(d) Filed on 03/01/2010.

Cao, L., & Li, L. (2015). The impact of cross-channel integration on retailers' sales growth. *Journal of Retailing, 91*(2), 198–216. https://doi.org/10.1016/j.jretai.2014.12.005.

Casadesus-Masanell, R., & Ricart, J. E. (2010). From strategy to business models and onto tactics. *Long Range Planning, 43*(2/3), 195–215. https://doi.org/10.1016/j.lrp.2010.01.004.

Chaffey, D. (2010). Applying organisational capability models to assess the maturity of digital-marketing governance. *Journal of Marketing Management, 26*(3-4), 187–196.

Corbin, J., & Strauss, A. (2008). *Basics of qualitative research: Techniques to developing grounded theory* (3rd ed.). Los Angeles, CA: Sage.

DSW Inc. (2009). Form 10-K (Annual Report) Filed 04/01/09.

Eisenhardt, K. M. (1989). Building theories from case study research. *Academy of Management Review, 14*(4), 532–550. https://doi.org/10.5465/AMR.1989.4308385.

Eisenhardt, K. M., & Graebner, M. E. (2007). Theory building from cases. Opportunities and challlenges. *Academy of Management Journal, 50*(1), 25–32. https://doi.org/10.5465/AMJ.2007.24160888.

Gulati, R., & Garino, J. (2000). Get the right mix of bricks & clicks (cover story). *Harvard Business Review, 78*(3), 107–114.

Hansen, R., & Sia, S. K. (2015). Hummel's digital transformation toward omnichannel retailing: Key lessons learned. *MIS Quarterly Executive, 14*(2), 51–66.

Herhausen, D., Binder, J., Schoegel, M., & Herrmann, A. (2015). Integrating bricks with clicks: Retailer-level and channel-level outcomes of online–offline channel integration. *Journal of Retailing, 91*(2), 309–325. https://doi.org/10.1016/j.jretai.2014.12.009.

hhgregg Inc. (2009). Form 10-K annual report pursuant to section 13 or 15(d) of the Securities Exchange Act of 1934 For the fiscal year ended, March 31 2008.

J C Penney Co Inc. (2008). 10-K Annual report pursuant to section 13 and 15(d) Filed on 04/01/2008.

J C Penney Co Inc. (2009). 10-K Annual report pursuant to section 13 and 15(d) Filed on 03/31/2009.

Kozlenkova, I. V., Hult, G. T. M., Lund, D. J., Mena, J. A., & Kekec, P. (2015). The role of marketing channels in supply chain management. *Journal of Retailing, 91*(4), 586–609. https://doi.org/10.1016/j.jretai.2015.03.003.

Levy, M., & Weitz, B. A. (2009). *Retailing management* (7th ed.). New York: The McGraw-Hill/Irwin Companies.

Lowes Companies Inc. (2011). 10-K Annual report pursuant to section 13 and 15(d) Filed on 03/29/2011.

Macy's Inc. (2009). Form10-K Annual Report Pursuant to Section 13 or 15(d) of the Securities Exchange Act of 1934 For the Fiscal Year Ended January 31 2009.

Neslin, S. A., & Shankar, V. (2009). Key issues in multichannel customer management: Current knowledge and future directions. *Journal of Interactive Marketing, 23*(1), 70–81. https://doi.org/10.1016/j.intmar.2008.10.005.

Neslin, S. A., Grewal, D., Leghorn, R., Shankar, V., Teerling, M. L., Thomas, J. S., & Verhoef, P. C. (2006). Challenges and opportunities in multichannel customer management. *Journal of Service Research, 9*(2), 95–112. https://doi.org/10.1177/1094670506293559.

Neslin, S. A., Jerath, K., Bodapati, A., Bradlow, E. T., Deighton, J., Gensler, S., et al. (2014). The interrelationships between brand and channel choice. *Marketing Letters, 25*(3), 319–330. https://doi.org/10.1007/s11002-014-9305-2.

Nordstorm Inc. (2010). Form 10-K annual report pursuant to section 13 or 15(d) of the Securities Exchange Act of 1934 For the fiscal year ended January 30 2010.

Piotrowicz, W., & Cuthbertson, R. (2014). Introduction to the special issue information technology in retail: Toward omnichannel retailing. *International Journal of Electronic Commerce, 18*(4), 5–16. https://doi.org/10.2753/JEC1086-4415180400.

Rigby, D. (2011). The future of shopping. *Harvard Business Review, 89*(12), 64–75.

Sorescu, A., Frambach, R. T., Singh, J., Rangaswamy, A., & Bridges, C. (2011). Innovations in retail business models. *Journal of Retailing, 87*, S3–S16. https://doi.org/10.1016/j.jretai.2011.04.005.

Sousa, R., & Voss, C. A. (2006). Service quality in multichannel services employing virtual channels. *Journal of Service Research, 8*(4), 356–371. https://doi.org/10.1177/1094670506286324.

The Home Depot Inc. (2011). Form 10-K annual report pursuant to section 13 or 15(d) of the Securities Exchange Act of 1934 For the fiscal year ended January 30 2011.

The Talbots Inc. (2008). Form 10-K annual report pursuant to section 13 or 15(d) of the Securities Exchange Act of 1934 For the Fiscal Year Ended February 2 2008.

Verhoef, P. C. (2012). Multichannel customer management strategy. In V. Shankar & G. S. Carpenter (Eds.), *Handbook of marketing strategy* (pp. 135–150). Cheltenham: Edward Elgar.

Verhoef, P. C., Kannan, P. K., & Inman, J. J. (2015). From multi-channel retailing to omnichannel retailing: Introduction to the special issue on multi-channel retailing. *Journal of Retailing, 91*(2), 174–181. https://doi.org/10.1016/j.jretai.2015.02.005.

Vitamin Shoppe Inc. (2011). Form 10-K annual report pursuant to section 13 or 15(d) of the Securities Exchange Act of 1934 for the fiscal year ended December 31 2011.

Wal Mart Stores. (2011). 10-K Annual report pursuant to section 13 and 15(d) Filed on 03/30/2011.

Xue, M., Hitt, L. M., & Chen, P. Y. (2011). Determinants and outcomes of internet banking adoption. *Management Science, 57*(2), 291–307. https://doi.org/10.1287/mnsc.1100.1187.

Yan, R., Wang, J., & Zhou, B. (2010). Channel integration and profit sharing in the dynamics of multi-channel firms. *Journal of Retailing & Consumer Services, 17*(5), 430–440. https://doi.org/10.1016/j.jretconser.2010.04.004.

Yin, R. K. (1994). *Case study research: Design and methods* (2nd ed.). Newbury Park, CA: Sage.

Zhang, J., Farris, P. W., Irvin, J. W., Kushwaha, T., Steenburgh, T. J., & Weitz, B. A. (2010). Crafting integrated multichannel retailing strategies. *Journal of Interactive Marketing, 24*, 168–180. https://doi.org/10.1016/j.intmar.2010.02.002.

Lanlan Cao is Associate Professor of Marketing at NEOMA Business School in France. Her research interests include Digital Retailing, Retail Innovation, International Retailing, Retail Business Model Innovation and Multichannel Retailing. Her works have appeared in Journal of Retailing, International Journal of Electronic Commerce, International Journal of Retail & Distribution Management, Journal of Strategic Marketing, Economie et Sociétés, Décisions Marketing, Journal of Asia-Pacific Business, International Review of Retail, Distribution and Consumer Research and other journals.

Does Service Quality Perception in Omnichannel Retailing Matter? A Systematic Review and Agenda for Future Research

Shahriar Akter, Muhammad Ismail Hossain, Steven Lu, Sutapa Aditya, Tasnim M. Taufique Hossain, and Uraiporn Kattiyapornpong

Abstract The retailing landscape has been transformed in the past decade with the emergence of web, mobile and social media. Multichannel retailers are focusing on establishing seamless omnichannel service experience. Omnichannel retailing is not only addition of channels, rather integration of service elements, price, promotion, product assortment, information and transactional data within all available channels of a company. Within omnichannel retailing, the concept of brand experience is highly specific as it includes interactive channels such as social media and review sites. To complete even a single purchase, customers nowadays are using multiple channels. Customers are trying out products in a physical store but at the same time ordering it online using smartphones after comparing price and checking reviews. Remember the customer who did not complete her purchase in store? She may have ordered similar product using other channels offered by competitors. To create a successful omnichannel strategy, companies need to integrate all the channels and customer touchpoints to provide a consistent experience. Whereas multi-channel has focused on enhancing customer value incorporating digital tools, omnichannel has introduced a wider perspective in influencing consumer decision making. With the emergence of omnichannel and related complexities, this study calls for a broader conceptualization of virtual, physical and integration quality. The study also puts forward challenges and future research directions for quality modelling in omnichannel research.

S. Akter (✉) · T. M. T. Hossain · U. Kattiyapornpong
University of Wollongong, Wollongong, NSW, Australia
e-mail: sakter@uow.edu.au

M. I. Hossain
University of Dhaka, Dhaka, Bangladesh

S. Lu
University of Sydney, Camperdown, NSW, Australia

S. Aditya
Long Island University, New York, NY, USA

© Springer Nature Switzerland AG 2019

W. Piotrowicz, R. Cuthbertson (eds.), *Exploring Omnichannel Retailing*,
https://doi.org/10.1007/978-3-319-98273-1_4

1 Introduction

Technology has not only changed retailing in the last two decades, but also created new channels of doing business. Specifically, in services marketing where economic activities are performed by one party to another (Wirtz and Lovelock 2016), the online channel has played a critical role in creating, offering and capturing value; for example, Booking.com in travel, Netflix in movie, and Amazon in the publication industries. To tackle the emerging challenges emanating from the digital disruption, many traditional retailers have embraced multi-channel strategies (Verhoef et al. 2015). However, both the traditional brick and mortar players and the new online players face constant challenges on how to deliver seamless quality experiences within and across multiple channels. The advent of mobile platforms (e.g., smartphone and tablet), social media (e.g., Facebook, Twitter or Instagram), and the integration of these channels in the retail mix has created a new phase in multi-channel retailing (Verhoef et al. 2015). This new channel mix basically indicates the emergence of an omnichannel retailing model (Rigby 2011) or seamless omnichannel experience by turning the world into a showroom without a wall (Brynjolfsson et al. 2013). As multi-channel is based on separate channels with no overlap, omnichannel aims to provide seamless experiences across all integrated channels including store, web, mobile, social media and direct marketing (Verhoef et al. 2015). Although omnichannel creates new opportunities, it also represents complexities in maintaining seamless service quality, which indicates excellence or superiority of the overall service delivery performance (Cao and Li 2015; Leeflang et al. 2014; Sousa and Voss 2006). There are growing concerns about the perceived quality of these channels due to a lack of reliability of the system, knowledge and competence of providers, privacy and security of information, and their effects on outcome constructs (Sousa and Voss 2006). A review of the literature reveals that this research stream has predominantly focused on the impact of the addition or deletion of channels on firm performance (Cao and Li 2015; Cheng et al. 2007; Homburg et al. 2014; Konuş et al. 2008; Xia and Zhang 2010), with little empirical evidence about the impact of perceived quality within and across omnichannels and their effects on service outcomes. Thus, this study fills these voids by aiming to conceptualize an omnichannel service quality model using a systematic review. As such, the current study seeks to answer the question.

RQ What are the dimensions of omnichannel service quality?

To answer this research question, we focus on perceived service quality to evaluate the effectiveness of omnichannel services marketing for two reasons: first, the extant literature identifies quality as a critical construct to measure service performance (Sousa and Voss 2006) and second, service quality is a significant predictor of various outcome constructs, such as satisfaction and customer lifetime value (Brady and Cronin 2001; Brady and Robertson 2001; Cronin et al. 2000; Dagger and Sweeney 2006; Dagger et al. 2007; Parasuraman and Grewal 2000; Parasuraman et al. 1988, 2005).

This research makes several contributions to omnichannel research by addressing the abovementioned research question. First, it offers a comprehensive theoretical framework of quality dimensions in omnichannel. Second, it extends knowledge on the 'quality' implications of omnichannel integration. The structure of this paper is as follows: first, we present the literature review by defining omnichannel retailing and illuminating the importance of quality in omnichannel retailing. Second, we discuss our research approach and findings in terms of in-store, digital and integration quality. Finally, we present challenges, opportunities and future research directions for omnichannel retailing.

2 Literature Review

2.1 Defining Omnichannel Retailing

The multichannel setting of the present world has dramatically changed the service industry and exposed us to a new set of complexities (e.g. in distribution, communication), which mandates a renewed conceptualization of services and service quality (Ackermann and von Wangenheim 2014; Sousa and Voss 2006; Van Bruggen et al. 2010). This calls for acknowledging customer experience to be formed across all moments of truth and/or contact with the firm through multiple channels (Neslin et al. 2006). Sousa and Voss (2006, p. 358) therefore define multichannel service as "*a service composed of components (physical and/or virtual) that are delivered through two or more channels*". This conceptualization of service and its quality is an extension of traditional service quality research that has been anchored on a single-channel mind set considering primarily the characteristics of either physical or virtual facilities associated with the service. The multichannel service can be contemplated as a point of departure from these single-channel mind-sets to conceiving service experience as a multi-interface system (Patrício et al. 2008) that has three components of quality: virtual (e.g. website, the Internet and smart phone apps), physical (e.g. people-delivered, including logistics), and integration quality (seamless service experience across channels) (Sousa and Voss 2006). Prior research finds that customers' experience in the virtual retail setting affects their behaviours and expectations in the physical retail setting (Burke 2002). In addition, in a multichannel service setting, the levels of virtual and physical service provided by service providers independently may be good, however, the overall perceived service and the consequent satisfaction may be low due to poor integration between different channels and their attributes (Hammerschmidt et al. 2016; Sousa and Voss 2006). Thus, the integration (i.e. consistency across service interactions, integration quality, integration of different channels and attributes) has been suggested as one of the keys to facilitate purchase and to provide uninterrupted service experience across the channels (see Banerjee 2014; Falk et al. 2007; Ganesh 2004; Johnston and Clark 2001; Montoya-Weiss et al. 2003; Patrício et al. 2008; Sousa and Voss 2006). Meanwhile the recent evidence suggests that the integration itself is not enough to offer a seamless customer experience due to a customer's need to have comparable/alienable channel features across every moments of truth in a typical service encounter (Hammerschmidt et al. 2016). This leads to the notion of omnichannel strategy.

In addition, a special issue on the role of technology in retailing by Piotrowicz and Cuthbertson (2014) has articulated factors impacting the current retailing landscape. The authors highlight the need for channel integration due to the growing role of social media, the changing role of physical brick and mortar stores, the impact of mobile technologies, the need to respond to diverse customer requirements, supply chain redesign, and the balance between personalization and privacy as key issues shaping today's retailing environment. Furthermore, the scope of multichannel marketing which is limited to offline, online and direct marketing (Verhoef et al. 2007, 2015) is not able to address the current trend in retailing. Hence, the retailing industry requires a new emerging theme, omnichannel marketing, in order to address the current revolution of technology in retailing (Piotrowicz and Cuthbertson 2014; Verhoef et al. 2015).

Additionally, the term *"Omni"* is a Latin word meaning *"all"* or *"universal"* which business practitioners introduce and define 'omnichannel' as an evolution of the multichannel where channels are used simultaneously rather than in parallel (Lazaris and Vrechopoulos 2014). In academia, Rigby (2011, p. 4) first coined the term 'omnichannel' by defining it as *"an integrated sales experience that melds the advantages of physical stores with the information-rich experience of online shopping"*. This definition is later extended by incorporating the simultaneous use of channels as well as the experience that derives from their integrated combination. Moreover, Levy et al. (2013) introduce the term *"omniretailing"* where multichannel offering is considered to be coordinated with the aim to provide a seamless service/ shopping experience using all of retailers' shopping channels. Besides, these omnichannel definitions have one thing in common; service/shopping experience must be integrated/seamless while using all channels. Although the traditional multichannel and e-commerce literature discusses about such integration and seamless experience across the channels, the firms' independent development and management of these channels in order to offer seamless experience across channels are still limited (Verhoef 2012).

The service and retail landscape in general is profoundly changing due to the proliferation of mobile channel, tablets, social media and the integration of these new channels in both online and offline settings which suggest a movement from multichannel to omnichannel (Rigby 2011; Verhoef et al. 2015). Brynjolfsson et al. (2013) thus rightly say that the distinction between physical and online settings is disappearing; it is instead transforming the world into a showroom without a wall. The change from multichannel phase facilitates the emergence of omnichannel that essentially involves more channels which eventually is affecting the competitive strategies of retailers, service providers and the supply-chain partners (Brynjolfsson et al. 2013; Verhoef et al. 2015). Unlike multichannel the traditional division between one-way and two-way communication channels appears less apparent in omnichannel due to the inclusion of customer touchpoints, for example, one-way or two-way interaction between customers and firms and even between Customer to Customer (Baxendale et al. 2015). In omnichannel context, media that once considered as parts of a broader channel are increasingly presumed to be separate channels facilitating one- or two-way communication or interaction. For example, search, display, email, affiliates and referral websites appear as separate channels within the online media as well as a branded app within the context of mobile medium (Li and Kannan 2014). While undertaking and/or undergoing a service or shopping experience, customers frequently switch across the different channels and devices (e.g. desktop, laptop, mobile). Therefore different channels and touchpoints that used continuously, interchangeably, and simultaneously by customers and firms/providers are needed to be taken into account by the firms/providers to provide a seamless service/shopping experience. In omnichannel environment, the interplay as well as the integration between customer-brand-channel-providers bear significant importance than the standalone consideration of multiple channels of multi-channel world (Verhoef et al. 2015).

The differences as laid down in the preceding paragraphs between omni- and multi-channel management lead Verhoef et al. (2015, p. 176) to define omnichannel management as *"the synergetic management of the numerous available channels and customer touchpoints, in such a way that the customer experience across channels and the performance over channels is optimized"*. Meanwhile as suggested by Neslin et al. (2006), this definition is generally applied in retail/brand rather than in customer management. Therefore, in order to have a holistic perspective regarding omnichannel and omnichannel management, we need to bypass the distinctions between different channels and consider them under a single umbrella. It consists of the conceptualization, planning, operation/implementation and monitoring of all different channels as components of a seamless, integrated single platform that will perform the task of creating, developing and maintaining awareness, interest, desire, conviction, action and post-action for a brand, product, and company. Marketers need to consider the shopping/service experience in omnichannel as an entire process where every customer touchpoint contributes towards the overall service/shopping process and/or experience. They should have the view of co-producer of services or co-shoppers in helping customers along the entire touchpoints across those media. Bagging these thoughts, the omnichannel can be defined as an integrated single system characterized by systematic interdependencies and a series of simultaneous and/or sequential value adding functions/services/touchpoints across channels serving both ends of the value chain- the customer and the marketer.

3 The Importance of Quality in Omnichannel Retailing

Now that we have defined omnichannel, it is important to establish the importance of quality for success in omnichannel setting. There are various definitions of quality (Crosby 2006). It differs for products and services, for different industries and for different levels of dimensionality (Wicks and Roethlein 2009). According to Kara et al. (2005), quality does not have a universally accepted definition. However, commonly accepted definition of quality can be stated as *"the degree to which a set of inherent characteristics fulfils requirements"* (International Organization for Standardization (ISO) 2005). Garvin (1988) segments quality into five categories: (1) Transcendent definitions-these definitions are subjective to individuals and related to emotional perceptions such as beauty and love, hence, are not measurable or follow a logical pattern; (2) Product-based definitions-quality is measured according to objective attributes of products such as reliability, durability; (3) User-based definitions-quality is measured according to the satisfaction level of individual users; (4) Manufacturing-based definitions-quality is seen as meeting production standards such as "zero defects"; and (5) Value-based definitions-quality is defined according to the benefit customers perceive compared to the cost they incur.

In regards to the usage of multiple channels, "Integration Quality" is important for organizations. One of the key premises of multichannel experience is the commitment to customers for channel choice and convenience. However, the breadth of channel choice is no longer a differentiator for companies in today's world, it rather has become a norm (Banerjee 2014). What rather differentiates companies from their competition is the integration quality of resources, infrastructures and processes to deliver highest customer value through these multichannel experiences. Integration quality relates to the level of seamlessness in customer experience a company can deliver within and across multiple channels (Sousa and Voss 2006). A company needs to achieve the highest level of cooperation between functional areas, processes and capabilities to deliver a seamless experience to their customers (Banerjee 2014). When customers interact with a company via any platforms in a multichannel setting, they evaluate the experience through the same set of quality standards they use for a traditional in-person interaction experience at a physical store. For instance, a retailer may have excellent customer service delivered in their physical stores, however, when customers shop from the same retailer through web or mobile platforms, the shopping or post purchase experience may not match with the level of quality delivered at physical stores. Such disconnection fails to deliver a seamless experience with the brand for the customers leading to lower perception of service quality and therefore, lower level of loyalty towards the brand.

Therefore, it is important to acknowledge that multichannel experience bring its own advantages and disadvantages. The multiple added touchpoints open up opportunities for companies to interact with customers via multiple channels of communication. When managed effectively and efficiently, this can possibly lead to stronger and deeper level of commitment between the company and its valued customers, and possibly develop more loyal relationship with the company. The comfort, convenience and habitual practices that customers develop through multichannel experiences increase the switching cost for them and lead to longer term relationship with the brand. However, on the down side, when not managed optimally, multiple touchpoints can open up possibilities for customers to perceive service failure and develop negative attitude and opinion about the company's service quality.

In addition to offering a wide breadth of channel choice, it is important for marketers to help customers manage their service expectations from each touchpoint in order to avoid dissatisfaction and disappointment. Marketers and managers need to understand the appropriateness and benefit of each channel as well as the different service attributes of each channel to manage customer expectations related to each channel experience accordingly (Banerjee 2014). Although all channels may not be capable of performing all activities, it is important for marketers to match channel capabilities with the tasks that are appropriate for each channel (Banerjee 2014). Implementation of the technology and infrastructure alone will not be sufficient in creating the seamless experience that is demanded from every company in today's world. Companies have to be transparent and specific about how each channel contributes to the delivery of optimal customer value.

4 Research Approach

The study followed a systematic literature review to synthesize the current knowledge on the definitional aspects and quality dimensions of omnichannel retailing in services marketing context. A systematic approach was applied throughout the review following the guidelines of Ngai and Wat (2002), Vaithianathan (2010) and Benedettini and Neely (2012). The protocol adopted by the review embraced a scientific and transparent process to establish its due rigor.

The review process aimed to answer the research question: *what are the dimensions of omnichannel service quality?* This question paved the path for proper identification of the subject areas, relevant studies, sources of materials, and the inclusion and exclusion criteria. The findings of the review also aimed to present pragmatic solutions to the research question by tapping into the omnichannel contexts with the support of empirical evidence. As such, the core components of omnichannel retailing (e.g., bricks and mortar, web, mobile and social media) were studied in relation to service outcomes. We have conducted a search from 2006–2016 (February) that was considered to be representative since the research on omnichannel is emerging. We set the lower boundary at 2006 because the seminal papers on "multi-channel retailing" were first published by Sousa and Voss (2006) and Neslin et al. (2006). In addition, the review protocol has identified these two papers as the triggers for subsequent multi-channel/omnichannel retailing research.

In order to identify the relevant publications, the study formed search strings that combined the keywords 'multi-channel retailing' with a different range of terms and phrases. Using wildcard symbols (*), the study reduced the number of search strings, for example, 'multi-channel retailing' could return hits for 'cross-channel retailing' and 'omni-channel retailing'. The study initially focused on marketing, retailing and services research fields as the source of relevant papers. A rigorous database search was conducted by combining the keywords 'multi-channel retailing' with the terms 'omni-channel retailing', 'digital services marketing' and 'interactive services marketing'. The study also constructed further search strings focusing on quality dimensions in multi-channel retailing such as, 'in-store quality' with the terms 'retailers', 'e-retailers'. An initial search was carried out for the two major keywords 'multi-channel retailing' and 'quality'. This search was supplemented by searches that focused on two specific areas where 'quality' was grounded, for example: (a) 'web quality', 'mobile quality', and 'social media quality', and (b) 'satisfaction value', 'loyalty'. The study also constructed analogous search strings on the area keywords 'omnichannel' OR 'quality'. Finally, the study used the search terms 'omnichannel' and 'quality' in combination with 'review'. The study came up with a total of 25 search strings to a panel of experts (n = 5) from marketing, retailing and services studies to validate the review protocol.

The search commenced on January 15, 2016 and ended on February 29, 2016. We reviewed scholarly peer reviewed journals, periodicals, and quality web content by exploring five databases: Scopus (Elsevier); Web of Knowledge (Thomson ISI); ABI/Inform Complete (ProQuest); Business Source Complete (EBSCO Host); and Emerald, IEEE Xplore and ScienceDirect (Taylor & Francis). The searches provided a total of 30,616 hits. We first analysed each citation by searching for the keyword 'multi-channel' or 'omnichannel quality' within titles and abstracts. We ensured the adequacy of screening criterion to confirm the relevance of the study to the research objective. To address any ambiguity, we downloaded the full papers and checked each paper's relevance in the context of omnichannel quality. Consequently, a total of 75 papers were downloaded and reviewed. As we aimed to gather the maximum number of papers in omnichannel quality, a screening criterion (i.e., what are the dimensions of omnichannel service quality?) was established aligning the target papers' contributions to the research questions (Birnik and Bowman 2007). Following this process 10 papers were identified. The study also found five more papers applying cross-referencing technique on seminal papers, yielding the final list of 15 papers in the context of omnichannel service quality.

5 Findings

Following the guidelines of thematic analysis of the literature review by Ezzy (2002) and Braun and Clarke (2006), the paper presented the following three themes of omnichannel quality dimension in services marketing. Firstly, we discuss in-store service quality dimensions. Secondly, we present digital (e.g., web, mobile or social media) service quality dimensions. Finally, we synthesize integration quality dimensions in the context of omnichannel service quality.

5.1 In-Store Quality Dimensions

Traditionally, generic models (Parasuraman et al. 1985; Rust and Oliver 1994) have played a predominant role in service quality literature and have been applied in different disciplines, such as, services marketing, information systems and health care. In fact, marketing literature has played a crucial role in establishing the foundation for traditional service quality theory (Brady and Cronin 2001). The following section discusses the study findings of key service quality theories in measuring in-store quality.

Firstly, the findings focus on the Nordic model which was introduced by Grönroos (1984). This model suggests that perceptions of service quality should be measured under two dimensions: functional quality (how) and technical quality (what). Although this is one of the foundational theories and famous for its seminal conceptualization among researchers, it has been seriously criticized for its limited dimensions (Oliver et al. 1997; Rust et al. 1994).

Secondly, the findings focus on the SERVQUAL model (Parasuraman et al. 1985). This model is quite dominant in services literature and applied widely in various industries such as, health care, public recreation centres, and banking which sometimes indicate that scholars around the world use SERVQUAL as a basis for their own industries (Parasuraman 1990). It may be noted that the initial exploratory research came up with 10 dimensions (*tangibles, reliability, responsiveness, communication, credibility, security, competence, courtesy, understanding and access*) for assessing any service by customers. Due to the overlapping nature of the initial dimensions, this model was later modified into five dimensions (*reliability, responsiveness, assurance, empathy* and *tangibles*) and named as the SERVQUAL model.

Thirdly, according to Rust and Oliver (1994), overall perception of service quality is influenced by three factors: customer-employee interaction (functional quality), service benefit (technical quality) and service environment. The model highlights the support for Grönroos (1984) model and service environment to measure service quality and solidify the positioning of this three-component model. Although the model was not tested empirically, similar models were applied in retail banking and health care settings (Dagger et al. 2007).

Finally, the findings focus on multilevel and multidimensional model introduced by Brady and Cronin (2001) which consists of three primary dimensions (*interaction quality, outcome quality* and *physical environment quality*) and nine sub-dimensions (*attitude, behaviour, expertise, ambient conditions, design, social factors, waiting time, tangibles* and *valence*) based on users' perceptions to capture overall service quality. This study successfully synthesized the previous works of Grönroos (1984) and Rust and Oliver (1994) and proposed a hierarchical service quality model.

Although the extant literature has evidenced multiple dimensions of in-store service quality, for example, two (e.g., Grönroos 1984), three (e.g., Brady and Cronin 2001; Rust and Oliver 1994), five (e.g., Parasuraman et al. 1988) and ten dimensions (Parasuraman et al. 1985), there is no standard agreement on the nature or content of dimensions in defining service quality (Brady and Cronin 2001; Dagger et al. 2007). Therefore, it is generally agreed that in-store service quality should be defined from the users' viewpoint and its conceptualization should result in multilevel, multidimensional constructs.

Most service quality literature has conceptualized quality dimensions of offline and online channels in an incoherent manner. However, indication of quality dimensions from an integrated perspective can be observed in some articles. Table 1 provides a snapshot of key literature in multichannel and omnichannel marketing and a brief overview of the quality dimensions addressed by each article.

5.2 Digital Quality Dimensions

In order to recognize the critical role of service quality in digital contexts, many researchers have initially adopted SERVQUAL to measure service performance, but they face enormous challenges because of the reliability and validity of the generic SERVQUAL measures and lack of Information Technology (IT) artifact in the Information Systems (IS) context (Jiang et al. 2000; Kettinger and Lee 1994; Orlikowski and Iacono 2001). Critics in IS, for example, Van Dyke et al. (1997) highlight that the confusion of SERVQUAL's expectation component and its difference score measurement approach make the model perform poorly in establishing discriminant validity for those five dimensions. Although such studies are important in explaining IT usage, they are relatively weak in capturing human–technology interactions and provide limited guidance for system designers (Nelson et al. 2005). Orlikowski and Iacono (2001) have highlighted that such IT research, which employs a "proxy view" of technology, has lost its connection to the field's core subject matter—the IT artifact itself. Besides, some researchers found that when applying the SERVQUAL model to e-services' collapse, most dimensions lose their reliability and validity (Gefen 2002). Overall, the extant literature on the SERVQUAL model in IS does not focus on *human–technology interaction (system quality), interpersonal interaction* and *outcome (or information) benefits* separately to measure overall IS service quality.

Service quality theories in a web-based electronic service strongly influence mobile service because in both cases, services are delivered over an electronic platform. Several powerful models have been developed to address the issues of service quality over this platform, such as SITEQUAL (Yoo and Donthu 2001), eQUAL (Barnes and Vidgen 2002), web quality (Aladwani and Palvia 2002), E-S-QUAL (Parasuraman et al. 2005). In order to overcome the pitfalls of the earlier models, Parasuraman et al. (2005) develop the E-S-QUAL or electronic service quality model to measure service quality of web-based electronic services. The uniqueness of the E-S-QUAL model lies in its capacity to capture perceptions on human–technology interaction for any web-based e-service platform (Sousa and Voss 2006). Similarly, (Fassnacht and Koese 2006) introduce quite a broad model by focusing on online electronic networks. They proposed to measure service quality through *environment quality, delivery quality* and *information quality*. However, this model does not address the unique characteristics of the mobile platform (e.g., network quality, interaction quality) and it is again restricted to measuring service quality of all web-related services.

Although service quality failures are frequently related to back office operations (i.e., information systems), most web-based electronic service quality studies are

Table 1 Quality dynamics in omnichannel

Studies	Theory and context	Quality dimensions		
		In-store quality	Digital quality	Integration quality
The Impact of Cross-channel Integration on Retailers' Sales Growth (Cao and Li 2015)	The paper proposed a conceptual framework to illustrate the firm-level conditions of cross-channel integration that impacts firms' sales growth.	Cross channel integration stimulates sales growth but firms with a stronger focus on a specific channel (i.e., online, or physical store as measured by physical store presence) benefit less from cross-channel integration.	N/A	Five mechanisms by which cross-channel integration affects firm sales growth have been proposed i.e. (1) improved trust, (2) increased customer loyalty, (3) higher customer conversion rates, (4) greater opportunities to cross-sell, and (5) the loss of special channel features
Integrating Bricks with Clicks: Retailer-Level and Channel-Level Outcomes of Online–Offline Channel Integration (Herhausen et al. 2015)	Utilizing technology adoption research and diffusion theory, this paper conceptualized a theoretical model to examine the impact of online–offline channel integration (OI).	OI does not negatively affect the physical store.	OI directly increases perceived service quality of the Internet store. Perceived service quality of the Internet store increases overall and Internet outcomes	OI indirectly increases overall and Internet outcomes via perceived service quality of the Internet store. OI is moderated by customers' Internet shopping experience.
Building with Bricks and Mortar: The Revenue Impact of Opening Physical Stores in a Multichannel Environment (Pauwels and Neslin 2015)	A multichannel customer management framework has been proposed which is used to identify revenue and cannibalization impact of adding a physical channel for a retailer with existing Internet and catalogue channel.	Study concluded that adding a physical channel would cannibalize catalogue sales but not Internet sales. Total number of returns and exchanges increased and was diverted towards store. Overall value of exchange increased; creating a positive net		N/A

(continued)

Table 1 (continued)

Studies	Theory and context	Quality dimensions		
		In-store quality	Digital quality	Integration quality
		impact on adding physical stores. Little impact on customer acquisition was observed. Overall, the study established that adding channels is definitely a way to grow revenue.		
Leveraging Distribution to Maximize Firm Performance in Emerging Markets (Kumar et al. 2015)	An econometric model encompassing own-marketing mix, competitive actions, brand-level heterogeneity, and dependencies has been proposed for firms developing a multichannel distribution strategy in emerging markets.	Firms must match store formats to the right customer segments to leverage brand. Study found that each distribution format affects sales differently and sales vary according to product form. Further, depending on the product form, price and advertising elasticities could vary even though the brand is essentially the same.	N/A	N/A
From Multi-Channel Retailing to Omnichannel Retailing: Introduction to the Special Issue on Multi-Channel Retailing (Verhoef et al. 2015)	This paper conceptually developed the omnichannel retailing notion and has discussed existing research in this multi-channel	N/A	N/A	Multi-channel retailing is shifting towards Omnichannel retailing. The contributions of the paper can be classified along two dimension:

(continued)

Table 1 (continued)

Studies	Theory and context	Quality dimensions		
		In-store quality	Digital quality	Integration quality
	retailing. Whereas the multi-channel world mainly considers retail channels, the Omnichannel environment is putting more emphasis on the interplay between channels and brands.			(1) Multi-channel versus omnichannel focus and (2) The three research streams i.e. (a) Impact of channels on performance (b) Shopper behaviour across channels and (c) Retail mix across channels
Managing Marketing Channel Multiplicity (Van Bruggen et al. 2010)	The authors proposed a notion "channel multiplicity" which is characterized by the customer's reliance on multiple sources of information and increasing demand for a seamless experience throughout the buying process.	N/A	Following Channel Multiplicity, issues have been proposed in the literature: (a) View of products and marketing channels (b) Channel leadership (c) Channel structure (d) Distribution intensity	N/A
Channels in the Mirror: An Alignable Model for Assessing Customer Satisfaction in Concurrent Channel Systems (Hammerschmidt et al. 2016)	The research paper utilized the structural alignment framework to conceptualize customer satisfaction in their concurrent channel system	The 5C Model-Choice (assortment breadth and depth), Charge (availability of fair prices), Convenience (efficiency of the purchase process), Confidence (security of transactions), and Care (assurance of promised quality)	N/A	N/A

(continued)

Table 1 (continued)

Studies	Theory and context	Quality dimensions		
		In-store quality	Digital quality	Integration quality
		have been proposed.		
Understanding consumers' multichannel choices across the different stages of the buying process (Gensler et al. 2012)	Developed a model that explains consumers' channel choices in the different stages of the buying process in a retail banking setting.	Accounted for channel experience and spillover effects and its impact on consumers' channel choices over and above channel attributes. This article provides a more integrative approach toward channel choice.	N/A	N/A
The value proposition in multichannel retailing (Helbling et al. 2011)	A report on consumers' inclination towards lower price in comparison to shoppers perceive value online and in stores.	Report concludes that price is not the only important factor while buying products, degree of trust on the retailer, its product assortment, and their previous buying experiences influences purchase significantly.	N/A	N/A
Multichannel Shopping: Causes and Consequences (Venkatesan et al. 2007)	Through a longitudinal analysis this paper explores the drivers of multichannel shopping for customer profitability.	Proposed a model of several interaction characteristics i.e. Channel-Related attributes, Purchase-Related attributes, Frequency-Related attributes and Customer Heterogeneity and their impact on Channel Adoption	N/A	N/A

(continued)

Table 1 (continued)

Studies	Theory and context	Quality dimensions		
		In-store quality	Digital quality	Integration quality
		Duration. Concluded that multichannel results in higher customer profitability, improved customer retention and customer growth.		
Service Quality in Multichannel Services Employing Virtual Channels (Sousa and Voss 2006)	This article developed a framework for conceptualizing multichannel service quality and has distinguished between virtual, physical, and integration quality.	Proposed Domain of the Physical Quality Construct: 1. Interpersonal service 1.1 Routine 1.2 Exception (customer support) 2. Logistics fulfilment	Proposed Domain of the Virtual Quality Construct: 1. Virtual fulfilment 2. Efficiency 2.1 Ease of use 2.2 Speed (response time) 3. System availability 4. Privacy	Proposed Domain of the Integration Quality Construct: Channel-service configuration 1.1 Breadth of channel choice 1.2 Transparency of channel- service configuration Integrated interactions 2.1 Content consistency 2.2 Process consistency
Misalignment and Its Influence on Integration Quality in Multichannel Services (Banerjee 2014)	Using a qualitative, multi-method, multisite, case research this study identified different factors affecting integration quality and how it impacts multichannel management.	N/A	N/A	Proposed the following dimensions of Integration Quality: Channel-service configuration Breadth of Channel Choice Transparency of channel-service configuration Appropriateness of channel-service configuration Integrated interactions

(continued)

Table 1 (continued)

Studies	Theory and context	Quality dimensions		
		In-store quality	Digital quality	Integration quality
				Content Consistency Transaction data and interaction data integration Process consistency Within channel and across channel integration

primarily based on front office (i.e., quality of interaction between the end-user and the virtual platform). Since overall customer satisfaction is strongly influenced by service quality at all moments of contact, few studies (e.g., Sousa and Voss 2006) integrate both front office and back office operations in evaluating service quality. In this case, Sousa and Voss (2006) proposed a powerful service quality model focusing on system quality, interpersonal quality and interaction quality to measure any service which contains both electronic (e.g., mobile channel) and physical components (service provided by persons). Therefore, they proposed the dimensions of the E-S-QUAL model (Parasuraman et al. 2005) to measure system quality and the SERVQUAL model (Parasuraman et al. 1985, 1988) to measure interpersonal interaction quality for any service over an electronic platform. However, Sousa and Voss (2006's) conceptual model was not empirically tested and, again, it was proposed as a generic model for all electronic services ignoring the contextual influence of service quality settings. In the case of mobile services, Chae et al. (2002) develop a quality model focusing on the characteristics of a generic mobile platform. They identified four primary quality dimensions and these were *connection quality, content quality, interaction quality* and *contextual quality.*

In addition to web and mobile, Social Media (SM) or Social Networking Sites (SNS) are affecting the lives of individuals across the globe in numerous ways which include but not limited to the way people communicate, socialize, learn, entertain themselves, or even the way they conduct their information search, make decisions and do their shopping (Constantinides and Fountain 2008; Mangold and Faulds 2009; Vollmer and Precourt 2008). These changes forced almost all marketers (e.g. B2B, B2C) to adopt social media as a central element while marketing their products and services. For example, in a recent survey 88.2% of B2C and 93% of B2B firms indicated that they have started social media initiatives and almost half of them fully integrates social media into their business strategies (Holden-Bache 2011; Insites 2011). Kim and Nitecki (2014)'s research on measuring the quality of social media services by adopting and modifying E-S-QUAL approach suggests four dimensions; namely, efficiency, system availability, privacy and fulfilment and two endogenous constructs; namely, perceived value and loyalty intentions. While defining the dimensions of online social value by utilizing Social Exchange Theory, Hu et al. (2015) suggests that utilitarian benefits (such as relational and informational), hedonic benefits (such as enjoyment and curiosity fulfilment), information risk and effort work as inputs in the assessment of online social value.

5.3   Integration Quality Dimensions

Organizations are increasingly linked to the proliferation of e-services, which are embedded in omnichannel environment, combining the web with physical facilities i.e. phone and other channels of service delivery. Evidence from different literature argue that companies which integrate their physical presence with internet based channels are more successful compared to companies operating in a single channel environment (Gulati and Garino 1999; Michael 2001; Vishwanath and Mulvin 2001). A seamless customer experience within and across physical and virtual channels reflects the integration quality of multichannel services.

Sousa and Voss (2006) develop a conceptual framework for multichannel service quality. They have illustrated the distinguishing factors of three service quality components; namely, virtual, physical and integration quality. Sousa and Voss (2006) argue that even though an organization offering good level of virtual and physical quality, they may lack in terms of the overall perception of multichannel service offering. Hence, they have proposed "Integration Quality", a third component of quality in multichannel services. Sousa and Voss (2006, p. 359) define integration quality as "*the quality of the overall service experienced by a customer, encompassing all the existing physical and virtual components*". The types of channels range from in-store (e.g., hotel reception desks, and retail stores), to digital (e.g., phone-based customer contact centres and airline self-check-in kiosks), and to virtual channels (e.g., the Internet and smart phone apps).

The first dimensions of integration quality proposed by Sousa and Voss (2006) is "*Channel-Service Configuration*". This refers to the quality of service combination of the existing channels. The first sub-dimension of channel service configuration is *breadth of channel choice* that refers to the degree to which customers can chose and accomplish specific tasks through alternative channels. The second sub-dimension proposed by Sousa and Voss (2006) is *transparency of the existing channel-service configuration* which refers to the degree to which customers are aware of the existence of all available channels and of differences between service features across different channels.

The second dimension of integration quality proposed by Sousa and Voss (2006) is "*Integrated Interactions*" which refers to the consistency of service provided through all the channels. Integrated interactions quality dimension has two components. The first component is *content consistency* referring to the consistency of both outgoing and incoming information between the service provider and the customer. The second component is *process consistency* referring to the consistency between

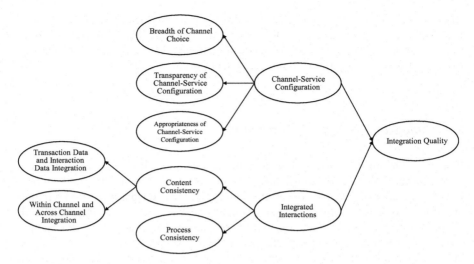

Fig. 1 Conceptual framework of quality dimensions in omnichannel (Adapted from: Banerjee 2014; Sousa and Voss 2006)

the relevant and comparable process aspects of the front offices linked with the different channels.

Extending the work of Sousa and Voss (2006), Banerjee (2014) reports several dimensions of integration quality using a qualitative, multimethod case research within a banking context. The study explores the misalignment between the organizational perception and the design of a multichannel system and customer expectations of a multichannel service experience in banking. The dimensions of integration quality proposed by Banerjee (2014) include *channel service configuration quality* (e.g., breadth of channel choice, transparency of channel-service configuration, appropriateness of channel-service configuration) and *integrated interaction quality* (e.g., content consistency, transaction data and interaction data integration, process consistency, within channel and across channel integration). Figure 1 illustrates a conceptual framework of integration quality dimensions proposed by Sousa and Voss (2006) and Banerjee (2014).

6 Future Research, Challenges and Opportunities

Omnichannel retailing is a step forward from multi-channel retailing as it aims to integrate all the relevant channels seamlessly aiming to provide a satisfying overall shopping experience (Verhoef et al. 2015) to multi-channel shoppers. It takes into account the customers' entire shopping process including: information search, purchase and post-purchase behaviour. Hypothetical examples are given to show how omnichannel can better serve customers during the purchasing process (Rigby

2011). Among different issues related to omnichannel retailing, integration quality is a major one. In this paper, we have developed a comprehensive conceptual framework of quality dimensions in omnichannel and demonstrated how they impact service outcomes. However, there are still issues and difficulties remaining for properly defining and measuring omnichannel service quality. We further include a general discussion of these challenges, which we believe are important for the future research agenda.

There are several challenges of having a comprehensive definition of service quality in an omnichannel setting. First, the cross-channel synergies of different channels within which customers purchase a product are important in the omnichannel environment (Montoya-Weiss et al. 2003). However, the synergy of the complementary platforms in the omnichannel setting and its dimensions are still not fully investigated. For example, customers may use an online channel mainly for information and go to a physical channel to make a purchase. One may check the quality of online information and ease of purchase in the store while measuring service quality. However, customers, who have obtained most of the information online, may still use the complementary information in the store to make a final purchase decision. Thus, there is a synergy between online and offline information, which requires more in-depth analysis in terms of conceptualizing the dimensions and finding out behavioural outcome related to synergy. Second, service quality in omnichannel environment is difficult to measure as it is not as straight forward as measuring physical or virtual channels, instead it involves the factors related to customer perception towards integration of physical and virtual channels. Research in omnichannel is still in its early stage. Firms are forming and implementing their omnichannel strategy. As a result, the structure of a firm's omnichannel is changing to achieve the best outcome. At the same time, the definition of service quality in an omnichannel setting is very dependent on the specific components of the channel, making it difficult to come up with a complete definition of service quality in the omnichannel in advance. Finally, technology is changing very fast in this era, making the definition of service quality even more difficult. For example, new technology is being developed to allow customers to have completely virtual online shopping experiences and even have virtual fitting room (Kim et al. 2017). This can dramatically influence how customers evaluate the quality of the service provided by a firm. Generally speaking, three channels have been considered in omnichannel retailing: online, offline and catalogues (Verhoef et al. 2015). However, within each channel, there are different platforms that function differently and appeal to different types of customers at different times. For example, within the context of online channel, customers who make online purchases through a computer and a mobile phone app may have different preferences, experience and expectation. The criteria that those customers use to judge service quality can vary as well. Therefore, it is important to consider these factors when firms measure service quality.

With the development of Web 2.0 technology, social media (e.g., Facebook, Twitter, and Instagram) have gained in popularity. Many firms adopt social media as their information distribution channel. Although social media allow firms to interact with the users, social media are also used as an information distribution (marketing) channel. Firms need to respond to their customers' inquires promptly and efficiently, and customers also generate lots of information online—referred to as user generated content (Goh et al. 2013), which firms do not have direct control over. As more and more customers go to social media to seek information and share their thoughts and experience, social media gains higher importance in service quality perception. Therefore, a firm's social media presence and performance should be considered while measuring its service quality in omnichannel environment.

7 Conclusion

Integration quality plays a vital role in omnichannel retailing. Research related to omnichannel retailing and integration quality is still at a conceptual level. Through extensive literature review, this study answered the research question: what are the dimensions of service quality in omnichannel retailing? Based on the findings of a systematic review, this study conceptualises several dimensions of integration quality within omnichannel retailing i.e. channel service configuration quality, integrated interactions quality and their sub-dimensions i.e. breadth of channel choice, transparency of channel-service configuration, appropriateness of channel-service configuration, content consistency and process consistency. This research is largely a first step towards understanding the service quality dimensions of omnichannel retailing. Using the knowledge of this research, future studies can investigate omnichannel implementation by integrating physical and virtual quality dimensions. Additionally, the findings of this research also lead to several contributions towards managerial and theoretical practice as discussed below.

7.1 Recommendations for Practice

Omnichannel retailing is becoming into a strategy for success. Managers need to introduce diverse channels and integrate all service components within these channels to provide higher customer satisfaction and avoid losing customers to competitors. The findings of this research will provide managers with valuable guideline to create a blueprint of service quality management process.

First, this research will enable managers to understand the role of integration within omnichannel. Identification of factors which influence integration quality will allow managers to allocate resources in those areas. Mangers should include diverse range of channels for customers to avail services from. Additionally, managers should also utilise the power of social media and interactive channels to inform and aware customers about available channels and their service capabilities. On the contrary, managers should be careful about appropriateness of channel service configuration. Organisations might be tempted to increase the number of channels. However, this research shows, adding channels without focusing on service appropriateness will cause customer dissatisfaction. Hence, addressing the appropriateness of the channel-service configuration will also play a vital role in designing omnichannel service pattern within organisations. Within an omnichannel environment it is critical to create a balance between number of channels offered with cost and benefit of each channels.

Moreover, the findings of this research indicate the importance of content consistency and process consistency to be achieved within the channels. Managers should create a database to collect information from customers and integrate the information within all the channels. This will help the firm to address customer individually through all customer touchpoints and ensure satisfaction within customers. Not only inbound information, but outbound information needs to be integrated as well. Managers should ensure consistency regarding price, features and other related information within all the channels.

Finally, this research has stressed highly on the importance of integration within channels. Customers want the advantages of digital shopping, such as wide selection, rich product information, feedback from customers as well as the advantages of physical stores such as personal service, and ability to experience the product. Therefore, the integration of multiple platforms to create a seamless shopping experience for customers has become the key to success in today's retailing world. Specifically, in industries were competitors are utilising and integrating multiple channels, a firm with disintegrated channels will create dissatisfied customers and eventually lose customers to competition. In this backdrop, companies need to invest their resources, in the form of human, capital and infrastructure, to create this seamless omnichannel experience for their customers.

Retailers can introduce Click and Collect service, where customers can order products online and collect in store, or even order in store from their mobile devices. Retailers can also incorporate technologies such as interactive screens, augmented realities or provide tablets to its staffs to address their customers. Customers will be able to order or do some research on products through different self-service kiosks, communicate with other customers and also receive reviews of different products in store. Retailers should also consider redesigning their stores to facilitate omnichannel integration.

7.2 Recommendation for Future Research

Future research should focus on developing specific measures to understand how marketers can conceptualize as well as measure quality perceptions of customers and other related business outcomes in an omnichannel setting. Research on channel performance, customer/shopper behaviour and retail mix should focus more on omnichannel services.

In regards to channel performance, issues such as, impact of store performance due to integration of different channels, impact on purchase behaviour due to integration of mobile channels within stores, importance of seamless channel experience among customers can be addressed in future research.

In regards to shopper behaviour, issues such as generalisation of important drivers of channel choice, generalisation of behavioural outcome of integration quality can be addressed in future research. In terms of retail mix across channels, issues such as the extent of integration of different channels, role of brands in relation to integration, shopper's control on integration (customisation), effect of promotions in omnichannel performance can also be addressed in future research.

In regards to integration quality, the next step in future research is to develop/ generate scale items for dimensions proposed in previous studies. In addition, future research can measure customer and organisational perception of integration quality and the similarities or differences between these viewpoints.

Questions for Review and Discussion

1. How can organizations better incorporate functional differences to implement integrated channel system?
2. Should firms integrate all components within all the channels or keep some services unique for specific channels? Such as, should price be same for all channels? Should there be specific promotion for utilizing specific channel?
3. How can organizations collect and integrate customer transaction data and customer interaction data within all its available channels?
4. How customer transaction data collected from different channels enable organizations to create more personalized products and services and offer dynamic pricing?
5. What factors influence consumer equity due to integration quality?
6. How can organizations better use data and insights from multiple channels to achieve operational excellence?
7. What are the different evaluation criteria and metrics appropriate for cross-channel performance measurement?
8. What is the cost of adding a new channel and whether channel integration results to net benefit for organizations—how to measure the benefits?
9. What factors influence security and privacy within multichannel usage and what steps multichannel service providers should undertake to mitigate these concerns?
10. What type of organizational culture is appropriate to adapt channel integration?

References

Ackermann, S., & von Wangenheim, F. (2014). Behavioural consequences of customer-initiated channel migration. *Journal of Service Research, 17*, 262–277.

Aladwani, A. M., & Palvia, P. C. (2002). Developing and validating an instrument for measuring user-perceived web quality. *Information Management, 39*, 467–476.

Banerjee, M. (2014). Misalignment and its influence on integration quality in multichannel services. *Journal of Service Research, 17*, 460–474.

Barnes, S. J., & Vidgen, R. T. (2002). An integrative approach to the assessment of E-commerce quality. *Journal of Electronic Commerce Research, 3*, 114–127.

Baxendale, S., Macdonald, E. K., & Wilson, H. N. (2015). The impact of different touchpoints on brand consideration. *Journal of Retailing, 91*, 235–253.

Benedettini, O., & Neely, A. (2012). Complexity in services: An interpretative framework. *POMS 23rd Annual Conference*.

Birnik, A., & Bowman, C. (2007). Marketing mix standardization in multinational corporations: A review of the evidence. *International Journal of Management Reviews, 9*, 303–324.

Brady, M. K., & Cronin, J. J. (2001). Some new thoughts on conceptualizing perceived service quality: A hierarchical approach. *The Journal of Marketing, 65*(3), 34–49.

Brady, M. K., & Robertson, C. J. (2001). Searching for a consensus on the antecedent role of service quality and satisfaction: An exploratory cross-national study. *Journal of Business Research, 51*, 53–60.

Braun, V., & Clarke, V. (2006). *Using thematic analysis in psychology qualitative research in psychology* (Vol. 3, pp. 77–101). Bristol: University of the West of England.

Brynjolfsson, E., Hu, Y. J., & Rahman, M. S. (2013). Competing in the age of omnichannel retailing. *MIT Sloan Management Review, 54*, 23–29.

Burke, R. (2002). Technology and the customer interface: What consumers want in the physical and virtual store. *Journal of the Academy of Marketing Science, 30*, 411–432.

Cao, L., & Li, L. (2015). The impact of cross-channel integration on retailers' sales growth. *Journal of Retailing, 91*, 198–216.

Chae, M., Kim, J., Kim, H., & Ryu, H. (2002). Information quality for mobile internet services: A theoretical model with empirical validation. *Electronic Markets, 12*, 38–46.

Cheng, J. M.-S., Tsao, S.-M., Tsai, W.-H., & Tu, H. H.-J. (2007). Will eChannel additions increase the financial performance of the firm?—The evidence from Taiwan. *Industrial Marketing Management, 36*, 50–57.

Constantinides, E., & Fountain, S. J. (2008). Web 2.0: Conceptual foundations and marketing issues. *Journal of Direct, Data and Digital Marketing Practice, 9*, 231–244.

Cronin, J. J., Brady, M. K., & Hult, G. T. M. (2000). Assessing the effects of quality, value, and customer satisfaction on consumer behavioural intentions in service environments. *Journal of Retailing, 76*, 193–218.

Crosby, D. C. (2006). Quality is easy. *Quality, 45*, 58.

Dagger, T. S., & Sweeney, J. C. (2006). The effect of service evaluations on behavioural intentions and quality of life. *Journal of Service Research, 9*, 3–18.

Dagger, T. S., Sweeney, J. C., & Johnson, L. W. (2007). A hierarchical model of health service quality scale development and investigation of an integrated model. *Journal of Service Research, 10*, 123–142.

Ezzy, D. (2002). *Qualitative analysis: Practice and innovation*. Crows Nest: Allen & Unwin.

Falk, T., Schepers, J., Hammerschmidt, M., & Bauer, H. H. (2007). Identifying cross-channel dissynergies for multichannel service providers. *Journal of Service Research, 10*, 143–160.

Fassnacht, M., & Koese, I. (2006). Quality of electronic services conceptualizing and testing a hierarchical model. *Journal of Service Research, 9*, 19–37.

Ganesh, J. (2004). Managing customer preferences in a multi-channel environment using Eeb services. *International Journal of Retail & Distribution Management, 32*, 140–146.

Garvin, D. A. (1988). *Managing quality: The strategic and competitive edge*. Simon and Schuster.

Gefen, D. (2002). Customer loyalty in e-commerce. *Journal of the Association for Information Systems, 3*, 27–51.

Gensler, S., Verhoef, P. C., & Böhm, M. (2012). Understanding consumers' multichannel choices across the different stages of the buying process. *Marketing Letters, 23*, 987–1003.

Goh, K.-Y., Heng, C.-S., & Lin, Z. (2013). Social media brand community and consumer behaviour: Quantifying the relative impact of user- and marketer-generated content. *Information Systems Research, 24*, 88–107.

Grönroos, C. (1984). A service quality model and its marketing implications. *European Journal of Marketing, 18*, 36–44.

Gulati, R., & Garino, J. (1999). Get the right mix of bricks & clicks. *Harvard Business Review, 78*, 107–114, 214.

Hammerschmidt, M., Falk, T., & Weijters, B. (2016). Channels in the mirror: An alignable model for assessing customer satisfaction in concurrent channel systems. *Journal of Service Research, 19*, 88–101.

Helbling, J., Leibowitz, J., Rettaliata, A. (2011). The value proposition in multichannel retailing. *McKinsey Quarterly.*

Herhausen, D., Binder, J., Schoegel, M., & Herrmann, A. (2015). Integrating bricks with clicks: Retailer-level and channel-level outcomes of online-offline channel integration. *Journal of Retailing, 91*, 309–325.

Holden-Bache, A. (2011). Study: 93% of B2B marketers use social media marketing. *BtoB Magazine.*

Homburg, C., Vollmayr, J., & Hahn, A. (2014). Firm value creation through major channel expansions: Evidence from an event study in the United States, Germany, and China. *Journal of Marketing, 78*, 38–61.

Hu, T., Kettinger, W. J., & Poston, R. S. (2015). The effect of online social value on satisfaction and continued use of social media. *European Journal of Information Systems, 24*, 391–410.

Insites, C. (2011). *Social integration survey.* Ghent, Belgium.

International Organization for Standardization (ISO). (2005). *Quality management systems – Fundamentals and vocabulary.* ISO Standard 9000/2005, Geneva.

Jiang, J. J., Klein, G., & Crampton, S. M. (2000). A note on SERVQUAL reliability and validity in information system service quality measurement. *Decision Sciences, 31*, 725–744.

Johnston, R., & Clark, G. (2001). *Service operations management.* Harlow: Pearson Education.

Kara, A., Lonial, S., Tarim, M., & Zaim, S. (2005). A paradox of service quality in Turkey: The seemingly contradictory relative importance of tangible and intangible determinants of service quality. *European Business Review, 17*, 5–20.

Kettinger, W. J., & Lee, C. C. (1994). Perceived service quality and user satisfaction with the information services function. *Decision Sciences, 25*, 737–766.

Kim, H. M., & Nitecki, D. A. (2014). *A proposed scale for measuring the quality of social media services: An E-S-QUAL approach.* Seattle, Washington: ASIST.

Kim, H.-Y., Lee, J. Y., Mun, J. M., & Johnson, K. K. (2017). Consumer adoption of smart in-store technology: Assessing the predictive value of attitude versus beliefs in the technology acceptance model. *International Journal of Fashion Design, Technology and Education, 10*, 26–36.

Konuş, U., Verhoef, P. C., & Neslin, S. A. (2008). Multichannel shopper segments and their covariates. *Journal of Retailing, 84*, 398–413.

Kumar, V., Sunder, S., & Sharma, A. (2015). Leveraging distribution to maximize firm performance in emerging markets. *Journal of Retailing, 91*, 627–643.

Lazaris, C., & Vrechopoulos, A. (2014). *From multichannel to "omnichannel" retailing: Review of the literature and calls for research 2nd International Conference on Contemporary Marketing Issues (ICCMI).* Greece: Athens.

Leeflang, P. S., Verhoef, P. C., Dahlström, P., & Freundt, T. (2014). Challenges and solutions for marketing in a digital era. *European Management Journal, 32*, 1–12.

Levy, M., Weitz, B., & Grewal, D. (2013). *Retailing management* (9th ed.). New York: McGraw-Hill Education.

Li, H., & Kannan, P. K. (2014). Attributing conversions in a multi-channel online marketing environment: An empirical model and a field experiment. *Journal of Marketing Research, 51*, 40–56.

Mangold, W. G., & Faulds, D. J. (2009). Social media: The new hybrid element of the promotion mix. *Business Horizons, 52*, 357–365.

Michael, P. (2001). Strategy and the internet. *Harvard Business Review, 79*, 63–78.

Montoya-Weiss, M. M., Voss, G. B., & Grewal, D. (2003). Determinants of online channel use and overall satisfaction with a relational, multichannel service provider. *Journal of the Academy of Marketing Science, 31*, 448–458.

Nelson, R. R., Todd, P. A., & Wixom, B. H. (2005). Antecedents of information and system quality: An empirical examination within the context of data warehousing. *Journal of Management Information Systems, 21*, 199–235.

Neslin, S. A., Grewal, D., Leghorn, R., Shankar, V., Teerling, M. L., Thomas, J. S., & Verhoef, P. C. (2006). Challenges and opportunities in multichannel customer management. *Journal of Service Research, 9*, 95–112.

Ngai, E. W. T., & Wat, F. K. T. (2002). A literature review and classification of electronic commerce research. *Information Management, 39*, 415–429.

Oliver, R. L., Rust, R. T., & Varki, S. (1997). Customer delight: Foundations, findings, and managerial insight. *Journal of Retailing, 73*, 311–336.

Orlikowski, W. J., & Iacono, C. S. (2001). Research commentary: Desperately seeking the "it" in it research—a call to theorizing the it artifact. *Information Systems Research, 12*, 121–134.

Parasuraman, A. (1990). *Delivering quality service: Balancing customer perceptions and expectations*. New York: Free Press; London: Collier Macmillan.

Parasuraman, A., & Grewal, D. (2000). The impact of technology on the quality-value-loyalty chain: A research agenda. *Journal of the Academy of Marketing Science, 28*, 168–174.

Parasuraman, A., Zeithaml, V. A., & Berry, L. L. (1985). A conceptual model of service quality and its implications for future research. *The Journal of Marketing, 49*, 41–50.

Parasuraman, A., Zeithaml, V. A., & Berry, L. L. (1988). Servqual. *Journal of Retailing, 64*, 12–40.

Parasuraman, A., Zeithaml, V. A., & Malhotra, A. (2005). E-S-QUAL: A multiple-item scale for assessing electronic service quality. *Journal of Service Research, 7*, 213–233.

Patrício, L., Fisk, R. P., & Falcão e Cunha, J. (2008). Designing multi-interface service experiences: The service experience blueprint. *Journal of Service Research, 10*, 318–334.

Pauwels, K., & Neslin, S. A. (2015). Building with bricks and mortar: The revenue impact of opening physical stores in a multichannel environment. *Journal of Retailing, 91*, 182–197.

Piotrowicz, W., & Cuthbertson, R. (2014). Introduction to the special issue information technology in retail: Toward omnichannel retailing. *International Journal of Electronic Commerce, 18*, 5–16.

Rigby, D. (2011). The future of shopping. *Harvard Business Review, 89*, 65–76.

Rust, R. T., & Oliver, R. L. (1994). *Service quality: New directions in theory and practice*. California: Sage.

Rust, R. T., Zahorik, A. J., & Keiningham, T. L. (1994). *Return on quality: Measuring the financial impact of your company's quest for quality*. Probus Chicago.

Sousa, R., & Voss, C. A. (2006). Service quality in multichannel services employing virtual channels. *Journal of Service Research, 8*, 356–371.

Vaithianathan, S. (2010). A review of e-commerce literature on India and research agenda for the future. *Electronic Commerce Research, 10*, 83–97.

Van Bruggen, G. H., Antia, K. D., Jap, S. D., Reinartz, W. J., & Pallas, F. (2010). Managing marketing channel multiplicity. *Journal of Service Research, 13*, 331–340.

Van Dyke, T. P., Kappelman, L. A., & Prybutok, V. R. (1997). Measuring information systems service quality: Concerns on the use of the SERVQUAL questionnaire. *MIS Quarterly*, 195–208.

Venkatesan, R., Kumar, V., & Ravishanker, N. (2007). Multichannel shopping: Causes and consequences. *Journal of Marketing, 71*, 114–132.

Verhoef, P. C. (2012). Multi-channel customer management strategy. In V. Shankar & G. Carpenter (Eds.), *Handbook of marketing strategy*. Cheltenham: Edward Elgar.

Verhoef, P. C., Neslin, S. A., & Vroomen, B. (2007). Multichannel customer management: Understanding the research-shopper phenomenon. *International Journal of Research in Marketing, 24*, 129–148.

Verhoef, P. C., Kannan, P., & Inman, J. J. (2015). From multi-channel retailing to omnichannel retailing: Introduction to the special issue on multi-channel retailing. *Journal of Retailing, 91*, 174–181.

Vishwanath, V., & Mulvin, G. (2001). Multi-Channels: The Real Winners in the B2C Internet Wars. *Business Strategy Review, 12*, 25–33.

Vollmer, C., & Precourt, G. (2008). *Always on: Advertising, marketing, and media in an era of consumer control*. New York: McGraw-Hill.

Wicks, A. M., & Roethlein, C. J. (2009). A satisfaction-based definition of quality. *The Journal of Business and Economic Studies, 15*, 82.

Wirtz, J., & Lovelock, C. (2016). *Services marketing: People, technology, strategy*.

Xia, Y., & Zhang, G. P. (2010). The impact of the online channel on retailers' performances: An empirical evaluation. *Decision Sciences, 41*, 517–546.

Yoo, B., & Donthu, N. (2001). Developing a scale to measure the perceived quality of an internet shopping (SITEQUAL). *Quarterly Journal of Electronic Commerce, 2*, 31–47.

Shahriar Akter is an Associate Professor at the Sydney Business School, University of Wollongong, Australia. Shahriar was awarded his PhD from the UNSW Business School, with a doctoral fellowship in research methods from the Oxford Internet Institute, University of Oxford. He completed his BBA in Marketing, MBA in Marketing and a Master by research degree in E-Business Management. Shahriar has published top ranked business journals including International Journal of Production Economics, Information & Management, Journal of the American Society for Information Science & Technology, International Journal of Operations and Production Management, Journal of Business Research, International Journal of Production Research, Behaviour & IT, and Electronic Markets. His research areas include big data analytics, digital and social media marketing, digital innovations, service systems and variance based SEM techniques.

Muhammad Ismail Hossain is a Professor at the Department of Marketing, Faculty of Business Studies, University of Dhaka, Bangladesh. He holds a Master in International Business from University of Melbourne, Australia and a PhD from Monash University in Melbourne, Australia. His academic research focuses on the role of emotions and age-based generational division in consumer behaviour and branding, in particular in service encounters across online and offline contexts. His industry related research work focuses on diverse social issues including employment and investment and their impact on Bangladesh and its wellbeing. He has over twenty five academic and industry publications. He presented his academic work at several local and international academic conferences. His industry based work is showcased to leading trade and investment bodies of the People's Republic of Bangladesh.

Steven Lu is the co-director of Consumer Insights Research Group at the University of Sydney Business School. He obtained his PhD in Marketing from the University of Toronto, and MA in Economics from York University. His research interests are: Multichannel Consumer Behavior and Insights: this stream of research examines the behavior of multichannel consumers and relevant marketing strategy. Big Data Analytics: this stream of research aims at extracting invaluable information from companies' big data. He has published in several internationally acclaimed journals such as Marketing Science, Statistical Science, Annals of Tourism Research, Journal of Business Research, Journal of Interactive Marketing, International Journal of Production Research, and Customer Needs and Solutions. He has served on the editorial board of Marketing Science.

Sutapa Aditya is an independent marketing consultant working in the Greater New York area. She worked as an assistant professor of marketing at LIU Brooklyn's School of Business, Public Administration and Information Sciences. In addition, she taught various marketing courses in different business schools in Canada and Bangladesh. She obtained her B.B.A. with a specialization in marketing at the Institute of Business Administration of the University of Dhaka in Bangladesh. Later, she obtained her M.B.A. degree from Simon Fraser University in Canada and her Ph.D. degree in marketing from the Schulich School of Business at York University in Canada. Her research focuses on consumer-to-consumer communication on brands, persuasion knowledge and implicit cognition and attitudes. She has presented at various conferences, including the Association of Consumer Research, Society of Consumer Psychology and Southern Ontario Behavioral Decision Research Conferences.

Taufique Hossain is a PhD candidate in Marketing at the University of Wollongong, NSW, Australia. His research focus is towards multichannel service quality, omnichannel marketing, customer engagement and customer equity. Have experience in teaching several marketing courses including marketing strategy and marketing communication. Worked as a strategic marketing analyst at a global telecommunication company in Bangladesh. Experienced in formulating company's marketing strategies, budgeting, forecasting, creating pricing models, preparing business models for new packages, segments and promotions. Completed Masters in Advertising and Marketing from University of Leeds, UK and Bachelors in Business majoring in Marketing and Finance from North South University, Bangladesh.

Uraiporn Kattiyapornpong or Ping is a Lecturer in Marketing at the School of Management, Operations and Marketing, Faculty of Business, University of Wollongong. She teaches a variety of marketing subjects at undergraduate and postgraduate levels. She holds a Bachelor of Arts in Business Administration (Marketing) (Bradford Business School, University of Bradford, UK), Master of Business (International Marketing) (University of Technology Sydney, Australian) and a Graduate Certificate in Higher Education (Deakin University, Australia).Ping completed her PhD (Marketing) at Thammasat University, Thailand. Ping's research interests are International Marketing, Business to Business Marketing, Services Marketing, Tourism Marketing, and Consumer Behaviour.

Drivers for Channel Integration and Omnichannel Strategy: Evidence from the Leading Grocery Retailer in Turkey

Işık Özge Yumurtacı Hüseyinoğlu

Abstract As retailing is amongst the most diverse and dynamic sectors, channel integration and omnichannel strategy have become prominent issues across the entire retail supply chain. Customers are seeking a seamless shopping experience, and insisting on uninterrupted business processes. In this regard, to improve service, it is clear that the Business-to-Business (B2B) context would benefit from a deeper understanding of the Business-to-Customer (B2C) relationships. Hence, the drivers for channel integration and omnichannel strategy are priorities for research.

This chapter aims to provide an understanding of channel integration and omnichannel strategy, highlighting the trends and future perspectives. Based on the content of the topic, primary and secondary data are used to provide evidence and present a broader view, using a Turkish grocery retailer as an example. The findings from focus groups revealed the drivers for channel integration and implementation of omnichannel strategy. The drivers for channel integration are related to the changing dynamics within the retail sector; changes in shopping habits and the need for high productivity in logistics and supply chain processes. Moreover, the implementation of an omnichannel strategy is examined, with the focus on advanced information technology, integration of business processes, and customer perception.

1 Introduction

In the past, retailing has been considered as an industry concerned mainly with the sale of consumer goods through shops; however, services became an equally important part of the retail offering (Cox and Brittain 2004). Retailing in the twenty-first century is very different from the twentieth century, just as retailing in the late twentieth century differed from earlier (Peterson and Balasubramanian 2002). Key trends in retailing include changing customer needs, an increasing desire

I. Ö. Y. Hüseyinoğlu (✉)
Department of Logistics Management, Business Faculty, Izmir University of Economics, Izmir, Turkey
e-mail: isik.yumurtaci@ieu.edu.tr

© Springer Nature Switzerland AG 2019
W. Piotrowicz, R. Cuthbertson (eds.), *Exploring Omnichannel Retailing*,
https://doi.org/10.1007/978-3-319-98273-1_5

for digital shopping experiences, retailer consolidation, technology driven channel strategies, competition between retail formats, and advances in social media (Krafft and Mantrala 2006).

The field of retailing unifies Business-to-Business (B2B) and Business-to-Customer (B2C) relationships (Dant and Brown 2008). For B2B, retailers perform a number of critical functions for suppliers, manufacturers and wholesalers, including displaying merchandise, providing expertise, working closely with manufacturers to develop promotions and managing operations (Ennis 2016). For B2C, the marketing channels provide products and services for end users, with a special focus on their overall satisfaction (Kozlenkova et al. 2015).

Advances in information technology (IT) have driven retailers to involve consumers in business processes through internet-based tools and interfaces. Rapid economic growth and widespread internet access have greatly changed shopping habits (Narwal and Sachdeva 2013). The consumer considers multichannel shopping as a given, and there is a great effort to provide integrated, customer-focused technology, which transforms the "channel" experience into a total retail experience (PWC 2014). This total retail and "channel" experience, omnichannel retailing, is considered to be an evolutionary aspect of multichannel retailing. It aims to provide consumers with a seamless shopping experience by using advanced and integrated IT in each channel (Verhoef et al. 2015). In addition to competition between retailers, traditional store based retailers also have to compete with pure online players, such as Amazon.

This chapter aims to discuss and examine the drivers for channel integration and omnichannel strategy by providing evidence from an organized chain retailer. Although internet penetration and advances in technology have spread globally, their impact on channel strategies varies across countries. Therefore, the aim of this study is to provide insights into the factors influencing omnichannel strategy, and to discuss the drivers for channel integration from an emerging country—Turkey.

The chapter is structured as follows: first, a summary of studies on channel integration and omnichannel strategy is provided, followed by the methodology and findings. The chapter ends with a critical discussion, comparing findings against the literature, and drawing conclusions both for practitioners and researchers.

2   Literature Review on Channel Integration and Omnichannel Strategy

In retailing, marketing channels enable retailers to access a wide range of consumers through touchpoints and the integration of channels. In this regard, this section discusses the drivers for channel integration and transition in a marketing channel strategy from a multichannel to an omnichannel strategy.

Marketing channels comprise interdependent organizations that provide products and services to the end user (Kumar et al. 1995). Today, most of these are multichannel retailers, displaying and selling in the various channels available. Therefore, the integration of different channels, providing a seamless customer experience, has become an emerging trend (Panigrahi 2013). Channel integration can be provided by the integration of online-available devices within physical stores, and the availability of physical store locators in mobile channels, so that the interaction between physical and digital channels will be enhanced (Herhausen et al. 2015). With integration between physical and digital channels, the consumer has the opportunity to benefit from all channels. The consumer has access to various channels whether using a physical store/mobile app or online web site. However, tracking and monitoring transaction information across channels requires infrastructure for data integration (Zhang et al. 2010).

Today, there has been a shift away from multichannel retailing evolving towards an omnichannel strategy (Rigby 2011; Piotrowicz and Cuthbertson 2014; Verhoef et al. 2015). Omnichannel management can be defined as, *"the synergetic management of the numerous available channels and customer touchpoints, in such a way that the customer experience across channels and the performance over channels is optimized"* (Verhoef et al. 2015, p. 176). In an omnichannel strategy, the retailer controls data and uses it to guide consumer purchases across all channels (Beck and Rygl 2015). An omnichannel strategy enables an uninterrupted and independent shopping experience for end users, and ensures multiple channel product availability (Kozlenkova et al. 2015). A major advantage of this strategy is the capacity to provide services targeted at particular consumer segments (Bell et al. 2013).

An omnichannel customer makes a single purchase using a combination of different channels, such as physical stores, websites, and mobile apps (Li et al. 2015). In this type of retailing, full interaction can be initiated by the customer, while full integration is under retailer control. The practices of omnichannel retailing can be characterized by three features: the opportunity to use discount coupons across all channels; the ability to return product through any channel regardless of its point of purchase; and the full integration of data relating to the customer, pricing, assortment, and consistency of merchandise and services (Beck and Rygl 2015).

An omnichannel strategy attracts customer attention, creates interaction through touchpoints, and supports marketing activities. Retailers following such a strategy need to utilize advanced information management technologies to facilitate the transfer of customers between channels (Rangaswamy and Van Bruggen 2005). Marketing activities enhance revenues in channels by creating interactions across different channels (Pauwels and Neslin 2015). Although an omnichannel strategy is a developed form of a multichannel strategy, it has more advanced requirements related to technology usage, logistics, and internal integration (Piotrowicz and Cuthbertson 2014).

The latest advances in technology, changing consumption habits and consumer demographics are making it possible for retailers to provide goods and services through a range of channels and touchpoints. However, this requires an integrated and effective omnichannel strategy. In this regard, we aim to provide evidence for the main drivers that cause retailers to integrate channels and adopt an omnichannel strategy. This is a popular trend across the retailing sector (Brynjolfsson et al. 2013;

Piotrowicz and Cuthbertson 2014; Frazer and Stiehler 2014; Verhoef et al. 2015, Li et al. 2015; Beck and Rygl 2015); nevertheless, its implementation is likely to differ according to context. Hence, it is important to examine the drivers of channel integration, omnichannel strategy, and its implementation among retailers. Thus, we developed the following research questions (RQ):

RQ1   What are the drivers of channel integration from a retailer perspective?

RQ2   How does a retailer manage their omnichannel strategy?

A series of focus group discussions were conducted with a grocery retailer in Turkey to address the research questions. The examined retailer is amongst the leading retailers in the Turkish market and operates both locally and abroad (Asia and Europe).

3   Turkish Retail Sector

Turkish retailing is an emerging market with great opportunities for both consumers and retailers. The total size of the retail sector reached approximately US$300 billion in 2015, and is expected to continue to grow (Perakende.org 2016). The Turkish retail industry consists of 67% conventional (traditional, not organised) and 33% modern organized retailing (TUIK 2016; AC Nielsen 2016; PWC 2016). Retail sales are increasing due to the young population and the fast rate of urbanization. The share of organized retailing is growing as a result of the acquisition of traditional independent retailers by national and global retailers, such as Migros and Carrefour (ATKearney 2016).

Turkey is amongst the top ten most attractive online markets in the world (Markafoni 2013). According to Deloitte (2014a), the total volume of online spending through online networks has reached US$18 billion. Turkey is a particularly suitable environment for e-commerce due to the high level of banking card acceptance, fast and reliable delivery of goods, and intense mobile, internet, and social media usage (ETicaretmag 2016). The most popular products bought from online retailers are electronics (40%), followed by clothing (16%), white goods and furniture (13%), books & music (11%), and grocery (2%) (ETicaretmag 2016). The total e-commerce market size was 7.4 billion USD (2.6 billion USD by pure online retail 1.2 billion USD by multichannel retail 2.7 billion USD travel & transportation, 0.8 billion USD online legal betting) (Deloitte 2014b). The B2C e-commerce market in Turkey is the second largest in Eastern Europe and mobile shopping and social media are increasingly important (yStats 2016). In 2015, approximately 35% of internet users in Turkey purchased goods or services online, which is up from 19% in 2011 (yStats 2016).

The leading top ten retailers, in order of net sales, are BİM (grocery), Migros (grocery), LC Waikiki (clothing), ŞOK Market (grocery), CarrefourSA (hypermarket), Teknosa (electronics), Bizim Market (grocery), Media Markt (electronics),

ATÜ duty free, and Koton (clothing) (Retailer.net 2017). Local players are still dominant in the list of the leading 100 retailers (according to net sales). The Turkish market has already attracted global retailers such as Ecco and Save My Bag, and others are considering entry, such as & Other Stories and Galeries Lafayette. Further growth is expected in Turkey, however, a number of global retailers have left the market, including Best Buy, Printemps, La Senza, Douglas, Tesco, and C&A (Ekotrent 2016). The emerging Turkish retailing industry continues its growth, with a total volume of sales approximately $225 billion (PWC 2016), and e-commerce is accelerating in parallel. The ratio of online retail to total retail is 1.3% in Turkey, and the proportion of consumers shopping online is 24% (TUBISAD 2013). Grocery retailers maintain market dominance in the national retailing industry (Euromonitor 2016).

4 Methodology

A series of focus group meetings were used to collect data related to the research questions. The focus group method is a qualitative approach that explores and examines the views, experiences, and predictions of the participants (Gibbs 1997; Edmunds 2000). This method was considered suitable for examining the leading retailer's processes of accomplishment of channel integration and implementation of omnichannel strategy. The focus group approach allowed for the discussion of experiences of these processes in the retail and grocery sector. Questions were prepared in advance in accordance with the literature on retail strategy. The moderator of the discussion was the author, who has previous experience of conducting such studies. Instead of posing direct questions, the moderator highlighted the main trends and terms for discussion in accordance with the study. The focus group study questions are listed in Appendix. The main limitations of this study are as follows: focus group studies were the only research methodology used, the primary data was collected from a single retailer type, and a purposive sample was selected for the research unit. Secondary data are used to provide general insight for the retail sector in Turkey. The focus on a single retailer in the research means that it is hard to generalise from the findings.

Because grocery retailers have the greatest market share in the organized Turkish retailing sector, a leading Turkish grocery retailer was selected as the unit of analysis to provide evidence for channel integration and an omnichannel strategy. This particular retailer was chosen due to its position as one of the most developed and organized retailer, and its introduction of many innovations to the Turkish retail industry, such as online sales, Click and Collect, and alternative delivery options.

Two meetings with different participants were carried out in 2016 at the company headquarters in Istanbul, Turkey. This location was selected based on the availability of key informants. There were 15 participants in total split into two groups of seven and eight. The participants had different roles, and included department managers from food marketing, customer experience, e-commerce, demand management, marketing, supply chain, business development, customer relationship management, and project management.

4.1 Data Analysis

Before the focus group studies, permission was granted from the participants to record and transcribe the conversations. The duration of the focus group studies was 70–80 minutes. Notes taken by the researcher were examined to support the transcription of the recordings. The transcriptions were open coded by the researcher to cover the insights that emerged during the focus group studies. The findings from the different focus groups were analysed in combination rather than separately due to their common purpose, i.e. to address the same research questions. The diversity of the participants provides broad insights for channel integration and omnichannel strategy. The findings were validated by triangulation of multiple data sources, including primary data, and various market research reports. After the initial analysis of the open codes, the next stage was to search for further evidence-based understanding of channel integration and an omnichannel strategy; axial coding was used to identify the various interactions, relationships, perceptions, responsibilities, and perspectives of the participants. This allowed for the identification of drivers and strategy enablers, and an understanding of the interaction between them.

The grocery retailer in this study has physical stores, an online store, and a mobile app, which enable shopping across the different channels. In addition, the retailer is widely using social media (Facebook, Instagram and Twitter) as communication tools, as well as having a loyalty programme. The physical stores are located in both rural and urban areas, with different store formats (size, number of SKUs, discounters, supermarkets, and hypermarkets). The retailer offers Click and Collect, shop online and pay at door (home delivery), and other combinations for multiple channel use in a single shopping transaction.

5 Findings

The findings from the focus group studies revealed the drivers for channel integration and implementation of an omnichannel strategy. Firstly, the drivers for the omnichannel are discussed; the changing dynamics in the retailing industry, changes in shopping habits, and the need for high productivity in logistics and supply chain processes. Following this, the implementation of an omnichannel strategy is examined, with the focus on advanced information technology as well as data and process integration. Finally, the customer perception is discussed.

5.1 Drivers for Channel Integration

5.1.1 Changing Dynamics in Retailing Industry

All focus group discussions started with general perceptions of the retail sector, both in Turkey, and throughout the world. In general, the participants believe that retailing is a very dynamic and challenging sector, in which the key issue is how consumers access products. It was often stated that competition in retailing would continue to increase in the short term. Additionally, operating in close proximity to residential areas was seen to maintain competitiveness.

There is currently a lack of a long-term perspective in this fast changing sector, in which even a period of 3 months is considered as long-term. The most powerful change is the mobile revolution, and the tendency is for transactions to be mass customized. Shopping activity has become an "experience", which provides added benefits to the consumer, and mobile/online shopping has led to easy access to information. The participants shared the view that, in the future, retailers will act as personal digital assistants to consumers, through various touchpoints. Among various touchpoints, the mobile application is considered to be the most popular.

5.1.2 Changing Shopping Habits

The changing shopping habits of Turkish consumers were considered as one of the main drivers for channel integration. One participant gave an example from his childhood to explain the alterations in the industry, stating that:

> Two decades ago we used to go to grocery shopping once a month after salaries were paid. All supplies were bought from a single grocery retailer, and afterwards no further shopping was performed [until the next month] (manager of food marketing department).

As a consumer, the participant classified himself as a dedicated mobile user, and even using the retailer's application inside the physical store, which was the main driver determining what he would buy. Another participant emphasized the growth in numbers of white collar workers, especially in big cities, which was responsible for a decline in time spent on grocery shopping from physical stores or from open bazaars, which are still very common in Turkey. Thus, mobile/online grocery shopping has increased. Most white-collar workers plan their grocery shopping and shop from online channels, leaving more time available for leisure activities. Nevertheless, despite a notable increase in online shopping, participants believe that physical store shopping will always exist, and remain important in the future. This is mainly due to the preference of consumers with more time (e.g. the retired, housewives) as well as for social reasons. This type of consumer is more likely to visit a physical store and compare prices and products. The customer segment which tends to shop both off and online comprises mainly families with small children. This group of customers represent the emerging middle class, and are generally in the 25 to 35 years old age range.

5.1.3   Increasing Need for Productivity in Logistics and Supply Chain Processes

Another driver that enables the sustainability of physical stores is the prevalence of unplanned shopping behaviour. The participants interpreted online grocery shopping as planned, in contrast to physical store shopping, which was more likely to be unplanned, the result of instantaneous consumption needs. Participants believed that, because instantaneous shopping is not likely to disappear in the future, there will always be a need for physical stores. In order to maintain physical stores, support of logistics and supply chain activities in certain locations is necessary. For instance, there will always be a need for on-shelf availability, continuous replenishment, and storage to display merchandise at stores. To achieve such goal, improvements across all business processes and substantial IT investment are required. Therefore, there is a clear need for greater productivity in all operations and processes. The participants perceived the main aims of retailing as being able to place products on the shelf, the efficient management of operations, and integrated logistics and supply chain planning. They considered that the prices of the stock keeping units (SKUs) would remain steady over the next decade and competition would mainly focus on supply chain management capabilities. It was regarded logistics and supply chain processes as the main drivers for channel integration. Apart from efficient supply chain management, other major trends reported were differentiation through branded products, specialty gourmet food, and niche market products.

Due to the rapid growth in online grocery shopping, retailers are facing challenges in operations planning and delivery schedules, especially in mega cities such as Istanbul. The participants emphasized the importance of IT and advances in technology for capturing and analysing real time data. They considered that channel integration would not work without efficient data collection and management. Moreover, all participants agreed that if a retailer was unable to provide the desired products on shelf, it would be impossible to be successful. The logistics and supply chain capability are therefore indispensable to support marketing.

5.2   Implementation of Omnichannel Strategy

In this section, implementation of an omnichannel strategy by the retailer is discussed in terms of changing channel strategy, advanced information technologies (IT), and the integration of data and business processes. In addition, the customer perspective of an omnichannel strategy is introduced. The surveyed retailer has implemented a formal omnichannel strategy, leads and organizes a number of activities to access consumers, and provides tailored solutions across all channels.

This retailer already operates an omnichannel strategy, by providing a range of services: Click and Collect, same day delivery, buy online, return offline, pay at door/pay with credit card; buy online, collect from the nearest petrol station; buy online, collect from a locker; and buy online, we bring to your office (a collaboration with some business centres in Istanbul). Moreover, the consumer can return products to a physical store or to online market personnel, as well as use the call centre for any complaints.

5.2.1 From Multichannel Strategy to Omnichannel Strategy

Before introducing a formal omnichannel strategy, this retailer had a long experience of multichannel management. Therefore, the participants believed that it was impossible to implement an omnichannel strategy without previous multichannel management experience. The drivers for omnichannel strategy originate from the intense competition in the industry. The strategy is based on accessing consumers through various touchpoints along multiple integrated channels. The participants stated that the customers' research to purchase journey could start in any channel(s), and end in any channel. Another aspect is that push notifications are used by marketing planners through touchpoints to encourage purchases.

An omnichannel approach enables consumers to find the desired products, check the availability of the product before purchase, and provides alternatives to the physical store for collection. In retailing, competition is not just among retailers, as manufacturers that supply retailers can also become competitors to retail channels. Recently, manufacturers have begun intensive TV campaigns to access consumers directly, operating an online store, and promising timely delivery. This also reaches those who are unable to access the manufacturers' products in store. An omnichannel strategy has become crucial for the retailers' survival in a changing market. The participants stated that when applying this innovative strategy, they are careful to standardize assortment and variety, prices, and promotional campaigns across channels. One participant stated that:

> In online, whether the consumer visits the online store or mobile app, he/she wants to spend the minimum time with the minimum number of clicks. In Turkey, especially online, consumers don't want to see any products that they don't need. Online consumers are goal-oriented, and the goal is clear; using the internet to do grocery shopping as fast as possible. However, offline consumers often like to spend time in the stores and want to enjoy the physical contact with products as much as possible (E-commerce manager).

Such observations are based on regular analysis of their customer database, by tracking and tracing every individual transaction; however, this requires advanced IT and the integration of data.

5.2.2 Advanced IT Solutions and Data Integration

Advanced IT and the integration of data are amongst the main enablers of implementation, because without this it is not possible to make decisions on channel strategies and channel alignment. With a large numbers of customers using a loyalty card, the retailer can obtain data that can be filtered and analysed for different purposes. The participants emphasized that their job is to analyse big data in retailing to reveal the channel preferences of the consumers, and offer promotions according to purchase history. The retailer can use a variety of communication channels, such as SMS (text messages), e-mail, MMS (multimedia messages), sales receipts, kiosks, social media, the mobile app, website, and direct mail. Participants stated, that based on the market basket analysis (i.e., data retrieved from loyalty cards), customized promotions are communicated to the consumer via their most frequently used channel, providing individualized offers based on preferences, favourites, most frequently purchased, and discounted products. The appropriate touchpoints to access each consumer is determined in line with the favoured response channel. For instance, the retailer sends discount/campaign notifications from various touchpoints and follows the response by tracing each transaction, in order to understand which channel(s) are used by the consumer.

During the discussion, it emerged that the performance of each marketing campaign was followed by social media experts within the marketing department. Campaigns for special days (e.g. Women's day), were followed by the social media team using statistics from the talks, hashtags, and the number of mentions. The participants agreed that social media has an important role within an omnichannel strategy, and acts as a powerful touchpoint. When there are a large number of users, loyalty cards provide big data, including consumer demographics and shopping habits, which can be mined to reveal individual shopping habits and brand/product preferences.

With the mobile application, the consumer can find the nearest store, learn about the campaigns and savings, receive a personalised offering—"absolutely for me campaigns"—and purchase via a QR code scan of the product. The participants did not consider that these features cannibalized sales channels; rather, that they enable access to different customer segments. One participant, a customer relationship manager, emphasized the role of mobile apps in the physical stores. With the mobile applications, and IBeacon technology used between shelves, instant notifications are sent during store visits, based on past shopping history and the location of the customer in the store. With WhatsApp Corporate, it will be possible to order products through online chats, impacting existing touchpoints, and allowing more varied omnichannel management practices.

5.2.3 Integration of Business Processes

Effectively designed and managed business processes are needed to enable the uninterrupted flow of goods, services, and information across the various retail channels. Therefore, certain business processes are by nature crucial for the implementation of an omnichannel strategy. In this regard the participants highlighted the role of procurement and delivery in grocery retailing. They agreed that there was no difference in the procurement models for physical and online store. Delivery options, on the other hand, are determined differently for the physical store, the online store, and omnichannel preferences. The retailer uses the same warehouses for all channels. The orders of online consumers are prepared in specific physical stores according to geographical segmentation. The physical stores receive orders from the retailer warehouses, and therefore support the operations and business processes of both online and offline consumers. The participants considered that pursuing an omnichannel strategy is especially suitable for grocery retailers, selling fast moving consumer goods. In grocery retailing, the profit margins are lower compared to other retail formats (e.g. fashion retailers); therefore, it is crucial to optimize logistics activities and supply chain processes. The participants expressed the views that their organization had advantages due to its in-house provision of IT solutions, with its own team to develop, for example, mobile applications and algorithms for the "absolutely for me campaigns". The IT insourcing is considered to be one of the main enablers for effective omnichannel management and efficient logistics management.

5.2.4   Customer Perception

The retailer was aware of the time needed for customers to evaluate the performance of their omnichannel strategy. The participants believed that customers would become aware of any interruptions or failures in the shopping process. This was important. To maintain existing customers and attract new ones, the retailer needs to provide a seamless shopping experience to a consistent standard. One participant stated that retailers and customers had different understandings of the omnichannel strategy. It was argued that, regardless of the channel used, the customer wants to be recognized, and immediately informed about ongoing campaigns, based on purchase history. The viewpoint of the customer focuses on their demand for convenient, fast, reliable, consistent, and budget-friendly grocery shopping. The key issue in accessibility is providing an uninterrupted shopping experience and uniform service levels across channels. While grocery shopping is by nature repetitive and frequent, customers prefer to be loyal to retailers that "value" them as frequent customers. When a retailer proposes distinctive "value" options to different customers, based on a diversified channel structure, it is very likely that it will have a significant market share in the sector. The participants stated that for a retailer the consideration of the consumer should be continuous to sustain competitive advantage.

6   Discussion

The purpose of this section is to briefly discuss the findings of the study in line with the literature review. The literature on channel integration and omnichannel strategy is consistent with the research findings. In our research, the participants highlighted the role of channel integration, as in Herhausen et al. (2015). The omnichannel strategy involves various aspects including data integration (Zhang et al. 2010), serving various consumer segments (Bell et al. 2013), providing an uninterrupted (seamless) shopping experience (Panigrahi 2013; Kozlenkova et al. 2015) and enabling easy switches between channels, and returning products through alternative channels (Beck and Rygl 2015). Moreover, during focus group discussions, participants referred to the definition of the content of omnichannel management (Verhoef et al. 2015, p. 176), *"the synergetic management of the numerous available channels and customer touchpoints, in such a way that the customer experience across channels and the performance over channels is optimized"*.

In addition to providing evidence supporting previous findings in the literature, two novel considerations are revealed. First, the changing shopping habits in a particular market should be comprehensively examined to enable effective channel integration. Also, the role of productivity in logistics and supply chain processes was raised as an important antecedent of channel integration. Another aspect was revealed as the need for the integration of business processes, and the adoption of advanced IT and integrated data. These should be supported through the continuous consideration of customer expectations. There is a need for a more detailed examination of interfaces between logistics, supply chain, and channel integration with retailing.

The second benefit of this research is the greater insight into an omnichannel strategy. A leading, experienced retailer provided valuable perceptions into the key role of their previous experience of a multichannel strategy. This study validates the role of advanced IT, data integration, big data, and touchpoints in omnichannel management. The participants revealed the role of the integration of business processes in enabling a seamless shopping experience, and described the continuing search for ways to enhance the performance of the existing channels through integration and advanced IT usage. At present, an omnichannel strategy is acknowledged as a powerful tool for competitive advantage; however, it is rapidly becoming a necessity for a retailer's survival in the market.

It is also evident that channel integration and omnichannel implementation requires the efficient use of resources, and also the integration of supply chain members into related business processes.

The findings of research provide support for both network theory (NT) and a resource based view (RBV). RBV focuses on gaining competitive advantage and superior performance through the use of a firm's distinctive resources and capabilities (Hoppner and Griffith 2015, p. 614). On the other hand, NT is interested in the alignment of actors in a network of specific stakeholders, and the management of the interrelationships among these actors (Hoppner and Girffith 2015). In line with these theories and findings, it is necessary to ensure the efficient management of resources, and of interrelationships between supply chain members to achieve channel integration and effective omnichannel implementation.

7   Conclusions

This study provides managerial implications for retailers transiting from a multichannel strategy to an omnichannel strategy, pointing to the need for the integrated use of customer data, and also to maximize the benefits from channels and touchpoints. Retailers should closely follow the changing consumption habits and invest in the necessary resources to implement an omnichannel strategy.

As part of recommended further research, it is evident that we need an effective theoretical grounding with which to evaluate the practices of retailers and attitudes of consumers, and thus to gain more comprehensive insights. In the examination of the transition from a multichannel strategy to an omnichannel strategy, different types of retailers should be considered. An omnichannel strategy needs the combined perspectives of customers and retail supply chain members, and can be considered as a strategy that unites B2B and B2C.

The evaluation of changing dynamics in the retail sector from the perspective of global retailers will provide greater insight into global trends. Changes in consumption habits differ, so that cross-country research can be considered for the future. Therefore, a longitudinal study would be beneficial to examine and compare the practices in this emerging field. Such longitudinal studies might be expected to provide greater insight if conducted in cross-cultural settings. The challenges of implementing an omnichannel strategy is another area for research, particularly the outsourcing and insourcing activities of retailers, to understand how they impact the implementation of an omnichannel strategy when control is enhanced. To gain insight into customer perceptions, it will be necessary to engage in qualitative research based on focus groups, interviews, and projective techniques with customers from different segments. This approach also requires support from quantitative research, based on surveys and mathematical modelling to predict and reveal customer preferences, further contributing to omnichannel implementation and strategy developments. Customers' perceptions on omnichannel practices needs better understanding; therefore, it is important to develop a survey instrument that can reveal their perceptions and expectations.

Questions for Review and Discussion

1. How has retailing changed in developed versus emerging markets in the last decades? What are the main trends?
2. Discuss how retailers' marketing channels have evolved during the last decades.
3. Explain the role of logistics and supply chain management in retailing.
4. Is it possible for every retailer to be an "omnichannel" strategy follower?
5. Discuss the role of Information Technologies in the implementation of an omnichannel strategy.
6. Is an omnichannel strategy possible without channel integration? Discuss.
7. Do you think grocery retailers use an omnichannel strategy differently compared to other retailer types? Discuss.

8. What are the main characteristics of consumers of the millennium, and what is their relationship to an omnichannel strategy?
9. Do you think physical stores will disappear in the future? Explain your reasoning.
10. What is the role of social media in omnichannel retailing?

Appendix: Questions for Focus Group Study

- What do you think about the past, present, and future of retailing?
- As an emerging country, how is retailing in Turkey different from developed countries?
- What does channel integration mean to you? In terms of channel integration, what are the main practices in the company?
- What are your views on the omnichannel strategy?
- What are the must haves/drivers of channel integration?
- What are the roles of logistics and supply chain management in retailing?
- How is social media managed, and what does it imply for channel integration and an omnichannel strategy?
- What has mobile commerce changed for the company and the sector?
- What do you think about location-based technologies, and how do they impact sales and customer loyalty?
- How do you differentiate your company from your competitors?
- From your point of view, what is the future of distribution channels?

References

AC Nielsen. (2016). http://www.nielsen.com/tr/tr.html. Accessed 15.04.2017.
AT Kearney. (2016). https://www.atkearney.com/documents/10192/8226719/Global+Retail+Expansion+at+a+Crossroads%E2%80%932016+GRDI.pdf/dc845ffc-fe28-4623-bdd4-b36f3a443787. Accessed 10.04.2017.
Beck, N., & Rygl, D. (2015). Categorization of multiplechannel retailing in multi-, cross-, and omni-channel retailing for retailers and retailing. *Journal of Retailing and Consumer Services, 27*, 170–178.
Bell, D. R., Gallino, S., & Moreno, A. (2013). *Inventory showrooms and customer migration in omnichannel retail: The effect of product information.* Available at SSRN 2370535.
Brynjolfsson, E., Hu, Y. J., & Rahman, M. S. (2013). Competing in the age of omnichannel retailing. *MIT Sloan Management Review, 54*(4), 23.
Cox, R., & Brittain, P. (2004). *Retailing: An introduction* (5th ed.). London: Pearson.
Dant, R. P., & Brown, J. R. (2008). Bridging the B2C and B2B research divide: The domain of retailing literature. *Journal of Retailing, 84*(4), 371–397.
Deloitte. (2014a). https://www2.deloitte.com/content/dam/Deloitte/tr/Documents/mergers-acqisitions/tr-retail-sector-update.pdf. Accessed 10.05.2016.

Deloitte. (2014b). https://www2.deloitte.com/content/dam/Deloitte/tr/Documents/technology-media-telecommunications/tr-e-commerce-in-turkey-market-definition%20and-sizing-eng.pdf. Accessed 05.05.2016.

Edmunds, H. (2000). *The focus group research handbook* (1st ed.). New York: McGraw-Hill.

Ekotrent. (2016). http://ekonomi.haber7.com/sirketler/haber/2066188-avrupali-perakende-devi-turkiyeden-cekiliyor. Accessed 10.04.2017.

Ennis, S. (2016). *Retail marketing* (1st ed.). Berkshire: McGraw-Hill.

ETicaretmag. (2016). http://eticaretmag.com/. Accessed 10.04.2017.

Euromonitor. (2016). http://www.euromonitor.com/retailing-in-turkey/report. Accessed 11.04.2017.

Frazer, M., & Stiehler, B. E. (2014). Omni channel retailing: The merging of the online and offline environment. In *Proceedings of the global conference on business and finance* (Vol. 9, No. 1, pp. 655–657).

Gibbs, A. (1997). *Focus groups, social research update 19*. http://sru.soc.surrey.ac.uk/SRU19. html. Accessed 30.01.2016.

Herhausen, D., Binder, J., Schögel, M., & Herrmann, A. (2015). Integrating bricks with clicks: Retailer-level and channel-level outcomes of online–offline channel integration. *Journal of Retailing, 91*(2), 309–325.

Hoppner, J. J., & Griffith, D. A. (2015). Looking back to move forward: A review of the evolution of research in international marketing channels. *Journal of Retailing, 91*(4), 610–626.

Kozlenkova, I. V., Hult, G. T., Lund, D. J., Mena, J. A., & Kekec, P. (2015). The role of marketing channels in supply chain management. *Journal of Retailing, 91*(4), 586–609.

Krafft, M., & Mantrala, M. K. (2006). *Retailing in the 21st century* (1st ed.). Berlin: Springer.

Kumar, N., Scheer, L. K., & Steenkamp, J.-B. E. M. (1995). The effects of perceived interdependence on dealer attitudes. *Journal of Marketing Research, 32*(August), 348–356.

Li, Q., Luo, H., Xie, P. X., Feng, X. Q., & Du, R. Y. (2015). Product whole life-cycle and omnichannels data convergence oriented enterprise networks integration in a sensing environ-ment. *Computers in Industry, 70*, 23–45.

Markafoni. (2013). http://www.markafoni.com/. Accessed 10.05.2016.

Narwal, M., & Sachdeva, G. (2013). Impact of information technology on consumer purchase behaviour. *Researchers World, 4*(3), 41.

Panigrahi, M. S. K. (2013). *Seamless purchase-an Insight into the issues*. ELK Asia.

Pauwels, K., & Neslin, S. A. (2015). Building with bricks and mortar: The revenue impact of opening physical stores in a multichannel environment. *Journal of Retailing, 91*(2), 182–197.

Perakende.org. (2016). http://www.perakende.org/dernekler/perakende-sektorunun-buyuklugu-turkiyeden-25-kat-fazla-1342802738h.html. Accessed 11.04.2017.

Peterson, R. A., & Balasubramanian, S. (2002). Retailing in the 21st century: Reflections and prologue to research. *Journal of Retailing, 78*, 9–16.

Piotrowicz, W., & Cuthbertson, R. (2014). Introduction to the special issue information technology in retail: Toward omni channel retailing. *International Journal of Electronic Commerce, 18*(4), 5–16.

PWC. (2014). https://www.pwc.com/gx/en/retail-consumer/assets/achieving-total-retail.pdf. Accessed 11.05.2016.

PWC. (2016). https://www.pwc.com.tr/tr/publications/industrial/retail-consumer/pdf/donusurken-buyuyen-turkiye-perakende-sektoru-raporu.pdf Accessed 11.05.2016.

Rangaswamy, A., & Van Bruggen, G. H. (2005). Opportunities and challenges in multichannel marketing: An introduction to the special issue. *Journal of Interactive Marketing, 19*(2), 5–11.

Retailer.net. (2017). http://www.retailler.net/turkiyenin-en-buyuk-100-perakendecisi-belirlendi/. Accessed 12.04.2017.

Rigby, D. (2011). The future of shopping. *Harvard Business Review, 89*(12), 65–76.

TUBISAD. (2013). Türkiye'de E-Ticaret Pazar Tanımlama ve 2013 Pazar Büyüklüğü Ölçümleme Çalışması. http://www.tubisad.org.tr/duyuru/2014/e-bulten/temmuz14/TUBISAD_E-Ticaret_Pazar_Buyuklugu_2013_Raporu.pdf. Accessed 10.05.2016.

TUIK. (2016). http://tuik.gov.tr/Start.do;jsessionid=4kR0YrCGvjc6kJWTFhzDTJ2Z9PG4L3SM THhkFbVVGzs5MTH8yPy2!-135332398. Accessed 12.04.2017.
Verhoef, P., Kannan, P., & Inman, J. (2015). From multichannel retailing to omnichannel retailing. Introduction to the special issue on multichannel retailing. *Journal of Retailing, 91*(2), 174–181.
YStats. (2016). https://www.ystats.com/wp-content/uploads/2016/04/20160329_Product-Bro chure-Order-Form_-Turkey-B2C-E-Commerce-Market-2016-by-yStats.com_.pdf. Accessed 10.04.2017.
Zhang, J., Farris, P. W., Irvin, J. W., Kushwaha, T., Steenburgh, T. J., & Weitz, B. A. (2010). Crafting integrated multichannel retailing strategies. *Journal of Interactive Marketing, 24*(2), 168–180.

Işık Özge Yumurtacı Hüseyinoğlu, PhD Associate Professor received B.S. degree in Business Administration in 2005, M.S. in Logistics Management in 2007 and PhD, Business Administration in 2011. During her doctoral studies, she was a visiting scholar at Cranfield University (UK), School of Management—Supply Chain Research Centre in 2008. As part of her post-doctoral research, she was at University of Bremen (Germany) logistics management department in 2014 and 2015. She has worked in several research projects funded by Ministry of Economy, Ministry of Transportation Maritime Affairs and Communication, Izmir Chamber of Commerce and Izmir University of Economics. Her research is focused on retail marketing, marketing channels, logistics management and supply chain management. Since 2012, she has worked at Izmir University of Economics as an Assistant Professor at Logistics Management department. Currently, she is an Associate Professor of Marketing at the same department.

Development of Omnichannel in India: Retail Landscape, Drivers and Challenges

Mohua Banerjee

Abstract This chapter presents the organised retail landscape in India with a special focus on the retail growth in online trade and the retailers' journey from physical stores to e-commerce, multi-channel, and omnichannel retailing. It highlights the steps that need to be contemplated by retailers moving towards building an omnichannel strategy. The challenges that e-commerce players face while operating in this retail landscape are examined. The characteristics of Indian consumers and their behaviour are also discussed as they further define India's markets and future growth opportunities. The business models that are evolving as retailers explore newer channel modalities to transform their businesses are discussed, along with the logistics innovations that facilitate such retail operations. There is also a comparison between the Indian and Chinese retail market. While India is a large market, with many potential customers, and a growing middle class that implies business opportunities, there also major challenges, such as access and quality of the transport infrastructure and logistics networks, as well as access to the rural population.

1 Introduction

India has a large consumer market and its retail sector is undergoing rapid changes to meet market requirements. Digital channels are also expanding at an unprecedented rate that is boosting the growth of e-commerce in the country. The mindset of consumers is undergoing a major psychological shift and a significant number of shoppers are buying online frequently. Consumers are now getting into a frame of mind where they are consistently expecting retailers to provide exceptional services in product delivery across all touchpoints. Implementing an omnichannel retail strategy is an appropriate step for retailers at this juncture. Technology trends like cloud services, big data, and real-time analytics will facilitate retailers in implementation though it will need substantial Information Technology (IT) budgets. The

M. Banerjee (✉)
International Management Institute Kolkata, Kolkata, West Bengal, India
e-mail: m.banerjee@imi-k.edu.in

© Springer Nature Switzerland AG 2019   115
W. Piotrowicz, R. Cuthbertson (eds.), *Exploring Omnichannel Retailing*,
https://doi.org/10.1007/978-3-319-98273-1_6

retailer's eventual aim is to merge the information-rich experience and the convenience of shopping online with the tangible atmosphere of shopping in physical stores.

This chapter delves into the Indian retail growth story and the retailers' journey from physical stores to e-commerce and multi-channel retailing. It highlights in detail the steps that may be ultimately contemplated by retailers towards building an omnichannel strategy. The challenges that e-commerce players face while operating in this retail landscape are examined. The typical nuances of Indian consumers are also discussed as they further define India's markets. The business models that are evolving as retailers explore newer channel modalities to transform their businesses are deliberated at length, along with the logistics innovations that facilitate retail operations. This chapter is based mainly on secondary sources.

2 Retail Landscape in India

India has a population of 1.34 billion people. With total retail sales of $1.01 trillion and retail sales CAGR[1] of 8.8% over the period of 2013–2015, the country shows prospects of a strong growth phase over the next coming years. Modern retail (or organized retail) is still at 8–10% of total retail sales. Traditional retail which is marked by *kirana* (or mom-and-pop) stores, wet markets, a public distribution system (PDS), and cooperative stores, still dominate the retail landscape. The evolution of organized retail is driven by the growth of an aspiring middle class with greater disposable income who are now seeking choice, access to branded goods, and an improved shopping experience. At the same time, the market is restricted by local regulations which limit the entry of foreign modern retailers. There were more than 15 million mom-and-pop stores in 2015. International retailers in India are still confined to the cash-and-carry and wholesale formats like Metro and Walmart, or the single-brand retail formats where 100% Foreign Direct Investment (FDI) is allowed. Currently many new entrants are choosing between partnerships with local companies (e.g. Gap, The Children's Place) and company-owned stores (e.g. Nike, IKEA, Sisley and H&M), as only 51% FDI is allowed in multi-brand retail at the time of writing, though with riders such as 30% mandatory local sourcing, minimum $100 million investment with 50% in the backend infrastructure, among others.

---

[1]Compound Annual Growth Rate (CAGR) is a measurement of growth over multiple time periods.

3 Market Penetration: Percentage of Traditional, Organized and Online to Total Trade

The emergence of online trade (or e-commerce, e-retail) has further changed the dynamics of the Indian retail sector, though the e-commerce market will remain challenging in the near future. Until 2015, India had remained unranked in major reports, such as A.T. Kearney's Global Retail E-commerce Index. Indian online retail is just 2.5% of the total Indian retail market (eMarketer Chart 2016). Only 69% of India's population has access to broadband and mobile Internet (A.T. Kearney 2015a, b). There are only 39 million online buyers in India, which is approximately just 3% of the whole Indian population; this indicates potential growth in online trade.

4 Online Retailing

Major e-commerce players are Flipkart, Amazon India, and Snapdeal. Their websites serve as *"Online Marketplaces"* for other retailers and other companies to sell their goods. Companies store their products in the online retailer's warehouses, but ownership of the product does not transfer to the online retailer. Companies pay the online retailer a fee for the storage and distribution of its products and for access to the website as a selling platform. In 2014, e-commerce spend in India increased by 27% to $3.8 billion, and it is expected to grow over the next 5 years by 21%, that is slightly higher than the global average. A KPMG-CII report has identified the e-commerce market in India at $27.5 billion in 2016 and is expected to reach $80 billion by 2020 with a CAGR of 31% (Tanwar and Doger 2016).

In the recent past, online retailers have wooed consumers with deep discounts and promotions causing a substantial dip in the revenues of brick and mortar (physical, offline) retailers, as the consumers shopped online. To cope with the competition, physical retailers like The Future Group, Spencer's Retail, and Aditya Birla Group are gradually shifting to e-commerce (Table 1). While some are launching their own websites, others are making their products available online through the marketplace platforms like Flipkart, Snapdeal and Amazon. The concept of omnichannel retailing in India thus originated as a response by offline retailers to mitigate the threat that was posed by the pure online retailers.

5 From Multi-Channel to Omnichannel Retailing

Technically omnichannel retailing refers to integrated multichannel touch points for consumers. The consumer decides where and when to shop and from which device. A consumer can look for a product in the physical store and if it is unavailable,

Table 1 Offerings from Major Retailers

	Big Bazaar	Food Bazaar	More	Reliance Fresh	Spencer's
Parent Organization (Retail Arm)	Future Group (Future Retail Limited)	Future Group (Future Retail Limited)	Aditya Birla Group (Aditya Birla Retail Limited)	Reliance Industries (Reliance Retail Limited)	RP-Sanjiv Goenka Group (Spencer's Retail Limited)
Website	bigbazaar.com	Webpage available in: futureretail.in	morestore.com	reliancefresh.co.in	spencersretail.com
Online Shopping	Separate website: bigbazaardirect.com	No	Link available on More's website that opens to separate website: mymorestore.com	Separate website: reliancefreshdirect.com	Separate website: spencers.in
Mobile App	Select cities only	No	No	No	Select cities only
Online Coupons	No	NA	Limited discount coupons available	Limited food coupons available	No
In-store Wi-Fi	No	No	No	No	No

Source: Author's own

browse for it on the website or through a mobile app to complete the order. The consumer may then pick up purchase from the store, at a delivery location or through home delivery, decide on appropriate delivery windows and is able to return purchased products in any of the retailer's physical stores without any encumbrances. Customers connect across the range of platforms, searching for means to integrate their buying experiencess, providing seamless interaction for the consumer across the various platforms, when the lines between channels are disappearing and focus is on brand, not channel management (Piotrowicz and Cuthbertson 2014). The physical and online formats are seamlessly developed so that the consumer's convenience remains the focal point of the retailer's strategy. Indian retailers are still in a reactive phase and it may take a some years before they can fully leverage the synergies between their physical stores and online presence to generate a competitive advantage.

6 Online Retail in India

Online retail growth has been broadly envisaged as a disruptive business model across the world. A disruptive innovation is described as *"an innovation that creates a new market and value network and eventually disrupts an existing market and value network, displacing established market leaders and alliances"* (Bower and Christensen 1995).

The factors that cause retail disruption are the changing nature of retail competition, the increase in the digitally-influenced shopping experience, and the availability of the numerous technologies as enablers.

6.1 E-Retail Growth Phases

Similar to other disruptive business models, e-retail growth has revealed three successive phases worldwide—the incubation phase, the inflexion phase and the acceleration phase (Sharma and Flamind 2015).

The incubation phase in India lasted broadly from 2007 to 2012 when India was marked by a period of slow growth in Tier-1 and Tier-2[2] cities, during which e-retailers developed new capabilities in technology and infrastructure, investors opened up funding the new businesses, and consumers adapted to the new forms of consumption. CAGR was relatively low at 38% during this period.

---

[2]Tier 1 cities are commercialized metropolitan cities and comprise of Delhi, Mumbai, Kolkata, Chennai, Bengaluru and Hyderabad. Tier 2 cities are smaller cities hubs with a population of one million approximately and are industrialized hubs or regional centers like Chandigarh, Bhubaneswar, Lucknow. Tier-3 and Tier-4 cities are the cities beyond Tier-1 and Tier-2. This is based on the X, Y and Z Classification of Cities by the Government of India.

   The inflexion phase was from 2012 to 2014 during which point of time the e-retailers reached the necessary level of development to match the market's needs. Growth increased remarkably with a CAGR of 80%.

   The acceleration phase from 2014 onwards is expected to be a longer phase during which the pace of growth will further increase, transforming e-retail into a conventional market space. India has already passed the inflexion phase and moved into the phase of accelerated growth. Presently though e-retail is less than 1% of the total retail sales, it is a matter of contemplation to many as to how fast e-retail can expand in this phase of development, given the huge size of the overall Indian market.

6.2   Similarities and Differences with the Chinese Market

A study by A.T. Kearney of the top 30 developing countries for retail investment ranks China and India at No.1 and No.2 respectively with scores of 72.5 and 71 (The 2016 Global Retail Development Index). Further comparisons of relevant retail-specific variables reveal certain similarities and contrasts that exist between the two countries. E-retail growth in India may be expected to mirror the growth path of China as studies show that both countries have a number of similar fundamental characteristics that facilitate its fast progression. In both countries, economic growth has fuelled growth in the number of consumers who have greater spending power, higher disposable income with more women entering the workforce, rising aspirations to buy brands and to shop in modern store formats. However, for the majority of consumers in both India and China, accessibility to desired products and brands is difficult as the organized retail landscape is not adequately developed. Data shows that organized retail is at 8% in India and 20% in China, while it has been more than 80% for over a decade in countries like the USA and the UK (Sharma and Flamind 2015). A plausible reason for this insufficient development is that both India and China are vast countries and have consumers coming from diverse social and cultural backgrounds, so it becomes very difficult for a retailer to address this immense diversity with product offerings and grow their brand nationally. Rather, the retailer expands their store footprint in distinct pockets where there is a higher density of target customers. This leads to a demand-supply gap and fragmentation of the overall physical retail landscape. It is possible for e-retail to meet this gap as it enables consumers to get access to products and brands that would otherwise have remained inaccessible to them through the existing retail stores. Another important feature common to both countries is that smartphones have been instrumental to the growth of online retail. As mobile internet usage is increasing, it is leading to the growth of e-retail.

   The marketplace platform is the major model through which e-retail operates in India and China, as compared to the inventory-based model or the online website presence of physical store retailers. In China, 90% of online sales happen through marketplaces whereas the figure is only 20 to 25% in the USA (Sharma and Flamind

2015). Marketplace platforms enable online retailers to expand rapidly as in these models it is the vendors present on the websites who are responsible for regularly increasing their product offerings, sourcing and stocking their inventory. This allows the online retailers to focus on improving their logistics infrastructure and delivery operations, especially in countries that are marked by rudimentary infrastructure mechanisms and inadequate accessibility to third party logistics (3PL) providers. Another focal point for online retailers is to establish the network effect, in which a greater number of visitors to the website attracts more vendors and vice versa. As the retailers build positive feedback through the network effect, they gain scale and are able to attract further investment for their business.

To attract visitors to their platforms, marketplaces initially offered deep discounts and sustained heavy losses in the process. In such a hyper-competitive environment, many small online retailers are forced to exit the market or consolidate and get acquired by larger players. This phase is currently evident in India with major players like Flipkart and Snapdeal acquiring not only other category specific e-retailers (Flipkart acquiring Myntra, Snapdeal acquiring Exclusively) but also companies that provide them with technological capabilities (Flipkart acquiring AdIQuity, Appiterate and DSYN Technologies; Snapdeal acquiring MartMobi, Letsgomo Labs) to capture the shift in customers' preferences for shopping through smartphones than from desktop computers and laptops.

6.3 Online Consumer Behaviour

In the Asia Pacific (APAC) region, the average millennial aged between 16 to 30 years spends 2.8 hours a day on their mobile phones. Across APAC mobile use among millennials differs. While Thailand has the highest daily usage at 4.2 hours, China is at 3.9 hours. India clocks 2.2 hours and Japan has the lowest daily usage rate at 1.6 hours (Connected Life—TNS 2015). 46% of millennials spend their time on mobiles browsing social media platforms, 42% watch videos, and 12% shop online. When compared to the other BRIC economies, India has a higher proportion of internet users between the age of 15 and 35 years though fewer women go online (Ernst & Young 2016). In fact, the women internet-user population in India is the lowest in comparison to the other BRIC economies. It implies that the 'high earning-high spending' women population aged above 35 years are currently more comfortable shopping offline than online. Similar to the other BRIC countries, internet usage in India is mainly an urban phenomenon though the user mix is currently shifting toward rural areas. This has been driven by the easy access to smartphones in rural areas. The rural segment is too significant for e-commerce players to ignore. A recent survey of 700 online users across six cities by Ernst & Young reveals that in India 71% of online shoppers prefer cashless payments and 64% of online shoppers have concerns about sharing card details. 55% do not want to pay for home delivery. 86% regularly look for discounts and 96% of women consumers below 21 years of age buy only for discounts. Most online high-spending individuals are above 35-years and are predominantly from cities. Room for e-commerce growth in Tier-1 and Tier-2 cities still exists.

It is also important to note that the older generations who generally have higher disposable income and established buying patterns, are spending more time online. This is where a major challenge is posed to marketers. They are exploring ways to market to the digitally most-advanced millennial consumers on the newest digital platforms and the need to make sure that they are focusing on the content-driven, shareable campaigns that are effective with this group. At the same time marketers have to bear in mind that the older customers cannot be targeted only through traditional media as their patterns of behaviour are also shifting. A tiered marketing strategy with tailored messaging and media plans that also takes into account the higher spending power of the older generations will best address the digital divide caused by the dual pace of consumer's digital media adoption rates. To reach out effectively to both segments, marketers will have to create relevant content for each segment, communicate in a significant manner to each segment using the media channels, and engage them with the brand.

6.4   Challenges Faced by e-Commerce Companies in India

Though the growth potential envisaged in e-commerce is promising, there are certain challenges that render major impediments to the sector. Among others, four key areas that can be identified are the Indian consumers' buying habits, lack of necessary infrastructure, predatory pricing strategies, and lack of readiness in omnichannel technology.

Consumers' Buying Habits Indian consumers have an innate preference to touch and feel a product before buying which is impracticable to fulfil by e-commerce companies. To some, shopping as an activity is not regarded as a chore but as a social activity that allows them to interact with friends and acquaintances that cannot be fully replicated in an online shopping environment. However, for customers who are time-constrained, online shopping tends to be less stressful than conventional shopping because it helps to evade delays in the queues and navigation of traffic in peak hours. Shopping at flexible times from the convenience of their homes as well as day-and-night product delivery services make e-commerce attractive to such customers. It is also thought that consumers spend less while shopping online as impulse buying happens predominantly while shopping in ambient environments in physical stores. Online shoppers have doubts on the reliability of the websites in portraying the actual product that they will receive after ordering. They are also apprehensive about the return policies and money refund should the need arise. Security of online payments also remains a cause of concern to buyers. Shoppers so far do not tend to have loyalty to any specific e-commerce platform. They are price-sensitive and compare prices between e-commerce platforms before choosing the best deal.

Lack of Necessary Infrastructure As India has a relatively low internet penetration of 34.8% of the country's total population (India Internet Users 2016), browsing products online and shopping is impaired. Success in e-commerce requires having a robust supply chain in place and ensuring last-mile delivery at the lowest possible cost. Distribution costs in Tier-2 and Tier-3 cities are very high as the physical infrastructure for e-commerce, such as warehouses or fulfilment centres and technological infrastructure like global positioning systems (GPS), is still fragmented and in a state of development. Road infrastructure is a critical issue. India's road and highway density is underdeveloped with many roads being unpaved and poorly maintained in the hinterlands. There is no standardized street address system for which building and street names and landmarks are often needed to locate a house. Other challenges faced by e-retailers include supply chain issues relating to delivery personnel and order-taking centres, inventory management, storage requirements for diverse product categories, errors in delivery, and timely delivery of products in good condition. A dearth of skilled manpower is another major challenge as e-commerce companies require a talent pool of specialized digital experts. The companies have to concentrate on building relevant capabilities by recruiting people with the right capabilities, especially in marketing and sales teams.

Predatory Pricing Strategies A key cause of concern is that currently e-retailers steeply discount their product prices to attract both online customers and customers of brick and mortar retailers. E-retailers undertake steep discounting to acquire customers, build customer loyalty, and increase their market share. Each player hopes that once the customer finds the lowest price on its portal and makes repeat purchases for a sustained time period, the customer will eventually stop comparing prices and have a higher brand recall towards that particular e-retailer, thereby building loyalty. But such steep discounting renders businesses unsustainable for e-retailers without deep pockets and drives existing players out of the market while creating a formidable entry barrier for new players. It also disrupts the physical retailers who do not have the financial muscle and have no intention to operate with severe losses. Product brand value is another issue for the physical retailers and manufacturers, as with the heavy discounts offered on the same products by the e-commerce players on their platforms, the image of the brand could be eroded. This would lead to an inability to effectively price the product even in the brick and mortar stores. It is a common perception that steep discounting is the result of the undue amount of funding that e-retailers are obtaining. Flipkart has raised $3.4 billion and Snapdeal $1.7 billion through investor funding since inception in 2007 and 2010 respectively, while Amazon has invested a total of $47.43 million in India since 2014. As Amazon continues to invest aggressively, Flipkart and Snapdeal continue to spend heavily on discounts, advertising and logistics to defend their market shares. To enable their activities the three companies require fresh funding at regular intervals. In reality, the deep discounts that are funded by investors' funds erode the e-retailer's bottom line, whereas the funds are ideally needed for investment in improving technology, hiring relevant talent, and acquiring new customers in a creative fashion.

Lack of Readiness in Omnichannel Technology Customers are steadily becoming channel agnostic and want a seamless experience across the channels that they choose to shop in. Yet retailers have some distance to go in upgrading and integrating their back-end systems that will help them to deliver the customers' expectations. Currently retailers are exploring technology projects in silos, in their attempt to providing new experiences to the customers, and not as part of an integrated road map.

Retailers are realizing that their existing core systems of merchandise planning, inventory management, order management, and POS (Point of Sale) will not be able to support an exhaustive omnichannel transformation and provide them with the long-term flexibility and agility that they will need to facilitate the transformation. To elaborate, omnichannel implementation entails that the retailer build a single view of the customer, of the product, of the inventory, as well as the orders. To obtain a single view of the customer, retailers can store the data from their sources like POS, merchandising, marketing, loyalty programmes, social media, blogs, social shopping services, and websites, in a common customer database and develop analytical capabilities to leverage that data. To obtain a single view of the product, retailers need to bring together product information, such as product attributes and descriptions, related content, such as manufacturer's information and instructions, digital assets like product images, and product relationships, such as recommendations and adjacencies, to enable better purchase decisions for the customers across channels. To obtain a single view of inventory and orders, retailers must integrate their supply chain, merchandising, store operations, and e-commerce solutions, as well as their order management systems. This will help retailers to optimize the location from which they select inventory to fulfil an order while minimizing costs and ensuring speedy delivery.

However, retailers' current systems have isolated software that result in fragmented views of their operations. So for retailers, this omnichannel transformation means a fundamental change in investments. Major IT infrastructure investment decisions need to be made and budgets have to be adjusted to factor in the transformation. These decisions need substantial deliberations as in the immediate future, when the transition to omnichannel is in process, it may be difficult to measure the individual contribution of the different channels to the retailer's return on investment: for example, measuring whether increased footfalls in the store have been caused by website communication or promotion in the store window. In due course though when the transition to omnichannel has been put into practice, store Wi-Fi devices and big data usage may help provide such answers.

7   Online Retail Terminology: Showrooming, Webrooming, m-Commerce, Apps

A study of shopping behaviour by market research firm Openbravo reveals that 52% of shoppers like to check the prices before selecting a product, 50% trust reviews and information, 39% believe in taking the opinion of a family member or friend, and 30.2% are traditional shoppers who prefer the in-store shopping experience. It is evident that consumer journeys are becoming increasingly complicated and that retail terminology now includes words such as "Showrooming" and "Webrooming". Showrooming is when a customer is in a store and checks on a mobile device whether a better price is available online. Webrooming is when a customer researches a product online, makes a purchase decision online and goes to the store to make the final purchase. Gradually consumers are seeking to control their shopping experiences and marketers strive for the consumers' loyalty by enabling them with multi-channel experiences.

The spurt in growth of m-commerce is increasingly more important than desktop-based sales. A report by Mary Meeker shows that India (at 41%) ranks higher than China (at 33%) in its mobile usage as a percentage of total e-commerce sales. It has also the highest share across major economies like Brazil (20%), Russia (13%), UK (20.5%) and USA (15%) (KPCB 2015). With smartphones becoming cheaper and more readily available, these upward trends are expected to continue further. A strong focus towards the development of m-commerce infrastructure is essential for a retail player as simply converting an active e-commerce website into a mobile website will not yield the desired outcome. It calls for reinvention and establishing a mobile-centric infrastructure. Providing targeted content such as personalized notifications to the customer at the right time through mobile apps would be a key value proposition. One major obstacle is the diverse regional languages in India. There is limited usage of the English language beyond the Tier-1 cities and marketers will have to invest considerably in localizing their content.

From the middle of 2014 e-commerce players have been promoting and offering discounts to customers on purchases made through their mobile apps. While smartphones are equipped with powerful web browsers that let a consumer do any activity that was once confined to a desktop computer, navigating through a URL bar on a mobile phone can prove to be a cumbersome experience. Online sites and services provide the app in an attempt to provide users with superior control and simpler usage techniques. Apps enhance the functionality in a simplistic yet more user-friendly manner. A study by Nielsen has shown that users with expensive handsets (exceeding INR 15,000) spend 1.6 times more time on shopping apps as compared to those with cheaper phones, and some correlation exists between higher time spent on mobile phones with higher spending in mobile shopping (Jha and Varma 2015). Flipkart is the leader in mobile shopping apps in terms of both penetration (35%) and engagement (60 min per month) followed closely by Snapdeal (penetration 20%, user engagement 35 min a month). Amazon India Shopping is a more recent launch and has ranked third.

With the emerging familiarity of shopping apps among consumers, it is an opportune time for the organized retailers to take the cue and develop mobile-based platforms and apps for their customers to browse, purchase, and have the goods delivered to them without requiring them to visit the physical stores. This will help the physical store retailers expand their markets.

Benefits of apps however do not negate the benefits of websites. A case in hand was when online fashion retailer Myntra shut down its website to operate as an app-only platform in February 2015 as its mobile sales had exceeded its sales from personal computer figures. Myntra's sales figures had indicated that 70% of its sales were generated from smartphones. Shutting down the website meant that users were not left with any alternative but to download the Myntra app. Within 6 months, the app-only strategy failed as Myntra faced a loss of sales. A plausible reason would be that the Indian shoppers were not ready to completely abandon shopping from their personal computers or mobile browsers and found the app-only option too restrictive. Myntra has thereafter reworked and come up with a mobile site, which is a lighter mobile version of its website, rather than being present on an app-only format. As Myntra still relies on Google searches for new users, being available on the website put Myntra back on the Google search platform.

8 Analysis of e-Retail Sector Using Porter's Five Forces Framework

In the ensuing chaotic market condition, it is necessary to assess where the power lies in the e-retail sector. This analysis will provide an understanding of the e-retailers' competitive situation in India and the position that they are attempting to move into, as well as the profitability and the attractiveness of the e-retail sector:

1. Competition in the industry—Overall industry rivalry is high with a large number of e-retailers entering the market who have low differentiation in terms of their product offerings. A high degree of polarization is evident with larger players like Flipkart, Snapdeal and Amazon existing with numerous small e-retailers. The market is showing signs of consolidation with bigger e-retailers acquiring smaller players who have developed certain competencies.
2. Power of suppliers—The suppliers in e-retail indicate the sellers, who generally have moderate power. The marketplace model provides an attractive channel for vendors to sell their products and they have several alternatives available to them in the online landscape. Should the e-retailers choose to change the technology providers to their websites, they will have to incur high switching costs. There is also a dearth of skilled manpower in e-commerce. Nevertheless, this model lets the e-retailer focus on being an efficient logistics provider and increase profitability through low cost, high volume opportunities while also expanding rapidly.
3. Power of customers—The overall power of customers is high as the products are seldom differentiated across the various platforms and there are few switching

costs. The differentiated services, like free home delivery for any billing amount, are fundamentally unsustainable and e-retailers are opting out of such service offerings. Mechanisms to lock-in customers are also largely absent.

4. Threat of new entrants—The threat of an existing player's market share depletion by new players joining the market is moderate. The regulatory framework is currently being drawn up and FDI investment is restricted for an inventory-based model. The number of product categories that are required to be developed for e-retail requires time as the e-retailer has to build the infrastructure and competencies. Gaining consumer trust also is time-consuming for a new entrant. However, compared to brick and mortar stores relatively low capital investment is required for online retail in such a vast country.

5. Threat of substitute products—The threat from substitute services is relatively low for e-retail. Though its market share is currently small, a lot of growth is expected to happen in this segment. Traditional retail, direct marketing by manufacturers, and tele-retailing exist as shopping substitutes to customers, yet the advantages of e-retailing have generated profound interest among the consumer base.

As the market is evolving, retailers are working out their business models on a trial-and-error basis. Which of the retailers will profitably survive will predominantly be governed by their ability to innovate and evolve in ways that can best serve today's empowered consumers.

9 Migration of Business Model from Owned-Inventory to Marketplace Platform for Online Retailers

Online retailers like Flipkart initially had a just-in-time delivery model where they received orders from customers and then placed orders with their suppliers. The existing courier partners lacked the organization, capability, scale, and capital to meet Flipkart's growing requirements which led to delays in delivery. In many cases shoppers abandoned carts due to delayed delivery. This prompted Flipkart to invest in its supply chain services. The distribution network in this owned-inventory setup was a hub-and-spoke model that had fulfilment centres (FC) in the pan-India metropolitan cities (Delhi in the north, Hyderabad and Bengaluru in the south, Kolkata in the east, and Mumbai in the west). The FCs were around 250,000 square feet each and undertook the initial sorting and packing. From FCs the goods were transported to the mother hubs that catered to four or five major cities and several smaller cities within a 200 km radius where additional sorting was done. From the mother hubs the goods were moved to the hubs, which were around 2500 square feet each, from which they were carried on motorcycles to the customers' homes by the delivery boys. Flipkart used algorithms to determine ideal warehouse locations and invested in technology to track packages and provide text alerts to customers before a scheduled delivery.

Flipkart had a Gross Merchandise Value (GMV)[3] close to \$1 billion in 2013 and very soon its competition intensified with Snapdeal and Amazon India leading to deep discounts and price wars. To meet the competition and enhance its market share, Flipkart undertook a strategic change to shift to a marketplace model and so opened up its platform to a large number of sellers. This thought process was supported by observing Airbnb and Uber on a global platform which were pure-platform companies that had scaled up using technology. The marketplace model was expected to enhance revenues for Flipkart as the company would earn relatively high-margins from the commissions that it charged on every transaction which occurred through their platform, without incurring any cost of holding inventory. Flipkart also proposed to earn substantial revenues from the search advertisements and display advertisements of the sellers on its platform. Sellers relied on the advertising on Flipkart's platform to draw customers. They could use their in-house labour for storing, shipping and packing functions for delivery or use the services of Flipkart for storage, packaging, cataloguing, delivery, and payment options, for which Flipkart charged the sellers a fee.

10 Shift from Multichannel Retailing to Omnichannel Retailing

The rise of marketplace platforms does not indicate that the other online or offline retail formats will become redundant in India. Rather, retailers are strategizing to become omnipresent and make their products available through multiple channels so that they can map their customers through the complete purchase process. An online-to-offline integration is gradually developing in the retail scenario where online retailers are opening physical stores. Simultaneously physical store retailers are building their online presence through both their own platforms and through marketplaces. The retailers are building their competitive advantage by streamlining their offers to ensure that consumers get the same brands at the same prices irrespective of the channel that they use. 'Online' and 'offline' are not regarded as mutually exclusive channels anymore but as highly integrated channels that can offer a unique value proposition to customers.

This transition is largely because retailers have realized that their businesses can no longer continue to connect with the customer in a unidirectional manner—from themselves to the consumers. With the advent of the internet, information is accessed and disseminated much faster, resulting in the customer being more conscious and having greater expectations. Companies are adopting the omnichannel approach so that they can remain engaged with the customer constantly and give the customer the

---

[3]Gross Merchandise Value—The total value of merchandise sold in an established time period before deducting fees or expenses. E-retailers use this measure to quantify business growth. It is also considered as gross revenue.

option to decide when, where, and how to shop. It provides customers with a single holistic view of the business through multiple channels that operate concurrently and offers the customer a seamless experience. Thus customers gain visibility of retailers' inventory and availability in their preferred channel. The difference with the multi-channel approach is that each channel in an omnichannel approach automatically knows details of the customer's interaction with another channel and uses it to guide and carry on the customer experience. The brand takes into account how one channel or message will affect the other and ensures that the experience is similar across platforms. The customers are then able to switch adeptly between the channels and receive a similar quality of experience wherever they go. According to a report by IDC Retail Insights, internationally retailers utilizing multiple channels in their marketing and retail activities saw an increase between 15 to 35% in average transaction size, along with a 5 to 10% increase in loyalty customers' profitability.

There is still a large number of people who prefer to touch and feel a product before purchasing it and for e-commerce players, brick and mortar stores are a way to capture the segment of customers that shop in physical formats. Physical stores provide a place for the company to differentiate itself through its ambience and also provide a network of after-sales centres where customers can get their purchases exchanged, repaired or refunded. These are the factors that are compelling e-commerce companies to look at establishing physical stores. Yet the road to establishing an omnichannel strategy is not without its inherent uncertainties. Online retailers have expertise in supply chain capabilities but lack an understanding of the telecommunication technology crucial to this domain. Efficient technology usage will help them make meaningful insights into customers shopping online. Also, the deep discounting that is done by e-commerce players will not be sustainable in physical formats. Hence they will need to identify the target audience, analyse how to reach out to them, and communicate relevant messages to gather maximum response. Providing customized solutions to customers based on real-time information and consumer data are effective tools for building a customer base and helps the companies bring the offline experience online to customers, though this can be a very complex and costly proposition in an omnichannel strategy. Companies like Lakmé and L'Oréal have been experimenting with apps like Lakmé Makeup Pro and L'Oréal Makeup Genius where customers upload their pictures and use virtual make-up to create different looks, receive suggestions, and purchase the products used for those looks.

While retailers are making inroads into newer channel modalities for growing their businesses, three trends are emerging as dominant: physical stores foraying into online retailing, online retailers opening physical stores, and the hyperlocal e-commerce model.

10.1 Physical Stores Foraying into Online Retailing

To compete with the threat posed by e-commerce, Future Group (the parent organization of Future Retail and Future Lifestyle Fashions) was one of the first physical store retailers to have come up with an online strategy. While a normal Big Bazaar hypermarket stocks 40,000 to 60,000 SKUs, the 'endless aisles' available online or in the in-store kiosks offers more than 250,000 SKUs. The physical stores hold the inventories and the products are home-delivered or customers pick them up from the stores. An initial investment of more than \$15 million[4] over a period of 18 months since September 2014 had been undertaken to implement the strategy. The same discounts that are available in the physical stores are also available to the online format and deep discounting is refrained from as incurring negative gross margins will render the business proposition unprofitable. What it lacks in terms of deep discounting, it hopes to compensate by mining the customer data of its 30 million customers alongside the purchase data that it has accumulated through its loyalty programmes. Big Bazaar caters to 20 to 30% of the consumer's overall shopping basket and aims to hike it to 60% of the overall basket, with the aid of the technology and data analytics that are becoming an integral part of the organization.

In a parallel omnichannel business model Future Group has introduced the Online Selling Agent model, where the agent plays the role of a trusted link between the physical and online retail. Customers browse the products on a tablet that is provided to the Agent and selects the products. The Agent places the order and a confirmation message is received in the customer's mobile. The agent only takes the payment from the customer. Delivery of purchased products to the customer and any after-sales queries are handled by the retailer through its Distribution Centres and the agent is not involved in this part of the process.

To venture into e-commerce and compete with strong online players in the food and grocery segment (like Grofers), RP-Sanjiv Goenka Group's Spencer's Retail Limited (SRL) acquired 100% stake in Omnipresent Retail India, which operates Meragrocer.com, an online grocery business that since 2014 delivers grocery items to consumers in the Northern Capital Region (NCR) of Delhi and Gurgaon. Customers can order online, through a mobile-app or interactive voice response (IVR), and pay online through an e-wallet or through cash-on-delivery while choosing their delivery slots. It is a scalable model and allows SRL to expand quickly into the e-commerce space. The synergies between the two companies are being realized as SRL is responsible for the merchandising and providing the back-end infrastructure from the Spencer's hypermarkets while Meragrocer is providing the technology platform along with their e-commerce expertise. It has provided SRL an accelerated learning curve in the e-commerce industry, as a green field venture would have taken 10 months to18 months to launch, along with significant cost-savings as the cost of development of a green field e-commerce venture would have been significantly higher (approximately \$25 million) than its cost of acquisition. Currently Spencer's

---

[4]Exchange rate of \$1 = Rs. 66.5275 has been used for conversion.

has 122 stores across 35 cities with 1.5 million square feet space and 3.7 million monthly footfalls. Spencer's will not adopt the deep discount model. This online format was initially providing grocery and food category only but will gradually enter into other product categories like homeware, electronics, and apparel. The online set-up would gradually provide delivery within a few hours while currently offering delivery within 1 day. Also, it is available only in those cities where Spencer's has an offline presence as the online model is expected to supplement Spencer's catchment area with a deeper penetration in an existing market.

Departmental retailer K. Raheja Corp Group's Shoppers Stop had invested in their online platform thrice—in 1999 2008 and 2011, but had to shut down each time. Shoppers Stop had been facing declining sales per square feet from Rs 8518 in 2010–11 to Rs 7837 in 2012–13, and a conversion ratio from 24% to 22% in the same period (CRISIL Research 2014). Currently Shoppers Stop is taking concerted efforts to implement their omnichannel strategy, to mitigate this declining trend. Fortune India magazine had ranked Shoppers Stop as the "No. 1 Social Networth Company" for 2 consecutive years (2011 and 2012) for its Facebook page and Shoppers Stop is attempting to connect these customers to its stores through the omnichannel route. The customer may browse through the trends on the store's Facebook page, view a YouTube video, shop from the physical Shoppers Stop stores in the neighbourhoods or airport stores, or online from the e-store. Customers are also able to shop online and exchange products in the physical stores. Shoppers Stop has been awarded the 'Most Admired Fashion Retailer of the Year: Omnichannel Initiative' by IMAGES Fashion Awards 2016 in recognition of its initiatives towards implementing an omnichannel strategy.

Some apparel brand manufacturers like Raymond Group and the Aditya Birla Group have launched their own e-commerce ventures (Raymondnext.com and trendin.com). Competition from online players may not have been their reason for getting into the online space and their e-commerce activities coincided with the growth of e-commerce in the market. The compelling motive for them has been the need to upgrade operations with investment in technology for which a centralized warehouse and distribution centre was put in place.

To alleviate competition from e-commerce, brands like Van Heusen, Puma and Allen Solly are also digitizing their stores. They need to keep reinventing themselves which assists them in increasing store footfalls and average ticket sizes. They are using technology solutions like digital display, summarizing day's new styles and fashion tips, booking trial rooms and selected items waiting in the changing room in their flagship stores to improve their brand images and create excitement among buyers. Brands undertake such initiatives to differentiate themselves and be perceived as tech-savvy by customers. However these creativities may be more relevant from the marketing perspective for creating enthusiasm among potential buyers rather than providing any additional benefit to customers or improving their shopping experience.

10.2   Online Retailers Opening Physical Stores

Online retailers are working on building their offline presence. India's largest e-commerce retailer Flipkart in conjunction with its logistic company eKart is providing customers with 'experience zones' to facilitate buying and pick-ups for consumers at their convenient time. In due course, these experience zones evolve to offer value-added services like spot trials, reverse pick-ups, instant returns, cash on returns, and exclusive product demos. The experience zone initiative stems from the customers' dissatisfaction with the delivery process due to unavailability of delivery at preferred timings and restricted entry of delivery persons into office complexes, gated communities, and educational institutions. Through the experience zones Flipkart is also contemplating its rural expansion strategy as it proposes to expand into Tier-4 towns and rural areas by making them serviceable from a pick-up centre. This is a reliable alternative to door-delivery in remote areas where logistics add significant costs.

Amazon, as a major competitor of Flipkart, has come up with a similar model and added pickup services with BPCL's In & Out stores and with *kirana* stores in Bangalore for in-store pickups by customers.

A leading online baby products portal called Firstcry.com is expanding with an offline presence and increasing the number of its stores, as a large proportion of baby product sales still happen offline. Currently they have around 70 stores through a franchisee model in Tier-1 2 and 3 cities across India. Similar to Flipkart's experience zones, Firstcry's stores act as experience centres and provide the touch-and-feel factor for customers. The physical stores display 300 to 400 brands, whereas through the kiosks in the physical stores customers can browse through approximately 70,000 SKUs, order online, and get the product in the store within 2–3 days.

The e-commerce industry is replete with examples of online retailers like Myntra.com (fashion), Zivame.com (innerwear), Bluestone.com (jeweller), Healthkart.com (fitness products), and Lenskart.com (eyewear), who are trying to start an offline presence by setting up stores and trial rooms with different modalities. The physical stores enable these retailers to reach buyers in smaller towns and cities as a major segment of sales for these companies happen in the smaller towns. The stores help to establish customer trust and build the brand as the buyers are reassured that there is an actual store to go to if they face problems with the products. In the long run, this offline strategy also helps the online companies to attract investors for funding.

10.3   The Hyperlocal e-Commerce Model

As per a report by retail consultancy firm Technopak, market share of the grocery e-store has been estimated at less than $100 million but is expected to cross $25 billion by 2020, growing at a rate of 25% to 30% year-on-year in major Indian cities. This segment has resultantly attracted funding and a few major players like

BigBasket, Local Banya, Grofers, Zopper and PepperTap have started operations in this space. While companies like BigBasket source from wholesalers and stock their inventory, players like Zopper, Grofers and PepperTap operate a hyperlocal model.

The hyperlocal model is an on-demand delivery model that takes groceries from a neighbourhood shop and brings it to the consumer's doorstep. Customers use the website/app of the hyperlocal retailer to order groceries and the retailer delivers the groceries through its delivery boys deployed at the mid-level grocery shops that have tied up with it. For its services rendered, the hyperlocal retailer charges a commission from the sellers. Ordinarily, the neighbourhood stores use their in-shop attendants to double as delivery boys when required. The hyperlocal retailer offers the owners of these neighbourhood stores professional logistics and technology support to attract customers and helps the grocery stores to compete with both the developing modern retail and e-commerce formats that are increasingly denting their business. For the hyperlocal grocers, it is a very asset-light business model as they do not need to carry their inventory (the products the retailers carry is their inventory), do not have any warehouse requirement (the retailers' shop is their warehouse), and does not involve any high-cost delivery infrastructure. They divide the area of operations into different zones, with one shop in each zone that caters to a catchment area of 3–4 km in the immediate vicinity. The available stock items of the shop are accessible on the website/app through which customers select their products.

Numerous challenges are faced by the hyperlocal retailer start-ups in identifying the right local stores for supply, right talent for vendor acquisition and fulfilment, maintaining the quality of the products to be delivered, logistics, retention of delivery staff, maintaining customer satisfaction, and raising investment funding to enable the growth of the company. Such business models have many crucial components that must work in tandem and it calls for adequate strategic planning to sustain the business. While Zopper with its focus on electronics category is looking at expanding its city reach and doubling its gross sales, PepperTap failed to raise sufficient funds to sustain its growth and closed down.

11   Logistics Innovations in the e-Commerce Industry

Currently there are 1 to 1.2 million transactions occurring daily in leading categories like apparel (43%), electronics (24%), and books (22%) and the logistics sector catering to e-commerce was valued at USD 0.2 billion in 2014 and is projected to reach $2.2 billion by 2020 with a CAGR of 48% (Dogar and Tanwar 2015).

Logistics is a critical aspect for the success of an e-commerce company and until a few years back it has been a fragmented process with scarce IT enablement and insufficient investment leading to operational inefficiencies. E-commerce companies are gradually foraying beyond the Tier-1 and Tier-2 cities and the emphasis on logistics will naturally increase with this progression into surrounding areas. Companies like Flipkart and Snapdeal reportedly get more than 60% of their businesses from the hinterland. Logistics infrastructure is also expected to get a substantial boost when international players like Alibaba (who has until now invested in Snapdeal and Paytm) make a full-fledged entry into the Indian market.

Numerous e-commerce companies have invested in building their logistics networks and capabilities and the e-commerce logistics market is replete with both in-house logistics firms (like Flipkart's Ekart) and third-party providers. As the emphasis shifts from standard to specialized deliveries, companies are growing their logistics businesses in the e-commerce industry in the form of secure locker deliveries, long-distance truck freighting, hyperlocal deliveries, software optimization platforms, and reverse logistics, among others.

To help e-commerce companies solve the critical problem of an individual last-mile delivery that is time-consuming and costly, new companies like QikPod are proposing to use lockers in places where consumers live, work, shop or travel through (like information technology parks, commercial and residential complexes) to help e-commerce companies ensure faster deliveries. The products are shipped to a secure locker and the customer is provided with a code through a text message to unlock the locker. In this case, the consumer also benefits as they are not required to stay at home or at work to receive a delivery and take recurrent calls from delivery agents for providing them directions.

Due to the broken road-freighting system in India, e-commerce deliveries usually take a week or more. To reform long distance truck freighting in India, Rigivo has come up with a new business model. Truckers have signed up with Rigivo and the company has set up pit stops (a stop during a trip for fuel, food, rest or for use of a restroom) for them where drivers change but the truck does not stop. This relay mechanism ensures that deliveries happen 50% to 70% faster while the driver returns home the same day.

Specialized logistics provider for e-commerce like Delivery are investing in newer capabilities and developing their automation sortation capacity, GPS mapping, and address systems to scale up to meet the demands of the e-commerce sector. The address and mapping systems are broken and require innovations for efficient delivery. Legacy logistics companies like Blue Dart have also taken initiatives like cash-on-delivery, hand-held devices for on-the-move usage, smart trucks, and mobile point-of-sale solutions for e-commerce. They commenced operations in their first eFulfilment centre in Delhi in 2015 and are undertaking initiatives to launch more such centres. Hyperlocal delivery businesses (like Opinio engaging in food delivery within a seven kilometer radius) have started to play a pivotal role in helping small businesses expand and build an online presence, though they too face similar challenges of broken address and mapping systems. Flipkart had initially set up its logistics arm eKart Logistics for its in-house deliveries only but now that its technology infrastructure has been established, eKart has opened its services for other e-commerce players and delivers packages for its competitors too.

Software platforms like Loginext provide solutions to logistics providers and focus on improving efficiency for e-commerce companies by automating route-planning through analysing their location, traffic, time, and carrying capacity. This translates to more deliveries, fewer missed deliveries and kilometres travelled thereby providing three to four percent cost savings to customers.

Reverse logistics is another crucial component in e-commerce as companies offer returns and exchanges as a part of their product promise of an enhanced customer experience, in an attempt to acquire and retain customers. Unlike conventional logistics, reverse logistics is under-served and a lot of ambiguities exist in areas like the condition of the product, packaging, how to deal with the owners. New companies like Blu Birch focus on reverse logistics and propose to use technology to improve efficiency across the reverse logistics chain by working on eliminating factors for which returns happen. They want to provide their customers with insights that will help the e-commerce companies reduce or eliminate product returns. Until now reverse logistics in e-commerce has been traditionally controlled by sundry middlemen and e-waste handlers.

Over the last 2 years the Department of Post through India Post has entered into tie-ups with the country's top online sellers—Amazon, Snapdeal and Flipkart-Myntra for offering them last-mile connectivity in areas outside of large cities and cash-on-delivery payments. India Post has unparalleled reach with 156 thousand post offices in all, out of which 125 thousand are in rural areas. India Post has set up 57 modern delivery centres to handle the e-commerce traffic. The deliveries are predominantly directed at Tier-2 towns and parts of the rural heartland. India Post handled cash-on-delivery showing a jump of 200%, as per Mr. Ravi Shankar Prasad (union minister for communications & IT).

The trend that can be observed is that the growth in e-commerce has led to the development of new service requirements and created a new section of logistics operators. All of the innovative logistics businesses are on a growth trajectory and have expectations of future growth. In spite of the projected potentials, the companies are not contemplating operations only in e-commerce and are aspiring to expand into new verticals and explore opportunities beyond e-commerce.

12 Recommendations and Conclusion

India is a country with extensive rural areas where online shopping may be difficult and product delivery may be a time-consuming affair for retailers. Yet the country has a market of 1.34 billion consumers who are discerning in their habits and view shopping as a personal journey of obtaining information and indicating their preferences seamlessly across several platforms. It is paradoxical that it is the consumers who appear to be orchestrating the change and not the retailers. The established retailers appear to have a reactive, not proactive, stance in this market evolution. The connotation of omnichannel suggests that the retailers be omnipresent to the consumers. Yet cognizance of transitional market dynamics has allowed 100% FDI in online retail of goods and services under the marketplace model through the automatic route in an attempt to legitimize the existing businesses of e-commerce companies operating in India. FDI is however prohibited in e-commerce companies that own inventories of goods and services and sell directly to consumers using online platforms. Also the marketplaces are prohibited from offering deep discounts on the products and warranty/guarantee of the goods. These can only be offered by the sellers and their contact details have to be displayed online in the marketplace platform. Sales from an individual vendor in such a marketplace is capped at 25% of the total sales. The e-commerce retailer can continue to provide support services like warehousing, logistics, order fulfilment, call centre, and payment collection to the individual sellers. These directives of the Government can potentially end the price wars in the e-commerce space and level the playing field with physical stores. As the retail players in the online space gear up towards implementing the transitions laid down by the Government, it is evident that their transformative role in the Indian market have been duly acknowledged. Over the next few years, it will be of much interest to monitor the retail landscape and analyse the market dynamics that unfurl among the dominant stakeholders.

Questions for Discussion and Review

1. Conduct a SWOT Analysis of the Indian e-retail sector. Match its strengths to opportunities and indicate any competitive advantage that the sector may have.
2. A customer notices that a particular product available at the store is cheaper on the retailer's website and requests to get the same price at the store. The salesman says that online offers are limited to those buying online. In this context, discuss the implications of a customer walking out of the store and buying online instead.
3. Analyse the evolution of e-retail as a disruptive business model and identify the stage of development that India has currently reached.
4. Is China the most relevant benchmark for global CEOs who are attempting to study future changes in Indian e-retail? Discuss.
5. Explain some of the current challenges encountered by e-commerce retailers in India.
6. Discuss the strategies that are being taken by online and offline retailers to build sustainable omnichannels for their organizations.
7. Delivery logistics is innovating to add value and provide delivery speed to customers. Discuss its impact of delivery the e-commerce business.
8. Indian consumers often abandon their online shopping carts because of unexpected costs such as high cost of shipping, tax rate, accessory charges at the point of payment. Explain how omnichannel retailing can help lessen this problem?
9. Critically evaluate the factors that may make the Indian e-commerce sector profitable in the long run.
10. Discuss the Government's policy regulations that are shaping the overall retail sector in India.

References

A.T. Kearney. (2015a). *The 2015 global retail development index. Global retail expansion: An unstoppable force.*

A.T. Kearney. (2015b). *The 2015 global retail e-commerce index. Global retail e-commerce clicks on clicking.*

Bower, J. L., & Christensen, C. M. (1995). Disruptive technologies: Catching the wave. *Harvard Business Review, 73,* 43–53.

Connected Life – TNS Mobile. (2015). *Millennials in Asia Pacific.* http://www.tnsglobal.com/sites/default/files/Millennials-on-Phone-A4.pdf

CRISIL Opinion, "e-tail eats into retail", CRISIL Research. (2014, February). http://www.crisil.com/pdf/research/CRISIL-Research-Article-Online-Retail-Feb14.pdf

Doger, K., & Tanwar, P. (2015, November). *Fulfilled! India's e-commerce retail logistics growth story.* KPMG and CII.

eMarketer Chart. (2016, August). *Total retail and retail ecommerce* sales in India 2015–2020 (billions, % change and % of total retail sales).* https://www.emarketer.com/Chart/Total-Retail-Retail-Ecommerce-Sales-India-2015-2020-billions-change-of-total-retail-sales/194284

Ernst & Young. (2016). *What will it take to sustain e-commerce growth?.*

India Internet Users. (2016). http://www.internetlivestats.com/internet-users/india/

Jha, D., & Varma, K. (2015). *Mobile shoppers turn App-happy – Delivering consumer clarity.* Nielsen India, Nielsen Informate Mobile Insights – India Smartphone Users Panel.

Piotrowicz, W., & Cuthbertson, R. (2014). Introduction to the special issue information technology in retail: Toward omnichannel retailing. *International Journal of Electronic Commerce, 18*(4), 5–16.

Sharma, D., & Flamind, V. (2015, September). *The Elephant charts the Dragon, charting the future of e-retail in India, images retail,* pgs. 46–53.

Tanwar, P., & Doger, K. (2016, August). *Fulfilled! India's e-commerce retail logistics growth story.* KPMG and CII.

Mohua Banerjee is Professor (Marketing) & Dean (Placements, Corporate & Alumni Relations) at International Management Institute Kolkata. She had completed her M.Com in Accountancy and Ph.D. from University of Calcutta. She teaches courses on Retail Marketing, Sales & Distribution and Marketing Communication in Kolkata and courses on Digital Marketing and Consumer Behaviour in foreign Universities like University of Bordeaux, Tours and Celsa-Sorbonne University in France. She has consulted in the telecom sector and has conducted practice-oriented retail research with Oxford Institute of Retail Management, Saïd Business School, University of Oxford. She had been actively involved in Retail Management curriculum development for National Skill Development Mission, NITTTR, Ministry of HRD. Her publications include research articles and cases in international journals and publishing houses. Currently she is working on a Joint Research Project with Leeds Beckett University, UK as a part of the 'UK-India Education Research Initiative' (UKIERI) Research Grant, on "Fostering Entrepreneurship for Sustainable and Inclusive Agri-Food Innovation: A comparative analysis of India and UK".

The Development of Digital Distribution Channels in Poland's Retail Pharmaceutical Market

Jana Pieriegud

Abstract Over the past 20 years, Poland's pharmaceutical industry has undergone privatization and fundamental modernization to become the second largest pharmaceutical market in Central and Eastern Europe. Pharmaceutical industry is one of the most innovative and fastest growing sectors in Poland, worth an estimated 6 billion euros in 2014. The over-the-counter (OTC) medicines market is significant and is expected to develop as the most attractive segment of Poland's pharmaceutical market in the next few years. The distribution of drugs, including OTC, is subject to stringent regulations: most OTCs must be sold in pharmacies, although a list of products that may be sold in other retail outlets is published by the authorities. In 2014, about 23% of OTC sales revenues came from non-pharmacy distribution channels, such as hypermarkets, supermarkets, and traditional grocers.

Electronic commerce in Poland is still at an early stage of development but has strong growth potential and includes online sales of pharmaceuticals and cosmetics. The first Polish online pharmacy was established in 2004. At the beginning of 2016, there were almost 300 pharmacies selling via online mail order, yet the channel had less than a 1% share of the OTC segment. Polish online pharmacies are run by traditional brick and mortar pharmacies under the relevant licenses and permits. This chapter examines the changes in Poland's pharmaceutical market, describing the evolution of online pharmacies and identifying barriers to the development of new business models utilizing the advantages of channel integration.

1 Introduction

The pharmaceutical industry is responsible for the development, production and distribution of medicines. Because drugs critically impact human health, as well as the quality and duration of life, this industry has a number of specific characteristics that differentiates it from other sectors, including the following:

J. Pieriegud (✉)
Department of Transport, Warsaw School of Economics, Warsaw, Poland
e-mail: jpiere@sgh.waw.pl

© Springer Nature Switzerland AG 2019
W. Piotrowicz, R. Cuthbertson (eds.), *Exploring Omnichannel Retailing*,
https://doi.org/10.1007/978-3-319-98273-1_7

- It is one of the largest and most profitable industries worldwide. As reported by the IMS Institute for Healthcare Informatics, in 2014 the global pharmaceutical market exceeded one trillion USD. North America and Europe (including Russia and Turkey) remained the world's two largest markets, with a 44.5% and a 25.3% share in global sales revenue respectively (IMS Health 2015).
- It is one of the most technology- and innovation-driven industries (Petrova 2014), with the highest ratio of Research and Development (R&D) investment to net sales. All new medicines introduced into the market are the result of lengthy, costly, and risky R&D conducted by pharmaceutical companies (EFPIA 2015). According to the 2015 EU Industrial R&D Investment Scoreboard, the pharmaceuticals and biotechnology sector, in conjunction with health care equipment and services, accounts for 18.2% of total business R&D expenditure worldwide (EC 2015).
- It is a multi-level market with numerous stakeholders: manufacturers and importers; wholesalers, including pre-wholesalers (e.g. customs warehouses); retailers, including pharmacies and other retailer outlets (shops, kiosks, petrol stations), and e-pharmacies; healthcare providers (hospitals, clinics, health centers, diagnostic centers); physicians and pharmaceutical representatives; health insurers; government agencies, regulatory bodies, inspectors, chambers of commerce; professional foundations and associations; universities, research institutes, and laboratories; technological parks and clusters; consulting firms and marketing agencies; and individual consumers, including patients.
- It is much more heavily regulated than any other industry due to its impact on human health. In addition, the regulatory regimes and distribution margins, which are generally fixed by governments, differ significantly both between the US and the EU and from country to country (Sifuentes and Giuffrida 2015). Depending on national legislation, digital pharmacies in the EU can be either be full pharmacies (including the prescription business) or limited para-pharmacies with non-prescription self-care (Dudley 2015).
- It is among the biggest spenders on marketing. Since product development, distribution, and pricing are highly regulated across the world, pharmaceutical firms are not as flexible as firms in other industries in using these elements of the marketing mix. Special focus is therefore placed on communication activities, spanning from sales calls (visits paid to physicians and pharmacists by sales representatives), through advertisements in medical journals, to TV and radio commercials targeted at end consumers, as well as other channels (Fischer 2014). As a result, pharmaceutical companies spend about one-third of all sales revenue on marketing their products—roughly twice as much as they spend on R&D.

It should also be observed that the pharmaceutical market is composed of two segments governed by different regulations: prescription-only and over-the-counter medicines.

Prescription-only medicines (POMs), also known as Rx, Rp, or ethical drugs, need permits from medical staff to purchase. The other segment is OTC (over-the-counter) pharmaceuticals, including products registered as medicines, dietary supplements, medical items, pharmacy cosmetics, which are distributed through different channels, depending on local regulations. Both POMs and OTCs can be marketed as innovative drugs under long-term patent protection, or as generic drugs having the same active chemical substances as the original innovative drug but produced only after the initial patent expires.

In moving specific groups of products from producers to end consumers (patients) it is possible to make simultaneous use of a number of distribution channels, thus practicing what is referred to as multi-channel distribution (Katsanis 2016). With the recent advances of information and communication technology (ICT), a variety of electronic distribution channels have become available, online, internet pharmacies, or mail-order pharmacies are businesses that operate over the Web and deliver orders to customers through mail or shipping companies. Meanwhile, as a result of integration between and across sales channels, so called omnichannels are emerging (Piotrowicz and Cuthbertson 2014), where traditional, online, and mobile channels are integrated.

The main objective of this chapter is to assess changes in the development of distribution channels in Poland's pharmaceutical market. The Polish market (with 6 billion euros net sales revenue in 2014) is the sixth-largest pharmaceutical market in the EU. First, the latest trends in the pharmaceutical industry are presented. The key macro-environmental factors influencing its development are identified using a PESTEL analysis, when political, economic, social, technological, ecological and legal factors are reviewed. The second part of this chapter provides an overview of the Polish drug distribution channels and market structure. The third section focuses on the development of the e-pharmacy business in Poland, analyzing the different models of channel integration and including a case study of the first Polish online pharmacy (DMZ) that went bankrupt in 2013. Further, the strategies of Poland's leading online pharmacies are outlined. The role of social media in marketing pharmaceuticals and the influence of consumer trends are also depicted. Finally, the major barriers to and opportunities for future growth of electronic distribution channels in Poland are discussed.

2   Methodology and Data Collection

The study of Poland's market delivered in this chapter spans the period 2004–2015. The key macro-environmental factors bearing on the development of the Polish pharmaceutical market were determined using a PESTEL analysis. In addition, a SWOT (Strengths, Weaknesses, Opportunities and Threats) analysis was employed to identify the opportunities for and the barriers to the development of electronic distribution channels for over-the-counter (OTC) medicines in Poland.

The chapter relies mainly on secondary data and information derived from books, academic papers, industry reports, and Internet sources available in the public domain. The principal sources of data on Poland's pharmaceutical market include official national medical registers, legal documents and GUS [the Central Statistical Office of Poland] statistics, Euromonitor reports, selected publicly available reports by pharmaceutical market research agencies (IMS Health, PMR), data compilations and documents published by consulting firms (PwC), listed companies' annual reports, publications by industry associations, and UOKiK [the Polish Office of Competition and Consumer Protection] reports.

The e-pharmacy market research was conducted using comparative content analysis and was based on data available through corporate websites. To illustrate consumer behaviors, the findings of research performed by Opinio.pl were employed alongside surveys of social media carried out by NapoleonCat.

3   Literature Review

Aspects related to the development of distribution channels in the pharmaceutical market are discussed at length in international (Rollins and Perri 2013; Katsanis 2016), as well as national (Mruk et al. 2014) publications. The sector is most influenced by legal changes (Sifuentes and Giuffrida 2015) and technological innovations. Hence, these factors have received special treatment in a number of studies (cf. Gassmann et al. 2008; Ding et al. 2014). Diversity in pharmaceutical distribution systems and its impact on the prices of reimbursable prescription-only medicines (POMs) in EU member states were investigated by Kanavos et al. (2011). In Poland, the distribution costs for reimbursable POMs and the effects of legal changes on the condition of the pharmaceutical market have been repeatedly investigated (IMF Health 2013; PwC 2013) after the new Reimbursement Law came into effect in 2012.

New technologies, such as the Internet, mobile communications, and social media have created novel technology-based communication channels that are designated as "digital channels" or "electronic channels". The typology of digital channels and touchpoints proposed by Straker et al. (2015) helps understand the relationships between the proliferation of digital channels and enabling connections within specific industries. In recent years, several studies have been published concerning the development of electronic distribution channels in the retail pharmaceutical markets of different countries. Comprehensive studies of mail-order and Internet pharmacies in Europe have been provided by Dudley since 2012. The 2015 edition introduces new and emerging issues that present both challenges and opportunities for healthcare retailers, suppliers, and their advisors operating in the complex European healthcare environment. It covers 17 European countries with around 7000 authorized pharmacy e-commerce websites, some of which operate as small-scale independent businesses while others are larger cross-border "pure play" mail-order pharmacies or have been integrated into the multi-channel strategies of leading pharmacy chains. Across Europe, a number of major retail groups are combining traditional with Internet-based pharmacy and online medical consultation services to capture specific target audiences seeking confidentiality, convenience, and low prices. The European market is significantly less mature than the USUS one, where nearly a quarter of pharmacy turnover is generated through online channels and where such channels are mostly developed by pharmaceutical chains. Major US drugstore chains are setting the agenda in response to the challenges of mail-order pharmacies by integrating the concept of a seamless shopping experience into their retail strategies through PCs, tablets, notebooks, and mobile apps, to create powerful omnichannel brands (Dudley 2015). There are also studies describing the development of online pharmacies and suitable retail channels in emerging markets, like those of India and China (cf. Meng et al. 2015).

An example of a digital channel that has impacted all sectors and companies is social media (Straker et al. 2015). A few researchers have already undertaken attempts to evaluate the presence of the pharmaceutical industry on social media platforms such as Facebook, Twitter and YouTube, and characterize the types of digital engagement strategies used (Costa 2014; Meyers 2012).

Despite the growth of e-commerce, electronic distribution channels utilized in retail pharmaceutical markets are still not sufficiently covered in international literature. In addition, no comprehensive studies have been performed on this field in Poland, this paper responds to the lack of such analyses.

4 Poland's Pharmaceutical Market

4.1 Industry Potential and Market Trends

Over the past two decades, Poland's pharmaceutical market has experienced a major transformation. Its ownership structure has changed significantly, evolving from state control production, distribution, and sales system towards prevalent private ownership, with substantial participation of foreign capital, primarily from Germany, France, and the United Kingdom. Investments are to a large extent associated with the need to comply with EU standards concerning the modernization of production facilities. As a result of heavy investment, Poland-based production plants merit the designation of state-of-the-art and are indubitably among the most modern throughout Europe as well as globally (PAIZ 2014). The public healthcare administration system has changed too (e.g. the network of regional Health Funds that existed prior to 2003 was transformed into the centralized National Health Fund), and the legal framework has been overhauled with a number of new regulations in place. According to GUS data, at the end of 2014 there were 897 hospitals, 19,500 health centers, and 140,000 licensed physicians.

The pharmaceutical industry in Poland is composed of domestic and international manufacturers with production facilities located across Poland, and of local branches of multinational concerns involved in pharmaceutical retailing in the Polish market. The wholesale market has recently undergone considerable consolidation, there has also been an increase in the number of retail outlets, and new distribution channels, such as mail order, have come into use. In 2013, Poland's market includes around 450 pharmaceutical companies (PwC 2013), 620 wholesale businesses (RHF 2015), 14,500 pharmacies, and 300 e-pharmacies (WIF 2015). Notwithstanding the large number of registered businesses, the degree of concentration is very high in all segments of the market.

Poland's pharmaceutical market is characterized by rapid growth dynamics, both in numerical and value terms. Manufacturers' sales revenues increased by 20.3% between 2008 and 2014, totaling PLN 12.3 billion. While the general trend is on the rise, in 2011–2013 the entire pharmaceutical sector was affected by the changes introduced by the Reimbursement Act of May 2011. The decline in sales in 2011 and 2012 was followed in 2013 by a recovery to the 2010 level. In 2013, imports amounted to around PLN 17.9 billion, while exports were at PLN 9.9 billion. It can be therefore estimated that the domestic market is worth some PLN 19.4 billion.

In quantitative terms, domestic drug production satisfies around 54% of demand, which corresponds to only 30% in terms of sales. The biggest producers of pharmaceuticals in the Polish market are international companies, such as the French group SANOFI, with a production facility based in Rzeszów (about 8.5% of the market in terms of sales value), Switzerland's Novartis with a plant in Stryków (some 8.2%), and Britain's GlaxoSmithKline (GSK), with drug production concentrated in Poznań (around 6.1%). Other major players in the Polish market include: Merck, Roche, Bayer, AstraZeneca Pharma Poland, Teva Group, KPKA Polska, Pfizer. The following are the leading domestic manufacturers: Polpharma of Starogard Gdański (5.2%), Grupa Adamed, AFLOFARM, Bioton, Biofarm, USP Zdrowie, Hasco Lek, and LEK-AM. In total, the five biggest manufacturers (Sanofi, Novartis, GSK, Polpharma, and Roche) accounted for 30% of the production volume in 2013.

What can be seen as unique to the Polish pharmaceutical market is the sizeable share of generic medicines, i.e. those that are offered as replacements for branded medicinal products and can be marketed no sooner than the expiry of relevant patents. In 2013, in value terms, they represented some 62% of the market. Meanwhile, international manufacturers continue to account for most of the sales of innovative products (60% of imports). This can be explained, in the first instance, by the expenditure on new drug research and the cost of marketing such products. Another important factor is the Polish patent protection system that constrains many manufacturers' production capacity in case they are not licensed to produce a specific drug. The cost to discover and patent a single substance is estimated at USD 1 billion. International manufacturing companies with a presence in the Polish market have therefore adopted either of two models, where one is to build and develop their own sales and distribution networks, and the other is to combine production with research, sales, and distribution, e.g. Astra Zeneca Pharma Poland and GSK (Mruk 2014).

Poland's drug producers spend around 13% of their profits on R&D every year. The leading Polpharma Group has six R&D centers in Poland. There are also a number of clusters and technology parks acting within the industry, which provide laboratory facilities for the development of innovative biotechnological and pharmacy related products. The largest clusters grouping producers and research institutions are located in Kraków, Gdańsk, Poznań, Łódź, Wrocław, and Warsaw (PAIZ 2014).

In terms of sales value, Poland's pharmaceutical market is the sixth largest market in Europe. In 2015, its market was worth PLN 34.3 billion in total, which represented a 7.3% increase relative to 2014. The pharmacy market constituted nearly 88% of the whole pharmaceutical market (PLN 30.2 billion). The share of OTC medicines was at about 40% of the pharmaceutical market. The OTC segment is dominated by Polish manufacturers: AFLOFARM (some 7.0% of the pharmacy market in 2014), USP Zdrowie (6.0%), and Polpharma (5.8%). For a number of years, AFLOFARM has been the greatest advertising spender in Poland (in the industry as well as outside it). According to Katar Media estimates, in 2014 the company spent more than PLN 1.2 billion on advertising. The advertising budgets of pharmaceutical firms have been expanding consistently for several years. This is attributable to the development of the OTC market, which is exceptional in that there are no legal constraints on advertising. A massive advertising campaign increases the odds for increasing sales, since more than 50% of pharmacy customers admit that commercials for OTC medicines are the primary motivation for purchase (Zarzeczna-Baran et al. 2013). According to Nielsen, the Top 10 list of most advertised OTC drugs is as follows: Nurofen, Theraflu, Otrivin, Pyralgina, Ibuprom, Polocard, Voltaren, Metafen, Gripex, and Desmoxan. Overall, painkillers represent 60% of sales in the OTC market in Poland.

4.2 Macro-environmental Factors Analysis

The factors influencing the state of Poland's pharmaceutical industry were investigated using the **PESTEL** tool, which considers political, economic, social, technological, ecological and legal factors. The findings of the author's research indicate that the greatest impact on the development of the pharmaceutical sector is currently being made by changes in law and technology (Table 1), and this is likely to remain the case for the near future.

The regulatory framework applies to all actors and processes involved in the Polish pharmaceutical sector's supply chain. Given the health hazards that its products may pose, it comes as a matter of fact that the industry is commonly regulated, with stringent and detailed rules imposed at all stages—from production to delivery to end consumers (patients). Industry-specific rules regulate not only the production and sales of drugs, but of dietary supplements and cosmetics as well. Further, there are by-laws that can also immediately affect the market pertaining to the circulation of such products, involving the POM reimbursement regime or permits issued to specific businesses or types of businesses.

Poland's pharmaceutical sector is essentially governed by the Act of September 6, 2001, Pharmaceutical Law (further in this chapter referred to as "UPF") (Journal of Laws, 2008, No. 45, item 271, as later amended). The law lays down the following:

Table 1 PESTEL analysis for Poland's pharmaceutical industry

Factor	Impact assessment	Description
Political	Medium	Unclear prospects for the National Health Fund and uncertainty over the directions of health policy Changes in reimbursement rates and regimes taking place on every political power shift Preference for domestic investors Anticipated lowering of the retirement age
Economic	Medium	Relatively stable economic situation, albeit vulnerable to fluctuations in currency exchange rates Forecasts of continued slight economic growth and decreasing unemployment Anticipated slight increase in population earnings Opportunities arising from the Transatlantic Trade and Investment Partnership (TTIP), e.g. access to new markets for European products, including pharmaceuticals In case the VAT rate on pharmaceuticals is raised (from 8 to 16%), an increase in prices and, consequently, a reduction in demand for drugs is to be expected
Social	Medium	Ageing society Growing incidence of chronic diseases Increasing popularity of healthy lifestyles and healthy foods (healthy diet) Increasing trend for self-medication, e.g. due to time constraints (not enough time to consult a physician) Society's susceptibility to marketing promotions concerning OTC medicines and dietary supplements
Technological	High	Advances in genetics, biotechnology, nanotechnology, and other emergent sciences Technological progress in IT/ICTs Progress in self-diagnostics—increasingly available tests and measuring devices, including wearables Poland government's stated commitment to supporting new technologies, e.g. in pharmaceutics Poland's large growth potential in digitalization and e-commerce Ongoing advances in Internet of Caring Things and e-health solutions
Ecological	Low	Negative environmental effects caused by disposal of pharmaceutical waste Pharmaceuticals call for advanced waste processing technologies
Legal	High	One of the most restrictive POM reimbursement systems across the EU Gradually increasing availability of OTC medicines outside pharmacies: retail stores, drugstores (chemist's), gas (petrol) stations, newsagent's, etc. Obscure rules for advertising Rx medicines

- rules and procedures for the sale of medicinal products,
- regulations for the conduct of clinical research and the making of medicinal products,
- requirements to be met by pharmacies, pharmaceutical wholesalers, and non-pharmacy channels (outlets),
- organization of the system for control and assurance of medical product safety,
- terms of reference for Pharmaceutical Inspections,
- standards for the advertising of medicinal products.

At the same time, national legislation governing the pharmaceutical sector must be regularly reviewed and amended for compliance with EU regulations. The blend of EU regulatory influence, the goals of government social policy, and the recurrent government budget process make the sector extremely vulnerable to legislative changes that can have an immediate impact on its profitability as a whole or at least of some of its segments.

The detailed requirements to be met in running a pharmacy business are set out in the Regulation by the Minister of Health of September 30, 2002. Polish, as well European, legislation also addresses a very broad range of aspects involved in wholesaling, specifying the detailed responsibilities of a pharmaceutical wholesaler (PwC 2013). The sale and advertising of pharmaceuticals is subject to supervision by the Main Pharmaceutical Inspectorate [Główny Inspektorat Farmaceutyczny—GIF]. At the same time, a medicine may not be marketed over-the-counter unless permission is granted by the Office for Registration of Medicinal Products, Medical Devices and Biocidal Products [Urząd Rejestracji Produktów Leczniczych, Wyrobów Medycznych i Produktów Biobójczych—URLP].

Other important actors in Poland's pharmaceutical market include: the Polish Chamber of Physicians and Dentists [Naczelna Izba Lekarska], the Polish Pharmaceutical Chamber [Naczelna Izba Aptekarska], the Polish Chamber of the Pharmaceutical Industry and Medical Products POLFARMED [Polska Izba Przemysłu Farmaceutycznego i Wyrobów Medycznych POLFARMED], and the Polish Association of the Self-Medication Industry [Polskie Stowarzyszenie Producentów Leków Dostępnych bez Recepty—PASMI].

The so called "Reimbursement Law"—the Act of May 12, 2011 on Reimbursement for the Purchase of Medicines, Special Purpose Foods, and Medical Products (Journal of Laws, 2011, No. 122, item 696)—came into force on January 1, 2012. The law introduced new rules for the reimbursement of pharmaceutical purchases, including regulated prices and margins for publicly funded medicines as well as restrictions on pharmacy advertising. The pharmaceutical law does not allow drug manufacturers to target advertisements for prescription-only medicines directly at patients, while it is possible to target these at physicians. Then law became more strict at the beginning of 2012 when a complete ban on advertising by pharmacies came into effect. The issue of Internet advertising for OTC drugs closely parallels that of alcohol advertising. Since the legislation does not address the new online medium directly, there are no explicit guidelines, such as those governing TV or radio commercials. This leaves much room for interpretation. As a result, regulations intended for other media are applied but prove inadequate or unintelligible in the context. Practices are therefore diverse, with each company endeavoring to do online whatever their law departments or firms deem acceptable (Loedl 2015).

An area that appears critical to the growth of online pharmacies is legislation on e-health, for example, on electronic prescribing. At the end of 2015, there were ten European countries that had already had some experience with e-prescriptions for reimbursable medicines, but Poland was not among them, thus there was an absence of legislation and links between the health care system and pharmacies.

A concern that has just recently afflicted the pharmaceutical market is that of parallel exports—a term denoting uncontrolled flow of pharmaceutical products to countries where they can be sold at a considerably higher price, resulting in a shortage of medicines in Poland. To mitigate the problem, on May 7, 2015 amendments were enacted to the UPF law. The amendments require companies to report their stock levels and sales figures daily, and impose an obligation to inform the pharmaceutical inspection authority of any intent to export pharmaceuticals (UOKIK 2015). In parallel, EU member states are working on regulations to prevent drug forgery, and Poland is not an exception here.

Technology advances constitute another major group of factors influencing the development of the pharmaceutical industry. Advances in genetics, biotechnology, nanotechnology, and other sciences will remain key drivers of growth in the sector. Simultaneously, the Internet revolution has triggered the emergence of e-commerce as a new drug marketing and distribution channel, including access via mobile devices, such as smartphones. In Poland, between 2004 and 2014, the total **e-commerce** market increased from PLN 2 bn to PLN 29 bn (interaktywnie.com 2015). According to the Centre for Retail Research, in 2015, online sales represented 3.3% of retail sales nationwide. This is still below the average for other European countries, where e-commerce contributes 8.4% of total sales (and at the higher end: 11.6% in Germany and 15.2% in the UK). However, the e-commerce segment of Poland's market is now catching up very quickly. Since 2010, its growth has run at an impressive two-digit rate, and is commonly believed to have further growth potential. In 2014, Poland was ranked 24th among the 30 European countries covered by the PI Research (2016) in terms of the expansion of e-commerce, primarily because most Polish customers continued to refrain from buying online. In a survey focused on the e-commerce sector and conducted at the request of the Chamber of Digital Economy [Izba Gospodarki Elektronicznej] only 55% of Polish Internet users admitted to having hands-on experience of online purchases. In terms of private sector digital services, digital competences of staff, and the quality of e-government, Poland stands as low as 28th place in the PI ranking. At the same time, it is one of the fastest countries to catch up across Europe (PI Research 2016).

The key **economic factors** are the following: GDP growth rate, inflation rate, average personal income, policy toward parallel trade, drug prices, and drug reimbursement rate. Prior to 2010, the pharmaceutical sector showed growth dynamics exceeding the annual GDP growth rate (Fig. 1). A decline in the sector's financial indicators was observed in 2011–2012 and was associated with changes in the drug reimbursement regime. Its condition improved in 2013–2015.

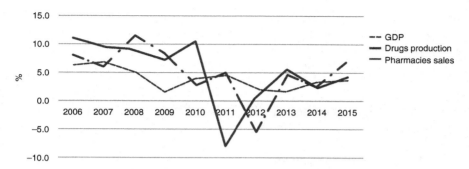

Fig. 1 Growth dynamics of GDP, pharmaceutical production, and pharmacy-based drug sales (%, year-on-year). Source: Based on GUS data

A **social factors** on which the development of the pharmaceutical sector is contingent are demographics, including population breakdown by sex, age, residence, as well as average life expectancy. In the future, Poland is going to increasingly see the overlapping of two trends: the average lifespan becoming longer on the one hand, and the ageing of society on the other. Compared to mid-twentieth century, the average life expectancy in Poland is 17–20 years longer, depending on sex, approximately 74 for men and 82 for women. Furthermore, elderly persons represent a larger proportion of society each year. It is estimated that, in 2035, 23% of Polish people will be above 65 years. In 2050, every third Pole will be above that age.

Surveys performed by GUS show that each year is marked with an increase in the number of patients suffering from chronic diseases. The prevalence of hypertension grows at a rate of 2%, and of diabetes—at 2.5% annually. Cardiovascular diseases account for nearly 27% of deaths below the age of 65 and for 24% of work disabilities. These factors obviously incur significant medical, social, and economic costs. More than 76% of Polish people use drugs and dietary supplements, of which 40% take painkillers; nearly 40% of the adult population do not use the services of physicians, half of whom indicate time constraints as the main reason, while the other half—long waiting-times for healthcare services. This means that this social group purchases OTC medicines. Opineo.pl has established that Poles take four pills per day on average. The French are the only nation across Europe to surpass Poles in their dependence on medicines.

Among **political factors**, it is the incumbent government's decisions that make the greatest impact on the pharmaceutical industry, such as those on the future evolution trajectory of the healthcare system, including the public health insurance fund (NFZ). In addition, the Polish government has to implement regulations defined at the EU level.

As with other economic sectors, the pharmaceutical industry must make more effort to conform to **natural environment protection** regulations and requirements. At the same time, specific weather conditions or changes of seasons tend to have adverse effects on health, causing illnesses and complaints and hence boosting demand for medication. There is also the issue of waste, unused and dumped out-of-date medicines, as well as disposal of pharmaceuticals returned to pharmacies requiring the management of reverse flows.

5 Distribution Channels in the Polish Pharmaceutical Market

5.1 General Characteristics

In the pharmaceutical market, distribution stands for the process of moving goods (medicines) from a production facility to end consumers (patients), spanning two principal areas: distribution channels between customers and sellers, and logistics, i.e. the physical movement of products. There are in fact several drug distribution channels including, in particular, direct selling, wholesaling, retailing through full and limited pharmacies, and non-pharmacy channels.

Distribution channels employed by the pharmaceutical market are multi-tier and complex, as they involve pre-wholesaling, wholesaling, and retailing. This is because many medicinal products are initially moved from manufacture to pre-wholesale storage, and only then distributed to wholesalers. As a next step, pharmaceutical wholesalers supply pharmacies and other retail outlets dealing in OTC drugs. Some drugs are also sold through hospital pharmacies, and certain medicines are available from groceries, super- and hypermarkets, discount and convenience stores (independent and chains), gas stations, newsagents (kiosks), and even pubs (Fig. 2).

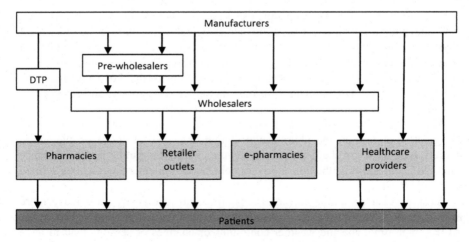

Fig. 2 Pharmaceutical distribution channels, based on Pilarczyk (2014)

Companies' decisions on the choice of distribution channels involve a complex set of criteria and are even further complicated by their financial resources and production capacities. More and more large manufacturers that can afford the extra investment choose to build their own direct sales systems (direct-to-pharmacy— DTP) alongside their collaboration with non-pharmacy outlets. Smaller businesses often prefer to work with intermediaries (wholesalers). Some make choices that are, to an extent, based on what their competitors do. For example, being concerned about their market share and brand reputation, a company may have to react to other businesses' decisions on expanding their distribution channels. Another factor that can influence companies' approaches is potential buyers' preferences and buying behaviors. Some target groups may be distrustful toward any channels other than traditional outlets for medicinal products, where they can be provided with advice and where sales personnel are perceived as having greater responsibility for their merchandise. What matters the most, however, is the kind of product being distributed, as some products simply imply or predetermine the distribution channel to be used. For example, costly innovative drugs are distributed predominantly through shorter channels; Rx medicines may not be marketed by mail order; and pharmaceutical products that may be administered under medical supervision only are delivered directly to hospitals.

5.2 Wholesaling

Wholesaling is defined as all sorts of activities involving procurement, storage, and delivery or export of medicinal products and engaging manufacturers or importers of medicinal products, or wholesalers of such products, or pharmacies, or veterinary clinics, or other duly authorized businesses, with the sole exception of supply to individual customers. Medicinal products, including products moved into or out of a country, may only be handled by pharmaceutical wholesalers or dedicated bonded warehouses and consignment stores.

Pharmaceutical wholesaling plays a major role in marketing medicinal products. Between 2006 and 2014, Poland's wholesale market (primarily supplying pharmacies and hospitals) grew by 66% to reach a total worth of PLN 30 billion. Its annual growth rate thus averaged 7.3%, with wholesale distribution to hospitals growing faster than supplies to pharmacies. In 2014, wholesale supplies to pharmacies were up 5.1%, totaling PLN 25.3 billion, while the wholesaler-to-hospital market soared by as much as 14.7%, totaling PLN 4.3 billion.

Despite the large number of actors (more than 600 wholesale businesses registered with WIF), Poland's pharmaceutical wholesale market is a highly concentrated one, being dominated by three capital groups whose total share of the wholesale market in medicinal products approximates 70% (UOKiK 2015). These groups are: Pelion Healthcare Group S.A. (based in Łódź), Neuca S.A. (based in Toruń), and Farmacol S.A. (based in Katowice). In 2013, their consolidated revenue from sales totaled PLN 18.3 billion, marking an 8% increase from the 2010 level.

The consolidation process in Poland's pharmaceutical wholesale business mirrors the horizontal integration process occurring between major and minor players whereby many local wholesalers have been taken over by market leaders. The process was initiated by Polska Grupa Farmaceutyczna (PGF) taking over ten wholesale businesses based in different parts of the country.

Pharmaceutical wholesalers keep a stock of more than 25,000 products, of which some 3500 are reimbursable medicines that are continuously available. The total worth of medicinal products in stock is estimated at PLN 1.6 billion (PwC 2013). Wholesalers are the key suppliers of medicines to pharmacies (around 80% of sales). In 2013, the NEUCA Capital Group, made up of more than 20 businesses, served some 10,000 pharmacies. However, the largest business in this segment is Grupa Pelion with a 30% share of the wholesale market in 2013.

PGF, part of the Pelion Healthcare Group and a leading pharmaceutical distributor working with some 600 drug manufacturers and more than 9000 pharmacies, operates 13 centrally managed modern storage facilities and sells in excess of one million items daily. The Group works closely with the specialized logistics operator PharmaLink providing warehouse management and drug distribution services to more than 100 pharmaceutical industry businesses, including mostly drug manufacturers and wholesalers, and pioneering the use of a state-of-the-art system for temperature tracking in transport (Pelion 2014). Attention should be given to Pelion's strategy adopted in 2014 and to be pursued in the forthcoming years. The strategy is explicitly founded on building close business partnerships in pharmaceutical distribution:

- PGF is focused on partnering with producers, therefore it does not own any medicine brands, nor is it going to build one in the future
- PGF partners with individual pharmacies and small pharmacy chains, therefore it does not own any pharmacies, nor is it going to build such a network in the future. Instead, it is launching the DOZ direct—an innovative manufacturer-to-patient drug distribution system
- PGF is developing an e-commerce channel.
- PGF is focused on the acquisition of new customers, particularly for its direct and dedicated distribution services.
- PGF is expanding into the cosmetics retail market.

At the end of 2014, Pelion made an entry into the new market segment of cosmetics by purchasing a 100% stake in Polbita Sp. z o.o., operator of the "Natura" drugstore chain, and Polbita Marketing Sp. z o.o. Natura is one of the largest chains of drugstores in Poland's cosmetics market and second best nationally in terms of brand recognition. At the beginning of 2016, it operated 270 stores countrywide, a central storage facility near Warsaw, and 14 local warehouses. The decision to take over a drugstore chain was underpinned by the need to diversify operations and hence improve performance in satisfying customers' changing expectations. Analyses of Poland's cosmetics market are indicative of its robust growth at an average annual rate of about 5% over the past 7 years.

5.3 Pharmacies

Pharmacy is designated as a business specialized in the sales of medicines and other medical products, having an exclusive right to sell prescription-only medicines and certain cosmetics. Full and limited pharmacies (the latter mostly set up in rural areas) play an important part in the healthcare system. At the beginning of 2016, there were 14,500 pharmacies in Poland. Most pharmacies are found in the regions of Mazowieckie and Śląskie, with 1500 pharmacies present in each. A single pharmacy serves 2600 to 2800 people on average. For comparison, the average for EU countries is 4500 people. The latter figure was achieved in Poland in 2000, with 8600 operational pharmacies countrywide.

Since 2005, the domestic market has been experiencing a gradual increase in the number of pharmacies operating within network structures (a chain being defined as composed of at least five outlets). According to IMS Health data, at the beginning of 2015 the number of network pharmacies reached 5400 to represent 37% of the total number of pharmacies and account for 53% of total sales in the market. It should be noted, too, that the biggest market share among pharmacy networks has been garnered by small chains of 5–14 outlets; a sizeable proportion has also been reaped by large countrywide chains comprised of more than 50 pharmacies. Compared to the wholesale market, the pharmacy market is relatively fragmented.

In 2015, the pharmacy market was worth PLN 30.2billion, up 7.1% from the previous year (Fig. 3). OTC drugs (including medicines, dietary supplements, other medical products, and pharmacy cosmetics) represented 40% of sales, reimbursable Rx medicines 37%, and non-reimbursable Rx medicines 23%.

In recent years, the demand for OTC drugs, dietary supplements, skin cosmetics, and medicinal preparations has been rising steadily. The increase in OTC drug sales has been to a large extent due to the 2011 Reimbursement Law that introduced fixed margins on reimbursable medicines (5% as from 2014). The average price of an

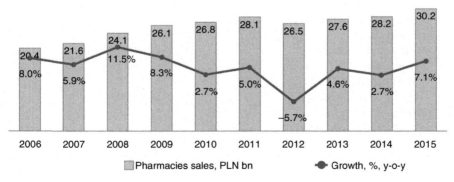

Fig. 3 Pharmacy sales market volume (in PLN bn, retail net prices) and dynamics (%, year-on-year). Source: Based on PMR data (2016)

OTC drug available from pharmacies was in January 2015 PLN 16.63 for an item/
packet (end consumer price), while the average pharmacy margin stood at 26.2%.

5.4 Non-pharmacy Retailing

Until just recently, the distribution of OTC drugs in Poland was concentrated in the
pharmacy channel. Non-pharmacy channels of drug distribution are, under paragraph 71 of UPF, construed as those retail channels that are only allowed to
distribute non-prescription products. These include: herbal stores, grocery retailers,
health and beauty shops, newsagents, gas stations, and (increasingly popular) online
retailers.

Table 2 show that in 2014 non-pharmacy channels accounted for some 23% of
OTC drug sales. These can be further broken down into: hyper- and supermarkets
10.1%, drugstores 7.5%, groceries and other retailers around 5%. Online sales are
insignificant at this time at 0.7%.

As the market for OTC medicines and dietary supplements is still on the rise
(largely due to massive advertising campaigns), and given the recent changes in
legislation easing restrictions on online retailers, e-pharmacies can be expected to
harvest an increasing share of the market. This is also reflected in analyses of OTC
drug distribution channels in other EU countries (Fig. 4). In Germany, for example,
the proportion of OTC medicines retailed through the online channel grew from
7.4% in 2009 to 10.7% in 2014.

Table 2 Market share per OTC drug retail distribution channel in Poland (%)

Outlets	2009	2011	2013	2014
Store-based retailing	**99.60**	**99.40**	**99.30**	**99.30**
Non-grocery retailers	86.30	86.00	85.70	85.70
Health and beauty specialist retailers	85.00	85.00	84.80	84.70
– **Pharmacies**	**78.10**	**77.90**	**77.40**	**77.20**
– Parapharmacies/Drugstores	6.90	7.10	7.30	7.50
– Other consumer health non-grocery retailers	1.40	0.90	1.00	0.90
Grocery retailers	13.20	13.50	13.60	13.60
Modern grocery retailers	9.70	9.80	10.00	10.10
– Hypermarkets	5.40	5.40	5.50	5.50
– Supermarkets	3.90	4.00	4.10	4.10
– Other (incl. discounters)	0.40	0.40	0.40	0.40
Traditional grocery retailers	3.50	3.70	3.60	3.50
– Food/drink/tobacco specialists	2.30	2.30	2.10	2.00
– Independent small grocers	1.30	1.40	1.50	1.50
Non-store retailing	**0.40**	**0.60**	**0.70**	**0.70**
Internet retailing	**0.40**	**0.50**	**0.60**	**0.70**

Source: Based on Customer Health/Trade sources/National statistics in Euromonitor International
2015/Passport. Retrieved June 30, 2015, from https://www.portal.euromonitor.com

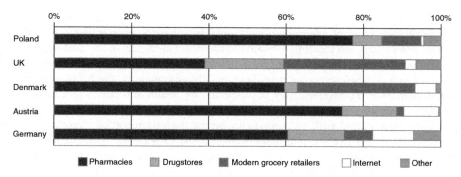

Fig. 4 Share of non-pharmacy distribution channels in OTC drug retailing in 2014 in selected EU countries (%). Source: Based on Customer Health/Trade sources/National statistics in: Euromonitor International 2015/Passport. Retrieved June 30, 2015, from https://www.portal.euromonitor.com

6 Online Pharmacies in Poland

6.1 Development of E-pharmacies in 2004–2015

Albeit in popular usage, names such as "online pharmacy" or "e-pharmacy" are alien to Polish law. For simplicity, they are, however, used throughout the following sections to refer to pharmacies selling medicinal products by mail order.

It became possible to retail medicinal products via the Internet on Poland's accession to the EU. Initially, e-pharmacies were launched by traditional pharmacies as an additional sales channel and operated under the relevant 2003 ruling by the European Court of Justice. In May 2004, the first Polish online pharmacy DomZdrowia.pl was established in Kraków. After a year in business, its monthly sales were several times the average (PLN 130,000) for a traditional brick and mortar pharmacy. The example of DomZdrowia.pl (later renamed Internetowy Dom Zdrowia) is spectacular because the pharmacy, having climbed to the market leader position in approximately ten years, declared bankruptcy in January 2014, while its website was eventually auctioned in January 2015.

I-apteka.pl (based near Łódź) was launched in December 2005, and is now among the leaders in online sales of OTC drugs, dietary supplements, and other products. Some of the e-pharmacies that commenced operations in 2006 are Aptecus (based in Gdańsk), AptekaZdrowia.pl (based in Rzeszów), e-farm, Apteka4u.pl, Cefarm24.pl (based in Białystok). In 2005–2006, two to three such pharmacies went into business somewhere in Poland every month, bringing their number up to 40 by the end of 2006.

In May 2007, the Pharmaceutical Law permitted mail-order sale of non-prescription medicinal products by owners of full and limited pharmacies. The terms and conditions applicable to mail-order sales of OTC products were laid down in the Regulation by the Minister of Health on March 14, 2008. The relevant Regulation in force is that published by the Minister of Health on March 26, 2015 ("concerning mail-order sales of medicinal products"). Polish legislation allows Internet-based sales of pharmaceuticals only by pharmacies running brick and mortar retail stores and meeting relevant requirements in respect of the qualifications of personnel, storage facilities, and so on. Such stores are supplied exclusively by pharmaceutical wholesalers or manufacturers' representatives. Each online pharmacy, like other pharmacies, may be inspected by health authorities and must be properly licensed. The Pharmaceutical Law stipulates that full details of each purchase order placed with an e-pharmacy be consistently recorded. Another legal requirement is that every e-pharmacy website must provide the name of the base store (establishment), its license (permit) number, a copy of the underlying license award document, and the pharmacy's official real-world address. For each medicine on offer, the website has to produce such information as: price, method of payment, terms and cost of delivery, and order processing time.

At the beginning of 2016 there were almost 300 pharmacies in Poland selling OTCs, skin cosmetics, and dietary supplements by mail order. However, in fact, the number of active market players is smaller, with around just 30 e-pharmacies that can be described as significant actors. According to IMS data, mail-order sales by e-pharmacies reached PLN 233 million in 2015. Despite the impressive growth dynamics (55.5%) relative to 2014, the share of this channel remains diminutive: 0.8% of the retail market and 1.9% of the OTC segment.

Based on customer opinion surveys, Opinio.pl compiles online pharmacy rankings. In evaluating a store, consumers can rate such characteristics as the order processing time, quality of customer service, and parcel packaging, as well as state whether they would recommend the store to their friends and acquaintances. In the 2014 survey, the following e-pharmacies were rated best (Opineo.pl 2014):

- *Aptekagemini.pl*, part of a pharmacy chain with 19 retail outlets across the region of Pomorze, employing 170 pharmacists. In business since 2008. What customers appreciate the most is its packaging and superb customer service;
- *Apteka-mellisa.pl* from Łódź, praised by its wide range of products and competitive prices as well as for free gifts attached to each order.
- *Cefarm24.pl*, an online store run by a pharmacy based in Białystok and having a high rate of recommendations from customers. Its greatest strengths are fast order processing and professional advice.

At the same time, a number of pharmacies are organized around the DOZ.pl website that enables consumers to place orders for medicines that can be then picked up in one of more than 2000 traditional pharmacies across the country. The pharmacy chain named "Dbam o zdrowie" has been built around PGF. By law, retailing through the platform known as "Platforma zamawiania leków" [Medicine Ordering Platform] does not constitute mail-order sale.

Research demonstrates that the product range and the cost of delivery for similar orders are comparable in most e-pharmacies. Attention can be drawn to just a few differences, such as the fact that prescription-only medicines can only be ordered (attaching a scan/photo of the prescription) through the websites of Apteka Melissa and DOZ, to be picked up in person at a retail store on producing the original prescription to the pharmacist. Apteka Melissa and Apteka Gemini do not accept international mail orders. The widest geographical coverage is provided by i-apteka that fills orders from Grodków, a small town in the region of Opolskie.

As far as interaction with the customer is concerned, a toll-free helpline is only available at DOZ.pl pharmacies. Differences between the pharmacies examined include online consultations from professionals, as only few of them provide such service through an instant messenger or discussion forum. Contact with the customer is critical to building customer relationships, since clients expect to be able to obtain instant help from a specialist and to be assured that the order will be shipped in just several hours to a pick-up point or to their homes. President of Opineo.pl Paweł Kucharzak observes that an online pharmacy that wants to be successful in retaining a group of loyal and satisfied customers should have the following characteristics: commitment to maintaining excellent customer relationships, competitive pricing, and an efficient and reliable stock and supply function (Opineo.pl 2015). In the opinion of Loopa.eu analysts, most revenue is derived by online pharmacies from the sales of such products as: toothbrushes, blood pressure meters, alternative medicine remedies, and vitamin-minerals supplements. Furthermore, the trend is for consumers to increasingly choose products from the upper price range. Another trend that was captured by the survey is that, interestingly, peak seasons for common colds do not cause increases in purchases from e-pharmacies (Opineo.pl 2015).

Besides e-pharmacies, there are other online stores where one can mail-order non-prescription drugs, skin cosmetics, dietary supplements, medical products. The largest such portal is an online marketplace Allegro.pl, which is used as sales channel by other companies.

While mail-ordering through a website is what all e-pharmacies have in common, specific businesses adopt different models of distribution:

- a single brick and mortar pharmacy, either full (e.g. i-apteka.pl) or limited (e.g. e-farm.pl),
- a single traditional pharmacy being part of a pharmacy chain (e.g. Apteki GEMINI, Apteki Melissa),
- a traditional pharmacy using an e-commerce platform such as Allegro.

Major e-pharmacies typically cooperate with a retail courier of their choice and/or the Polish national postal service to ensure speedy and safe delivery. The total order processing time is conditional on parcel packaging time that, in turn, depends on the availability of a product in stock. Hence, physical proximity of a storage facility is essential for the efficient operations of an e-pharmacy. An interesting example to illustrate the point is provided by the e-pharmacy Cefarm24.pl, controlled by CEFARM Białystok S.A. (member of the Katowice-based group Farmacol S.A.) until May 2015, one of the biggest players in Poland's pharmaceutical sector. Farmacol S.A. group runs its own pharmaceutical warehouses located throughout the country and a nationwide chain of nearly 200 pharmacies. As of May 22, 2015, the Internet-based pharmacy Cefarm24.pl is wholly owned by SK-Farm II Sp z o.o. headquartered in Katowice. The proximity of a storage facility can be an important edge over competitors, enabling an e-pharmacy to offer a broad range of products at affordable prices and deliver them quickly to a consumer-designated address.

According to the findings of an IMS survey, in 2015 the total value of transactions finalized through e-pharmacies exceeded that of purchases from traditional brick and mortar pharmacies. An e-pharmacy sold three times as many items per transaction as would a network or stand-alone pharmacy. This is of course associated with the cost of delivery that is calculated on a per-order basis.

6.2 Case Study: DMZ[1]

Domzdrowia.pl Spółka Akcyjna (DMZ) was founded in 1999. On Poland's EU accession in May 2004 the company, inspired by the proliferation of online pharmacies in western European countries, undertook to start a similar business in Poland. In June 2004, the company obtained a permit to open and run a limited pharmacy in Zielonki near Kraków and began selling medicinal products via the Internet. Initially, its product range was limited to OTC drugs and dietary supplements. As a first step, a simple Web application was developed to handle transactions, and foundations were laid for a logistics system. Next, the e-commerce software was substantially enhanced and integrated with the pharmacy's inventory management system; a high-performance logistics system was also put in place. In October 2005, on acquiring a shareholding by the investment fund MCI Management SA, the company was transformed into "Domzdrowia.pl" Sp. z o.o.

In 2006–2007, the company focused on further extending the functionalities of its e-commerce platform, streamlining its logistics operations, and refining its financial and accounting system. Vertical portals were created in conjunction with Internet platforms Interia and Wirtualna Polska (WP), and partnerships or cooperative links were established with other Web portals. The company expanded its product range to over 15,000 items by incorporating cosmetics and Rx medicines and took an active approach towards search engine optimization, which resulted in a considerable increase in the number of customers.

In 2008, the company continued to expand its services portfolio and significantly strengthened its leadership position in online sales of pharmaceuticals and cosmetics (to approximately 15%), with more than 300,000 unique users monthly. At the same time, work was underway on further vertical portals and a novel website combining online shopping with social networking to foster the formation of an active community around the store, utilizing the social shopping model. In addition, a partnership program was launched to bring together businesses running traditional pharmacies, whether full or limited, in an effort to optimize logistics processes. It was estimated that in the first quarter of 2008 there were around 100 pharmacies in the Polish

---

[1]Based on information available from NewConnect (2008).

market, but few could effectively compete with DMZ. These included: i-apteka.pl, Cefarm24.pl, Vitanea.pl, aptecus.pl, and e-lek.pl.

The key suppliers to DMZ were at the same time the country's major pharmaceutical wholesalers, providing a complete range of drugs, dietary supplements, and pharmacy cosmetics. The business terms and conditions were similar with all the suppliers, including a standing discount of 10–11% from the wholesale price on virtually all items and standard payment terms of 30 days. Most orders were placed automatically twice a day using a computer application capable of comparing the prices at which an item could be purchased from specific wholesalers. Orders were also delivered twice a day against an electronic invoice. Inputting the underlying sales documents into the system was almost fully automated, too. The procurement process was organized in much the same way as in the case of cosmetics wholesalers, only with slightly less automation due to the absence of a consistent product code system.

In 2007, a process was inaugurated whereby smaller suppliers were brought in (Prosper, Phoenix, Slawex, Salus). The company implemented a policy of sourcing only selected items from small wholesalers and negotiating terms that would make room for higher mark-ups than on products bought from major suppliers. Because such purchases were not automated and therefore time-consuming, the company never aimed to make more than a certain part of their purchases that way. An increasing proportion of supplies was procured under direct-to-pharmacy schemes or, even if bought through wholesalers, on conditions agreed directly with manufacturers. In 2006–2007, the so called "manufacturer promotions" were, on average, worth more than 10% per purchase. The largest supplier to DMZ was Polska Grupa Farmaceutyczna (PGF), yet its share of total supplies declined over the years (from 58% in 2006 to just 36% in 2007)—a trend that was to continue. Other 'Top 5' wholesalers were TORFRAM SA (some 17% of the purchases in 2007, ACP PHARMA SA (16%), and Polska Grupa Kosmetyczna (6%).

In September 2008, DMZ made its debut on the NewConnect stock market, raising PLN 1.4million of equity. The funds were spent on developing the proprietary e-commerce platform that was finally launched in November 2009. Under its strategy, DMZ pursues the goal of maintaining its number one position in online shopping for healthcare and beauty products in Poland alongside developing its partner network and a chain of its own pharmacies with a view to expanding its distribution channels and optimizing its logistics processes. Prior to that, the company was solely focused on selling via its own e-commerce platform; alternatively, customers had an option of placing orders on the premises (in a partner or DMZ-operated pharmacy) that would then be transmitted electronically and filled by delivering the purchased items to a DMZ pharmacy of the customer's choice. Consideration was also given to a blended model where the order would be placed at a pharmacy and delivered to the customer's home address. The company's network of partner pharmacies and DMZ-branded outlets covering the country's largest agglomerations was supposed to streamline logistics processes and minimize the delivery time through the use of urban services.

Alongside the e-commerce platform, the company owed a pharmacy situated in Zabierzów and a limited pharmacy in Zielonki (both locations are within the precincts of Kraków) that branched out into a network of DMZ and partner pharmacies supporting the company's online operations and at the same time providing for compliance with regulations on handling transactions in pharmaceuticals. To cater to its pharmacy chain, the company opened a wholesale warehouse in Zielonki near Kraków. Besides generating a wholesale margin, the key benefits included increased flexibility in filling orders, and more consistent pricing.

DMZ's strategic objectives were defined as, on the one hand, maintaining its industry leader position in Poland with an online market share of at least 15% and, on the other, expanding its chain of partner pharmacies in an endeavor to diversify its business model and optimize its logistics processes. Further enhancements to its e-commerce platform were contemplated, such as the addition of new functionalities and the launch of satellite content websites to accelerate lead generation. The websites were to be based on the social shopping model and targeted at the most attractive groups of commodities associated with specific themes. There were also plans to earmark additional funds for Internet search engine optimization and customer loyalty programs. In an attempt to boost growth in the offline segment, the company intended to build its own logistics platforms in Kraków and Warsaw and to develop partner networks around its proprietary e-commerce platform (with partners from Wrocław and Łódź).

In 2008, it was estimated that in the next few years the online pharmacy market will grow at a rate of around 6% per year to exceed PLN 500 million and attain a share of some 1.5% of the pharmaceutical market. In fact, this sales channel did not grow any faster than 1% until 2011, up to a total worth of around PLN 80 million. As the online pharmacy business clearly did not work out and failed to generate expected profits, the company altered its strategy and sought to improve performance by taking over drugstore chains. One of them—Fabrykazdrowia.pl—dealt primarily in cosmetics, but also retailed dietary supplements and medications, making a net profit of nearly PLN 2.8 million in 2011. To be able to buy out the Fabrykazdrowia.pl website, the pharmacy Dom Zdrowia issued bonds to the value of PLN 5 million. Besides www.domzdrowia.pl and www.fabrykazdrowia.pl, the company controlled such electronic retail channels as: www.101promocji.pl, www.dbamyoceny.pl, www.sexizdrowie.pl, and www.pretty.pl. For this reason, a decision was made to rename the company Internetowy Dom Zdrowia (IDZ).

However, these moves did not lead to much improvement in the company's financial performance. In 2006–2011, IDZ managed to bring its net loss down to PLN 0.1million from PLN 1.3 million but failed to significantly increase its revenue that stayed below PLN 7.5 million even after 2008. In 2012, the company made a net loss of PLN 803,000.

In February 2013, a majority interest in IDZ (62.5%), hitherto held by MCI Management, was purchased by Frisco SA, the Warsaw-based operator of the food e-store frisco.pl. Midway through 2013, IDZ had incurred nearly PLN 3.5 million in liabilities and a negative equity. On October 9, 2013, IDZ filed for bankruptcy proceedings, primarily due to an inability to service its cash debt. In

January 2015, the official receiver announced the sale of the company's intangible assets, including its title to the online store IDZ and the six other websites that it controlled.

Arguably, IDZ's bankruptcy stemmed partly from such externalities as, in the first place, the unstable regulatory environment (although the relevant risks were correctly identified by the company). At the same time, however, the company was overly optimistic about the growth potential of the e-commerce market in the pharmaceutical sector and pursued a flawed strategy that included taking a long time to mitigate some of the burden of transport costs, an emphasis on prescription-only medicines, and an insistence on operating a pharmacy chain of its own. Some industry experts point to legal disputes that cost the company time and money, the competitors' over aggressive pricing policy, and inefficient logistics impinging on the quality of customer service (eapteki.info 2015).

6.3 Consumer Trends and Omnichannel

This section will discuss the pharmaceutical and cosmetics markets and the development of omnichannel customer interaction and sales. Consumer buying behaviors and habits are among the key factors determining how much business online stores are able to take on. The findings of research conducted by NapoleonCat at the end of 2014 reveal that a vast majority of individuals admitting to making purchases at online pharmacies and drugstores were men (56%) aged 25–34 and living in major urban areas. Those of them who recommended online shopping typically indicated perfumes (43%) and pharmaceuticals (31%) as the kinds of merchandise that they shopped for on the Internet. It seems that the prevalence of men among online shoppers could be explained by their reluctance to pick up products at traditional brick and mortar stores as well as the convenience of shopping online (NapoleonCat 2015).

Women buying pharmaceuticals and cosmetics online are mostly younger (up to 24 years) and a greater percentage of them live in small towns. Women also tend to provide Web testimonials and recommendations for cosmetic products rather than for pharmaceuticals. Medications come up in just one out of ten opinions posted in the Web by a woman. Furthermore, women give a much higher priority to price as a factor influencing their online purchase decisions. To seek price information, they communicate with other women through discussion forums and social networking sites, sharing their lists of recommended products or even making joint shopping lists to benefit from economies of scale—a behavior known as social shopping.

Surveys show that the websites iPerfumy.pl and Perfumeria.pl are the most popular destinations for online purchases of pharmaceuticals and cosmetics. One out of three respondents who shopped for such products online in 2014 acknowledged having made a purchase from one of these online stores. The largest increase in purchases was captured by surveys in early spring, which could be attributed to a promotional campaign run by DOZ.pl and targeted at senior buyers. This appears to

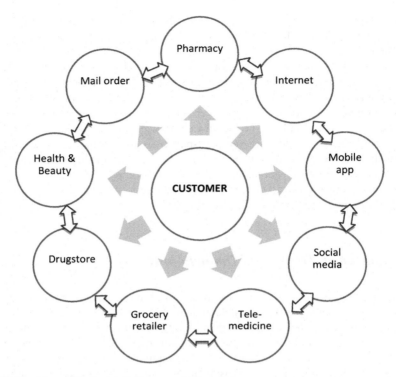

Fig. 5 Omnichannel in the retail pharmaceutical market

be an emergent category of online shoppers, more significant among men (6% of buyers aged 60+) than among women (3% only).

A number of studies concur on the trend towards portals combining e-pharmacy (home delivery of medicines) with online medical and pharmaceutical consultation services. Figure 5 draws on Polish customers' experiences to illustrate the presence of omnichannel in the retail pharmaceutical market.

7 Summary and Conclusions

This chapter has shown that the Polish pharmaceutical market has the following characteristics:

- Generic drug sales account for about 2/3 of market value.
- Retail and wholesale margins for pharmaceuticals are fixed by the Reimbursement Act of 2011.

- Concentration in the wholesale market is extremely high. Increasingly more wholesalers are joining forces with retailers to create pharmacy chains and form wholesale-retail conglomerates.
- Pharmacies remain the main retail channel; the share of pharmacy chains is on the increase.
- Direct marketing is restricted or completely prohibited.
- Online pharmacies are run by traditional pharmacies under relevant licenses and permits.

In 2015, the pharmacy market was worth PLN 30.2 billion, with OTC pharmaceuticals accounting for 40%. At the beginning of 2016, there were almost 300 pharmacies in Poland selling OTCs, skin cosmetics, and dietary supplements by mail order. According to IMS data, mail-order sales by e-pharmacies reached PLN 233 million in 2015. The share of this channel remains small: 0.8% of the retail market and 1.9% of the OTC segment. The major online pharmacies (around 30) have a very similar product range. What differentiates them is delivery time, price, and service quality.

In Poland, like in many other countries, the evolution of the pharmaceutical sector is to a large extent determined by regulatory and legal factors. New distribution models using electronic channels seem to be emerging in many EU member states, although their uptake is influenced by market conditions or may be compromised by regulatory constraints on wholesaling and retailing (Kanavos et al. 2011). The penetration of the Internet and new forms of digital media challenges the traditional communication model of pharmaceutical firms (Fischer 2014). Like other European customers, most Polish online pharmacy shoppers buy skincare products, medical devices, cosmetics, dietary supplements, and OTC medicines (Dudley 2015).

Today, the Internet and mail-order channel in pharmacy retailing is breaking through as a new, rapidly growing challenger. Businesses contemplating entry into this market should be aware of the opportunities and threats associated with the future growth of e-pharmacies in Poland (Table 3).

It must be added that the key considerations for the adoption of a retail omnichannel strategy are as follows (PAC 2015):

- developing a long-term channel integration strategy,
- aligning, or making adjustments to, the organizational structure,
- understanding client activity across different channels,
- a single customer retention system across channels.

Market research reveals that most e-pharmacy patrons are millennials, i.e. individuals belonging to Generation Y, residents of big cities and conurbations, and that in the near future the growth of the e-pharmacy market will be fuelled by an increased number of Internet users among the senior population. One of the marketing goals that e-pharmacies should aim at is therefore to reach those users of the Internet who have not yet discovered or recognized the conveniences of online shopping.

Table 3 SWOT Analysis for e-pharmacies

Strengths	Weaknesses
OTC pharmaceuticals are marketed online at least 10–15% (up to 30%) below the prices charged by traditional pharmacies. Larger stock and (two or three times) broader range of products than traditional pharmacies. More convenient access and home delivery. Offer patients more privacy and confidentiality. Can advertise and build brand recognition. Very high growth dynamics of the e-commerce and e-pharmacy markets in Poland expected in the years to come.	The online channel is not yet popular enough with Polish customers. Order delivery times from Polish e-pharmacies are still far from satisfactory. Not all e-pharmacies provide professional (pharmacist's) consultation.
Opportunities	Threats
Consolidation of the online pharmacy market. Continued development of social media channels. Advances in mobile technologies as well as in the Internet of Things and in health monitoring (e-health). Implementation of innovative solutions in drug distribution. Combining medicine retailing with physician and pharmacist advice.	Ambiguities concerning the legal framework of the e-pharmacy business; more stringent regulations might be enacted. Upward movement in reimbursement rates for Rx medicines.

Questions for Review and Discussion

1. Which unique characteristics make the pharmaceutical sector stand out among other industry sectors online?
2. Explain the range of distribution channels used in the pharmaceutical industry.
3. What factors make the greatest impact on the omnichannel operation of the pharmaceutical market?
4. Explain why major European pharmaceutical distributors and pharmacy chains are investing in digital distribution channels.
5. Discuss why mail-order and online pharmacies are evolving along different trajectories to provide patients with access to medicines, health information, medical advice, and associated products.
6. Describe how regulatory frameworks and the competitive strategies of traditional pharmacies are shaping the mail-order and Internet pharmacy landscape.
7. What factors should be considered in developing a long-term channel integration strategy?
8. How is the role of social media in omnichannel likely to change in the years to come?

References

Act of May 12, 2011 on Reimbursement for the Purchase of Medicines, Special Purpose Foods and Medical Products. *Journal of Laws, 2011*, No. 122, item 696.

Act of September 6, 2001 – Pharmaceutical Law. *Journal of Laws, 2008*, No. 45, item 271, as later amended.

Aptekagemini.pl. (2016). Retrieved March 20, 2016 from http://www.aptekagemini.pl

Apteka-mellisa.pl. (2016). Retrieved March 20, 2016 from http://www.apteka-melissa.pl

Cefarm24.pl. (2016). Retrieved March 20, 2016 from http://www.cefarm24.pl

Cerafarm24.pl. (2016). Retrieved March 20, 2016 from http://www.cefarm24.pl

Costa, T. F. T. (2014). *Pharmaceutical Marketing and Social Media: A Facebook, Twitter and Youtube Analysis.* MBA thesis, Universidade dos Açores, 2014. Retrieved February 25, 2016 from https://www.google.pl/url?sa=t&rct=j&q=&esrc=s&source=web&cd=4&ved=0ahUKEwivxZGzk4XMAhVrApoKHUN-AEIQFgg0MAM&url=https%3A%2F%2Frepositorio.uac.pt%2Fbitstream%2F10400.3%2F3246%2F4%2FDissertMestradoTiagoFilipeTavaresCosta2014.pdf&usg=AFQjCNGS5xYV_dydXjfZfHlYBKMkVeD5xg&sig2=AMKl41vJgNP-r6FkBbyPwQ

Ding, M., Eliashberg, J., & Stremersch, S. (Vol. eds), & Eliashberg, J. (Series ed.). (2014). *International series in quantitative marketing: Vol. 20. Innovation and marketing in the pharmaceutical industry. Emerging practices, research, and policies.* New York: Springer.

Domzdrowia.pl. (2016). Retrieved March 20, 2016 from http://www.domzdrowia.pl

DOZ.pl. (2016). Retrieved March 20, 2016 from http://www.doz.pl

Dudley, J. (2015). *The Future for Pharmacy Exploring Strategies for Competitive Success.* Presentation. Retrieved March 15, 2016 from Linkedin Slide-Share.

eapteki.info (2015). *Kup Pan Sklep – smutna historia upadku Domzdrowia.pl.* Retrieved February 15, 2016 from http://www.eapteki.info/kup-pan-sklep---smutna-historia-upadku-domzdrowia-pl/

EC. (2015). *The 2015 EU Industrial R&D Investment Scoreboard.* JRC/DG RTD. Retrieved June 30, 2015 from http://iri.jrc.ec.europa.eu/scoreboard15.html

e-farm.pl. (2016). Retrieved March 20, 2016 from http://www.e-farm.pl

EFPIA. (2015). *The Pharmaceutical Industry in Figures. Key Data.* Retrieved March 10, 2016, from http://publications.jrc.ec.europa.eu/repository/bitstream/JRC98287/ipts jrc 98287 (online) completo.pdf

Euromonitor. (2015). Customer Health/Trade sources/National statictics in Euromonitor International 2015/Passport. Retrieved June 30, 2015, from https://www.portal.euromonitor.com

Fischer, M. (2014). Marketing spending models. In: Eliashberg, J. (Series ed.) & Ding, M., Eliashberg, J., & Stremersch, S. (Vol. eds), *International series in quantitative marketing: Vol. 20. Innovation and marketing in the pharmaceutical industry. Emerging practices, research, and policies* (pp. 557–589). New York: Springer.

Gassmann, O., Reepmeyer, G., & von Zedtwitz, M. (2008). *Leading pharmaceutical innovation. Trends and drivers for growth in the pharmaceutical industry.* Berlin: Springer.

GIF. (2016). Retrieved March 20, 2016 from https://www.gif.gov.pl

GUS. (2014). *Zdrowie i ochrona zdrowia w 2013 r.* Warszawa: GUS. Retrieved July 15, 2015 from http://stat.gov.pl/obszary-tematyczne/zdrowie/zdrowie/zdrowie-i-ochrona-zdrowia-w-2013-r-,1,4.html

i-apteka.pl. http://www.i-apteka.pl

IMF Health. (2013). *Obraz polskiego rynku farmaceutycznego i kondycji aptek po wprowadzeniu nowej ustawy refundacyjnej. Podsumowanie roku 2012 oraz perspektywy na przyszłość.* Warszawa. Retrieved July 20, 2015 from http://www.farmacja-polska.org.pl/cms/uploads/dokumenty/OBRAZ_POLSKIEGO_RYNKU_FARMACEUTYCZNEGO.pdf

IMS Health. (2015). Retrieved March 20, 2016 from http://www.imshealth.com

interaktywnie.com. (2015). Raport e-commerce. Retrieved January 20, 2016 from http://
    interaktywnie.com/biznes/artykuly/raporty-interaktywnie-com/raport-interaktywnie-com-e-
    commerce-2015-252160
Kanavos, P., Schurer, W., & Vogler, S. (2011). *The pharmaceutical distribution chain in the
    European Union: Structure and impact on pharmaceutical prices*. Brussels: European Com-
    mission. Retrivied February 20, 2016 from http://eprints.lse.ac.uk/51051/
Katsanis, L. P. (2016). *Global issues in pharmaceutical marketing*. New York: Rouledge.
Loedl, P. (2015). W reklamach leków od przepisów ważniejsza ich interpretacja. In: NapoleonCat
    (2015). *Social footprint*. Retrieved July 2015 from http://napoleoncat.com/blog/wp-content/
    uploads/2015/02/RAPORT_styczen-2015.pdf, 38.
Meng, L.-Q., et al. (2015). Online pharmacy model choice of pharmaceutical retail chain enter-
    prises. *Asian Journal of Social Pharmacy, 10*(1), 23–29.
Meyers, S. D. (2012). Facebook and pharmaceutical companies: An industry in need of guidance.
    Online Journal of Communication and Media Technologies, 2(3), 48–70. Retrieved March
    20, 2016, from http://www.ojcmt.net/articles/23/234.pdf
Mruk, H. (2014). Orientacja marketingowa na rynku farmaceutycznym. In: Mruk, H., Pilarczyk, B.,
    Michalik, M. (Eds.), *Marketing strategiczny na rynku farmaceutycznym*. Warszawa: Wolters
    Kluwer Polska, 19; 48.
Mruk, H., Pilarczyk, B., & Michalik, M. (Eds.). (2014). *Marketing strategiczny na rynku
    farmaceutycznym*. Warszawa: Wolters Kluwer Polska.
NapoleonCat. (2015). *Social footprint*. Retrieved July 2015 from http://napoleoncat.com/blog/wp-
    content/uploads/2015/02/RAPORT_styczen-2015.pdf
NewConnect. (2008). *Dokument Informacyjny Dom Zdrowia SA*. Retrieved July 15, 2015, from
    https://www.bdm.com.pl/files/Dokument_Informacyjny_Domzdrowia_pl_SA_BC.pdf
Opineo.pl. (2014). *Ranking aptek internetowych 2014*. Retrieved July 20, 2015 from http://static.
    opineo.pl/press/dl/ranking-aptek-internetowych-2014-pelen-raport.pdf, 9.
Opineo.pl. (2015). *Ranking sklepów internetowych 2015*. Retrieved February 20, 2016 from http://
    static.opineo.pl/press/dl/ranking-sklepow-internetowych-opineo-2015.pdf
PAC. (2015). *Omnichannel Retail in Europe. Strategies, Challenfges and Measuring Success*.
    Presentation. Retrieved March 15, 2016 from https://www.google.pl/search?client=safari&
    rls=en&q=Omnichannel+Retail+in+Europe.+Strategies,+Challenfges+%
    26+Measuring+Success&ie=UTF-8&oe=UTF-8&gfe_rd=cr&ei=7uAKV9nbBuOv8weO_
    5CIAw#
PAIZ. (2014). *Pharmaceutical sector in Poland*. Warszawa. Retrieved July 30, 2015 from http://
    www.paiz.gov.pl/files/?id_plik=24338
Pelion. (2014). *Raport roczny 2014*. Retrieved July 30, 2015 from http://raport2014.pelion.eu/pl/
    otoczenie_rynkowe
Petrova, E. (2014). Innovation in the pharmaceutical industry: The process of drug discovery and
    development. In: Eliashberg J. (Series ed.) & Ding, M., Eliashberg, J., & Stremersch, S. (Vol.
    eds), *International series in quantitative marketing: Vol. 20. Innovation and marketing in the
    pharmaceutical industry. Emerging practices, research, and policies* (pp. 19–81). New York:
    Springer.
PI Research. (2016). *Czas na przyśpieszenie. Cyfryzacja gospodarki Polski*. Warszawa. Retrieved
    January 20, 2016 from http://zasoby.politykainsight.pl/politykainsight.pl/public/Czas-na-
    przyspieszenie%2D%2DCyfryzacja-gospodarki-Polski.pdf
Pilarczyk, B. (2014). Uwarunkowania działań marketingowych na rynku farmaceutycznym. In
    H. Mruk, B. Pilarczyk, & M. Michalik (Eds.), *Marketing strategiczny na rynku
    farmaceutycznym* (pp. 49–50). Warszawa: Wolters Kluwer SA.
Piotrowicz, W., & Cuthbertson, R. (2014). Introduction to the special issue information technology
    in retail: Toward omnichannel retailing. *International Journal of Electronic Commerce, 18*(4),
    5–16.
PMR. (2016). Retrieved March 20, 2106 from http://www.research-pmr.com/pl/

PwC. (2013). *Analiza kosztów hurtowej dystrybucji leków refundowanych w Polsce w latach 2012-2014*. Retrieved July 30, 2015, from http://www.pwc.pl/pl_PL/pl/publikacje/assets/hurtowa-dystrybucja-lekow-refundowanych-w-polsce-analiza-2012-2014-raport-pwc.pdf

Regulation by the Minister of Health of March 26, 2015 on the Mail Order Sales of Medicinal Products. *Journal of Laws*, 2015, item 481.

RHF. (2015). Retrieved March 20, 2015 from http://rhf.rejestrymedyczne.csioz.gov.pl

Rollins, B. L., & Perri, M. (2013). *Pharmaceutical marketing*. Burlington: Jones & Bartlett Learning.

Sifuentes, M.M., & Giuffrida, A. (2015). Drug review differences across the United States and the European Union. *Pharmaceutical Regulatory Affairs, 4*(4), 1000e156. Retrieved February 20, 2016 from https://doi.org/10.4172/2167-7689.1000e156

Straker, K., Wrigley, C., & Rosemann, M. (2015). Typologies and touchpoints: Designing multi-channel digital strategies. *Journal of Research in Interactive Marketing, 9*(2), 110–128.

UOKIK. (2015). *Streszczenie raportu dotyczącego detalicznej sprzedaży aptek*. Warszawa. Retrieved July 30, 2015, from https://uokik.gov.pl/aktualnosci.php?news_id=11636

WIF. (2015). Retrieved March 20, 2015 from http://www.wiif.waw.pl

Zarzeczna-Baran, M. et al. (2013). Wpływ reklamy na zakup leków dostępnych bez recepty. *Annales Academiae Medicae Gedanensis, 43*. Retrieved January 8, 2016 from http://annales.gumed.edu.pl/attachment/attachment/23599/07_O_Zarzeczna_Baran.pdf

Jana Pieriegud is a Professor at the Department of Transport, Warsaw School of Economics. Her areas of research include: megatrends, network industries, transport corridors, railway market, intermodal transport, smart cities, e-mobility, retail supply chains, new business models in digital economy. She has authored more than 150 articles and book chapters, including the co-editing of the titles such as: 'E-mobility—Vision and Development Scenarios', 'Digitalisation of Economy and Society—Chances and Challenges for Network Industries'. She is a versatile researcher as well as a market intelligence analyst, also an independent expert of the European Commission, The Austrian Research Promotion Agency (FFG), The National Centre of Research and Development (NCBR, Poland). She was a member of the Horizon 2020 Transport Advisory Group for the years 2013–2015. She is a member of the Scientific Committee of the Shift2Rail Joint Undertaking, the Transport Economists' Group (TEG, UK), and the Jury for the 'Innovative Product—Logistics, Transport, Manufacturing' Eurologistics' Award (Poland).

The Use of Mobile Technologies in Physical Stores: The Case of Fashion Retailing

Patsy Perry, Anthony Kent, and Francesca Bonetti

Abstract This chapter considers the value of consumer-facing mobile technologies as a component of the in-store shopping experience and their role in bridging digital and physical retail environments. Mobile technology is increasingly integrated into the physical retail store. By incorporating digital features into the store environment, retailers aim to exceed customer expectations, compete more effectively with online pure-players and offer a unique shopping experience. This chapter reviews various technologies employed in the retail fashion sector and considers their benefits and challenges alongside a discussion of theoretical models that may be used to indicate the success of such technologies from a consumer adoption perspective. Three mini-cases show how fashion retailers with different customer objectives integrate consumer-facing mobile technology into their store experience.

1 Introduction

Mobile technology is increasingly integrated into the physical retail store experience (Google 2013), as part of the continuing evolution of omnichannel retailing. By incorporating digital features into the store environment, retailers aim to exceed customer expectations, compete more effectively with online pure-players and offer a unique, sensory and personalised shopping experience (eConsultancy 2016). Consumers increasingly use their mobile devices to research information while shopping in-store (Verdict 2013; eMarketer 2014b), as they enhance their ability to research and exchange product and brand information (Berman 2012), compare prices (Piotrowicz and Cuthbertson 2014) and purchase at any time and place (Brynjolfsson et al. 2013). As technological advances improve the effectiveness and efficiency of the online channel, and penetration of mobile devices increases to

P. Perry (✉) · F. Bonetti
School of Materials, University of Manchester, Manchester, UK
e-mail: patsy.perry@manchester.ac.uk

A. Kent
Nottingham Trent University, Nottingham, UK

© Springer Nature Switzerland AG 2019
W. Piotrowicz, R. Cuthbertson (eds.), *Exploring Omnichannel Retailing*,
https://doi.org/10.1007/978-3-319-98273-1_8

allow more consumers to shop anytime and anywhere, how do consumer-facing mobile technologies in the physical store contribute to the omnichannel retail experience? This chapter considers the value of consumer-facing mobile technologies as a component of the in-store shopping experience and their role in bridging digital and physical retail environments. We begin with a review of the various types of these technologies currently utilised in the fashion retail sector, their benefits and challenges, and a discussion of relevant theoretical models, which may be used to predict the success of the technologies from a consumer adoption perspective. Three mini-cases show how fashion retailers at different levels of the marketplace integrate consumer-facing mobile technology into their store experience.

2   Omnichannel Retailing

Retailers are increasingly required to offer products and services through multiple channels (Verhoef et al. 2015). Using more than one channel to sell to customers is described as multichannel retailing (Beck and Rygl 2015). Alternatively, Bagge (2007) proposed a definition that distinguishes between retailers with multiple channels and multichannel retailers. Essentially, a multichannel retailer aims to achieve brand consistency not only in each channel but across all channels to the consumer. More recently, the concept of omnichannel retailing has arisen from the need for retailers to extend their multichannel activities (Retail Week 2014a, b; Brynjolfsson et al. 2013). This refers to "*a channel-agnostic view of how consumers experience the retailer brand*" (PWC 2012, p. 30) and allows the consumer to be served by any channel at any point throughout the shopping journey (Napolitano 2013). Since a single consumer shopping journey may well consist of multiple channel interactions, retail channels can no longer work independently of one another (McCormick et al. 2014). An integrated experience between channels may be achieved through the development and use of innovative technology, such as Click and Collect services or interactive fitting rooms that connect with social media platforms (Blázquez 2014). This focus on integration and consistent experience across all customer touchpoints and a single view of inventory and customers defines an omnichannel approach (Retail Week 2014a, b). It allows consumers to look for, purchase or reserve products across all channels, while being able to collect or return the items at a convenient place (Verdict 2013). Consequently, omnichannel retailing must be organised as a synchronised operating model presenting a single face to the customer (Carroll and Guzman 2015; Fujitsu 2016).

Experiential shopping spaces are becoming increasingly important for retailers (Antéblian et al. 2014) and the use of consumer-facing technologies in-store represents one way of enabling an enhanced customer experience (Verhoef et al. 2009). The physical retail environment can be used as a theatre to display, entertain and delight consumers through the increasing use of innovative in-store technology (Kozinets et al. 2002; Kent 2007). Interactive displays and other engaging forms of information technology evoke emotions and other sensations that make consumers' experiences unique and individual (Kozinets et al. 2002; Pantano 2015). Concept stores use multi-sensory experiences, with an emphasis on design and consumer-facing in-store technology, to create retail environments for interactivity, socialisation and communication (Kent 2007). Experiential retail environments refer to spaces where the consumer is totally immersed in a fantasy world and undergoes an extraordinary experience through service value, great store interiors and product display (Antéblian et al. 2014). These witness an increasing use of consumer-facing in-store technology and innovations, used to enhance the shopping experience and store environment through the stimulation of consumers' interaction to confer a pleasant and entertaining experience. In addition, in-store mobile technology innovations present retailers with an opportunity to offer an improved in-store experience, blending the best of digital and physical retail (Retail Week 2014a).

3   The Mobile Device in Omnichannel Retail

The mobile channel is both an online retail channel in its own right and also facilitates the integration of the physical and digital retail experience (Brynjolfsson et al. 2013; Blázquez 2014). It encompasses three dimensions: connectivity, the physical devices themselves and the content, usually delivered via mobile applications (apps). Mobile becomes a channel by combining all three dimensions:

Connectivity is enabled by the penetration of faster 4G networks in developed areas, the falling cost of sending and receiving data on mobile devices, and the increasing provision of free Wi-Fi in public spaces such as shopping centres, food outlets and retail stores, which allow consumers to get online more easily when out of their home or workplace.

With regard to the physical device itself, modern mobile devices generally accompany the user and are nearly always switched on, thus symbolically placing the retailer in the consumer's palm throughout the day and night. The key features and unique value propositions of the mobile medium include ubiquity, convenience, personalisation, localisation, flexibility, spontaneity, immediacy, accessibility, time-criticality and instant connectivity (Chaffey and Ellis-Chadwick 2015).The trajectory of technological development has led to larger screens, lighter weight, greater interactivity, longer battery life and more powerful processors that allow consumers to perform many more functions on their mobile devices than ever before.

Content for the mobile channel is delivered via a mobile web browser or a mobile app. Mobile apps are defined as *"end-user software that are designed for a cell phone operating system and which extend the phone's capabilities by enabling users to perform particular tasks"* (Purcell et al. 2010, p. 2). These include interactive information, entertainment or location-based services (Chaffey and Ellis-Chadwick 2015) to pay for goods, take and share photos or videos, and use maps to find locations. Mobile apps are a key development in mobile communications as they highlight a change in the method of delivering interactive services and content via mobile phones. Before mobile apps, the web browser was the main method. However, viewing websites via a web browser on the smaller screen of a mobile device can be frustrating if the website is not optimised for mobile. Mobile optimisation involves designing and coding web pages to provide the user with the best possible experience on their device, for example by ensuring content is legible and fits on the page without the need for horizontal scrolling or zooming.

Consumer purchasing patterns have changed significantly due to technological advances in e-commerce, the rise of social media marketing and mobile device penetration, with many consumers now searching online for ideas and inspiration, to compare prices and to discover new retailers and brands (McCormick et al. 2014; Barclays 2016). Market penetration of internet-enabled mobile devices is facilitated by the falling prices of entry-level smartphones and tablets in recent years, making mobile devices accessible to more consumer segments. In October 2016, global mobile internet traffic eclipsed desktop internet traffic for the first time (Statcounter 2016). Since they have become a central component of consumers' daily lives (PWC 2012; Google 2013), mobile devices have taken a significant place in the consumer shopping journey, empowering consumers with access to greater information and more choice than ever before (eConsultancy 2016; Barclays 2016). Retail Week (2014, p. 3) thus described UK consumers as "ultraconnected, mega-mobile and extraordinarily well-informed". Empowered by digital connectivity, knowledgeable consumers are now more judicious in their purchasing behaviour by conducting research prior to purchase and considering a wider range of information, examining user reviews and seeking advice (Aubrey and Judge 2012), with mobile devices increasingly used for many of these activities (Fujitsu 2016). Millenials (born between 1980 and 2000) are highlighted as a digital generation for whom online and mobile channels are particularly important, providing the information they need to find the best products and services (Accenture 2013).

Mobile devices provide a unique synergy between physical and digital shopping environments as they can be used in both contexts, separately or simultaneously (Piotrowicz and Cuthbertson 2014; Kearney 2012). Outside of the store, they can be used as a retail channel for purchasing items as well as everything related with the buying decision such as price comparison, finding stores, researching products and availability. Within the store, consumers may also use their mobile devices for information and research purposes (Verdict 2013; eMarketer 2014b), for example photographing products, comparing prices and barcode scanning (Holmes et al. 2013; Nielsen 2013, 2016). Even if consumers ultimately purchase an item in a store, they may have researched options online first, reading reviews and acquiring input from others through social media to find the best price and availability for the chosen solution (Table 1) (RSR 2016; Nielsen 2013, 2016; Berman 2012). Evidence suggests that the mobile channel's share of total online spend is increasing, but its main potential is to provide consumers a valuable medium for research, comparison shopping and retailer interaction (Verdict 2013; Nielsen 2016).

Figure 1 shows the prevalence of shopper mobile behaviours amongst different segments of the retail sector. Data show retailers response to questions about how

Table 1 The uses of mobile devices in the consumer purchase journey (based on Nielsen 2013, 2016; RSR 2016)

Shopping stage	Activity	Performed in-store	Performed outside store
Pre-purchase stage	Find and research items before buying		x
	Access product ratings and reviews	x	x
	Pre-transaction customer service		x
	Create a wishlist or shopping list		x
	Use store locator		x
	Search for and select merchandise		x
	Take photos of merchandise in-store	x	
	Check price and/or availability	x	x
During shopping stage	Receive/redeem coupons or offers	x	
	Purchase/redeem gift cards	x	x
	Pay for product	x	x
	Schedule and reschedule Click and Collect (in-store pickup of online order)	x	x
Post-purchase stage	Check order status		x
	Check loyalty programme status		x
	Use social media to comment on a purchase		x
	Write a review of a purchase		x
	Post-transaction customer service		x

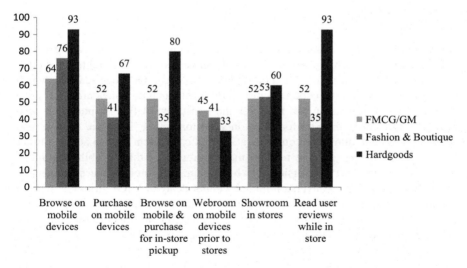

Fig. 1 Consumer mobile retail behaviours by retail sector (RSR 2016, p. 2)

often their customers carry out mobile retail behaviours. Whilst user reviews are less important for fashion consumers, it is clear that mobile devices are important for researching before and during visits to physical stores.

4   Consumer-Facing Mobile Technologies in the Retail Store

In order to compete with online retailers, traditional retailing must consider offering products, services but also experiences to encourage consumers to come to the store (Kurutz 2015). Despite the benefits of shopping online, which include lower search costs, wider choice of merchandise and lack of temporal or spatial barriers to browse or purchase, a visit to a physical store enables consumers to touch and try on the product, feel the brand come to life and engage with trained employees who can help them achieve their shopping objectives (RSR 2016; Fujitsu 2016). The consumer journey through the store presents many opportunities to engage with the retail brand, and may involve numerous touchpoints before the final transaction. These touchpoints increasingly involve new digital media and links to the online channel, such as social networking or electronic and mobile device channels, including blogs, communities, video, and location-based services. As more fashion retailers adopt technology-based innovations in-store and online to communicate with consumers throughout their shopping journey, the key to success lies in exploiting synergies with the online channel to drive footfall to physical stores (McCormick et al. 2014). Some of the benefits of the online channel can now be brought to the traditional bricks-and-mortar store via the capabilities of consumer-facing mobile technologies such as QR codes, RFID tags, provision of in-store Wi-Fi, retailer or staff use of mobile devices, beacon technology, mobile payment tools, mobile apps, virtual reality (VR) and augmented reality (AR). As the most commonly found consumer-facing mobile technologies, these will be discussed in further detail in the following subsections.

QR Codes Originally designed for industrial uses, QR codes are increasingly used in consumer contexts to provide a direct link between offline and online marketing communications. Consumers use their mobile device as a QR-code scanner, which displays and converts the code to some useful form (such as a standard URL for a website, thereby obviating the need for the consumer to type it into their web browser). QR codes may be found on in-store marketing literature, signage and shop windows and allow the consumer a fast and convenient way to access further brand-related content. For the retailer, the importance of this capability is that it increases the customer conversion rate by encouraging prospective customers to move further down the conversion funnel without delay or effort, bringing them to the advertiser's site immediately, where a longer and more targeted sales pitch may continue. It is a pull mechanism for already-interested consumers to find out more and engage with the brand, rather than a push communication to the mass-market. Several fashion retailers have utilised QR codes to provide a connection between their physical and digital offerings, for example Diesel put QR codes on product labels which then took consumers to the brand's social media platforms, whilst UGG put QR codes on its shop window to enable consumers to purchase the season's most popular items digitally (Giorgetti 2014). However, the effectiveness of in-store QR codes depends on the willingness of consumers to scan them. Current evidence suggests males are more likely than females to use their mobile devices to scan QR codes in the UK (eMarketer 2014a). There are regional variations too; Giorgetti (2014) noted that QR codes are more likely to be scanned in China than in Europe, since consumers already use them on key social media platforms such as WeChat, which allows consumers to seamlessly scan a QR code and pay for the item on their mobile device.

RFID Tags Radio-frequency identification (RFID) technology has been used upstream in retail logistics and supply chain management for some time, but their application to improve the consumer's shopping experience is more recent (McCormick et al. 2014). RFID tags are tiny microchips hooked up to miniature antennas which contain a unique ID number that identifies the item to which the tag is attached (Ustundag and Tanyas 2009). They can be used to enhance customer experience by targeting consumers and providing more useful and personalised real-time information through push communication (for example customised recommendations) sent by the retailer, thus saving time as well as customising consumers' in-store shopping experience (McCormick et al. 2014). This can be done by integrating RFID tags into mirrors, labels, shopping trolleys, scanners, products such as shoes or bags to track the consumer's movements during and after purchase (Albrecht and McIntyre 2015; Lee et al. 2012; Kowatsch and Maas 2010). Implementing an RFID-enabled system can alter the service offered. It can result in an organisation relying completely on self-service, whereby the consumer enters the store, selects products to purchase, then exits the store through a system reader that automatically recognises all the products and charges the consumer's credit card or store account, avoiding checkout queues (Lee et al. 2012). Department stores have introduced self-service technologies equipped with RFID systems for self-checkouts (Pantano 2015). In this way, the consumer-employee interaction would be entirely removed, or else this system could enable the retailer to utilise its employees in the form of roaming customer service representatives, thus providing a one-to-one experience with consumers to serve individual consumer needs more effectively than having them stand stationary at checkout counters (Lee et al. 2012). US fashion retailer Rebecca Minkoff installed interactive digital dressing room mirrors into its flagship store, where RFID tags recognise each item brought in by shoppers and when placed close to the mirror, show the item styled with different looks and other sizes and colour available, making recommendations and giving style advice (Greenwald 2015; Zaryouni 2015; McCormick et al. 2014; Milnes 2015). This consumer-facing technology is used not only to enhance the in-store experience but also to gather data and keep track of consumer behaviour in-store, by finding out which items are taken into the fitting rooms, and which ones are purchased or rejected (Milnes 2015).

Integration of RFID tags into the store environment can provide consumers a window into the retailer's inner workings. In this way, Burberry used tags to create imaginative and personalised experiences. Customers can walk up to magic fitting room mirrors with items in hand and receive pop-up information about its craftsmanship; moreover, if the item is in a fashion show, a catwalk show appears, showing consumers how to style the item (McCormick et al. 2014; Ascharya 2016). Although RFID could help retailers target consumers and offer a better in-store experience, Boeck et al. (2011) noted that perceived intrusion is a resistance to adopt this technology; consumers were concerned about privacy issues, which could be due to misunderstanding how the retailer can access their location and thus perceiving it as an invasion of privacy. Further, consumers were happy to be identified from a distance from the store and also to have their movements and behaviour tracked in-store, but their identification on entering the store was perceived to be intrusive. This suggests that consumers are open to RFID tags that identify them from a distance, but more discreetly in-store. Lee et al. (2012) also stressed that the tagging of individual items could raise privacy issues, as although the tags can be removed from clothing and packages, they can still remain active and be tracked. Privacy concerns are therefore a significant barrier for the adoption of this technology (Turri et al. 2017).

Mini-Case Study in Context: Luxury Retail
Luxury—Burberry

Burberry's flagship store on London's Regent Street is one of the most technologically advanced stores in the UK, blurring the physical and digital world to create Burberry World Live, which offers consumers the physical expression of the brand's digital prowess. It integrates the online and offline customer experience via digital retail theatre to replicate the Burberry.com digital experience in a physical space. The store features include a 22ft-high screen, 500 hidden speakers and a hydraulic stage. There are also RFID microchips in some garments, so that when a customer wears the microchipped item in front of a magic mirror in the changing room, the mirror transforms into a screen which shows the garment on the catwalk. Digital rain showers fall on the many digital screens in store, with an enormous video display unit also reinforcing the store's unique experiential scope (Ascharya 2016; Pantano 2015). In addition, there is a digitally enabled gallery and events space. At the flagship launch in 2012, Angela Ahrendts (then Burberry's chief executive officer) said: "Burberry Regent Street brings our digital world to life in a physical space for the first time, where customers can experience every facet of the brand through immersive multimedia content, exactly as they do online. Walking through the doors is just like walking into our website. It is Burberry World Live" (Alexander 2012).

In-store Wi-Fi: Many retailers now offer free wireless local area networking technology (Wi-Fi) in store for consumers to access via their own mobile devices (McCormick et al. 2014). Although showrooming is still a concern, many retailers are trying to make it easier for consumers to use their Wi-Fi services, so that they can engage in an active dialogue with consumers while they browse in the digital space, to observe what consumers are doing in that space as a way of gauging demand, and to provide more customer-facing

(continued)

benefits by leveraging consumers' own devices (RSR 2016). Since consumers have to register and log in to receive Wi-Fi, retailers can thus capture their details, with the consumers' consent, which allows a more precise way to track consumers' activities in-store and enhance the in-store shopping experience (McCormick et al. 2014). Location analysis software can monitor consumers through the Wi-Fi network, providing information such as footfall outside the store, engagement (visitor duration time), whether consumers are repeat shoppers, in-store sales conversions and drivers, walks-by and bounce rates (Datoo 2014; Euclid Analytics 2016). Other techniques involve tracking consumers' Bluetooth connection to follow their movements around the store (ShopperTrak 2016). The aim is to optimise the in-store experience through retail analytics to create a profile of the consumer including the number of recent visits, the products they previously browsed online and their purchase history (Henry 2013; Nomi 2016). However, as in the case of information collected through RFID tags, privacy or security concerns over how retailers collect or use their data may prevent consumers from connecting to the retailer's free Wi-Fi (Mintel 2016; Datoo 2014). Age plays an important role in the acceptance of this technology, with younger cohorts most likely to adopt it and share data with retailers in exchange for access to special deals (Mintel 2016). 15–34 year olds are most likely to use their mobile devices to look for reviews, find detailed product information and compare prices online (McCormick et al. 2014).

Retailer/Staff use of mobile devices: By being able to use their mobile devices when shopping in physical stores, consumers have arguably outpaced retail store staff in terms of having access to information on the web (Severs 2013). In order to improve in-store customer service, the use of mobile devices by staff is an increasingly common sight in retail stores such as Topshop and Marks & Spencer. These devices empower employees to be more service-oriented and to become more relevant to in-store shoppers by providing them with the same tools as consumers (Severs 2013). Providing store staff with the means to access information on the web quickly and accurately whilst they are serving the consumer brings one of the best features of the online experience into the physical store (Fujitsu 2016). Retail Week (2014b) suggested that human interaction between store employees and consumers is paramount and therefore retailers should focus investment on digital tools for staff to increase engagement and expertise. Mobile capabilities for store staff include access to corporate information about products and services, assisted selling and access to the same search and social media information used by consumers (RSR 2016). In 2017, Zara introduced iPads in changing rooms in its flagship Madrid store so consumers could request additional items more easily (Chan 2017; Smith 2015). The intention was to create new interactions with

(continued)

individual consumers, as they would first have to scan items in the changing room, and then request different sizes or colours to be brought to them by a sales associate.

Beacons: Beacon technology is a type of geo-targeting technology and is used for location-based interactive marketing and to help retailers understand in-store traffic flows, dwell time and conversion (RSR 2016; eConsultancy 2016). It capitalises on some of the key features and unique value propositions of the mobile medium outlined previously: personalisation, localisation, spontaneity, immediacy, accessibility, and time-criticality. Beacons work with mobile devices that allow users the option of sharing their location, and thus provide brands with the opportunity to use proximity or location-based marketing to deliver relevant offers and messages to consumers, as well as collect data about their preferences and behaviour (Chaffey and Ellis-Chadwick 2015).

Beacons can be detected by smartphones or tablets and their technology enables users to access beacon signals using a mobile app to opt-in. As mobile apps are limited to the type of device consumers use, for example Android or Apple iOS, this means the apps will not work across platforms unless the platform is of the same brand or the brand has created separate mobile apps for each platform. Whilst users can rely on mobile apps as they work offline, there are potential difficulties online with incompatible software. Therefore, although beacon technology works across iOS, Android and Windows, it is possible that the mobile app may not.

iBeacon is a brand name created by Apple for a specific technology that allows mobile apps to recognise when an iPhone using iOS 7 or above is near a small wireless sensor called a beacon (or iBeacon). The beacon can transmit data to an iPhone—and vice versa—using Bluetooth Low Energy (BLE), so consumers can receive relevant and personalised notifications when they are in a physical store. When the consumer enters the beacon's zone, the beacon can transmit special promotions, coupons, item recommendations, product reviews or in-store layout maps, to their iPhone via the retailer's app, as well as accept payments (Maycotte 2015). It allows more targeted and specific messaging, which could relate to a particular area of the store (Lunden 2014). In 2014, American Eagle Outfitters partnered with Shopkick, location-based offers start-up business, to roll out iBeacons across its US store network. The beacons sent a welcome message to shoppers on entry along with details of location-specific rewards, deals, discounts and product recommendations, without the need for consumers to open the retailer's mobile app (Lunden 2014). Significantly, beacon technology can be used to send push notifications to the consumer's mobile device outside the store (Milnes 2015). Elle

(continued)

magazine in the USA pioneered an initiative to make its editors' product recommendations more shoppable and help drive traffic into those physical stores stocking the magazine's editorial picks, by reaching potential customers within a mile of a store.

Mobile POS (Point of Sale): This includes contactless payment with NFC-enabled smartphones or contactless bank cards, as well as staff use of mobile devices to offer a roving mobile payment option so that consumers need not wait in a queue. A mobile payment is a transfer of funds between two parties using a mobile device. There are two main forms of mobile payments: proximity and remote. Proximity mobile payments occur at the point of sale, where customers use a mobile device or bank card with built-in near field communication (NFC) technology to make a contactless purchase at an NFC-equipped point of sale terminal, which could be staffed (e.g. traditional till) or unstaffed (e.g. self-service checkout). This technology offers an easier and faster payment process and also to enhance customer experience. The mobile POS can be implemented in-store where staff use iPads, which act as POS systems to help reduce queues, for example in Coast, Oasis and Warehouse (Severs 2013). Remote mobile payments do not require NFC technology or a POS terminal. Instead, consumers use their mobile device's SMS or wireless application protocol (WAP) technology to make payments. However, although the technology is effective, consumer adoption levels remain very small due to a lack of trust in the technology (eMarketer 2016). Barclays' (2016) survey of UK consumers indicated that shoppers view mobile payment options as useful, rather than gimmicky, new technology. It demonstrated the potential for mobile app-based payment via smartphones to gradually enter everyday usage, just as contactless payments have done.

Mobile apps: Branded mobile apps can be defined as "*software downloadable to a mobile device which prominently displays a brand identity, often via the name of the app and the appearance of a brand logo through the user experience*" (Bellman et al. 2011, p. 191), which could be the retailer's own or a third party app. Designed for use on mobile devices, they deliver interactive services and content, providing users with information, entertainment or location-based services. They may be downloaded, often for free, through app distribution platforms such as Apple's App Store, Google Play or Windows, or may be charged, as 'paid apps'.

For retailers, deeper insights into shopper behaviour can be gained through app insights, summarised as:

> ". . ..the ability to geographically pinpoint where a customer is browsing from and tailor content for someone who is near a store, or a competitor's store, actively pushing content to an app for offers and vouchers, provides fantastic opportunities

(continued)

for contextual marketing and communications" (Gavin Masters, Head of E-commerce Consulting at Maginus, cited in Severs 2013)

It has been argued that the best way for marketers to reach their target audiences through the mobile channel is via mobile apps (Kim et al. 2013), because users spend more of their time on them than on the mobile web (Arthur 2014). Mobile apps are faster than the mobile web and are necessary to facilitate the complex integration of users with mobile payment and loyalty programmes. Further they permit push notifications, text-message style pop-ups, that app users can opt-in to receive. As email open-rates steadily decline, push notification is an appealing new marketing communication channel for fashion brands. Given the significant increase in use of mobile apps, they have the potential to further develop mobile shopping as an online sale channel in fashion marketing (Magrath and McCormick 2013).

For consumers, mobile apps facilitate a variety of browsing and shopping tasks, including price comparisons, customer reviews and recommendations, the creation of wishlists as well as viewing and purchasing items (McCormick et al. 2014; Magrath and McCormick 2013; Kim et al. 2013; Ascharya 2016; Pantano 2015). Mobile apps generate a high level of user engagement as they are ubiquitous, personal and interactive and available 24/7, (Bellman et al. 2011). Magrath and McCormick (2013) developed the following framework of the design elements commonly found in fashion retail mobile apps:

- Multimedia product viewing—including catwalk video, graphics and image interactivity technology (IIT) such as zoom or spin
- Informative content—including practical product information (such as fabric composition), practical services information (such as delivery times), trend information, style advice, social media
- Product promotions—including vouchers, incentives, rewards, discounts, competitions and social media promotion
- Consumer-led interactions—including personalisation, customisation and augmented reality (AR)

Innovation in image recognition technology has enabled fashion apps to include a visual search option using the mobile device's camera. This allows consumers to take a picture of clothing they see in the real world and then link to a retailer where they can buy that piece or something similar online, for example using US department store retailer Macy's app. Snapfashion and ASAP54 are examples of third party visual search apps, which use an underlying mobile technology called Slyce and build it into their app platforms to enable visual search. The value of visual search depends on the programme being able to accurately recognise items and return results which are perceived as relevant by consumers. Third party apps also include consumer-to-consumer apps such as eBay, ASOS Marketplace, Depop and Schpock, which

(continued)

allow consumers to purchase from each other, thus representing a source of competition for retailers (McCormick et al. 2014). Other third party apps offer consumers a one-stop shop for all their favourite brands, for example Divalicious helps consumers to pick and mix items and virtually try on outfits from over 300 clothing and accessories brands in one place. Shoppers upload a full body image of themselves to virtually try on items from any brand in the selection list. If they decide to buy, the app redirects them to the appropriate online store.

The success of user engagement with mobile apps is ultimately predicated on connectivity issues and the characteristics of the physical device itself. Consumers may be dissuaded by the small size of mobile screens and problems connecting to the internet in-store due to weak signal/low speed or the need to register to use a Wi-Fi network in-store (Kent and Schwarz 2015).

Mini-Case Study in Context: Fast Fashion
Fast fashion—Topshop

In 2013, Topshop's digital initiative "The Future of the Fashion Show" exemplified new ways of integrating technology into fashion shows to reach a global audience and create more immersive experiences. Topshop was one of the first brands to transmit London Fashion Week live through headsets to customers in its flagship London store at Oxford Circus. Real-time 'model cams' enabled Topshop to capture and transmit the experience of walking the catwalk. In addition, a mobile app called "Be the Buyer" allowed users to compose, remix and share mood boards featuring their favourite pieces. A Google+ Hangout gave fans the chance to view and interact with the Topshop design team as they put the finishing touches to the collection. Driving social buzz is part of Topshop's strategy, but equally important was the large amount of data generated by millions of consumers interacting with the various elements of "The Future of the Fashion Show". The "Be the Buyer" app provided insights into consumer preferences, before products reached the store. This data could be used to inform buying and merchandising decisions, such as how many pieces of a particular style to manufacture and in which colours (Kansara 2013).

In 2015, Topshop partnered with Twitter to showcase key trends emerging from London Fashion Week. Real-time tweet data was fed through to billboards around the country to be displayed as a word cloud and placed alongside corresponding shoppable Topshop product. Consumers were also invited to tweet @Topshop to receive a curated shopping list in return. Six billboards within a 10 minute walk of a store were utilised and the experience was replicated in one of Topshop's Oxford Circus store windows, as well as via its website. Twitter's vast listening power enables the global consumer to

(continued)

shop the trends as and when they happen, and gives them insight and access into catwalk shows (Arthur 2015).

Mini-Case Study in Context: Department Store Retailing
Department Store—Harrods

Harrods brought its service to the iPhone for the first time in 2011, with 26,000 downloads of its mobile app in the first 6 weeks from launch. Customers were able to browse daily updated luxury brand news, add in-store events to their calendars and discover the latest 'must-have' merchandise. They could also discover the history of Harrods, take an audio tour around points of interest and create shopping lists for their visits. The purpose was to provide visitors with a modern guide to the store. A member of staff noted the overseas customers in store, in particular affluent Chinese customers as well as the need to attract a younger customer. This pushed the business into creating a mobile app as these groups of customers "... are much more into technologies than any other customer category" and use it to browse and research at home, later taking advantage of the store to successfully complete their purchase. Customers then know exactly what they want, where it is located in the store and shop assistants can promptly show them the products they want to see (Kent et al. 2016).

The potential for online and physical store integration was later demonstrated by Ralph Lauren's use of fifteen window displays to support its Polo line through the use of mobile proximity technology. The promotion drew on Harrods' previous experience with digital marketing to enhance the luxury shopping experience, by connecting with customers' smartphones to offer interactive and exclusive content. The initiative allowed window shoppers to scan or tap the window display with their mobiles, which directed them to the Fashion Lab Harrods webpage, from where they could navigate to the in-store location of the Ralph Lauren Polo collection (Skeldon 2014). This enabled Harrods to access potential customers even when the store was closed, and once they were drawn into the store, to build brand loyalty. The versatility of this interactive technology is demonstrated by its success in a marketing collabouration between a luxury fashion brand and an internationally recognised department store.

Augmented Reality (AR): This technology provides the user with an enhanced view of the real world, supplemented by various elements such as sound, graphics, GPS data and videos. As consumers become increasingly desensitised to traditional marketing communications, AR provides a creative and innovative way to capture their attention. AR blends real-world digital data capture typically with a digital camera in a webcam or mobile phone to create a browser-based digital representation or experience mimicking that of the real world (Chaffey and Ellis-Chadwick 2015) and thus enables the

(continued)

consumer to virtually interact with the brand, with a number of examples seen across luxury, sportswear and beauty sectors. Within the luxury industry, sales associates use iPads featuring a range of digital technologies, including augmented reality, to encourage customers to try on and engage with jewellery and watches virtually (Adler 2013). In 2010, Swiss watchmaker Hublot launched an iPhone app called Hublotista that allowed consumers to view the Hublot collection, design their own models and digitally try them on. GoldRun is an augmented reality mobile platform comprised of an app that enables users to locate, interact with and take photos of GPS-linked virtual objects positioned in the real world. It aims to drive traffic to physical and online destinations, increase product sales and enhance brand engagement within a certain geographic location for a predetermined amount of time. Beauty retailer Sephora created a virtual try-on feature app for lipstick (Pasquarelli 2016). In certain Karl Lagerfeld stores, fitting rooms were equipped with photo booths where consumers could apply filters to their images and share on social media (Retail Week 2014a). In 2014, Topshop partnered with Kinect to create AR fitting rooms, so consumers could virtually try on clothing quickly and easily. AR can also be used for interactive entertainment, for example as Adidas Originals did with their Augmented Reality Game Pack. Adidas turned Originals sneakers into a game control device by adding an AR code on the shoe's tongue. When held in front of a webcam, the code provided access to a number of different interactive games on the Adidas website which the players could navigate with their shoe.

Virtual Reality (VR): This technology comprises a wearable device, typically headgear, which blocks out the real world and immerses the user in a virtual one. Its application to fashion can be seen in a trial by The North Face, which piloted VR in a US concept store, providing consumers with immersive, 360-degree 3D video and audio experiences to mimic extreme outdoor landscapes, such as the Himalayas (Mintel 2016). VR can thus be distinguished from AR, where one or more layers of digital content are overlaid on the real world through an intermediary device: AR allows access to both the virtual and real world. Whilst AR can work with mobile devices, for VR to succeed, the headwear needs to be comfortable, stylish and powered by software that creates credible immersive visual effects. Some fashion brands have directly addressed this requirement. In 2015, French couture house Dior created its own high fashion VR headset equipped with high-definition image resolution and holophonic[1] audio to bring Dior Eyes, an immersive 360° experience of

(continued)

---

[1]Holophonic sound recording was developed by Hugo Zuccarelli in the 1980s and creates a hyper-realistic recorded sound which can stimulate other sensations and smells in the brain that usually accompany that sound.

Dior's runway and craftsmanship, to its boutique visitors (LVMH 2015). However, it raised concerns about whether typical luxury consumers would wear such a conspicuous headset in public, and whether Dior would provide hairdressing and make-up touch-up services once the consumer had taken the headset off. VR's success may depend on more scaled-down headsets, with Facebook founder Mark Zuckerberg predicting that future VR headsets would look like a normal pair of glasses (Lopez 2016).

Developmental trends point to the expansion of interactive shop windows and in-store communication that draw on the combination of GPS, various types of transmitters such as Apple's iBeacon and consumers' own smartphones. These take personalisation and micro-marketing to a new level with real-time offers, new product updates and post-purchase customer support. To support their brand, retailers will increasingly look at their customer relationships, in which stories, images, videos and news-fashion blogs have been particularly successful. These should provide new interactive opportunities, for example the conceptualisation and delivery of immersive scenarios.

The development of VR will involve further trials of devices, content and contexts combined with advances in technologies and retailer expertise. New devices will create more realistic immersive environments and add movement to the user experience. Engagement with the virtual world may be further enhanced through other senses, for example touch and the use of hand controls, for example to pick things up. VR provides an opportunity for consumers to visit retailers' fashion shows, events and exhibitions, and for the retailer to extend the lifespan of selected promotions to individual customers. They no longer have to present a view from a single point in the store, so users will virtually control where they go and what they see and interact with. However, VR is at early stage of implementation, and along with other forms innovative forms of in-store retail technology, may take time to be accepted by consumers (Barclays 2016).

Despite great advances in technological innovation and the potential of current technologies to add value to the omnichannel shopping experience, the success of consumer-facing mobile technologies in retail stores is dependent upon consumer acceptance of and attitudes toward the technology. Levels of acceptance of a technology can predict their actual use and consequently, many different theories about technology acceptance have been developed over time. The following section reviews key theoretical models of technology adoption that may be used to understand consumer adoption of mobile technology and guide retailers' strategic implementation decisions.

5   Theoretical Models of Technology Adoption

User attitude to online shopping can be explained by consumer behaviour theories, and in particular the influential Theory of Reasoned Action (Fishbein and Ajzen 1975), the Theory of Planned Behaviour (Ajzen 1991) and Innovation Diffusion

Theory (Rogers 1962). These became significant in understanding and theorising about technology adoption and its uses, as demonstrated in the Technology Acceptance Model (Davis 1989), the Unified Theory of Acceptance and Use of Technology (Venkatesh et al. 2003) and the Unified Theory of Acceptance and Use of Technology 2 (Venkatesh et al. 2012).

The Theory of Reasoned Action underpins many later theories commonly found in this field (Fishbein and Ajzen 1975). Its central factor is intention, the motivation to perform a behaviour, for example how hard individuals try to perform a given behaviour. The core constructs of attitude toward behaviour and subjective norm determine behavioural intention. Individuals' positive or negative evaluations about performing the behaviour with technology will determine their attitude towards it. The subjective norm is the individual's perception of significant other people's or individual's approval or disapproval about performing the behaviour. If the individual believes these people think they should perform the behaviour, then they are more likely to do so. In the context of social media, online groups and tribes, the theory can help explain why individuals use mobile communications and their behaviour in adopting new technologies, from the behaviour of friends and other social groups.

The Theory of Planned Behaviour (TPB) extends the Theory of Reasoned Action with the addition of perceived behavioural control, which concerns the individual's perception of the ease or difficulty in performing a behaviour, for example learning to use a new technology. It can also vary in different situations and activities. In the TPB perceived behavioural control along with behavioural intention can be used to predict behavioural achievement (Ajzen 1991). With the aim of explaining behaviour, the theory deals with antecedents of behaviour of which the most salient are behavioural, normative (underlying beliefs) and control beliefs. These three beliefs influence behavioural intention, which affects actual behaviour and can determine the extent to which an individual perceives the performance of the behaviour to be easy or difficult. Such perceived external and internal factors act as constraints on behaviour where an underlying foundation of beliefs determines attitudes, subjective norms and perceived behavioural control.

The acceptance of information technologies amongst consumers can be supplemented by an understanding of their diffusion, through the Diffusion of Innovations Theory (Rogers 1962). It provides a consumer-centric explanation of when and how innovations, for example new ideas or technologies, are adopted. Rogers (1962, p. 5) defined diffusion as *"the process by which an innovation is communicated through certain channels over time among the members of a social system"*. An innovation can be an idea, object or practice, and its characteristics explain different rates of adoption by members of a social system:

- Relative advantage: the extent to which the innovation is perceived as better than its predecessors
- Compatibility: the extent to which the technology relates to users existing or future needs
- Trialability: the basis on which an experimenter can experiment with an innovation

- Complexity: the perceived difficult in understanding and using an innovation
- Observability: the extent to which the outcomes of using the innovation can be observed (Rogers 1962, p. 16).

The theory explains communication as part of a two-way process between individuals with time as the third element, from an individual's first knowledge of the innovation, to decision-making and adoption. Finally the social system involves interrelationships in "*joint problem solving to accomplish a common goal*" (Rogers 1962, p. 23). Thus innovations are not adopted outside a social system of leaders, networks and structures, but are defined by and expedited by it. Adopter categories classify members of the social system on the basis of how early they adopt new ideas, and are defined as innovators, early adopters, early majority, late majority and laggards.

The expansion of online retailing through a multiplicity of technologically-enabled channels may disrupt existing business models since technological changes in disruptive innovations present a different set of performance attributes that are either valued by existing customers or that attract new customers. The theory of Disruptive Innovation (Christensen and Tedlow 2000) provides a framework for explaining how technology is often the source of disruptive innovation in service industries, as evidenced by the rise of computers, mobile phones, iKiosks and other electronic devices, which have replaced traditional means of interaction between firms and customers (Padgett and Mulvey 2007). It follows that the expansion of e-channels and e-channel touchpoints have the power to disrupt by fragmenting prevailing modes of online retailing and thus demanding a change of perspective by retailers (Wagner et al. 2015).

The Theory of Reasoned Action (Fishbein and Ajzen 1975) subsequently informed the development of a model to more specifically explain the use of technologies: the Technology Acceptance Model (Davis 1989; Davis et al. 1989). The Technology Acceptance Model (TAM) was originally applied to workplace tasks, rather than consumer behaviour, and in its simplest form shows that a user's perceptions of usefulness and ease of use of a technology determines their attitudes and hence their likelihood to adopt the technology as a way of life (Davis 1989). The user's intention to adopt is determined by their attitude toward using the technology, focusing on general technology perceptions, the direct and indirect adoption drivers. The direct adoption drivers are perceived usefulness (PU) and perceived ease of use (PEOU) whilst the indirect adoption drivers refer to external variables (Li et al. 2012).

The model has been used widely to predict individuals' behavioural intention to buy and use a particular piece of technology (Ko et al. 2009), and has been applied to the acceptance of online retailing (O'Cass and Fenech 2003) and m-commerce (Wu and Wang 2005). TAM has been continually re-developed and new factors added to reflect the increasing adoption of the internet and continuing evolution of online retailing. Thus, factors such as trust, enjoyment, intrinsic and extrinsic motivation, and human and social change process variables have been applied in more recent iterations of the model, namely the TAM2 (Venkatesh and Davis 2000) and the TAM3 (Venkatesh and Bala 2008). These new factors reflect the combination of hedonic as well as utilitarian motivations, which influence consumer behaviour.

Further theoretical development through the synthesis of technology usage models and the need for greater parsimony led to the Unified Theory of Acceptance and Use of Technology (UTAUT) (Venkatesh et al. 2003). The generalisability of the theory has been used and verified in other contexts and cultural settings to investigate different types of technologies. The UTAUT has four key constructs that influence behavioural intention and actual use of technology:

Performance expectancy is the degree to which the use of technology helps consumers perform certain activities;

Effort expectancy is the ease of using the technology;

Social influence is the extent to which consumers believe that important others think they should use a particular technology;

Facilitating conditions refer to consumers' perceptions of the resources and support available to perform the behaviour (Venkatesh et al. 2003; Al-Qeisi et al. 2014).

Venkatesh et al. (2012) extended the UTAUT by incorporating constructs related to consumer behaviour, creating the UTAUT2 model that scales technology acceptance in terms of mobile internet in a consumer context. UTAUT2 has been applied in a multitude of different contexts including mobile phone technology, mobile learning, mobile payments and online gaming. The consumer behaviour related constructs were hedonic motivation, cost and habit. Hedonic motivation has been found to detrimentally affect consumer products and technology use (Brown and Venkatesh 2005; Nysveen et al. 2005). Habit was introduced, and appears in other theories of behaviour (notably Triandis's (1977) Theory of Interpersonal Behaviour) because it admits lower levels of consciousness to explain and predict social behaviour. It has been found to predict technology use in multiple consumer contexts (Venkatesh et al. 2012).

6   Discussion

Adoption and use of the internet, computers, mobile devices and services have formed the focus of different strands of research using these theories and models. For online shopping, TAM has been used to research attitudes and behaviours concerning the question of *"how online shopping gained prevalence"* (Eroglu 2014, p. 37) and investigations into the confidence of consumers' acceptance of e-commerce, perceived risk, usability, and usefulness (Pavlou 2003). More generally TAM has been used to examine factors, which influence information gathering and consumer behaviour towards online marketing (Eroglu 2014). In these activities, the quality of a website and its design, including access, navigation and speed can determine its usefulness, adoption and acceptance (Al-Qeisi et al. 2014). For smartphones, websites need to successfully scale down to fit the smaller size of screen to avoid problems with access and navigation, while speed is in part determined by the device but also the availability and quality of connectivity to the internet. This aspect is addressed through the increasing provision of in-store Wi-Fi and the expansion of the web and 4G mobile network technology. However, other in-store factors contribute to consumers' intention to engage with technologies, including their perceived ability to interact with technologies, anxiety, level of self-consciousness, and desire for innovation (Stuart 2013). These factors suggest that increasing familiarity and confidence with personal and retailer-based technologies will result in more consumers interacting with retail brands through a diversity of touchpoints.

With the m-channel, TAM explains how mobile technology will be adopted primarily because of its ease of use and usefulness (Ko et al. 2009). In particular, the model has shown that perceived usefulness is a strong determinant of user acceptance and usage behaviour (Kim and Garrison 2009). Many TAM studies consider that usefulness may reflect the rational benefits of an information technology and the expected positive outcomes obtained (Hernández et al. 2010). Utilitarian motivations such as convenience, the width of the product assortment and 24/7 availability mainly determine the intention to buy online.

In addition, the m-channel has other valuable adoption qualities because of "value-for-time" to users (Clarke 2008, p. 41) such as ubiquity, convenience, localisation and personalisation. Perceived Ubiquity and Perceived Reachability are later additions to m-commerce research, where Perceived Ubiquity refers to the perception of the extent to which the mobile channel provides personalised and uninterrupted connection and communications between individuals and networks (Kim and Garrison 2009). Perceived Reachability is an individual's perception of engaging with other individuals 'anytime and anywhere' (Kim and Garrison 2009). These elements are evident in the extensive adoption of smartphones, new product development in hardware and software, and higher internet access speeds. In particular, the growth of social media has enabled more personalised and interactive communication between brands and consumers to take place.

The effects over time are important, as most consumers when using a specific computer system will change their perception of ease of use (Wu and Wang 2005). During the adoption phase, less experienced customers may base their perception on a relatively superficial knowledge of the features, which may easily change. More experienced customers have a stronger perception of ease of use, as previous experience of technology adoption reduces uncertainty and increases the ability to use a new medium (Rice and Katz 2003). In the later post-adoption phase, past experiences are important in perceptions of ease of use (Hernández et al. 2010).

The effects of other people and technologies on adoption are clearly significant; external factors may determine how and why an individual uses mobile technologies. Social influence plays a part in adopting an innovation and has an effect on consumer's intention to engage with innovative technology (Kulviwat et al. 2007). Fashion stores provide physical and through their online connectivity, digital channels to communicate with a social system of fashion consumers. Diffusion may depend on the role of functionally similar technologies. In particular, technology clusters help to distinguish boundaries for technology adoption (Rogers 1962) and innovations diffusing at the same time are often interdependent. Communication technology research tends to examine one technology in isolation, even though people tend to use functionally similar innovations (Sawhney 2007). Both the social dimension and the interdependence of innovations can be seen in the diffusion of smartphones and tablets, and may be used to assess the acceptance and diffusion of the emerging technologies of VR and AR. Both applications are at an earlier stage of development and adoption. Consequently their relative advantage is less clear and trialability is limited by device design, technologies and availability.

7 Conclusions for Practice

Consumer-facing mobile technologies provide a personal and accessible way for retailers to integrate their brands through digital and physical retail channels. For consumers, this enhances their shopping experience and provides retailers with valuable data to better target consumers in a more personalised way. However, consumers' perceptual barriers such as trust and privacy issues can result in resistance to adopt the technology, notwithstanding its potential for adding value to their shopping experience. Retailers should therefore seek to address consumer concerns by providing greater transparency on security and privacy issues, and ensuring there is a sufficient value exchange to encourage consumers to share their data while minimising risks to their security.

8 Conclusions for Academia and Future Research Directions

Extended versions of classic theoretical models help to explain adoption, use and perceived benefits of consumer-facing mobile technologies. In a dynamic and fast-changing area, it is almost certain that further iterations of the classic models will be developed to reflect the 'new normal' of consumer behaviour in an omnichannel world. Consumer-facing mobile technologies clearly contribute to omnichannel integration and provide utilitarian as well as hedonic benefits to shoppers. However, it is difficult to generalise conclusions across all types of mobile technologies, due to their unique characteristics, benefits and challenges. There is a need to more clearly understand the consumer and retailer perceived value of some of the newer technologies that have entered the retail sector, such as AR and VR. Future research could also extend the subject area beyond existing consumer-based studies by exploring managerial perspectives on integration of mobile technologies in the physical store by considering, for example, whether these technologies are considered to be primarily revenue-generating, brand image building or a tool for marketing communications.

Questions for Discussion and Review

1. Explain the various forms of consumer-facing mobile technology which currently exist in the fashion retail sector.
2. From a consumer perspective, compare and contrast the benefits and disadvantages of various forms of in-store mobile technology.
3. From a retailer perspective, discuss the benefits, disadvantages and risks of various forms of in-store mobile technology.
4. How do in-store mobile technologies contribute to omnichannel retailing?
5. Which elements of the Technology Acceptance Model could help to explain consumer adoption of in-store mobile technologies?
6. How have the theoretical models been adapted over time, to reflect the changing technology landscape?
7. How are in-store mobile technologies utilised in different levels of the fashion retail market? For example, compare and contrast their use in mid-market and luxury retailers.
8. Observe the in-store mobile technologies used by a selection of retailers on your local high street or shopping centre. Compare and contrast their effectiveness for each retailer's target consumer.

References

Accenture. (2013). *Who are the Millennial shoppers? And what do they really want?* Accessed Nov 1, 2016 from https://www.accenture.com/us-en/insight-outlook-who-are-millennial-shoppers-what-do-they-really-want-retail

Adler, C. (2013). *The iPad effect: How to unite physical and digital worlds.* Accessed Nov 1, 2016 from http://www.ft.com/cms/s/0/7b7d8f1a-598e-11e2-ae03-00144feab49a.html#axzz2IiLUql43

Ajzen, I. (1991). The theory of planned behaviour. *Organizational Behaviour and Human Decision Processes, 50,* 179–211.

Albrecht, K., & McIntyre, L. (2015). Protect yourself from RFID: Fend off frightening tracking tech. *Consumer Electronics Magazine, IEEE, 4*(2), 95–96.

Alexander, E. (2012). *Burberry opens Regent Street flagship.* Accessed Nov 1, 2016 from http://www.vogue.co.uk/gallery/burberry-regent-street-flagship-opens

Al-Qeisi, K., Dennis, C., Alamanos, E., & Jayawardhena, C. (2014). Website design quality and usage behaviour: Unified theory of acceptance and use of technology. *Journal of Business Research, 67*(11), 2282–2290.

Antéblian, B., Filser, M., & Roederer, C. (2014). Consumption experience in retail environments: A literature review. *Recherche et Applications en Marketing, 28*(3), 82–109.

Arthur, C. (2014). *Apps more popular than the mobile web, data shows.* Accessed Nov 1, 2016 from https://www.theguardian.com/technology/appsblog/2014/apr/02/apps-more-popular-than-the-mobile-web-data-shows

Arthur, R. (2015). *British brands enabling fans to shop real-time #LFW trends by leveraging outdoor advertising.* Accessed Nov 1, 2016 from http://www.forbes.com/sites/rachelarthur/2015/02/17/british-brands-enabling-fans-to-shop-real-time-lfw-trends-by-leveraging-outdoor-advertising/#441f55132356

Ascharya, K. (2016). *See how Burberry turns its stores into immersive websites – The results will amaze you.* Accessed Nov 1, 2016 from http://2machines.com/179111/

Aubrey, C., & Judge, D. (2012). Re-imagine retail: Why store innovation is key to a brand's growth in the 'new normal', digitally-connected and transparent world. *Journal of Brand Strategy, 1*(1), 31–39.

Barclays. (2016). *The new retail reality*. London: Barclays.

Beck, N., & Rygl, D. (2015). Categorization of multiple channel retailing in multi-, cross-, and omni-channel retailing for retailers and retailing. *Journal of Retailing and Consumer Services, 27*, 170–178.

Bellman, S., Potter, R. F., Treleaven-Hassard, S., Robinson, J. A., & Varan, D. (2011). The effectiveness of branded mobile phone apps. *Journal of Interactive Marketing, 25*, 191–200.

Berman, S. J. (2012). Digital transformation: Opportunities to create new business models. *Strategy and Leadership, 40*(2), 16–24.

Blázquez, M. (2014). Fashion shopping in multichannel retail: The role of technology in enhancing the customer experience. *International Journal of Electronic Commerce, 18*(4), 97–116.

Boeck, H., Roy, J., Durif, F., & Gregoire, M. (2011). The effect of perceived intrusion on consumers' attitude towards using an RFID-based marketing program. *Procedia Computer Science, 5*, 841–848.

Brown, S. A., & Venkatesh, V. (2005). Model of adoption of technology in households: A baseline model test and extension incorporating household life cycle. *MIS Quarterly, 29*(3), 399–426.

Brynjolfsson, E., Hu, Y. J., & Rahman, M. (2013). Competing in the age of omnichannel retailing. *MIT Sloan Management Review, 54*(4), 23–29.

Carroll, D., & Guzman, I. (2015). *The new omnichannel approach to serving customers*. Accenture.

Chaffey, D., & Ellis-Chadwick, F. (2015). *Digital marketing: Strategy, implementation and practice*. Pearson.

Chan, L. (2017). *The world's largest Zara store has opened and its incredible*. Accessed May 1, 2017 from http://www.elle.my/fashion/News/Largest-Zara-store-in-the-world-has-opened-and-its-incredible

Christensen, C. M., & Tedlow, R. S. (2000). Patterns of disruption in retailing. *Harvard Business Review, 78*(1), 42–45.

Clarke, I. (2008). Emerging value propositions for m-commerce. *Journal of Business Strategies, 25*(2), 41–57.

Datoo, S. (2014). *How tracking customers in-store will soon be the norm*. Accessed Nov 1, 2016 from http://www.theguardian.com/technology/datablog/2014/jan/10/how-tracking-customers-in-store-will-soon-be-the-norm

Davis, F. D. (1989). Perceived usefulness, perceived ease of use, and user acceptance of information technology. *MIS Quarterly, 13*(3), 319–340.

Davis, F. D., Bagozzi, R. P., & Warshaw, P. R. (1989). User acceptance of computer technology: A comparison of two theoretical models. *Management Science, 35*, 982–1003.

eConsultancy. (2016). *Digital transformation in the retail sector*. Accessed Nov 1, 2016 from https://econsultancy.com/reports/digital-transformation-in-the-retail-sector/

eMarketer. (2014a). *UK males are far more likely to scan QR codes*. Accessed Nov 1, 2016 from https://www.emarketer.com/Article/UK-Males-Far-More-Likely-Scan-QR-Codes/1010568

eMarketer. (2014b). *Smartphones are in-store shopping companions*. Accessed Nov 1, 2016 https://www.emarketer.com/Article/Smartphones-In-Store-Shopping-Companions/1010800

eMarketer. (2016). *UK trust in smartphone wallets stuck in stasis*. Accessed Nov 1, 2016 from https://www.emarketer.com/Article/UK-Trust-Smartphone-Wallets-Stuck-Stasis/1013712 ()

Eroglu, E. (2014). The changing shopping culture: Internet consumer behaviour. *Review of Business Information Systems, 18*(1), 35–40.

Euclid Analytics. (2016). *Wi-Fi is on the rise*. Accessed Nov 1, 2016 from http://www.euclidanalytics.com

Fishbein, M., & Ajzen, I. (1975). *Belief, attitude, intention, and behaviour*. Reading, MA: Addison-Wesley.

Fujitsu. (2016). *Shopping in the real world: Is the physical store dead?* London: Fujitsu.

Giorgetti, L. (2014). *QR codes in fashion retail: East versus West*. Accessed Nov 1, 2016 from http://fashionbi.com/insights/marketing-analysis/qr-codes-in-fashion-retail-east-versus-west

Google. (2013). *Shopping then and now: Five ways retail has changed and how businesses can adapt*. Accessed Nov 1, 2016 from http://www.google.com/think/articles/five-ways-retailhas-changed-and-how-businesses-can-adapt.html

Greenwald, M. (2015). *7 of the best strategic uses of consumer-facing tech in retail & hospitality*. Accessed November 1, 2016, from http://www.forbes.com/sites/michellegreenwald/2015/05/18/7-of-the-best-strategic-uses-of-consumer-facing-tech-in-retail-hospitality/#2715e4857a0b572daed95ade

Henry, A. (2013). *How retail stores track you using your smartphone (and how to stop it)*. Accessed Nov 1, 2016 from http://lifehacker.com/how-retail-stores-track-you-using-your-smartphone-and-827512308

Hernández, B., Jiménez, J., & Martín, M. J. (2010). Customer behaviour in electronic commerce: The moderating effect of e-purchasing experience. *Journal of Business Research, 63*(9–10), 964–971.

Holmes, A., Byrne, A., & Rowley, J. (2013). Mobile shopping behaviour: Insights into attitudes, shopping process involvement and location. *International Journal of Retail and Distribution Management, 42*(1), 25–39.

Kansara, V. A. (2013). *Topshop and Google plan data-savvy digital runway*. Accessed Nov 1, 2016 from https://www.businessoffashion.com/articles/fashion-tech/fashion-2-0-topshop-and-google-plan-data-savvy-digital-runway

Kearney, A. T. (2012). *Engaging multichannel consumers*. Accessed Nov 1, 2016 from https://www.atkearney.com/documents/10192/666269/Engaging+Multichannel+Consumers.pdf

Kent, A. (2007). Creative space: Design and the retail environment. *International Journal of Retail and Distribution Management, 35*(9), 734–745.

Kent, A., & Schwarz, E. (2015). The role of mobile devices within the customers' shopping journey in the omnichannel environment of UK fashion high-street retailers. In *Proceedings of the 18th EAERCD Conference*, Rennes.

Kent, A., Vianello, M., Blazquez-Cano, M., & Schwarz, E. (2016). Omnichannel fashion retail and channel integration: The case of department stores. In A. Vecchi & C. Buckley (Eds.), *Handbook of research on global fashion management and merchandising* (pp. 398–419). Hershey, PA: IGI Global.

Kim, S., & Garrison, G. (2009). Investigating mobile wireless technology adoption: An extension of the technology acceptance model. *Information System Frontiers, 11*, 323–333.

Kim, E., Lin, J.-S., & Sung, Y. (2013). To app or not to app: Engaging consumers via branded mobile apps. *Journal of Interactive Advertising, 13*(1), 53–65.

Ko, E., Kim, E. Y., & Lee, E. K. (2009). Modeling consumer adoption of mobile shopping for fashion products in Korea. *Journal of Psychology and Marketing, 26*(7), 669–687.

Kowatsch, T., & Maas, W. (2010). In-store consumer behaviour: How mobile recommendation agents influence usage intentions, product purchases, and store preferences. *Computers in Human Behaviour, 26*(4), 697–704.

Kozinets, R. V., Sherry, J. F., DeBerry-Spence, B., Duhachek, A., Nuttavuthisit, K., & Storm, D. (2002). Themed flagship brand stores in the new millennium: Theory, practice, prospects. *Journal of Retailing, 78*(1), 17–29.

Kulviwat, S., Bruner, G. C., Kumar, A., Nasco, S. A., & Clark, T. (2007). Toward a Unified theory of consumer acceptance technology. *Psychology and Marketing, 24*(12), 1059–1084.

Kurutz, S. (2015). *For brands like Toms, it's all about the experience*. Accessed Nov 1, 2016 from http://www.nytimes.com/2015/11/15/fashion/for-brands-like-toms-its-all-about-the-experience.html

Lee, L., Meyer, T., & Smith, J. S. (2012). *Reinventing the customer experience: Technology and the service marketing mix, in Service Management* (pp. 143–160). New York: Springer.

Li, M., Dong, Z. Y., & Chen, X. (2012). Factors influencing consumption experience of mobile commerce: A study from experiential view. *Internet Research, 22*(2), 120–141.

Lopez, N. (2016). *Facebook says VR headsets will look like Ray-Bans in 10 years.* Accessed Nov 1, 2016 from http://thenextweb.com/facebook/2016/04/12/facebook-says-will-vr-headsets-size-normal-glasses-next-10-years/#gref

Lunden, I. (2014). *Shopkick starts 100-store iBeacon trial for American Eagle, biggest apparel rollout yet.* Accessed Nov 1, 2016 from http://techcrunch.com/2014/01/16/shopkick-starts-100-store-ibeacon-trial-for-american-eagle-outfitters-the-biggest-apparel-rollout-yet

LVMH. (2015). *Dior creates its own virtual reality headset.* Accessed Nov 1, 2016 from https://www.lvmh.com/news-documents/news/dior-creates-its-own-virtual-reality-headset/

Magrath, V., & McCormick, H. (2013). Marketing design elements of mobile fashion retail apps. *Journal of Fashion Marketing and Management, 17*(1), 115–134.

Maycotte, H. O. (2015). *Beacon technology: The where, what, who, how and why.* Accessed Nov 1, 2016 from http://www.forbes.com/sites/homaycotte/2015/09/01/beacontechnology-the-what-who-how-why-and-where/

McCormick, H., Cartwright, J., Perry, P., Barnes, L., Lynch, S., & Ball, G. (2014). Fashion retailing – Past, present and future. *Textile Progress, 46*(3), 227–321.

Milnes, H. (2015). *Elle uses beacon technology to drive 500,000 retail store visits.* Accessed Nov 1, 2016 from http://digiday.com/publishers/elle-uses-beacon-technology-drive-500000-retail-store-visits/

Mintel. (2016). *Fashion: Technology and innovation.* London: Mintel Group.

Napolitano, B. (2013). *Omnichannel distribution: Moving at the speed of now.* Warehouse/DC Management, WMS Update, June.

Nielsen. (2013). *A mobile shopper's journey: From the couch to the store (and back again).* Accessed Nov 1, 2016 from http://www.nielsen.com/us/en/newswire/2013/a-mobile-shoppers-journey%2D%2Dfrom-the-couch-to-the-store%2D%2Dand-back.html

Nielsen. (2016). *Shop til they drop . . . or at least until their thumbs hurt: Getting to know mobile shoppers.* Accessed May 1, 2017 from http://www.nielsen.com/us/en/insights/news/2016/shop-til-they-drop-or-at-least-until-their-thumbs-hurt-getting-to-know-mobile-shoppers.html

Nomi. (2016). *Case Studies.* Accessed Nov 1, 2016 from http://www.nomi.com/resources/case-studies/

Nysveen, H., Pedersen, P. E., & Thorbjørnsen, H. (2005). Intentions to use mobile services: Antecedents and cross-service comparisons. *Journal of the Academy of Marketing Science, 33*(3), 330–346.

O'Cass, A., & Fenech, T. (2003). Web retailing adoption: Exploring the nature of internet users web retailing behaviour. *Journal of Retailing and Consumer Services, 10,* 81–94.

Padgett, D., & Mulvey, M. S. (2007). Differentiation via technology: Strategic positioning of services following the introduction of disruptive technology. *Journal of Retailing, 83*(4), 375–391.

Pantano, E. (2015). *Successful technological integration for competitive advantage in retail settings.* Hershey, PA: IGI Global.

Pasquarelli, A. (2016). *Why retailers are missing out on mobile with Millennials.* Accessed November 1, 2016, from http://adage.com/article/digital/retailers-missing-mobile-millennials/302755/

Pavlou, P. A. (2003). Consumer acceptance of electronic commerce: Integrating trust and risk with the technology acceptance model. *International Journal of Electronic Commerce, 7*(3), 101–134.

Piotrowicz, W., & Cuthbertson, R. (2014). Introduction to the special issue: Information technology in retail: Toward omnichannel retailing. *International Journal of Electronic Commerce, 18*(4), 5–16.

Purcell, K., Entner, R., & Henderson, N. (2010). *The rise of apps culture.* Accessed Nov 1, 2016 from http://www.pewinternet.org/2010/09/14/the-rise-of-apps-culture/

PWC. (2012). *Retailing 2020: Winning in a polarized world.* Accessed Nov 1, 2016 from http://www.pwc.com/us/en/retail-consumer/publications/assets/pwc-retailing-2020.pdf

Retail Week. (2014a). *Fashion retailing in an omnichannel world.* Accessed Nov 1, 2016 from http://guides.retail-week.com/147.guide

Retail Week. (2014b). *Connecting with today's fashion consumers: Digital marketing innovations in the retail sector.*

Rice, R. E., & Katz, J. E. (2003). Comparing Internet and mobile phone usage: Digital divides of usage, adoption, and dropouts. *Telecommunications Policy, 27,* 597–623.

Rogers, E. M. (1962). *Diffusion of innovations.* New York: The Free Press.

RSR. (2016). *Mobile in retail: The new normal: Benchmark Report 2016, Retail Systems Research LLC.*

Sawhney, H. (2007). Strategies for increasing the conceptual yield of new technologies research. *Communication Monographs, 74,* 395–401.

Severs, J. (2013). *Analysis: How can retailers prepare for the mobile revolution?* Accessed Nov 1, 2016 from http://www.retail-week.com/multichannel/analysis-how-can-retailers-prepare-for-the-mobile-revolution/5053033.article

ShopperTrak. (2016). *Our customers.* Accessed Nov 1, 2016 from http://www.shoppertrak.com/our-customers/

Skeldon, P. (2014). *Ralph Lauren connects shoppers through mobile with iconic Harrods window display.* Accessed Nov 1, 2016 from http://internetretailing.new2014/ralph-lauren-connects-shoppers-through-mobile-with-iconic-harrods-window-display/

Smith, G. (2015). *Zara is going to install iPads in its changing rooms.* Accessed Nov 1, 2016 from http://fortune.com/2015/12/01/zara-is-going-to-install-ipads-in-its-changing-rooms/

Statcounter. (2016). *Mobile and tablet internet usage exceeds desktop for first time worldwide.* Accessed Nov 1, 2016 from http://gs.statcounter.com/press/mobile-and-tablet-internet-usage-exceeds-desktop-for-first-time-worldwide#g1

Stuart, R. (2013). *An analysis of the antecedents to and dimensions of consumption experience in fashion stores.* Unpublished thesis. The University of Manchester, Manchester.

Triandis, H. C. (1977). *Interpersonal behaviour.* Monterey, CA: Brooks/Cole.

Turri, A. M., Smith, R. J., & Kopp, S. W. (2017). Privacy and RFID technology: A review of regulatory efforts. *Journal of Consumer Affairs.* https://doi.org/10.1111/joca.12133.

Ustundag, A., & Tanyas, M. (2009). The impacts of radio frequency identification (RFID) technology on supply chain costs. *Transportation Research Part E: Logistics and Transportation Review, 45*(1), 29–38.

Venkatesh, V., & Bala, H. (2008). Technology acceptance model 3 and a research agenda on interventions. *Decision Sciences, 39*(2), 273–315.

Venkatesh, V., & Davis, F. D. (2000). A theoretical extension of the technology acceptance model: Four longitudinal field studies. *Management Science, 46*(2), 186–204.

Venkatesh, V., Morris, M. G., Davis, G. B., & Davis, F. D. (2003). User acceptance of information technology: Toward a unified view. *MIS Quarterly, 27*(3), 425–478.

Venkatesh, V., Thong, J. Y. L., & Xu, X. (2012). Consumer acceptance and use of information technology: Extending the unified theory of acceptance and use of technology. *MIS Quarterly, 36*(1), 157–178.

Verdict. (2013). *Mobile and tablet retailing in the UK: Mobile device shopping journey.* London: Verdict.

Verhoef, P. C., Kannan, P. K., & Inman, J. J. (2015). From multi-channel retailing to omni-channel retailing: Introduction to the special issue on multi-channel retailing. *Journal of Retailing, 91*(2), 174–181.

Verhoef, P. C., Lemon, K. N., Parasuraman, A., Roggeveen, A., Tsiro, M., & Schlesinger, L. A. (2009). Customer experience creation: Determinants, dynamics and management strategies. *Journal of Retailing, 85*(1), 31–41.

Wagner, G., Schramm-Kleine, H., & Steinmann, S. (2015). E-tailing in a connected devices world: A review and research agenda. *Proceedings of the 18th EAERCD Conference,* Rennes.

Wu, J.-H., & Wang, S.-C. (2005). What drives mobile commerce? An empirical evaluation of the revised technology acceptance model. *Information and Management, 42,* 719–729.

Zaryouni, H. (2015). *Behind digital genius Burberry: Mobile, social, personal.* Accessed November 1, 2016, from http://www.l2inc.com/burberry-mobile-social/2015/blog

Patsy Perry is a Senior Lecturer in Fashion Marketing in the School of Materials at The University of Manchester. She has industry experience in retailing and market research, and gained her PhD in Corporate Social Responsibility in fashion supply chains from Heriot-Watt University in 2012. Since then, her research interests have expanded to fashion ecommerce and the application of digital technology to online fashion retailing, and she was awarded ESRC funding in 2013 for her project on the application of gestural interactivity technology to online fashion retail. She has presented her work at a number of international conferences including the European Marketing Academy Conference, Academy of Marketing Science, Fashion Colloquia and the Global Fashion Management Conference. She has published a number of book chapters and papers in academic journals including the Journal of Business Ethics, the Journal of Business Research, Computers in Human Behavior and the Journal of Fashion Marketing and Management, and she currently supervises PhD and DBA students in the areas of digital fashion marketing and retailing, luxury consumption and ethical consumer behaviour.

Anthony Kent is Professor of Fashion Marketing at Nottingham Trent University. He holds a degree in Modern History from Oxford University, an MBA, and PhD from the University of the Arts London. He began his career in the shoe industry as a graduate with K Shoes before moving into the retail industry. His current research interests are in the convergence between digital and physical environments with a focus on fashion retailing, and his second area of interest is in design management, where he is currently working on the personalisation of design and the marketing of smart textiles. Professor Kent has delivered academic papers at a wide range of conferences including Fashion Colloquia, Design Management International, the British Academy of Management and the International Foundation for Fashion Technology Institutions, where he won the senior research prize at their annual conference in 2015 in Florence, Italy. His most recent publication is the edited book 'Retail Design: Theoretical Perspectives' published by Routledge in January 2017.

Francesca Bonetti is a PhD Researcher in fashion retailing and consumer-facing technology in the School of Materials at The University of Manchester. She is also a part-time Lecturer in Fashion Marketing at London College of Fashion, University of the Arts London. Her research interests focus on the digital transformation of retailing and her PhD explores the adoption of consumer-facing technologies in fashion retail settings from a managerial perspective. Her interests also include luxury fashion retailing in China and the consumption of fashion goods by Asian consumers. She has international industry experience in marketing communications and business development in the fashion and apparel sector and consults for fashion brands and retailers on retailing and wholesaling, communications strategies and the use of consumer-facing technology across retail channels. She was awarded her Master's Degree in Marketing with Distinction from the University of St Andrews in 2012. She can be contacted by email at francesca.bonetti@postgrad.manchester.ac.uk

Futurising the Physical Store in the Omnichannel Retail Environment

Bethan Alexander and Marta Blazquez Cano

Abstract This chapter aims to gain a better understanding of the role that the physical store plays in the current multichannel offering and the expected omnichannel evolution of the format in the near future, from an industry perspective. This chapter has two main objectives: firstly, to explore the current situation of the physical store format in terms of experience, integration with other channels, the role of technology, and consumer' expectations; secondly, to establish relevant guidelines regarding the future evolution of the format. Interviews with industry experts enabled rich data on the topic to be collected, analysed, and presented. The work confirms that the role of the physical store so far seems to be evolving from places for transaction to places for interaction in which the different channels of the retailer come together via the technology. This challenges the traditional notions of retail format, retail place, and retail design.

1 Introduction

The retail scene has considerably changed in the last few years due to the growth of online retail and ongoing digitalisation (Verhoef et al. 2015) with consequences in the role that the physical store plays in the omnichannel scenario. While some experts state that the number of physical stores will diminish and many will become mere showrooms (Rigby 2011; Retail Week 2014) other voices situate the physical store as the focus of the brand experience and the point of integration of the different channels of the company. The reality is that the role of the physical store is being redefined but the future evolution of the format is uncertain. In the omnichannel environment, the store is considered as part of a bigger and more connected shopping experience, which involves the delivery of an integrated and seamless experience

B. Alexander (✉)
Fashion Business School, London College of Fashion, University of the Arts, London, UK
e-mail: b.alexander@fashion.arts.ac.uk

M. B. Cano
School of Materials, University of Manchester, Manchester, UK

without considering e-commerce and the physical store as separate channels (Cao and Li 2015). While a considerable amount of industry research has explored the evolution of physical formats, there is still a lack of academic research that addresses this issue.

In order to provide more insight into the process, this research aims to gain a better understanding about the role that the physical store plays in the current multichannel offering and the expected evolution of the format in the near future into omnichannel, from an industry perspective. This chapter conveys two main objectives: firstly, to explore the current situation of the physical store format in terms of experience, integration with other channels, role of technology and consumer' expectations; secondly, to establish relevant guidelines about the future evolution of the format. Interviews with industry experts enabled rich data on the topic to be collected, analysed and presented.

The chapter is structured as follows. First, the literature review provides the academic and industry background about the issues considered. Then, the methodology that guided the data collection is briefly explained followed by the results and discussion. Finally, conclusions and recommendations are stated.

2 Literature Review

2.1 The Role of the Physical Store in the Omnichannel Scenario

In the UK, the total clothing market (including womenswear, menswear, childrenswear and accessories) is currently valued at £44.2 billion and expected to reach £55.9 billion by 2021 with online sales accounting for £10 billion or 22.6% of total clothing spending in 2016 (Verdict 2016). The increasing growth of online channels has resulted in many retailers embracing multi-channel strategies that include aspects such as the integration of the retail mix across channels or the consideration of the consumer experience across those channels (Verhoef et al. 2015; Neslin and Shankar 2009). Not just e-commerce but the development of mobile technology has created another important change in the retail environment, changing consumer behaviour and expectations (Rigby 2011; Brynjolfsson et al. 2013).

The current retail scenario is dominated by the so called multichannel retailers who need to manage their different channels altogether and create a compelling experience for consumers. Some of the issues involved are the development of specific strategies to design the shopping experience and build relationships with customers (Brynjolfsson et al. 2013). In fact, multichannel has evolved to "omnichannel" to designate those retailers that offer an integrated sales experience and are able to interact with customers through multiple channels offering an interaction with the brand more than with the channels (Rigby 2011; Piotrowicz and Cuthbertson 2014). The most recent conceptualization of the term defines omnichannel retailing as *"the set of activities involved in selling merchandise or services through more than one channel or all widespread channels, whereby the customer can trigger full channel interaction and/or the retailer controls full channel integration"* (Beck and Rygl 2015, p. 175). When the consumer can trigger just partial interaction or the retailer controls just part of channel integration the authors talk about "cross-channel" retail.

One of the main drivers for channel interaction and integration in the physical store which includes Click and Collect services, that allows the ability to order goods online and return or exchange them in-store (Piotrowicz and Cuthbertson 2014). The availability and promotion of specific Click and Collect service points indicate their emergence as a significant interface with customers (Kent et al. 2015). Their location ranges from not having a specific place and using the regular check-out points to having specific areas designed for Click and Collect. In the latter, some retailers reserve a specific space to collect online orders prioritizing the utilitarian aspects of the experience, whilst others such as Harvey Nichols, claim their intention to take *"Click and Collect to another level, and create a luxury experience for the consumer"* (Deveaux 2014, p. 5). Westfield's Collect+ @ Westfield Lounge exemplifies this shift to an elevated experience, offering a luxurious environment with fitting rooms for customers to collect and try on their purchases from over 260 retailers in one place (Bearne 2014). There is a lack of specific research about the advantages and disadvantages of the different options, which makes it an issue worth investigating.

The provision of free Wi-Fi network access in the physical store is another key element to facilitate channel integration especially considering that mobiles are currently redefining the in-store experience (Blázquez 2014). Wi-Fi connects with an important dimension of the experience that is the social experience (Kent et al. 2015). That way, it enables co-created services but it is under developed in co-creating social communities and accessing social communities.

Wi-Fi is an important facilitator of 'showrooming' which refers to the type of consumer behaviour that consists of gathering information through a physical store but buying the product online (Mehra et al. 2013) and is becoming increasingly popular (Neslin et al. 2014). Rapp et al. (2015, p. 360) define showrooming as *"a practice whereby consumers visit a brick and mortar store to (1) evaluate products/ services first hand and (2) use mobile technology while in-store to compare products for potential purchase via any number of channels"*. The availability of online connectivity and mobile devices to get access to the Internet makes the information about the product readily available (Mehra et al. 2013). As a consequence, the use of the physical store as a purely information channel has increased. But the reverse showrooming, known as webrooming, also exists and involves doing the research online and purchasing the product in the physical store (Bell et al. 2014). Showrooming is strongly related with the quality of the experience provided in the physical store, which will be considered next.

2.2 The Store Experience

With the evolution of the retail sector the physical store is not just a point for transaction anymore. It has become a place for interaction and entertainment through the creation of an experiential setting.

From an experiential perspective, the point of sale is defined as the space where the interaction between the firm and the customer takes place; a cognitive and emotional scenario where emotional change can occur. The physical store must create value for customers and generate brand awareness (Russo Spena et al. 2012). The store atmosphere is the result of the layout and the environment and has an important influence on consumers' shopping behaviour (Parsons 2011). The layout of the store acts as a signal of store intentions for consumers and has a strong influence on the perception gained about the rest of the environment (Ballantine et al. 2010). The store design must be able to translate the brand identity from the products and services into the customer experience (Jones et al. 2010). That way, both layout and staff, draw customers into the brand experience.

Customer service is one of the most influential reasons to go to a physical setting where consumers expect a more personal shopping experience through engaging with a staff member in the store (Bäckström and Johansson 2006; Drapers 2015). However, employees can act as an inhibitor factor if consumers feel pressure when interacting with products. Accordingly, factors such as the location of employees or the use of technologies to assist customer service must be considered (Puccinelli et al. 2009; Ballantine et al. 2010). A relationship has been established between consumers' showrooming behaviour and retail salesperson performance in the way that the perception of consumers' showrooming behaviour leads to a decrease of salesperson's performance which can be overcome through cross-selling strategies that will diminish the impact of showrooming on sales performance (Rapp et al. 2015). The relationship with staff is one of the social elements of the physical store, another is the connection with other consumers that fulfil certain social needs and have a positive overall effect on consumers (Bäckström and Johansson 2006).

The store environment creates a holistic cognitive experience that must be emotionally engaging based on entertainment, design, customer involvement, and sensory attributes (Rigby 2011; Russo Spena et al. 2012). It must inspire consumers through the presentation of products in interesting and stimulating ways (Bäckström and Johansson 2006). This is especially evident in the fashion sector due to its symbolic properties related to consumers' personal image and self-concept (Levy 1959). However, Bäckström and Johansson (2006) found that while retailers are focused in providing a hedonic store experience, understood in the perceived entertainment and emotional worth provided through shopping activities (Babin et al. 1994), consumers seem motivated by more utilitarian and practical issues. So both sides, hedonic and utilitarian, must be considered when designing the store experience.

In relation to the use of sensory cues, it must be consistent and congruent in order to offer optimal levels of stimulation and a more pleasant shopping experience

(Spence et al. 2014). One of the best examples in the use of multisensory store settings is the use of 'experience stores'. They aim to provide *"cutting edge experiences for their increasingly sophisticated consumers and to develop store designs that translate their brand identity from their products and services into the customer experience of a retail environment"*. In fact, the concept of experience stores has been reserved for specific formats such as flagship and pop-up stores that encourage consumers to experience and communicate with the merchandise and to develop an emotional bond with the brand (Jones et al. 2010). Pop-up stores or temporary stores are *"short-lasting brand stores located in highly representative locations that aim to develop brand awareness and strengthen brand loyalty and value through a recreational happening"* (Russo Spena et al. 2012, p. 22). This format provides an interactive and relational platform that promotes co-creation processes, which is something they share in common with the flagship store format. Flagship stores are a way to establish brands' heritage and identity and display the depth of brand offering. It is defined by the stores' architecture, location, design and collaborations (Manlow and Nobbs 2013). Related to the flagship store format emerges the concept of the third place, described by Oldenburg (1999) as somewhere that is not home, the first place, or work, the second place, but as a comfortable space to browse, relax and meet people. This evolved into the commercial third place, designed to attract customers and increase their dwell-time in store (Crick 2015) and more recently to what Mikunda (2007) asserts as 'spectacular' third places, more experiential and emotionally charged retail places, which many brands are experimenting with today, like Melissa's Galeria London, a fusion of commerce, culture and social space (Saunter 2014; Alexander 2016). Some authors have explored possible tensions between these formats and retailers' conventional stores (Jones et al. 2010) and the danger of focussing too much on the experience instead of on the core offering (Spence et al. 2014).

2.3 The Use of Technology

The introduction of technology in the physical store responds to consumer preferences and retailers' needs and expectations (Renko and Druzijanic 2014). This research focuses on consumers' interface with in-store technology and considers technologies that facilitate the interaction between the consumer and the retailer and contributes to experience creation in the physical store (Pantano 2015). These forms of technology include technological solutions such as plasma screens, interactive screens, iPads, or interactive product displays (Ballantine et al. 2010) and more advanced and interactive technologies like virtual fitting rooms (Bell et al. 2014).

Technology redefines the store experience and store layouts and provides an opportunity to introduce new services, customised messages to consumers, and new entertaining tools (Pantano and Naccarato 2010; Merle et al. 2012). Also, technology demonstrates the capacity to blur the boundaries between traditional and internet retail, making omnichannel retail possible (Brynjolfsson et al. 2013).

The emphasis on experience creation has lead retailers to introduce advanced technologies in physical settings (Bäckström and Johansson 2006) and to develop immersive retail experiences that connect with consumers on an emotional level, giving them control over the shopping experience. These retail experiences are created through the use of immersive technologies that appeal to the senses and make consumers feel they are interacting with the brand more than merely browsing items. Augmented reality is one of these technologies that can help to increase cross-selling and conversion, reduce returns and increase the revenue per transaction with clear consequences for customer satisfaction (IBM 2008). Also, intelligent/virtual fitting rooms in online settings have been demonstrated to reduce returns and increase conversion rates and its use has spread to physical stores even when their presence is marginal (Bell et al. 2014). Other technologies that could contribute to create a more immersive shopping experience are virtual reality, wearable technology, and 3D printing, which are still in an experimental phase (Piotrowicz and Cuthbertson 2014).

Other retail service innovations are the PSA (electronic personal shopping assistant) that provides store information and check-out services for consumers, enhancing the shopping experience and providing a personal service. As a consequence, shoppers spend more time in the store when using these devices (Evanschitzky et al. 2015). Also, RFID (Radio Frequency Identification) assists retailers with better inventory management while for consumers it produces a more pleasurable shopping experience and improves service and convenience (Renko and Druzijanic 2014). Convenience and the perception of speed are the main strengths of self-service checkouts along with the ability of freeing employees for other customer service tasks (Renko and Druzijanic 2014).

Employees should receive adequate training and be provided with technology to make the shopping experience more relevant (Piotrowicz and Cuthbertson 2014). One technology that can empower the role of staff members in the store are mobile points of sale (mPOS) that can assist in delivering a more convenient payment experience. These mPOS used with a unified omnichannel payment solution can help retailers to access cross-channel shopper data and offer a personalised service with consequences for sales growth and customer loyalty (Drapers 2015).

In order to illustrate how these technologies are currently applied, Table 1 identifies the forms of new and emerging technologies utilised by a range of experimental fashion and lifestyle retailers.

In any case, technology must be a facilitator to create a superior customer experience in the store and a consistent and integrated experience between channels (Blázquez 2014; Alexander and Alvarado 2014). Considering the role of technology in physical store settings involves the consideration of the role played by consumers' own mobile phones which contribute to eliminate barriers between channels (Piotrowicz and Cuthbertson 2014).

Table 1 Technology forms utilised in the physical store, Source: authors own based on Jobling (Aug 2014), Rumsey (May 2015), Righetto (Feb 2015), Marian (Aug 2016)

Retailer	Technology forms	Example
Selfridges	Interactive screen, VR (virtual reality), AR (augmented reality), 3D printing & wearable technology, body scanning	Denim studio digital bar, Immersive virtual world by Gareth Pugh & Inition, Festival of Imagination
Burberry	100 screens, iPads, interactive mirrors, AR, RFID, Click and Collect, Apps; mPOS, iBeacons, Innovation lab—'What If' group.	London flagship store
New Look	iPads, paddiquins, QR codes, mobile app, mPOS (mobile point of sale), Click and Collect, interactive screens, AR (Blippar), body scanning, app.	London flagship store
Topshop/ Topman	VR, QR codes, mobile app, innovation lab, tech enabled personal shopping, mPOS	Virtual reality catwalk
Debenhams	Digital screens & kiosks, Wi-Fi, Click and Collect, app.	Oxford Circus London flagship store
Macy's	i-beacons; wearable tech shop, 3D printing, interactive photobooth, customisation	Trial with Shopkick app to alert customers about deals/products of interest; Millenial floor.
Nordstrom	Personal book software; innovation lab; apps, mPOS; personalised service; social app integration	Pinned items in-store
M&S	Virtual rail, browse & buy hub, mPOS, iPads, digital signage, digital lab, Wi-Fi, RFID (radio frequency identification) tag trials, mobile app.	Virtual rail trialled in Amsterdam 150 browse and buy hubs 1500 assisted sellers.
Uniqlo	Magic mirrors, AR, LED (light-emitting diode) tickers, rotating mannequins, Click & Collect	Colour changing technology. UK, Japan, US stores.
Westfield	Collect+ Westfield Lounge	Click and Collect from 260 brands in 1 place
John Lewis	Innovation lab, Click and Collect, mPOS, app, Wi-Fi, chargebox, virtual store guide, iBeacons	Integrated within John Lewis stores, UK
Rebecca Minkoff	RFID, magic mirrors, iPads.	Connected fitting rooms, smart walls
Disney	RFID magic band	Fast-laning customers
Nike	Mass personalisation, iPads, interactive touch screens, video screens, AR, digital mannequins, digitised treadmill, mPOS	Nike FuelStation, Shoreditch & Niketown
Sephora	iPad stations, personalised consultations,	Beauty interactive workshops

2.4 The Consumer

Digital disruption has created empowered consumers whose demands for convenience, speed, efficiency, flexibility, and consistency across channels has created
fundamental challenges for retailers (Blázquez 2014). Regarding their use of retail
channels, consumers are omnichannel in their thinking and behaviour and will
choose the channel that best fit their needs in every moment (Bell et al. 2014).
They want brands to speak to them with the same level of relevance no matter what
channel they chose to interact with the brand. In relation to their expectations, they
want the advantages of online shopping such as a broad selection or rich product
information along with the advantages of the physical store like personal service, the
ability to touch the product or the experience (Rigby 2011).

Fashion consumers expect and demand superior experiences in physical stores
even when this experience is not always provided by retailers (Blázquez 2014;
Alexander and Alvarado 2014). They want to be treated as individuals and expect
their shopping experiences to be relevant, accessible and lifestyle oriented. Retailers
that can connect with customers through experiences that meet these expectations
are more likely to increase sales and brand loyalty (IBM 2008). Customers have high
expectations from customer service, expecting retailers to meet their individual
needs online, in-store, and via mobile (Drapers 2015). However, they tend to get
easily bored of the same type of stimuli, necessitating frequent change in the store
experience (Parsons 2011).

In a recent study (2015) conducted in the UK, almost half of shoppers declared
that they want to be served by people in physical stores and not by technology, with
another 20% of shoppers wanting to use technology that makes the shopping
experience more convenient, faster and easier with payment technologies gaining
acceptance (Drapers 2015). They declared that the Click and Collect experience
must be effortless overall with nearly 30% of consumers expecting a more comfortable and hedonic experience. However, it seems that shoppers do not consider their
own mobile phones and the use of mobile applications as a form of in-store
technology. In this respect, retail experts state that it is necessary to consider the
role of mobile applications in the shopping experience because they act as the link
between the physical store and the online channel (Drapers 2015). Also, through
mobile devices, consumers take their social networks into the store where they
expect to find direct links so that they can share and comment in real time
(Piotrowicz and Cuthbertson 2014). It is especially relevant for fashion retailers to
consider the Millennial segment. These consumers, born after 1980, have grown up
in a technological environment. They adopt innovations quickly and have a fast
paced and socially connected lifestyle (Shankar et al. 2010) which makes them more
receptive to in-store technologies and online shopping channels compared to older
consumers.

Therefore, the literature shows that the role of the physical store is evolving
towards a more connected shopping experience, where the role of the experience
within the physical space, the use of technologies, and the integration of different

channels play a crucial role. Next, the research methodology is explained followed by the experts' view about the different issues discussed in the literature.

3 Methodology

Even when the evolution of retail formats is a research priority with clear implications for practice, academic research fails to provide a comprehensive view about the future prospects for fashion stores from an omnichannel perspective. Because of that, this chapter adopts an exploratory approach, and aims to develop a clearer understanding of the different ways in which the physical fashion store will evolve in the future. According to Maxwell and Loomis (2003), qualitative research includes the study of natural real life settings, a focus on participants' meanings and context, providing insights gained through a process of analysis and data integration. This is consistent with an interpretivist approach, which enables researchers to be more engaged with the world in which we live (Bryman and Bell 2007).

The data was obtained using semi structured industry expert interviews which allowed for deeper exploration and discussion of the topic (Silverman 2010). The topic guide was built on the literature review previously discussed and comprises three main areas: the role of the physical store and its evolution in the omnichannel scenario, the role of technology in the fashion store, and how the shopping experience will evolve in physical settings. In total, six industry informants, representing senior directors within retail design, experience or retail technology consultancies were recruited to take part in the study. Informants were selected using purposive and convenience sampling approaches respectively (Yin 2014). Senior managers who hold strategic direction roles and work with a cross-section of different industries on delivering retail design solutions were contacted and interviewed in order to explore the different ways in which the fashion store will evolve in the future. As Table 2 depicts, the interviews were conducted face-to face with each lasting 60 minutes.

Table 2 Informant selection

Informant	Company	Role	Interviewee code
Kate Shepherd	Checkland Kindleysides	Director of Strategy & Insight	1
Kevin Jackson	Engage Works	Sales & Marketing Director	2
Hannah Carter-Owers	Universal Design Studio	Co-director	3
Andrew Patterson	Mynt	Founder, Director	4
Erika Loch	Avenue Imperial	Head of business development	5
Alastair Kean	Dalziel & Pow	Group Development Director	6

Interviews were audio recorded and additional notes were taken, from which full transcripts were developed. From this full set of data, themes and sub-themes that emerged from the data were identified and analysed utilising word (thematic) tables based on the themes and subjects arising from the literature review. These categories were summarised and key quotes added, established by the pattern of transcripts in order to gain interpretive understanding (Silverman 2010; Miles and Huberman 1994).

4 Findings and Discussion

This section is structured around the themes deduced from the literature and empirical interviews. First the findings are presented, using thematic quote tables to support the suppositions. Then, the findings are discussed in relation to the literature.

4.1 Role of the Physical Store in the Omnichannel Scenario

An overriding sentiment that the retail experience will be enhanced within the physical store was asserted from all experts, with an increasing shift away from a place to transact towards a place to interact, socialise, and engage with the brand, which concurs with the literature (Bäckström and Johansson 2006; Jones et al. 2010; Alexander 2016). *"What people are seeking and what they value and what they talk about are experiences"* (expert 2). Within this scenario the role of the store is perceived as being more important than ever as the central "hub" for channel integration and poignantly, as the *"embodiment of the brand experience"* (expert 6). The limitations of the web as a conveyer of brand experience were shared by most, as a *"flat experience"* (expert 6) and the unique ability of the physical store to deliver a multi-sensory approach—sound, smell, touch—elevates its strategic position within the omnichannel offer, supporting Spence et al. (2014) and Ballantine et al. (2015). Moreover, the requirement for human interaction within the physical store, expressed through an elevated, personal customer service and the store enabling and empowering socialisation, community and connectivity was strongly conveyed and aligns to the work of Ballantine et al. (2010) and Alexander (2016) (Table 3).

All respondents reiterated the requirement for customer instant gratification that only the physical store provides, even though ecommerce has optimised same day delivery, it doesn't replicate the immediacy of bricks and mortar. Whilst the scale of the physical store and where it happens may be different in the future, the importance of delivering a customer experience, regardless of channel was considered critical, reinforcing Rigby (2011) and Bell et al.'s (2014) assertions. As experts 6 and 5 cited *"Stores are still going to be important for visibility. . . it's the holistic experience that is crucial"* and *"people don't shop channels they shop the brand. . . joining*

Table 3 Role of physical store in the omnichannel scenario

Physical store as experience	"It's not about fulfilment anymore it's about a sense of wellbeing & entertainment" (expert 6). "The epicentre is brand experience" (expert 5). "Physically immerse yourself in the brand experience" (expert 4) "The role of the store is to embody the brand" (expert 1) "Curating experiences is key within the physical store" (expert 3).
Physical store as multi-sensory	"The ability to touch, see, feel, experience the product and service—to interact" (expert 4).
Physical store as place to connect	"The store becomes a place people can meet, a social environment" (expert 6) "The ability to speak to a human being, as opposed to the kind of service you get online" (expert 1) "It's about creating a sense of belonging… unique moments…retail spaces will be more social spaces" (expert 3) "We're social animals… so these experiential retail hubs will be the centre of the social and retail experience" (expert 2).

Table 4 Contribution of the physical store

Instant gratification	"There is still a need for going in and buying now" (expert 4).
Communicate brand story	"In 1994 we designed Levi's flagship in Regent Street which was heralded as a new way in retail design…it's about the brand not the product" (expert 1) "Educating consumers about the brand story in-store is crucial" (expert 5).
Shaping of retailscape	"The brand & retail sector plays an important role in location development. Working with developers, planners, how retail offers social spaces within cities is important. Our cities need texture, colour and retail adds this" (expert 3).

everything up and maintaining a level of authenticity is important with the physical store at the centre". Two additional facets of the brick & mortar store emerged: the communication of a brand's story and the broader role it plays in the organisation and design of urban retailscapes (Table 4).

4.2   Evolution of Physical Retail Formats

Change is a constant and the need to be agile and responsive to format evolution was consistently expressed by the majority (5 of 6) of interviewees. Most did not perceive more suitable physical formats in the future but rather thought of it as an ecosystem, *"one doesn't exist without the other"* (expert 1). Most inferred a shift to smaller store footprints, driven not only by digital but by their ability to garner relationships, build community within certain locales, their flexibility to experiment (e.g. with customisation, collaboration), and their ability to deliver return on investment. Within this, the pop up store was cited as providing a lot of scope in *"bringing the brand to the customer"* rather than the traditional notion of the customer going to

Table 5 Physical store format evolution expressed by experts

Physical format evolution	*"When we've worked with brands rolling out internationally, the small format is how they build relationships and where they make most of their money"* (expert 3) *"All those formats are points on the way to somewhere else... the most important thing being brand experience"* (expert 2) "Being dynamic and trail blazing format innovation is important" (expert 5).
Taking the format to the customer	*"It's about you (the brand) going to them (customer) and not the other way around"* (expert 6) "Doing something that is more experiential, that may not be around forever, that brings the brand to the customer... can be the most creative" (expert 1).
Flagship format	*"Even the likes of Louis Vuitton, Prada, Chanel...the focus is on cultural experiences rather than commerce"* (expert 3) *"The idea of flagships as your biggest store, with the most amount of money spent on it – that's old fashioned"* (expert 6).

it. A recent project for Adidas Originals in China, Shanghai Disney Park by Mynt, whereby customers can customise clothing based on their Disney experience and the memory is transported home within days of returning, raises interesting ideas on retail places (expert 4). Moreover, Starbucks was cited as an interesting example of "place (format) positioning", with their Roastery attracting the coffee connoisseur to their small expresso format—each format telling a different brand story (expert 1). The flagship format was seen as evolving from a place of *"ostentation, show of wealth and commerce"* into a space for cultural and social absorption (expert 3) (Table 5).

4.3 Current and Future Role of Technology in the Physical Store

Most experts (4 of 6) highlighted the steep learning curve that retailers have been on with technology, with a tendency to use it without fully comprehending the need-benefit of it, supporting Bäckström and Johansson 2006's study (2006). This has resulted in "gimmicky tech" and many "disasters" (expert 1 & 2). A more strategic approach is now being realised, with a focus on the retail problem and what solution is required to solve it. In this scenario, technology is last in the decision making process and is often not the solution enabler. Experts also highlighted technology requirements and inhibitors. Requirements included the financial and human investment; technology's relevancy, brand fit, customer first solutions, and creativity first. Inhibitors included, the need for internal capabilities (staff expertise and know-how), the long term commitment required to on-going investment in technology, budget, timescale, technology inertia, and the back-end support required to support the technology. Five salient emotional roles of technology within the physical store

Table 6 Role of technology in the physical store

Shift to strategic role	*"We've been through a painful teething process, where technology was available so everyone used it, even if they didn't know what they were doing or didn't need it"* (expert 1) *"A client had a touchscreen mirror that they invested heavily in.. nobody used it"* (expert 4) *"It's about being smart with the technology you use"* (expert 4) *"Technology is never a solution, its an enabler of the solution"* (expert 2)
Enabler of customer service	*"Any tech that empowers customer service"* (expert 5) *"We're doing a lot of work integrating physical and digital experience, but its not about building technology in the space but about communicating information, improving service aspects"* (expert 3).
Elevating the experience	*"It highlights and accentuates the brand experience"* (expert 4) *"It's about storytelling, feeling more engaged and building on the experience"* (expert 6). *"Role for entertainment, heightening the experience, making it more immersive and more sensorial. It can also help understand the product offer better"* (expert 1). *"Emotions is where everything should be. . . and digital in-store can elevate that experience"* (expert 6).
Functional role	*"Fulfilment side of technology has such a practical role to play. . . being clear about your tech objectives is vital"* (expert 1). *"Operations: making it easier for sales staff to do their job and for customers speed and efficiency"* (expert 5).

were inferred: as brand educator, an enabler of customer service, elevating the experience, enhancing the senses, and heightening brand immersion (Table 6). The hedonic role of technology took precedence, with two experts referring to it as a means of making, *"magical moments"* (experts 2 & 6). In addition, three functional roles were cited, but situated as secondary to the emotional facets of technology. Under general fulfilment, convenience, flexibility, and speed (e.g. ability to check stock) that technology enables, were seen to play an important operational role.

4.4 Forms of Technology Used in the Physical Store

The prevailing perception when considering forms of technology was to consider the customer journey first, and the need to understand how consumers buy, what is important to them, and what would be beneficial. Apple was highlighted as a technology business that has not focused on developing new technology, but has excelled as experts in taking existing technology and perfecting it, making it fit for purpose, and delivering a real consumer benefit (expert 2). It was inferred that this *customer first* approach is therefore vital in selecting the form; no one size fits all. The issues of customer privacy (iBeacons), customer irritation, and the environmental impact of technology were raised as concerns, with the latter specifically being a drain in terms of energy and expenditure. Irritation was discussed in terms of useless, broken or dysfunctional tech, which may sever any attempt at delivering emotional engagement. Interestingly, many experts offered many more examples of poor technology implementation than good, corroborating Alexander and Alvarado

Table 7 Forms of technology used in-store

Form	Expert viewpoint	Retail examples cited by experts
Contactless payment	*"Great, speeds up the process. . .real consumer benefit"* (expert 2) *"This will be a given in the next few years"* (expert 1)	Apple pay
iPads	*"We used to collect examples of retailer's broken iPads"* (expert 1)	*"Nordstrom: elevated customer service using iPads"* (expert 5)
Kiosks	*"Invented gimmick that we haven't really worked out what they do yet"* (expert 2)	
Virtual mirrors	*"Again, a gimmick"* (expert 2) *"Mirrors in fitting rooms, that really help you connect when alone, E.g. other colours/sizes, could add real value"* (expert 1)	*"Jack and Jones invested in a social mirror and it was a waste of time and money"* (expert 4)
QR codes	*"QR codes are dead"* (expert 2) *"Uptake is really bad. . .no real traction"* (expert 1)	
iBeacons	*"No-one has really worked out what they do, what benefit is there for the consumer. Pushing more product at them is a retail not consumer benefit"* (expert 2) *"Issues concerning personal data protection"* (expert 3)	
Virtual reality (VR)/ Augmented Reality (AR)	*"VR just amplifies the role of aspirational retail"* (expert 5) *"AR can bring to life an uninteresting iPad in-store"* (expert 2)	*"Nike's mountain experience—live it, feel it, buy the product. VR immersion"* (expert 6), *"BMW"* (expert 2)

(2014) and Blazquez et al. (2014) extant research. Table 7 presents the key forms discussed and examples cited by experts, which concurs with the emerging forms cited in the literature (Table 1).

4.5   Presence of Other Channels in the Physical Store and How Are They Integrated

Seamless interaction across channels was strongly cited as being important by all experts. An emphasis on "intuitive" communication enabled by technology was stressed, removing the friction in the purchasing journey and starting with customer needs first. As expert 6 stated *"it'll be much more intelligent, more targeted, more bespoke"*. Click and Collect was highlighted as being effective for some retailers, mainly those of scale, who have the operational capabilities to activate it well, yet has room for improvement in fundamental areas: integration and experience, as well

Table 8 Omnichannel integration in the physical store

Cross-channel	Expert viewpoint	Example cited by experts
Click and Collect (CnC)	*"Click and Collect has to be a richer experience than you ever had online, you have to be engaged"* (expert 2)	*"Westfield Plus, I love, with CnC next to fitting rooms"* (expert 1 *"Kurt Geiger example of annoying CnC—clunky unconnected process, what was supposed to save me time, cost me time and money"* (expert 5)
Wi-Fi	*"Why do we even talk about free Wi-Fi in-store? It's like saying there is free air, it should just be a given"* (expert 1)	
Mobile devices	*"Everything is going to be mobile. . . we need to connect a mobile life with a retail life"* (expert 2) *"Unless technology is useful in-store e.g. get my size—why would I be on my mobile in store? Usefulness critical"* (expert 5) *"Checking availability is one thing, what's more interesting is from a brand engagement perspective, how you activate via mobile and attract a consumer"* (expert 4)	*"I don't know of any app that is actually useful to me in-store"* (expert 5).

as immediacy and instinctiveness. The former relates to spatial integration within store and delivering the same consistent experience. Too often it is relegated to, *"some weird space at the back of the store, a warehouse feel"* (expert 3), more associated with commoditisation and facility than experience. Immediacy and instinctiveness relates to recognition enabled technology on store arrival, removing the need to wait, rather the product is ready and waiting, thus removing the barriers to purchase. John Lewis (United Kingdom) often cited as Click and Collect industry best practice (Thomson 2014) was criticised in the past for not offering this, thus suggesting opportunities for possible further integration. Mobile was seen as vital yet there was a unanimous sentiment that there is much opportunity for improvement in the integration, usefulness, and experience enrichment of it across channels. This reinforces Piotrowicz and Cuthbertson's (2014) assertion that mobile contributes to barrier elimination between channels (Table 8).

4.6 The Future Experience in Physical Stores

Two key themes emerged when experts were asked to consider the future experience within physical stores: the importance of customer service and design in delivering the experience. Within the latter, four prerequisites became apparent: strategic brand led design, flexible stores, third places, and fitting rooms. These are discussed sequentially and completed with a case study on retailer, *& Other Stories*, exemplified by some experts as good practice of the aforementioned.

4.6.1 Customer Service

All experts reinforced the increasing importance of customer service in delivering an elevated in-store experience and the role of technology in activating a more personalised approach. Within the service journey, technology was seen as stimulating dialogue and elevating the quality of the human interaction. As expert 6 cited *"it's about service, it's about experience, they are so interwoven"*. The challenge of managing service was raised and how technology can help elevate this by equipping staff with the right tools and right information. Having the right service proposition based on market focus was also emphasised, with technology empowering value retailers by offering the possibilities of a virtual self-service to enhance customer service, whereas more luxury or bespoke retailers may place greater emphasis on the human connection. The elevation of the service proposition beyond the expertise of selling featured as being important in the future, with more clients introducing a concierge level of service, connecting consumers not only with products but the broader lifestyle within which it sits. The ongoing credence given to the human relationship was emphasised by all experts as something that could not be replaced by technology and the watch brand Nixon was used to exemplify the heightened service experience from buying in-store compared to buying online (expert 1). Table 9 evidences the above.

4.6.2 Delivering Experience Through the Design of the Physical Space

Four features emerged regarding delivered experience via design: brand led strategic design, flexible-multi-functional stores, delivering experiences in traditionally neglected areas, and growth in third places, the latter resonating with Crick (2015),

Table 9 Customer service in the physical store

Importance of customer service	*"Service is absolutely at the centre of what we do"* (expert 6) *"Service is going to be increasingly important"* (expert 5) *"I'm so passionate about this, aside from experience, it's about service"* (expert 1).
Role of technology in customer service delivery	*"Technology enabled service is the future of retail"* (expert 6) *"Technology is there to enhance the experience"* (expert 4)
Human interaction in service delivery	*"Service elevates the product massively, it's a ritual... the art of shopkeeping, it's the real human touch that's vital"* (expert 1).

Mikunda (2007) and Alexander (2016). A shift towards a more intelligent, intrinsic, sophisticated and strategic consideration of *designed experience* was echoed by all experts. A front end focus on creativity and the conveyance of brand stories and brand moments was emphasised or as expert 6 asserted *"an emphasis on reasons rather than results"*. The need to really understand the brand, the brand archetype, the role it plays in customers' lives and its intended impact was considered essential to translating this into an appropriate brandscape, supporting Kirby and Kent (2010). The requirement for stores to offer something unique to differentiate it from other channels was expressed, manifest in a *"clear, inspirational proposition"* (experts 1 and 4). The ability of the store to morph and evolve was considered a prerequisite in future store design, with an emphasis on flexibility, integration, entertainment, and enjoyment. This is highlighted in the statement that stores today *"are now in constant beta mode. . . a testbed for trying different things"* (expert 1). A focus on traditionally neglected areas, like fitting rooms, was identified as an opportunity to engage in that moment of trying before buying. Moreover, greater consideration to the emotional impact of design and how a store might create pace, a sense of journey, and how the brand might reveal itself through that journey was stressed. Interestingly, the broader socio-cultural role a physical store plays in connecting people is translating through design; thus the store assuming a more sociable role was highlighted. The necessity to build these sociable third places around the brand and to be relevant to the lifestyles and values of the customer were echoed by many experts. However, the difficulty of developing 'social stores' was also raised, described as a "magical mix" between creating buzz but converting consumers from comfortable customers who dwell to those who shop (expert 3). The need to programme spaces to attract customers in, immerse them but get them out again was considered essential. & Other Stories (curated space), Lindex (designed fitting rooms) Hunter (story led design), Topshop and Burberry (experiential & exciting design), Patagonia (story led design & third place), Selfridges (crafting experiential moments), and Apple (programmed space) were cited as retail examples that encompassed good practice in delivering experience through these various *designed experiences* (Table 10).

Mini Case Study: Delivering Experience Through Design: & Other Stories

Background
H&M's new retail concept, & Other Stories first launched in London in March 2013 to fill a market gap between the group's fast fashion mainline and its contemporary brand, COS (Anon 2013a, b). The concept brings to life, Brand Managing Director, Samuel Fernstrom's vision to create a store for women who want to develop their personal style, eclectically mixing and matching items based on their own personal 'story' (Anon, Mar 2013a). The retail launch was initially limited to 20 stores across selected cities, including

(continued)

London, Berlin, Stockholm, Paris, Madrid, Rome, Copenhagen, New York and Toronto. Whilst generating only a small percentage of the group's annual revenue (less than 1% in 2014), & Other Stories premium positioning makes a strategic contribution to portfolio diversity and thus towards growing brand equity for the group (Anon 2015).

Proposition
& Other Stories was conceived for customers to create their own look inspired by street style blogs, social media, like Tumblr and behind-the scenes at fashion shows. The product offer is divided into four mini-collections or 'stories' that evolve each season. Each of these stories offers a selection of clothing, shoes, accessories and beauty products. The idea being not only the ability to create a more personalized shopping experience but to achieve the spontaneous, 'get the look' popularized by bloggers (Anon 2013a, b; Buchanan 2013). A key differentiator is that the design teams are based in Stockholm and Paris, enabling the retailer to achieve the level of design diversity and democratisation desired (Buchanan 2013). Alongside these key stories is a rolling list of co-collaborating designers, referred to by the retailer as their 'Co-labs' which adds a further element of surprise (Anon 2013a, b).

Store Design
The street style, blogger inspired concept translates to the store design and visual merchandising (Buchanan 2013). Intentionally designing-in imperfections gives personality to the store (Fernstrom, cited by Buchanan 2013, p. 3). Each store is designed to be different, in response to the city, location and building that it inhabits. Stores are generally open plan and paired back with clear vistas between each 'story' conveyed. Resembling a flea market or pop-up store setting, from the busy shelving units, simple runner rails, random shoot inspired displays to low-tech postcard and poster signage, it is designed to be democratic, analogue, and mix and match (Buchanan 2013; Anon 2013a, b). The coordinated 'stories' act as in-store stylists with products curated to reflect a magazine layout or Pinterest board. This is replicated on the retailer's website, stories.com, reinforcing the retailer's deliberate mix and match, lo-fi, temporary feel narrative, and enabling customers to touch and feel, interact and engage in a more personalized store experience (Anon 2013a, b).

4.7 Physical Store ROI Measurement Shift

With the shifting emphasis towards delivering brand experiences, some experts highlighted a change in how physical stores' Return on Investment (ROI) is now being measured with greater emphasis placed on brand equity effects like brand awareness and loyalty, brand perception, recall and recognition, and brand reach.

Table 10 Delivering experience through store design

Brand led strategic design	*"These little moments of joy bring experiences to life"* (expert 3) *"It needs to be a pleasurable, enjoyable experience"* (expert 4) *"Design is changing, much more emphasis on content, strategy, creativity. . .much more holistic"* (expert 6).
Flexible store design	*"Agile, that sense that it can flex and evolve, ability to move around when you need it too"* (expert 1) *"For years we've been persuading clients to use furniture than store fit because of the ability to flex spaces. . . most of the spaces we design need some kind of event function"* (expert 3).
Third places	*"Social is kind of difficult, you don't want people just taking up space in store"* (expert 3). *"Third places are the way forward but they need to be built around your brand"* (expert 6). *"Keep your message clear"* (expert 3).
Fitting rooms	*"The fitting rooms are everything, but some retailers really neglect that part of the store"* (expert 1) *"Making them really beautiful, really luxurious, involving technology, social aspects. . . giving a new life to the store in the future"* (expert 5).

Whilst these are not displacing traditional metrics for conventional bricks and mortar stores they are emerging as equally, if not more important for many retailers. Described as the *"halo effect"*, it is harder to quantify but viewed more valuable in the long run (expert 1, 4, and 6).

4.8   Role of the Consumer in the Physical Store

Whilst a consumer centric design approach was shared by most experts, all highlighted the changing role of the consumer in the physical store, with an emphasis on shifts in consumption expectations and consumer typologies (Table 11). Consumption must be considered in its broadest sense, transcending transactional and increasingly shifting to experiential. The desire to consume information and inspiration from a retail brand places greater emphasis on curated spaces, showcasing products, and constantly updating to present newness, personalisation, and added value.

Many experts (4 of 6) emphasised the importance of *role* being customer dependent, specifically, driven by age, gender, need, and expectations. Millennials for example, were cited as having a very different relationship with a brand, often craving the offline experience because much of their world is online and relishing the emotive connectors to a brand (expert 1). The aging UK population was identified as being often ignored from a design perspective, yet raised interesting questions in terms of type of store design required to meet their specific needs. The shift in men's buying behaviours, mimicking those of women with a growing openness to shopping and browsing, resulting in destination locations dedicated to menswear, liked Lambs, Conduit Street, London. New menswear concepts were seen as experimenting with store design with an increasing emphasis on lifestyle led

Table 11 Customer role in the physical store

Shift in consumption expectations	*"It's consuming in a broader sense"* (expert 3) *"It's not about selling clothes, its selling a brand, selling a journey, the experience, the education"* (expert 5) "Personalisation, individuality, authenticity of service will determine success" (expert 5) *"They want to walk into a place, be understood, brand connects with something valuable to their lives"* (expert 2).
Customer typology dependencies	*"It depends on the age and gender of a person"* (expert 1) *"Men are becoming more like women in how they shop"* (expert 1) *"Brands like Ted Baker doing barber shops, this is an enormous growth area"* (expert 1).

formats and the usage of third places like barbers or grooming within traditional bricks and mortar stores, which concurs with Alexander (2016). Ultimately, understanding what customers want from a retail brand and translating that into a physical store was seen as vital. One expert felt that the connection between selling something and adding value to a customer's life was *"still the missing bit in retail"* (expert 2).

4.9 Best Practice Fashion Physical Stores

The majority of experts provided non-technological examples of fashion physical store design best practice (Table 12), raising questions about the value of technology in connecting with customers but also, poignantly that more analogue brand expressions are equally, if not more, innovative in delivering an experience. This is consistent with Bäckström and Johansson 2006' (2006) and Alexander's (2016) assertions about the need to provide in-store experiences that are relevant for consumers without the need to implement advanced technologies. & Other Stories was cited by two experts because it *"felt different, fresh, like a much better way of shopping, yet simple ideas"* (experts 1 & 6). Service was amplified in examples like Uniqlo, Armani and Argos, ranging from a one-to-one bespoke human personal relationship (Armani) to technology enabled convenience, speed, and self-service (Argos, Uniqlo). They highlight two distinct approaches: added value in design experimentation, greater focus on individuality, brand personality, storytelling, personalisation, and curated spaces to create moments of intimacy and intrigue that create hedonic, emotional experiences or alternatively added value through convenience, speed, and flexibility that deliver functional utilitarian experiences. Both approaches encompass the need to understand the nuances of the target customer and retail brand.

Table 12 Best practice fashion physical stores according to experts

Retailer	Industry/Type/Target	Reason
& Other Stories	*Fashion, mid market, womenswear*	*"I just really love the simple things they are doing, in a low key kind of way" (expert 1)* *"It's a wonderful experience, it's really good fashion, product design and it feels contemporary"* (expert 6).
Uniqlo	Fashion, mass market, menswear, womenswear, childrenswear	*"Customer service is excellent. . .well educated, happy to service you"* (expert 5).
Dover Street Market	Fashion, luxury market, menswear & womenswear	*"Beautiful, inspirational and authentic"* (expert 5).
Armani	Fashion, luxury market, menswear & womenswear	*"There's no technology interface, but its personal, they know me by name. . . technology can enable that personal connection on a mass scale, we're just not doing it yet"* (expert 2).
Patagonia	Outdoor, premium market, menswear and womenswear	*"Its believable, its tangible, they live and breath it, it's a true expression of the brand"* (expert 4).
H-Sport	Sports, value market, menswear, womenswear, childrenswear	*"A value proposition that is truly aspirational. . . we haven't changed the proposition but elevated it by categorising it, creating the sports lifestyle that surrounds the proposition"* (expert 4).
Argos	Catalogue retailer, multi-category, all consumers	*"The most integrated technology retail experience I've seen is Argos"* (expert 6).

4.10 Future Change in Fashion Shopping Experience

Most experts saw retail change as evolutionary rather than revolutionary, one citing, *"the future is already here, it's just not evenly distributed"* (attributed to William Gibson 1993). Thus whilst no seismic shift was predicted, three significant forecasts were inferred: heightened experience, more conscious design, and more personalisation, as Table 13 depicts. These are expressed through harnessing culture and commerce, pop ups or more flexible formats, co-created collaborative places, both analogue and technologically enabled.

5 Conclusions and Recommendations

The increasing growth of digital channels and the higher expectations of consumers regarding their shopping experiences are producing a change in the role that the physical store plays in the omnichannel landscape. The physical store has been reconceptualised as the place to harness the best of both physical and digital worlds, that is, the multi-sensorial experience of the offline with the access, interactivity, and

Table 13 Physical retail future forecasts according to experts

Heightened experience	"*Topshop shows that if you connect with the cultural facets that surround what you sell in a really exciting way, you can really hook in an audience*" (expert 1). "*It's going to be more dynamic, less formulaic, more pop up activity, clever collaborations*" (expert 5). "*More enjoyable, more inspirational*" (*expert 6*). "*Making the whole experience ridiculously pleasurable*" (expert 4).
Conscious design	"*The industry standard of 5–10 year store interior lifespan before ripping out is shocking... there has to be a better way of thinking about creating spaces, updatable, responsible approach*" (expert 3).
More personalisation	"*Greater scope for fitting room experience, offering advise*" (*expert 1*). "*Depends on market level, but more customisation, personal service, interaction with the individual*" (expert 4).

convenience of the online (Alexander and Alvarado 2014). The role of the physical store thus seems to be evolving from places for transaction to places for interaction in which the different channels of the retailer comes together joined by the technology. This, in turn, has profoundly challenged the traditional notions of retail format, retail place and retail design.

In terms of interaction, the physical store is considered to be a conveyor of the brand experience. That involves strengthening the brick and mortar stores' unique propositions, such as customer service and the creation of spaces for socialization. Customer service must be enhanced by technology but not replaced by it. Thus, the sense of community becomes more prominent and also the continuous development of a multisensory experience. Some formats naturally lend themselves to encompassing these aspects, such as a flagship store, but it is expected to extend to other experimental formats like pop-ups, showrooms, and Click and Collect spaces. Pop-ups are a format with good prospects for the future in the opinion of the experts due to its short-term life which makes it a flexible space that can be adapted to a brand's needs. Indeed, the flexibility of the space is one of the requirements of the store of the future: flexibility to adapt to the needs of consumers, to morph, adapt, and go to different places. The idea of the development of the third place is fitting here.

Regarding the role of the physical store in the omnichannel scenario, there is a need to re-think the role of cross-channel capabilities such as Click and Collect. If it takes a prominent place in the physical store, acting as a driver to develop a more luxurious experience will depend on the retailers' positioning and its target market. Also, the provision of free Wi-Fi should be a commodity to facilitate the interaction with online channels, mainly through the use of mobile devices. The mobile channel represents a challenge in the design of the physical experience and involves the development of mobile applications, mobile enabled websites, and interaction with social media (Blázquez 2014).

It is necessary to understand the benefit of technology prior to implementing it. In this sense, one relevant contribution of this chapter relates to the different roles of technology exposed, including enabler of customer service, brand educator,

Table 14 Summary of research findings

Omnichannel retail		
Store and retail strategy	*Contribution of store*	*Evolution*
Experience	Instant gratification	Format innovation
Multisensory	Brand history	Brand to customer
Place to connect	Retailscape	Flagship/cultural
In-store technology		
Role of technology	*Forms of technology*	*Cross-channel*
Strategic	Contactless payment	Click and Collect
Customer service enabler	iPads	WiFi
Experience elevator	Virtual Mirrors	Mobile devices
Functional	QR codes	
	iBeacons	
	Virtual Reality	
	Kiosks	
Future drivers of store experience		
Customer service	*Store design*	*Consumer*
Importance of CS	Brand-led strategic design	Shift in expectations
Technology influences CS	Flexible store design	Consumer typology
Human interactions in CS	Third Places	
Shopping experience		
	Heightened service	
	Conscious design	
	Personalisation	

experience elevator, enhancing the senses, and heightening brand immersion. Technology must be an enabler, enhancing but not replacing the role of the experience in physical stores. Also there is a need for consistency in consumer and retailer approaches regarding the presence of technology in brick and mortar stores.

Consumers shop the brand not the channel. They expect the physical store to deliver a customer experience, regardless of the channel. That means that they perceive a holistic view of the brand that is the sum of technology, interaction, design of space, and multisensory experience in the physical place. One important conclusion from the experts' views is the need to pay more attention to other consumer targets than millennials, who seems to be neglected in the design of the shopping experience. Relevant issues that need to be considered include the authenticity of the experience, personalisation, experiential consumption, development of curated spaces, as well as hedonic and emotional experiences. Table 14 summarizes the main findings of the research.

6 Limitations and Further Research

The exploratory nature of the study limits the generalisation of the results. The sampling was limited in size, scale, country and confined to design-tech-experiential consultancies only. There is merit in expanding the number of participants and including the retailers' perspectives in future research.

It would also be recommendable to extend this research and incorporate the consumer's view in order to determine if there is any consistency between the experience offered in physical stores and the experience expected by them. While qualitative research is preferred in order to get in-depth insight about their perceptions in relation to the store experience, quantitative enquiry could help to objectively measure specific attitudes regarding the interaction with technology.

Questions for Discussion and Review

1. What is the current role of the physical store within omnichannel and how do you predict this evolving in the future?
2. What role does technology currently assume within the physical store and how might this evolve in the store of the future?
3. What forms of technology add greatest value? Evaluate from both the retail brand and customer perspectives.
4. What is the best strategy to follow in terms of Click and Collect service integration within the physical store?
5. How important is customer experience in the physical store and how might this change in 5 years time?
6. What types of experience do consumers need or expect from a fashion retailer? Create an experiential matrix to measure the relative importance of each type of experience to consumers and products
7. Which fashion retailer would you cite as 'best practice' and why? What dimensions have you used to assess best practice?
8. What purpose does design play in creating a consumer experience? How might store design translate offline to online?
9. Which fashion retailers offer an omnichannel experience? How is this exemplified across their channels and service proposition?
10. What are your predictions for post omnichannel in the retail scenario?

References

Alexander, B. (2016). Retail as social experiences: Fashion third places from traditional to the virtual. conference proceedings. *ACRA2016 Annual Conference, Sponsored by the American Collegiate Retailing Association, Secaucus 13th–16th April 2016.*

Alexander, B., & Alvarado, D. O. (2014). Blurring of the channel boundaries: The impact of advanced technologies in the physical fashion store on consumer experience. *International Journal of Advanced Information Science and Technology, 30*(30), 29–42.

Anon. (15 Mar 2013a). *H&M's new narrative: & Other stories*. London: WGSN.

Anon. (14 Jun 2013b) *& Other stories*. Berlin: WGSN.

Anon. (Apr 2015). *H&M Hennes & Mauritz AB in apparel & footwear (world)*. Euromonitor

Babin, B., Darden, W., & Griffin, M. (1994). Work and/or fun: Measuring hedonic and utilitarian shopping value. *Journal of Consumer Research, 20*, 644–656.

Bäckström, K., & Johansson, U. (2006). Creating and consuming experiences in retail store environments: Comparing retailer and consumer perspectives. *Journal of Retailing and Consumer Services, 13*(6), 417–430.

Ballantine, P. W., Jack, R., & Parsons, A. G. (2010). Atmospheric cues and their effect on the hedonic retail experience. *International Journal of Retail and Distribution Management, 38*(8), 641–653.

Ballantine, P. W., Parsons, A., & Comeskey, K. (2015). A conceptual model of the holistic effects of atmospheric cues in fashion retailing. *International Journal of Retail and Distribution Management, 43*(6), 503–517.

Bearne, S. (Jan 2014). Westfield London moves into click and collect. *Drapers*.

Beck, N., & Rygl, D. (2015). Categorization of multiple channel retailing in multi, cross and omnichannel retailing for retailers and retailing. *Journal of Retailing and Consumer Services, 27*, 170–178.

Bell, D. R., Gallino, S., & Moreno, A. (2014). How to win in an omnichannel world. *MIT Sloan Management Review, 56*(1), 45.

Blázquez, M. (2014). Fashion shopping in multichannel retail: The role of technology in enhancing the customer experience. *International Journal of Electronic Commerce, 18*(4), 97–116.

Blazquez, M., Kent, T., Schwarz, E. (2014). Retail experiences and the role of in-store technologies and fashion apps. Conference proceedings. *Oxford Retail Futures Conference, Innovation in Retail and Distribution, 8th–9th December 2014*.

Bryman, A., & Bell, E. (2007). *Business research methods*. New York: Oxford University Press.

Brynjolfsson, E., Hu, Y. J., & Rahman, M. S. (2013). Competing in the age of multichannel retailing. *MIT Sloan Management Review, 54*(4), 23–29.

Buchanan, V. (11 Mar 2013). Retail analysis: & Other stories combined storytelling with street style, *L:SN Global*.

Cao, L., & Li, L. (2015). The impact of cross-channel integration on retailers' sales growth. *Journal of Retailing, 91*(2), 198–216.

Crick, A. (2015). New third places: Opportunities and challenges. *Advances in Culture, Tourism & Hospitality Research, 5*, 66–77.

Deveaux, S. (2014). Customer insight report, *Drapers*, May 2014, p. 5.

Drapers. (2015). Multichannel report. *Drapers*, September 2015.

Evanschitzky, H., Iyer, G. R., Pillai, K. G., Kenning, P., & Schütte, R. (2015). Consumer trial, continuous use, and economic benefits of a retail service innovation: The case of the personal shopping assistant. *Journal of Product Innovation Management, 32*(3), 459–475.

IBM. (2008). *How immersive technology can revitalize the shopping experience. Immersive retailing, executive brief*. IMB Corporation.

Jobling, A. (Aug 2014). *Digital commerce: Four areas of investment*. WGSN.

Jones, P., Comfort, D., Clarke-Hill, C., & Hillier, D. (2010). Retail experience stores: Experiencing the brand at first hand. *Marketing Intelligence and Planning, 28*(3), 241–248.

Kent, A., Dennis, C., Blazquez, M., Helberger, E., & Brakus, J. (2015). Branding, marketing, and design: Experiential in-store digital environments. In E. Pantano (Ed.), *Successful technological integration for competitive advantage in retail settings* (Vol. 1). London: Middlesex University.

Kirby, A. E., & Kent, A. (2010). Architecture as brand: Store design and brand identity. *Journal of Product and Brand Management, 19*(6), 432–439.

Levy, S. (1959). Symbols for sale. *Harvard Business Review, 37*, 117–124.

Manlow, V., & Nobbs, K. (2013). Form and function of luxury flagships: An international exploratory study of the meaning of the flagship store for managers and customers. *Journal of Fashion Marketing and Management: An International Journal, 17*(1), 49–64.

Marian, P. (Aug 2016). *The future of retail 2016*. WGSN

Maxwell, J., & Loomis, D. (2003). Mixed method design: An alternative approach. In A. Tashakkori & C. Teddle (Eds.), *Handbook of mixed methods in social and behavioral research* (pp. 241–272). Thousand Oaks, CA: Sage.

Mehra, A., Kumar, S., & Raju, J. S. (2013). *'Showrooming' and the competition between store and online retailers*. Available at SSRN 2200420.

Merle, A., Senecal, S., & St-Onge, A. (2012). Whether and how virtual try-on influences consumer responses to an apparel web site. *International Journal of Electronic Commerce, 16*(3), 41–64.

Mikunda, C. (2007). *Brand lands, hot spots and cool spaces: Welcome to the third place and the total marketing experience*. London: Kogan Page.

Miles, M. B., & Huberman, M. A. (1994). *Qualitative data analysis – An expanded source book*. Thousand Oaks, CA: Sage.

Neslin, S. A., & Shankar, V. (2009). Key issues in multichannel customer management: Current knowledge and future directions. *Journal of Interactive Marketing, 23*(1), 70–81.

Neslin, S. A., Jerath, K., Bodapati, A., Bradlow, E. T., Deighton, J., Gensler, S., & Verhoef, P. C. (2014). The interrelationships between brand and channel choice. *Marketing Letters, 25*(3), 319–330.

Oldenburg, R. (1999). *The great good place: Cafes, coffee shops, bookstores, bars, hair salons and other hangouts at the heart of a community*. New York, NY: Marlowe & Company.

Pantano, E. (2015). Pantano, E. (2016). Engaging consumer through the storefront: Evidences from integrating interactive technologies. *Journal of Retailing and Consumer Services, 28*, 149–154.

Pantano, E., & Naccarato, G. (2010). Entertainment in retailing: The influences of advanced technologies. *Journal of Retailing and Consumer Services, 17*(3), 200–204.

Parsons, A. G. (2011). Atmosphere in fashion stores: Do you need to change? *Journal of Fashion Marketing and Management: An International Journal, 15*(4), 428–445.

Piotrowicz, W., & Cuthbertson, R. (2014). Introduction to the special issue information technology in retail: Toward omnichannel retailing. *International Journal of Electronic Commerce, 18*(4), 5–16.

Puccinelli, N. M., Goodstein, R. C., Grewal, D., Price, R., Raghubir, P., & Stewart, D. (2009). Customer experience management in retailing: Understanding the buying process. *Journal of Retailing, 85*(1), 15–30.

Rapp, A., Baker, T. L., Bachrach, D. G., Ogilvie, J., & Beitelspacher, L. S. (2015). Perceived customer showrooming behaviour and the effect on retail salesperson self-efficacy and performance. *Journal of Retailing, 91*(2), 358–369.

Renko, S., & Druzijanic, M. (2014). Perceived usefulness of innovative technology in retailing: Consumers' and retailers' point of view. *Journal of Retailing and Consumer Services, 21*(5), 836–843.

Retail Week. (2014). Fashion retail 2014. The future of fashion retailing in a digital age. *Retail Week Reports* 2014

Rigby, D. (2011). The future of shopping. *Harvard Business Review, 89*(12), 65–76.

Righetto, H. (Feb 2015). *In-store technology: Interiors and lifestyle*. WGSN.

Rumsey, A. (May 2015). *Extreme engagement*. WGSN

Russo Spena, T., Caridà, A., Colurcio, M., & Melia, M. (2012). Store experience and co-creation: The case of temporary shop. *International Journal of Retail and Distribution Management, 40*(1), 21–40.

Saunter, L. (2014). *Eight ways retail is capitalising on culture*. WGSN. 15 December.

Shankar, V., Venkatesh, A., Hofacker, C., & Naik, P. (2010). Mobile marketing in the retailing environment: Current insights and future research avenues. *Journal of Interactive Marketing, 24*(2), 111–120.

Silverman, D. (2010). *Doing qualitative research* (4th ed.). London: Sage.

Spence, C., Puccinelli, N. M., Grewal, D., & Roggeveen, A. L. (2014). Store atmospherics: A multisensory perspective. *Psychology and Marketing, 31*(7), 472–488.

Thomson, R. (Mar 2014). Oracle retail week awards, John Lewis – Multichannel retailer of the year winner. *Retail week.*

Verdict (Mar 2016). *The UK clothing market 2016-2021.* Verdict.

Verhoef, P. C., Kannan, P. K., & Inman, J. J. (2015). From multi-channel retailing to omnichannel retailing: Introduction to the special issue on multi-channel retailing. *Journal of Retailing, 91*(2), 174–181.

Yin, R. (2014). *Case study research: Design and methods* (5th ed.). Thousand Oaks, CA: Sage.

Bethan Alexander is a passionate spokesperson, consultant and lecturer with a specific lens on maximising customer engagement through multi-sensorial fashion brand experiences. Having spent 18 years working internationally with fashion brands including Converse, Elle, Kangol and establishing her own consultancy business, Brand Baker, Bethan now brings the same verve to her academic role. Within Higher Education, Bethan has held senior lecturing positions at London College of Fashion, University of East London and has guest lectured at more than 20 global institutions. Bethan is a published author, international conference presenter and active researcher. Her research spans Multi-Sensory Fashion Retailing, Customer Brand Experiences Online and Offline and Innovative Retail Formats.

Marta Blazquez Cano is a Lecturer in Fashion Marketing at the School of Materials, University of Manchester. Marta holds a BA in Advertising and PR and has developed a career in the advertising a marketing industry for more than 10 years. She was awarded European PhD in Marketing with Cum Laude mention. Marta's research interest includes omnichannel retail, experiential retail, channel integration, in-store technology, social media marketing, mobile marketing and consumer behaviour. She has published in leading journals, contributed to edited books, and presented her work at various national and international conferences. Marta has been visiting researcher in the Oxford Institute of Research Management (OXIRM), University of Oxford, and has been invited lecturer on several occasions in China and Spain. She supervises a number of PhD and MSc students in the areas of fashion marketing and retailing.

Retail Promotional Communication: The Comparative Effectiveness of Print Versus Online

Cristina Ziliani, Marco Ieva, Juan Carlos Gázquez-Abad, and Ida D'Attoma

Abstract New promotional tools such as digital reward platforms, virtual loyalty currencies, and digital wallets are being introduced and some are being adopted quickly by consumers. These tools are increasingly accessed via mobile devices: for example, digital wallets developed in the form of apps. Despite the market increase in the popularity of new digital channels for purchasing and for information and promotion search, there is a scarcity of studies on the comparison between customer response to traditional (i.e. offline) channels versus new digital channels in the context of retail promotional communication. This chapter compares print versus online retail promotional communication; provides an overview of flyer evolution from print to digital thanks to customer insight and "flyer aggregators"; and discusses a field experiment implemented with the cooperation of an Italian retail chain aiming to measure the effectiveness of print versus online store flyers. Findings indicate that 80% of customers respond equally to print versus online, while 20% of the customers display a higher response to print.

1 Introduction

Consumers use multiple channels (Rangaswamy and Van Bruggen 2005; Verhoef et al. 2007): a PricewaterhouseCoopers (PwC) global survey on multichannel shopping (2012) reports that 86% of global respondents shop across online and offline channels and 25% of respondents use four or five channels to shop. The availability of new digital channels and touchpoints is having a strong effect on

C. Ziliani (✉) · M. Ieva
Department of Economics and Management, University of Parma, Parma, Italy
e-mail: cristina.ziliani@unipr.it

J. C. Gázquez-Abad
Faculty of Business and Economics, Department of Economics and Business, Agrifood Campus of International Excellence ceiA3, University of Almería, Almería, Spain

I. D'Attoma
Department of Statistical Sciences, University of Bologna, Bologna, Italy

© Springer Nature Switzerland AG 2019
W. Piotrowicz, R. Cuthbertson (eds.), *Exploring Omnichannel Retailing*,
https://doi.org/10.1007/978-3-319-98273-1_10

consumers, brand manufacturers and retailers. Brand manufacturers and retailers are reviewing their communication and promotional strategies because of the decreasing effectiveness of "traditional" promotion and because retail and brand activities are increasingly moving online (Ailawadi et al. 2009; Leeflang et al. 2014). For example, retailers are increasingly investing in online advertising. Their global spend was predicted to reach $200 billion at the end of 2015, a 15% increase on 2014 (Juniper Research 2015).

To sustain sales during the recent period of economic crisis, manufacturers and retailers have increased their promotional spending. A common metric, the incidence of sales on promotion on total grocery sales, rose from 20% in 2004 to 29% in 2013 in Italy. Overall, the proportion of product sales on promotion has reached 28.7% for food and 28.1% for non-food on average across Europe in 2015 (IRI 2015). However, promotional effectiveness is decreasing: 67% of Europeans have reduced their spending and the IRI index of promotional effectiveness dropped from 106.9 to 100.7 in the 2008–2011 period (Lugli 2014). At the same time, digital channels and customer insight gained from individual customer information (e.g. available through loyalty program databases) and new intermediaries opened opportunities for innovation in communication and promotional strategies. New promotional tools such as digital reward platforms, virtual loyalty currencies and digital wallets are introduced and some are being adopted quickly by consumers. These tools are increasingly being accessed via mobile devices: for example, digital wallets developed in the form of apps. Starbucks is one of the most popular examples of mobile loyalty, enabling its My Starbucks Rewards members to collect stars for their purchases and redeem them for free drinks. The fact that consumers do not need to input personal credit card information to participate in the program is an attractive factor for many people. According to a Gallup survey, more than half of individuals not using a mobile wallet listed security as their primary concern (Samuely 2016). To drive up mobile wallet usage and adoption rates, brands must therefore offer an added incentive. Many are in fact offering mobile wallet-reward program hybrids.

Despite the market increase in the popularity of new digital channels for purchasing and for information and promotion search, there is a scarcity of studies on the comparison between customer response to traditional (i.e. offline) channels versus new digital channels in the context of retail promotional communication. This lack of research comparing promotional media is surprising because the topic appears as one of the most pressing marketing issues (Danaher and Dagger 2013). Several separate reviews of new areas of retailing research conducted in 2009 and 2011 pointed to the comparison in terms of effectiveness between promotions via traditional media and promotions via online channels as an emerging issue in communication and promotion research (see Ailawadi et al. 2009; Grewal et al. 2011). The study described in this chapter addresses the comparative effect of print and online promotional communication on customer purchase behaviour. The retail communication tool under investigation in this study is the promotional flyer.

In many countries a substantial part of promotional communication budgets is commanded by store flyers (Gázquez-Abad et al. 2014). Managers are therefore concerned with the improvement of store flyer efficiency and effectiveness. In this context, the shift from traditional print to online flyers—i.e. the online version of the print flyer, available on the retailer website or via a mobile app—represents an interesting area for both academics and practitioners.

Retailers are increasingly introducing online flyers because millions of households search today for retail flyers online (Ziliani and Ieva 2015). Retailers are concerned with taking correct decisions with regard to online versus print to improve budget allocation. However, they have no evidence on the comparative effectiveness of print versus online. Previous scarce comparisons on medium effectiveness revealed conflicting results, as discussed below in the literature review. Most of what is currently known on this topic consists of industry studies performed by marketing agencies on behalf of retailers or manufacturers.

In this context, the present chapter aims to provide: (1) a review of the print versus online comparison in the area of retail promotional communication; (2) an overview of flyer evolution from print to digital thanks to customer insight and "flyer aggregators"; (3) the discussion of a field experiment implemented with the cooperation of an Italian retail chain aimed to measure the effectiveness of print versus online store flyers on the purchase behaviour of 5000 customers. Results shows that 80% of customers respond equally to print versus online, while 20% of the customers display a higher response to print; (4) managerial recommendations, pointing to the benefits of targeted distribution of print and online flyers.

2 Print Versus Online: The Role of the Medium

Academic contributions on the effect of new online media on customer response in comparison with traditional media started to appear during the late 1990s.

A medium has been defined as "a transmission vehicle, channel or device through which messages are transmitted from senders to receivers" (Sundar et al. 1998, p. 823). A medium is able to create a context in which consumers are exposed to and can process a marketing communication (Valacich et al. 1993; Bryant and Zillmann 2002).

Media technologies have been recognized to exert a psychological effect on customer response (Sundar et al. 1998). Theory—such as the theory of cognitive involvement and the theory of interface involvement—and empirical evidence suggest that psychological differences exist in processing content delivered by means of different media (e.g. Griffith et al. 2001; Suri et al. 2004).

Each medium includes a wide variety of attributes (Eveland 2003): interactivity, organisation (or structure), control, channel, textuality and content are listed as main but not exhaustive media attributes. Identifying the relevant medium attributes has been considered a challenging task because there is no structured approach and no conclusive list of key media attributes (Eveland 2003; Magee 2013). Consequently, analysing the medium from a holistic perspective enables the inclusion of all possible media attributes in the analysis. This is a common approach in applied marketing communication research (Magee 2013) and has been employed in several studies concerned with media comparison (e.g. Suri et al. 2004; Jones et al. 2005). In our work we adopt this perspective.

The print versus online comparison has been studied in the field of communication and advertising with the aim of evaluating which media is more effective. Compared to the print medium, the online medium has been found to be more interactive and vivid (Coyle and Thorson 2001). Consumers can exert a greater control on browsing online content and are more active in processing information online (Berthon et al. 1996; Hoffman and Novak 1996). When processing information on the internet, users have been shown to personalize the information flow and jump from one website to another while actively seeking information (Suri et al. 2004). Mobile devices are changing the way users process information online. Because mobile devices provide a narrow view and require a higher number of scrolling movements than PCs, they might lead users to lose the global perspective of the task they are involved in and to face higher cognitive load (Ghose et al. 2012). The small screens of mobile phones are reported to create a serious obstacle to users' navigation activities and perceptions (Chae and Kim 2004).

When processing content on print, consumers are exposed to the information in a more linear and passive way (Bezjian-Avery et al. 1998; Singer and Alexander 2016). Print texts let readers perceive the spatial extension of the text and be in contact with physical and tactile cues to the length of the passage (Mangen et al. 2013; Sellen and Harper 2002). Finally, reading on print has been found to decrease the likelihood, for readers, to multitask (e.g. checking their emails) when compared to online reading (Rideout et al. 2010).

3   Theoretical Background

Two main theories have been developed to explain how print and online affect customer response on a cognitive and attitudinal level: theory of cognitive involvement and theory of interface involvement. These theories are different but not rival in their explanation of the effect of print versus online on memory, attitude and purchase intention.

Theory of cognitive involvement points to the role of cognitive involvement in media effects (Eagly and Chaiken 1993; Suri et al. 2004). Cognitive involvement is defined as *"the extent of cognitive elabouration which occurs in a communication process"* (Liu and Shrum 2002, p. 60). This elabouration process has a key impact on memory for the presented content: a more thorough processing of information might lead to higher memory for the processed content (Suri et al. 2004). Cognitive involvement varies depending on the type of situation. In fact, motivation to process information and other contextual variables, such as the medium itself, might affect cognitive involvement (Batra and Ray 1986; Liu and Shrum 2002). The theory of cognitive involvement claims that motivation to process information interacts with the medium to influence the elabouration of information. For instance, the online medium will create a context with high cognitive involvement for consumers with low motivation to process information: it will lead to a more accurate evaluation of the marketing communication and eventually to higher memory for the content. Conversely, for consumers with high motivation to process information, the online medium will create a low cognitive involvement because the additional motivation induced by the medium is able to debilitate consumers in their elabouration process. Consequently, information processing for these consumers will be less accurate, leading to a lower level of memory.

Theory of interface involvement points to the role of interface. Interfaces can be decomposed into two basic elements: the physical medium through which information is transmitted, and the presentation of the content (Hartson 1998; Shneiderman 2010). For instance, the physical medium for print is the page, and the content presentation includes static pictures and text. The physical medium for online is the system employed to display the information while the content presentation is the manner in which the information is presented (e.g. videos, pictures, text). Interface involvement is "the ability of a user interface to facilitate users' involvement with the information content presented to them" (Griffith et al. 2001, p. 136). Theory of interface involvement claims that interface elements can exert an influence on user attitudes towards both the interface itself and the presented content (e.g. Rice 1993; Shneiderman 2010). When a user interacts with an interface, he might be involved in two environments: (1) the physical environment which is the actual environment where the information is processed, and (2) a virtual environment which corresponds to the content being read or viewed (Steuer 1992). If the involvement produced by the interaction with the interface is high, the user becomes more engaged with the content rather than with the physical environment (Nass and Steuer 1993). The theory of interface involvement claims that web-based physical-medium interfaces (e.g. display screens and keyboards) create barriers and limit consumer involvement with the presented offer. This, in turn, leads to a negative effect on attitude and purchase intention (Jacob 1996; Griffith et al. 2001; Jones et al. 2005). Hence, theory of interface involvement points to the role of the technical limitations of the web-based physical-medium interface (e.g. input devices and screen size) as the main source of the print superiority against online (e.g. Cook and Coupey 1998).

We now provide a brief description of the main studies comparing print and online. The reviewed studies employed informative and persuasive content across different industries (e.g. food, fashion, health), measuring media effects on several outcomes (e.g. recall, attitude). They share two main features:

- Only short term effects have been estimated, in terms of memory, attitude towards the offer or the ad, and purchase intention.
- Most of them were conducted by means of lab experiments.

These studies largely involved student samples in forced exposure conditions. Laboratory studies are indeed useful in theory testing, but their internal, ecological and external validity is severely reduced (Nan and Faber 2004). Moreover, no study has measured customer response to print versus online in terms of actual purchase behaviour. The main studies are summarized in following section.

Sundar et al. (1998) found higher memory for a print ad featured in a newspaper versus an online ad, and no difference in memory for an article (i.e. informative content) in the same newspaper between the two media. Griffith et al. (2001) found print superiority in terms of attitude and involvement as far as the content of an apparel retailer catalogue was concerned. Jones et al. (2005) reported print superiority for informative and persuasive content in the context of the communication of drugs and medications. Gallagher et al. (2001) found no overall medium superiority. Suri et al. (2004) compared online versus print coupons. According to their results, subjects processed information more accurately online in a low-motivation scenario (i.e. a low-involving situation such as grocery shopping) and on print in a high-motivation scenario. Wakolbinger et al. (2009) reported that print and online advertising are equally effective in terms of memory and showed that a cross-media campaign featuring both print and online ads might be more effective than a single-medium campaign. Finally, Magee (2013) conducted the only field experiment in this area and found a higher memory for an informative print publication (a university publication) sent via mail to university alumni rather than for the same publication sent via e-mail.

In sum, comparisons of print versus online presentation of the same content to comparable audiences (randomization has ensured that subjects exposed to print and online did not differ in term of their attributes and characteristics, such as age, gender, familiarity with technology and other unobservable characteristics) have shown a weak superiority of print.

This was attributed by most authors to physical interface differences (Magee 2013; Jones et al. 2005; Griffith et al. 2001; Sundar et al. 1998). However, superiority of print emerging from previous research might also be attributed to potential biases, as in Jones et al. (2005): information retrieval was assessed by means of an on-paper retrieval cue, which shared the same modality as one level of the independent variable (print).

Finally, age and comfort with using a screen have been shown to influence the relationship between medium and memory. Age has been found be a significant moderator of the effect of medium on memory: younger and older subjects exposed to print reported higher free recall than online, while no difference between print and online free recall was found among middle-aged subjects (Magee 2013). Moreover, comfort with using a screen (which expresses the degree of confidence in using the internet via a PC) was found to be a (weak) moderator of the effect of medium on memory: subjects less confident with the PC reported higher recall for the print content with respect to the online content (Jones et al. 2005).

Current academic research regarding print versus online leaves managers without a clear understanding of which medium is superior in terms of customer response and how the promotional budget should be assigned between print and online media to improve effectiveness.

4 Innovation in Promotion and Store Flyers

In this section the new promotional tools adopted by brands and retailers are introduced. They are enabled by digital technology. Then, store flyers are discussed as traditional promotional tools that are undergoing major changes due to the shift from print to online and to the rise of flyer aggregator platforms.

Brands and retailers are experimenting with innovation in promotion, thanks to new digital channels, and customer insight gained from individual customer information and new intermediaries (Ziliani and Ieva 2014). Consequently, shoppers are offered a plethora of promotional opportunities, accessible at various phases of the shopping cycle, deployed by a growing number of players across several channels (Shankar et al. 2011). Brand coupons, for example, are available on brand and retailer websites, coupon websites, mobile location-based coupon services and group deals sites (e.g. Groupon). In 2013, 80% of US internet users downloaded coupons from brand, retail or intermediary websites and over 60% of consumers looked online for a coupon/deal/offer before making a purchase (eMarketer 2013).

At the same time, brands compete for customer loyalty by offering loyalty schemes and clubs, loyalty apps, subscription-based schemes and branded currency wallets (e.g. Starbucks). "Price" and "loyalty" promotion (Fig. 1), once separate domains, are merging into hybrid strategies that make use of "the best of both worlds" to attract shoppers and make them stay.

Alongside retailers and manufacturers many "deal intermediaries" have emerged. They range from the long established providers of targeted coupons-at-till based on shoppers' history such as Catalina Marketing (www.catalina.com) to coupon websites, mobile location-based coupon services, group deals sites (e.g. Groupon) and group deals aggregators (e.g. Yipit.com). A very interesting case is that of virtual wallets such as Google Wallet and Apple's Passbook where coupons, loyalty points, customer data and methods of payment coexist (see Ziliani and Ieva 2014 for a detailed description of the new promotional tools).

Digital platforms are a powerful source of innovation in price promotion (Fig. 1), enabling new promotion types such as group deals and flash sales. At the same time, digital technology is transforming traditional tools, such as coupons and flyers, by shifting them online and enabling their customization. In the next section we focus on the digital evolution of promotional flyers.

4.1 Traditional Flyers

The promotional flyer, taking its original name from the times when wartime aircrafts dropped leaflets onto enemy cities for propaganda purposes, is a printed means of regular (e.g. weekly/monthly) one-way communication between retailers and customers, distributed both in store and out of store and employed to communicate deals and retailer image (Pieters et al. 2007).

Loyalty tools	Price promotion tools
Loyalty cards	Digital flyers
Brands loyalty programs	Digital coupons
Coalition loyalty programs	Save-to- card discounts for LP members
Loyalty apps	Promotional e-newsletter/e-mail
Digital rewards platforms	Retail web specials
Mobile payment wallets/branded currency	Coupon websites
Subscription based services	Mobile coupon services
Loyalty wallets	Flyer intermediaries
	Group deals websites
	Flash sales websites
	Deal aggregators

Fig. 1 The new promotional landscape, source Ziliani and Ieva (2015)

The flyer commands a substantial part of a retailer's budget in many countries (Parguel et al. 2009; De Camillis 2012; Gazquez-Abad and Sanchez-Perez 2009). In 2002, flyers accounted for 50% of the average retail marketing budget in Italy, while in France they accounted for 60% and 65% in the US (De Camillis 2012). Flyers are an important retail promotion tool because they influence shoppers both at home and in store and are source of marketing contributions from manufacturers who rely heavily on them to reach consumers directly (Srinivasan et al. 1995; Volle 1997; Arnold et al. 2001; Mimouni-Chaabane et al. 2010).

Due to the relevance of investment in flyers, the reduced effectiveness of promotions, the growing tide of new promotional opportunities and the emergence of new players, managers are concerned with the improvement of store flyer efficiency and effectiveness. The following critical aspects of flyers as retail marketing tools emerge from previous research (Ziliani and Ieva 2015):

Time to Market It takes up to 2 months from concept to delivery, and no last minute changes can be made.

Environmental Impact The twelve billion flyers printed and distributed in Italy every year account for 500,000 tons of carbon emissions (De Camillis 2012); it can be expected that more and more cities will rule against flyer distribution.

Poor Measurability At present, retailers track overall promotional sales lift of in-flyer items but have no means to relate this to customers' actual exposure to the flyer itself. Neither do they assess the impact of flyer page length, in-flyer brand mix, and other features.

Buyer Driven Process Within the retail organisation, the process of flyer production involves buyers and category managers more than marketing people, who usually collabourate on design elements and overall flyer theme only, and have little saying as far as the choice of products is concerned.

Retailers are concerned with the above problems, and they are aware that today's promotional scenario (Fig. 1) offers consumers numerous alternatives to print flyers (Ziliani and Ieva 2015).

So far, academic research on flyers has investigated: impact of flyer design on store traffic and on store sales (Gijsbrechts et al. 2003; Mimouni-Chaabane et al. 2010), flyer design optimisation (Pieters et al. 2007), profile of flyer-prone consumer (Martínez and Montaner 2006), and flyer as information source (Zhang 2006). Little or no attention has been paid by academic research to the flyer management process and its organisational dimensions. Ziliani and Ieva (2015) identify the decision centres involved in planning this essential part of retail promotion, and the information sources used for flyer creation and management. They found that flyers have evolved drastically in recent years thanks to the availability of customer insight for the flyer planning process and to digitalization.

To improve the flyer design and management process, some retailers have been applying customer insight derived from loyalty card data, as shown by the following applications (Ziliani and Ieva 2015):

Optimisation of Flyer Geographical Distribution By knowing where customers live, flyer distribution can be better planned.

Analysis of Flyer Performance in Different Customer Segments of Interests, and Customer Segmentation Based on "Flyer Proneness" Insight results in substituting the flyer (for customers who score low in terms of flyer influenced purchases or other measure of flyer impact) with new communication channels such as serving customised promotions on till receipts, kiosks, website, apps and others.

Shopping Basket Analysis This can be applied to understanding flyer impact, e.g. by computing the percentage of loyal families who repurchase the promoted good after having tried it due to a flyer. Shopping basket "gap" analysis can suggest categories and SKUs (stock keeping units) to promote on flyers in order to stimulate customers to fill such gaps.

Extracting insight from customer databases to improve print flyer effectiveness and efficiency, however, is evidently not an easy nor fast option. It is not surprising, therefore, that many retailers are turning to digital channels in search of a shortcut.

4.2   Digital Flyers

Digital flyers are the online version of the print flyer, available on the retailer website or mobile app, which have been identified by business press as a recent addition to retailers' digital assets (Ray 2011). Making the flyer available online, however, means different things for different retailers. Some digital flyers recall the early days of the web, when websites were "brochureware", i.e. pdf versions of print ads. Some retailers, on the other hand, have seized the opportunity to enhance flyers by "augmenting" them with digital features such as:

- Search engine internal to flyer, to enable in-flyer search of product offers by brand, category, and even percentage-off product price;
- Electronic coupons associated with each featured product that the customer can download or save electronically (i.e. to an online shopping list);
- Save item to shopping list, for printing, sharing, e-mailing;
- Product details that can be accessed by clicking on the product image: nutritional values, traceability, ratings by other shoppers;
- Recipes featuring the flyer products accessible as videos, QR codes and links;
- Send flyer via e-mail;
- Share flyer or single offer via text message or social plugins;
- Make flyer printable and downloadable, whole or single page;
- Flyer app: an app that allows for flyer push receiving, browsing and other flyer interactions and services (forward, share, save item to shopping list);
- "Shop through flyer": by connecting to e-commerce functionalities consumers can click on the image of products featured in the online flyer and access the retailer's (or manufacturer's or third party's) e-commerce website where the item can immediately be purchased.

Retailers who can leverage their customer information database for insight can go much further in the exploitation of the opportunities offered by digital channels. For example, the US Stop and Shop supermarket chain has combined loyalty data with a program from Datalogix that enables the retailer to find its customers while they are surfing the web and deliver the flyer online to them in real time by displaying a targeted ad that links to the retailer's online flyer (Alaymo 2011). In-store visits and sales can be directly attributed to the online campaign through the shopper card data. The retailer reported strong return on the campaigns.

A new type of information intermediary, the flyer aggregator, provides an opportunity for retailers who want to develop a digital presence for their flyers and extend their reach, as discussed below.

4.3   Flyer Aggregators

Flyer intermediaries have been on the market for over a decade, and have expanded rapidly in recent years. Some are in essence price comparison services, as they basically help customers find the cheapest store for their shopping list by calculating price indexes for store comparison. Others play the "discovery" key as they aim to enhance flyer browsing convenience and enjoyment. One leading player, Shopfully, owner of several flyer browsing services in different countries, defines its business as: "the last mile media, the first source of geolocalized information on promotions, new products, shops, opening times and contacts of the main retailers and brands in all shopping categories, from grocery and drugstores to discount, clothing, electronics, office supplies, sporting goods, hardware and home and many others." (www. shopfully.com).

Retailers cooperate with flyer aggregators because of consumer interest in finding flyers online, and because at the same time only a fraction of a retailer's customer base log on to their websites to read flyers. Customers enlisted in loyalty card databases can be reached directly. Other customer segments such as cherry pickers, "shared customers" and prospects are more difficult to reach and pull to the retailer's website to read the flyer. An effective way to do this seems to be by leveraging the new online flyer intermediaries. Consumers enjoy the convenience of browsing only flyers relevant to their search, i.e. those featuring the desired category/product/brand, on offer for the period of their choice, and in the preferred geographical area. Consumers who register with the aggregator get notified immediately of the release of new relevant flyers: an advantage in the common case of limited available quantities of promoted products.

- Flyer aggregators compute new metrics for flyers such as:
- Bounce-back rate (% of customers leaving the flyer after seeing the first page)
- Time spent with flyer
- Time spent in zoom mode
- Views by device: % of views through smartphone, tablet, desktop PC
- Number of page views per page

Percentage of viewers who zoomed on featured items per page: as it is assumed that viewers zoom on a product when it is of interest, the number of zoom actions or number/percentage of viewers who zoomed on each page provides information on how attractive each page is, hence supporting the improvement of the flyer construction process Heatmap of zooms per page: with each page featuring many products, it is relevant to understand where viewers' attention fixates on each page. As zooms are considered a proxy for attention and, consequently, interest, a "heatmap" representation—similar to eye tracking research heatmaps—generates insight into which item/items or area/areas of the page command greater attention

Retailers can use these metrics to address the above mentioned problem of poor measurability of flyers.

Insight provided by aggregators can support informed decisions on the optimal number of flyer pages, number of items per page and more. As flyer aggregator services are available on a variety of platforms, such as smartphones and tablets, metrics can be computed for browsing activities taking place both at home, in the store or on the go, shedding light on the flyer role at different stages of the consumer path to purchase and on device preferences among customers.

By polling the subscribers' database, the aggregator knows how many customers visited a store after browsing the flyer online, how many switched store, whether they also browse print flyers. By asking subscribers for additional personal information (or partnering with retailers to merge customer database information with the aggregator's own data on customers' use of the platform) the aggregator gains valuable insight for targeting, such as demographics and shopping behaviour. The Italian leading platform Doveconviene.it discovered that users of digital flyers live in smaller towns where print flyers are less intensely distributed due to higher costs, and where distance to store is greater, making it a worthwhile customer choice to determine the destination store based on the information of available offers. Doveconviene.it also confirmed the US finding (Nielsen 2011) that users of flyer intermediaries are retailer's "non-loyal" customers—a different audience from the retailer's own digital assets visitors. Metrics and insight could also support a retailer's negotiation of advertising contribution with brand manufacturers based on "quality" of flyer space, number of views ("reach" of the flyer), number of zooms ("interest in the product") and more.

At present, the promotional strategy scenario is one where traditional flyers are widely used in many markets and a growing number of retailers are popularizing the new digital flyer. Intuitively, traditional flyers will not require integration with the company's other channels whereas the advanced features of digital flyers described above are only available for retailers who adopt an omnichannel approach. The scenario described so far encourages more research into the effectiveness of digital versus print flyers. Findings from literature concerning the print versus online effectiveness comparison provide only weak support for an overall superiority of print. It is unclear to what extent print may be considered more effective than online. To our knowledge, no studies have been conducted, neither in the advertising nor in retailing, estimating the effect of print versus online on customer responses in terms of actual behaviour. Therefore, we formulated the following research question:

RQ: Do online and print flyers show a different effect on customer purchase behaviour?

5   Methodology

The present section details the research process that was followed to answer the question of whether print and online promotional communications are equally effective. It also discusses the limitations of the process, while results are discussed in the following section.

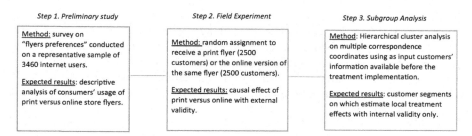

Fig. 2 Research design, main steps

Figure 2 details the implemented steps: (1) a preliminary study was useful to explore consumers' usage of print and online store flyers in the country of the study; (2) a field experimental design was adopted to test the effect of online vs print flyers on selected outcomes of interest; (3) a subgroup analysis on experimental data was employed to examine (at a descriptive level only), the various effects across heterogeneous subgroups.

In order to gain a general understanding of customer preference for print and online flyers in Italy, prior to the development of the experiment that we present in this chapter, we ran a preliminary study. The study consists of a survey of the Nielsen online consumer panel which is representative of the total Italian population. The panel includes 3460 subjects who are internet users and over 14 years old. Among these 2304 responses were collected from subjects who are in charge of, or cooperate with, the household's grocery shopping. Respondents were asked whether they preferred to receive store flyers in print, online, both forms, either form, or neither. This multi-item question, previously employed by Magee (2013), was used as the measure of medium preference.

5.1   Experiment: Research Design

After the preliminary study, we ran an effectiveness field study that employed a between-subject experimental design with partial treatment implementation (Shadish et al. 2002). A 37-supermarket retail chain currently active in Italy was the setting for this study. We compared two treatments, print versus online. The experiment was carried out on customers owning the retailer's loyalty card and a valid postal address and a valid e-mail address. Subjects were randomly assigned to one of two groups: 2500 customers were assigned to receive a print flyer and 2500 to receive the online version of the same flyer (which could be accessed via PC or mobile device). The offers featured in the flyer had a validity of 14 days.[1]

---

[1]The flyer was 32 pages long and featured 268 products: 85% were national brands and 15% were private labels.

Customers' purchase behaviour was recorded during these 14 days in terms of: (1) number of store visits; (2) amount spent on flyer-promoted products and amount spent on in-store promoted products; (3) number of flyer-promoted products bought and number of in-store promoted products bought. Products featured in the flyer were also promoted in the store by means of in-store reminders, whereas products we refer to as "in-store promoted products" were highlighted in store only. Using the experimental data, we have first estimated the average causal effect of print versus online flyers on some selected outcome of interest; then, we have implemented a Subgroup Analysis (SA) in order to determine whether and how print versus online effects vary across customer clusters (i.e. subgroups).

5.2   Subgroup Analysis

A variety of Subgroup Analysis (SA) applications to experimental data is largely found in the field of social experiments (e.g. Beecroft and Lee 2000; Gibson 2003; Peck 2003, 2005) or in clinical trials (see Olten and Gagnier 2015 for a recent review). Commonly, it is conducted by dividing treatment groups into subgroups on the basis of a single trait and, then, by exploring the interaction between the treatment and that covariate by repeated testing (Bonetti and Gelber 2004). In the present work, instead of using a single trait, following Peck (2005), we conducted SA by means of Hierarchical Cluster Analysis (e.g. Everitt et al. 2011). According to Peck's proposal, the use of Cluster Analysis (CA) applied to experimental data offers some advantages: (a) the identification of subgroups according to a complex set of characteristics rather than one trait at a time; (b) because of the use of pre-treatment characteristics to identify subgroups, the resulting comparison maintains the integrity of an experiment.

We collected all the customer information available before the treatment implementation (the sending of the flyer). Then, we employed a variant of the two-step tandem analysis (Arabie and Hubert 1994) to conduct cluster analysis. As a first step, we employed a Multiple Correspondence Analysis (MCA) on nine variables in order to transform categorical variables into a continuous space. As a second step, we ran hierarchical CA employing a Ward algorithm on all the MCA coordinates, exploiting the link existing between the two approaches (e.g. Greenacre 1988; Lebart and Mirkin 1993). To choose the number of groups we used the practical criterion of the dendrogram "cut" and we evaluated several indexes.[2] Then, within the selected clusters we estimated the effect of being assigned to a print versus online flyer[3] on

---

[2]Pseudo-T, Root-Mean-Square Standard Deviation, Cubic Clustering Criterion, R2 and Pseudo-F.

[3]To estimate effects, we employed a negative binomial regression for count outcomes (e.g. store visits, number of products) and a t-test on the log-transformed continuous outcomes (e.g. amount spent).

purchase behaviour outcomes collected during the 14-day promotional period. The analyses were carried out in SAS 9.4 application.

5.3 Research Limitations

First of all, the number of subgroups to be examined in the Subgroup Analysis are subjective. Different clustering algorithms and different "quality of clustering" criteria might lead to different results. Because "external validity may be limited" when a CA is employed (Peck 2005), we used CA at a descriptive level simply to have an idea of the direction and the magnitude of effects by subgroups. Moreover, we did not collect data on type of flyer-promoted and in-store promoted products bought (e.g. national brands versus private labels). In this experiment, before randomizing, we sampled subjects belonging to a population of customers with an active email. Thus, considerations on the comparative effectiveness of print versus online flyers are limited to the considered audience. We did not collect data on memory and attitude towards the presented offers. Hence, we were not able to estimate whether print and online have different effects on memory and attitudinal outcomes. Finally, external validity of findings is limited to this context of study: short-term media effects in a grocery setting.

6 Findings

6.1 Preliminary Study: Print Versus Online Flyers in Italy

Results from the preliminary study (Table 1) show that customers strongly prefer receiving print flyers only (54%), while 11% of customers declare an exclusive preference for online flyers. This might suggest that customer response to flyers might be in favour of print rather than online. Twenty-two % of customers actually prefer receiving both print and online, while 6% are reluctant to be addressed with flyers.

Table 1 Preference for print versus online flyers

Flyer medium	Respondents
Print	54%
Online	11%
Both print and online	22%
Either print or online	7%
Neither print nor online	6%

Table 2 Descriptive statistics of print and online groups

Variable	Print group mean	Online group mean
Number of store visits [ns]	1.55	1.56
Amount spent (€) on flyer-promoted products [ns]	11.44	10.77
Number of flyer-promoted products bought [ns]	7.14	6.92
Amount spent (€) on in-store promoted products [ns]	3.94	3.65
Number of in-store promoted products bought [ns]	1.86	1.77
N	2500	2500

[ns]= no significant difference found

6.2 Results from the Experiment

Table 2 shows the average causal effectiveness of print versus online flyers. For each selected outcome of interest, no significant difference was found between print and online groups.

The Subgroup Analysis includes as a first step the Cluster Analysis to identify clusters based on the following variables (for period of last 6 months):

- Number of store visits
- Amount spent (€) on flyer-promoted products
- Number of flyer-promoted products bought
- Amount spent (€) on in-store promoted products
- Number of in-store promoted products bought
- Amount spent (€) not on promotion
- Number of products bought not on promotion
- Subscription to the retailer newsletter
- Registration to the retailer website

The practical criterion of the dendrogram "cut" and the other indexes suggested an 8-cluster solution. Within each cluster, subjects are similar with respect to the variables employed in the analysis. However, subjects within a cluster differ from those belonging to any other cluster. Within each of these 8 clusters, we compared subjects assigned to the print flyer versus those assigned to the online. Clusters are described according to their characteristics and size in Table 3. Clusters differ in term of customer value (high spending versus low spending).

We compared subjects assigned to the print flyer versus those assigned to the online flyer within each segment (Table 4) in order to detect differences in the effect of print versus online flyer on purchase behaviour.

Cluster 4 and cluster 8 showed significant differences in customer response in favour of print. These two clusters include "intermediate-to-low" spending customers and represent about 20% of the total sample. However, the other six clusters did not display any difference. We shall now move on to discuss flyer effects in the light of each cluster characteristics. Several insights for research and management emerge.

Table 3 Means and frequencies of the identified customer clusters

Variable	Cluster 1	Cluster 2	Cluster 3	Cluster 4	Cluster 5	Cluster 6	Cluster 7	Cluster 8
Number of store visits in the last 6 months	64	53	3	30	40	25	9	16
Amount spent (€) on flyer-promoted products in the last 6 months	509	225	15	194	396	94	48	41
Number of flyer-promoted products bought in the last 6 months	307	128	9	119	248	56	29	22
Amount spent (€) on in-store promoted products in the last 6 months	118	66	3	42	79	54	1	14
Number of in-store promoted products bought in the last 6 months	240	143	6	83	156	26	21	31
Amount spent (€) on products not on promotion in the last 6 months	1554	1437	31	505	613	500	130	350
Number of in-store products bought not on promotion in the last 6 months	817	716	16	268	331	331	67	167
Subscription to the retailer newsletter	51%	38%	20%	41%	49%	32%	24%	23%
Registration on the retailer website	27%	18%	11%	27%	24%	17%	13%	14%
Subjects assigned to the online flyer	275	161	492	319	210	373	499	183
Subjects assigned to the print flyer	272	164	499	298	212	381	482	180
Total N	547	325	991	617	422	754	981	363

Table 4 Means of outcome variables between print and online within the identified clusters

	Flyer	Number of store visits	Amount spent (€) on flyer-promoted products	Number of flyer-promoted products bought	Amount spent (€) on in-store promoted products	Number of in-store promoted products bought	N
Cluster 1	Online	4.02	37.60	23.39	11.69	5.77	275
	Print	3.95	35.56	22.10	12.63	6.03	272
Cluster 2	Online	3.45	16.47	10.83	6.85	3.31	161
	Print	3.09	15.98	9.48	8.50	3.74	164
Cluster 3	Online	0.27	1.54	1.02	0.62	0.32	492
	Print	0.26	1.94	1.20	0.48	0.22	499
Cluster 4	Online	1.73	11.70	7.81	3.63	1.69	319
	Print	**2.03***	16.32	**10.04***	**4.71***	**2.17***	298
Cluster 5	Online	2.40	21.32	14.55	6.66	3.38	210
	Print	2.25	24.06	16.28	7.21	3.50	212
Cluster 6	Online	1.61	6.91	4.08	2.74	1.18	373
	Print	1.51	6.91	4.01	2.61	1.27	381
Cluster 7	Online	0.58	3.54	2.41	1.38	0.70	499
	Print	0.69	4.05	2.57	1.08	0.53	482
Cluster 8	Online	0.91	3.50	1.98	1.27	0.61	183
	Print	1.00	**4.26***	2.46	**1.86***	0.84	180

*statistically significant, $p < 0.05$

7 Discussion

This study compares the effect of print versus online flyers within each cluster, thus taking into account heterogeneity of customer response to flyers. The comparison between print and online groups reveals that there is no difference in customer response to print versus online as far as purchase behaviour is concerned. In this respect, online and print can be regarded as equally effective. Subgroup analysis shows that six customer segments (namely clusters 1 2, 3, 5, 6 and 7), representing 80% of customers, respond equally to print versus online flyers in terms of purchase behaviour. We call these clusters "Medium neutrals". "Medium neutrals" customers include: (1) high-spending customers (across all the spending variables), who also display higher subscription rates to the retailer newsletter and higher registration rates to the retailer website, and (2) low-spending customers (across all the spending variables), who also display the lowest levels of subscription rate to the retailer newsletter and registration to the retailer website.

Twenty percent of customers (clusters 4 and 8) are more responsive to print rather than to online flyers. We call them "Sensitive to print" customers. They appear to be "average-to-low" spending customers. Customers in cluster 4 display average frequency and spending across all spending variables. Moreover, this cluster displays a high subscription rate to the retailer newsletter and high registration rate to the retailer website. Customers in cluster 8 visit the store less frequently and are low-spending across all spending variables. Moreover, subscription rates to the retailer newsletter and website are low.

Our findings extend previous studies on media effects by measuring the effect of medium on purchase behaviour. Several studies found a weak superiority of print as far as memory is concerned (Magee 2013; Jones et al. 2005; Griffith et al. 2001; Sundar et al. 1998). We show that this superiority varies across customer clusters: only 20% of customers display higher response to print versus online. The majority of customers respond equally to print versus online. This finding is in line with results from Gallagher et al. (2001) and Wakolbinger et al. (2009), who found that print and online elicit the same response in terms of memory.

As far as the theory of interface involvement is concerned, that has been widely employed in the above research stream and our findings do not support it in full. Previous studies claimed the superiority of print in the development of a positive attitude and purchase intention towards the presented content. This was attributed to the physical interface elements of the online medium (e.g. keyboards, mouse) that worked as "barriers", thus limiting involvement with the content. Our results do not provide evidence for an absolute superiority of print. This might suggest that for 80% of subjects, physical medium interface attributes are not barriers to content impact on behavioural response.

It could be hypothesized that technological improvements that occurred over the last decade have simplified the way we interact with the online medium. Physical interfaces of the numerous available devices (e.g. laptops, smartphones or tablets) are now easy to use for consumers compared to the recent past. The large adoption of mobile devices and apps has intuitively played in favour of consumer familiarity with these new technologies and, at the same time, it offers new opportunities for retailers. In fact, studies have found that order size and rate increase as customers become mobile shoppers (Wang et al. 2015). Moreover, "touch" devices such as tablets and smartphones might lead to more positive product evaluations compared to "traditional" devices such as laptops (Brasel and Gips 2014).

In sum, new technological developments might have lowered the barriers between the user and the content presented through the online medium. Therefore, theory of interface involvement might not be appropriate to explain how customers develop an attitude towards content presented through an online medium.

8   Conclusions and Future Research Directions

In this section we highlight managerial implications for retailers arising from the study and we discuss areas for further academic and business research.

As different customer segments display a different response to print and online, retailers can increase the effectiveness of their promotional communications by targeting segments of interest with the appropriate medium. For instance, because intermediate-to-low-spending customers are found to be more responsive to print, retailers are advised to employ print flyers to target this segment, which has an up-selling potential. As high-spending customers respond equally to online and print content, they could usefully be targeted with online flyers. A shift to online flyers would also enable the gaining of useful information on browsing behaviour of these valuable customers. In-page analytics (e.g. click and zoom rates on different brands) would offer meaningful insights that retailers could employ for targeting promotional offers to customers displaying interest in specific brands/categories and at the same time for promotional fee negotiation with suppliers. Retailers are therefore encouraged to find ways to capture such analytics, be it by means of internally managed tools or by flyer aggregators. Finally, retailers could increase the effectiveness of their promotional communication efforts by stopping or reducing the frequency of print flyer distribution to occasional customers, as this has proved to be ineffective. At the same time, addressing occasional customers with online flyers would reduce the cost of communication.

In sum, to the extent that the online option is less costly than print, employing a customer segmentation approach in flyer distribution might lead to both cost reduction and improved effectiveness.

As far as omnichannel strategies for retailers are concerned our findings provide useful guidance. Retailers who are adopting an undifferentiated promotional communication strategy (e.g. the "one size fits all" print flyer), find little incremental value in moving to omnichannel as their promotional activity cannot be leveraged for targeting individual customers with specific content across channels. In this case, the undifferentiated promotional strategy is well fitted for a "simpler" multichannel approach. Retailers could establish an online version of the print flyer and make both available via the respective channels. Our study, indeed, shows that 80% of customers respond equally to print and online.

However, retailers who are showing an interest for the adoption of digital flyers enhanced with information intensive features such as those described earlier, will quickly grasp the need for an omnichannel strategy to enable the new promotional communication approach. In fact, several of the described features of digital flyers require a seamless integration of the retailer's channels. For example, saving an in-flyer coupon to the customer loyalty card profile to enable redemption in store, requires connection between flyer data and the loyalty database. Even more so, enabling the one-click purchase of a flyer featured product through the retailer ecommerce facility requires integration with the latter systems. In sum, retailers who are currently multi-channel will not be able to exploit to the full potential of digital flyers. As long as flyers are a major source of suppliers' funding and a favourite of consumers, retailers will strive to enable the potential of digital flyers and this will tilt the balance towards their investment into omnichannel.

Our work opens up several opportunities for further research. Considering the emerging stream of studies on the effect of touch interfaces on customer attitudes and behaviours (e.g. Brasel and Gips 2014; De Canio et al. 2015), exploration of the effect of type of device (tablet versus laptop versus mobile) in promotional communication is highly advisable.

With reference to the theory of cognitive involvement, future studies should contribute to investigating which medium is currently more effective in terms of memory as far as the promotional context is concerned. It can be argued that both theories of cognitive involvement and of interface involvement are challenged by continuous technological change. There is the need for improving and updating the theoretical understanding of how consumers interact through different devices with the same online promotion. Finally, as consumers' familiarity with the online medium is a dynamic process that will evolve across time, it will be of key relevance to evaluate print versus online effectiveness over the longer term.

Questions for Discussion and Review

1. What challenges are retail promotion strategies facing in today's scenario?
2. What is a "medium"?
3. What are the key points of main theories on print versus online effects?
4. What findings emerge from previous experimental research on print versus online?
5. What are the strengths and weaknesses of print versus online flyers?
6. What are flyer aggregators?
7. What are the main benefits for marketers of running a subgroup analysis?
8. What is the comparative effectiveness of print versus online flyers in terms of purchase behaviour?
9. What recommendations for retailers arise from the study presented in this chapter?
10. What is your experience with traditional and online flyers?

References

Ailawadi, K., Beauchamp, J. P., Donthu, N., Gauri, D., & Shankar, V. (2009). Communication and promotion decisions in retailing: A review and directions for future research. *Journal of Retailing, 85*(1), 42–55.

Alaymo, D. (2011). Circular logic. *Progressive Grocer*, November, Accessed February 14, 2014 from www.progressivegrocer.com/inprint/article/id2346/circular-logic/

Arabie, P., & Hubert, L. (1994). Cluster analysis in marketing research. In R. P. Bagozzi (Ed.), *Advanced Methods of Marketing Research* (pp. 160–189). Oxford: Blackwell.

Arnold, S., Kozinets, R., & Handelman, J. (2001). Hometown ideology and retailer legitimization: The institutional semiotics of Wal-Mart flyers. *Journal of Retailing, 77*, 243–271.

Batra, R., & Ray, M. L. (1986). Affective responses mediating acceptance of advertising. *Journal of Consumer Research*, 234–249.

Beecroft, E., & Lee, W. S. (2000). *Looking beyond mean impacts to see who gains and who loses with time-limited welfare: Evidence from the Indiana Welfare Reform Evaluation*. Paper presented at the Annual Meeting of the National Association for Welfare Research and Statistics, Scottsdale, AZ, August.

Berthon, P., Pitt, L. F., & Watson, R. T. (1996). The World Wide Web as an advertising medium. *Journal of Advertising Research, 36*(01), 43–54.

Bezjian-Avery, A., Calder, B., & Iacobucci, D. (1998). New media interactive advertising vs. traditional advertising. *Journal of Advertising Research, 38*, 23–32.

Bonetti, M., & Gelber, R. D. (2004). Patterns of treatment effects in subsets of patients in clinical trials. *Biostatistics, 5*(3), 465–481.

Brasel, S. A., & Gips, J. (2014). Tablets, touchscreens, and touchpads: How varying touch interfaces trigger psychological ownership and endowment. *Journal of Consumer Psychology, 24*(2), 226–233.

Bryant, J., & Zillmann, D. (2002). *Media effects. Advances in theory and research.* New Jersey: LEA.

Chae, M., & Kim, J. (2004). Do size and structure matter to mobile users? An empirical study of the effects of screen size, information structure, and task complexity on user activities with standard web phones. *Behaviour and Information Technology, 23*(3), 165–181.

Cook, D. L., & Coupey, E. (1998). Consumer behaviour and unresolved regulatory issues in electronic marketing. *Journal of Business Research, 41*(3), 231–238.

Coyle, J. R., & Thorson, E. (2001). The effects of progressive levels of interactivity and vividness in web marketing sites. *Journal of Advertising, 30*(3), 65–77.

Danaher, P. J., & Dagger, T. S. (2013). Comparing the relative effectiveness of advertising channels: A case study of a multimedia blitz campaign. *Journal of Marketing Research, 50* (4), 517–534.

De Camillis, R. (Ed.) (2012). Promozioni Efficaci? Il Volantino: Istruzioni per l'Uso. *Conference Proceedings Parma: Università degli Studi di Parma and Nielsen 24 February 2012*, pp. 1–5.

De Canio, F., Ieva, M., & Ziliani, C. (2015). *Device usage patterns and online shopping behaviour XII Convegno annuale della Società Italiana Marketing*, Torino.

Eagly, A. H., & Chaiken, S. (1993). *The psychology of attitudes.* Orlando, FL: Harcourt Brace Jovanovich College Publishers.

eMarketer. (2013). *Majority of US internet users will redeem digital coupons in 2013.* Accessed February 14, 2014 from www.emarketer.com/Article/Majority-of-US-Internet-Users-Will-Redeem-DigitalCoupons-2013/1010313#OdmfcBc1XC7yMjZP.99

Eveland, W. P. (2003). A "mix of attributes" approach to the study of media effects and new communication technologies. *Journal of Communication, 53*(3), 395–410.

Everitt, B., Landau, S., Leese, M., & Stahl, D. (2011). *Cluster analysis.* Chichester: Wiley.

Gallagher, K., Parsons, J., & Foster, K. D. (2001). A tale of two studies: Replicating 'advertising effectiveness and content evaluation in print and on the web'. *Journal of Advertising Research, 41*(4), 71–81.

Gazquez-Abad, J. C., & Sanchez-Perez, M. (2009). Characterising the deal-proneness of consumers by analysis of price sensitivity and brand loyalty: An analysis in the retail environment. *The International Review of Retail, Distribution and Consumer Research, 19*(1), 1–28.

Gázquez-Abad, J. C., Martínez-López, F. J., & Barrales-Molina, V. (2014). Profiling the flyer-prone consumer. *Journal of Retailing and Consumer Services, 21*(6), 966–975.

Ghose, A., Goldfarb, A., & Han, S. P. (2012). How is the mobile Internet different? Search costs and local activities. *Information Systems Research, 24*(3), 613–631.

Gibson, C. M. (2003). Privileging the participant: The importance of sub-group analysis in social wel-fare evaluations. *American Journal of Evaluation, 24*(4), 443–469.

Gijsbrechts, E., Campo, K., & Goossens, T. (2003). The impact of store flyers on store traffic and store sales: A geo-marketing approach. *Journal of Retailing, 79*, 1–16.

Greenacre, M. J. (1988). Clustering the rows and columns of a contingency table. *Journal of Classification, 5*, 39–51.

Grewal, D., Ailawadi, K. L., Gauri, D., Hall, K., Kopalle, P., & Robertson, J. R. (2011). Innovations in retail pricing and promotions. *Journal of Retailing, 87*, S43–S52.

Griffith, D. A., Krampf, R. F., & Palmer, J. W. (2001). The role of interface in electronic commerce: Consumer involvement with print versus on-line catalogs. *International Journal of Electronic Commerce, 5*(4), 135–153.

Hartson, H. R. (1998). Human–computer interaction: Interdisciplinary roots and trends. *Journal of Systems and Software, 43*(2), 103–118.

Hoffman, D. L., & Novak, T. P. (1996). Marketing in hypermedia computer-mediated environments: Conceptual foundations. *The Journal of Marketing, 60,* 50–68.

IRI. (2015). *Price and promotion in Western Europe: Encouraging signs of recovery.* Special Report IRI Worldwide. Accessed April 14, 2016 from https://www.iriworldwide.com/fr-FR/insights/Publications/Price-and-Promotion-in-Western-Europe-Encouraging

Jacob, R. (1996). *Human-computer interaction: Input devices. ACM computing interaction* (3rd ed.). Reading, MA: Addison-Wesley.

Jones, M. Y., Pentecost, R., & Requena, G. (2005). Memory for advertising and information content: Comparing the printed page to the computer screen. *Psychology and Marketing, 22* (8), 623–648.

Juniper Research. (2015). *Digital advertising. Online, mobile and wearables 2015-2019.* Accessed 01/06/2015 from http://www.juniperresearch.com/researchstore/strategy-competition/digital-advertising/online-mobile-wearables

Lebart, L., & Mirkin, B. G. (1993). Correspondence analysis and classification. In C. Cuadras & C. R. Rao (Eds.), *Multivariate analysis, future directions* (pp. 341–357). Amsterdam: North Holland.

Leeflang, P. S., Verhoef, P. C., Dahlström, P., & Freundt, T. (2014). Challenges and solutions for marketing in a digital era. *European Management Journal, 32*(1), 1–12.

Liu, Y., & Shrum, L. J. (2002). What is interactivity and is it always such a good thing? Implications of definition, person, and situation for the influence of interactivity on advertising effectiveness. *Journal of advertising, 31*(4), 53–64.

Lugli, G. (Ed.) (2014). *Quale Futuro per la promozione delle vendite?* Parma: Area Marketing Economia Università di Parma Com. Prom.re Manifestazioni Sc. di Marketing. ISBN 978-88-906195-2-6.

Magee, R. G. (2013). Can a print publication be equally effective online? Testing the effect of medium type on marketing communications. *Marketing Letters, 24*(1), 85–95.

Mangen, A., Walgermo, B. R., & Brønnick, K. (2013). Reading linear texts on paper versus computer screen: Effects on reading comprehension. *International Journal of Educational Research, 58,* 61–68.

Martínez, E., & Montaner, T. (2006). The effect of consumer's psychographic variables upon deal-proneness. *Journal of Retailing and Consumer Services, 13*(3), 157–168.

Mimouni-Chaabane, A., Sabri, O., & Praguel, B. (2010). Competitive advertising within store flyers: a win-win strategy? *Journal of Retailing and Consumer Services, 17,* 478–486.

Nan, X., & Faber, R. J. (2004). Advertising theory: Reconceptualizing the building blocks. *Marketing Theory, 4*(1–2), 7–30.

Nass, C., & Steuer, J. (1993). Voices, boxes, and sources of messages. *Human Communication Research, 19*(4), 504–527.

Nielsen. (2011). *Evolution of the circular: From print to digital Q4.* Accessed online at: http://www.nielsen.com/us/en/insights/reports/2011/the-evolution-of-circulars-q42011.html

Olten, H., & Gagnier, J. (2015). Use of clustering analysi in randomized controlled trials in orthopaedic surgery. *BMC Medical Research Methodology, 15,* 17.

Parguel, B., Sabri-Zaraaoui, O., & Mimouni-Chaabane, A. (2009) *L'influence relative des caractéristiques perçues du prospectus sur son efficacité pour le distributeur.* Actes du Colloque Etienne Thil – Colloque Etienne Thil, La Rochelle, 7 Octobre. Accessed February 14, 2014 from http://halshs.archives-ouvertes.fr/halshs-00636212

Peck, L. R. (2003). Subgroup analysis in social experiments: Measuring program impacts based on post-treatment choice. *American Journal of Evaluation, 24*(2), 157–187.

Peck, L. R. (2005). Using cluster analysis in program evaluation. *Evaluation Review, 29*(2), 178–196.

Pieters, R., Wedel, M., & Zhang, J. (2007). Optimal feature advertising design under competitive clutter. *Management Science, 53*(11), 1815–1828.

PricewaterhouseCoopers. (2012). *Understanding how US online shoppers are reshaping the retail experience*. Accessed 01/06/2015 from http://www.pwc.com/en_us/us/retail-consumer/publica tions/assets/pwc-us-multichannel-shopping-survey.pdf

Rangaswamy, A., & Van Bruggen, G. H. (2005). Opportunities and challenges in multichannel marketing: An introduction to the special issue. *Journal of Interactive Marketing, 19*(2), 5–11.

Ray, J. (2011). Moving circulars into the digital age. *Direct Marketing News*, 21 November. Accessed February 14, 2014 from www.dmnews.com/moving-circulars-into-the-digital-age/article/217267/#

Rice, R. E. (1993). Media appropriateness. *Human Communication Research, 19*(4), 451–484.

Rideout, V. J., Foehr, U. G., & Roberts, D. F. (2010). *Generation M² : Media in the lives of 8-to 18-year-olds*. Henry J. Kaiser Family Foundation.

Samuely, A. (2016). Why loyalty points may become mobile wallets' primary currency. *Mobile Commerce Daily*, 29 January. Accessed September 20, 2016 from http://www.mobilecommercedaily.com/why-loyalty-points-may-become-mobile-wallets-primary-currency

Sellen, A., & Harper, R. (2002). *The myth of the paperless office*. Cambridge, MA: MIT Press.

Shadish, W. R., Cook, T. D., & Campbell, D. T. (2002). *Experimental and quasi-experimental designs for generalized causal inference*. Belmont, CA: Wadsworth Cengage Learning.

Shankar, V., Inman, J., Mantrala, M., Kelley, E., & Rizley, R. (2011). Innovations in shopper marketing: Current insights and future research issues. *Journal of Retailing, 87S*(1), S29–S42.

Shneiderman, B. (2010). *Designing the user interface: Strategies for effective human-computer interaction*. Pearson Education India.

Singer, L. M., & Alexander, P. A. (2016). Reading across mediums: Effects of reading digital and print texts on comprehension and calibration. *The Journal of Experimental Education, 85* (1), 1–18.

Srinivasan, S., Leone, R., & Mulhern, F. (1995). The advertising exposure effect of free standing inserts. *Journal of Advertising, 24*(1), 29–40.

Steuer, J. (1992). Defining virtual reality: Dimensions determining telepresence. *Journal of Communication, 42*(4), 73–93.

Sundar, S. S., Narayan, S., Obregon, R., & Uppal, C. (1998). Does web advertising work? Memory for print vs. online media. *Journalism and Mass Communication Quarterly, 75*(4), 822–835.

Suri, R., Swaminathan, S., & Monroe, K. B. (2004). Price communications in online and print coupons: An empirical investigation. *Journal of Interactive Marketing, 18*(4), 74–86.

Valacich, J. S., Pranka, D., George, J. F., & Nunamaker, J. F. (1993). Communication concurrency and the new media: A new dimension for media richness. *Communication Research, 20*(2), 249–276.

Verhoef, P. C., Neslin, S. A., & Vroomen, B. (2007). Multichannel customer management: Understanding the research-shopper phenomenon. *International Journal of Research in Marketing, 24*(2), 129–148.

Volle, P. (1997). Quelles perspectives de développement pour les prospectus promotionnels des distributeurs. *Décisions Marketing, 12*(September), 39–46.

Wakolbinger, L. M., Denk, M., & Oberecker, K. (2009). The effectiveness of combining online and print advertisements. *Journal of Advertising Research, 49*(3), 360–372.

Wang, R. J. H., Malthouse, E. C., & Krishnamurthi, L. (2015). On the go: How mobile shopping affects customer purchase behaviour. *Journal of Retailing, 91*(2), 217–234.

Zhang, J. (2006). An integrated choice model incorporating alternative mechanisms for consumers' reactions to in-store display and feature advertising. *Marketing Science, 25*(3), 278–290.

Ziliani, C., & Ieva, M. (2014). Innovation in brand promotion: reacting to the economic crisis with digital channels and customer insight. *National Brands and Private Labels in Retailing*. Springer International Publishing, pp. 151–159.

Ziliani, C., & Ieva, M. (2015). Retail shopper marketing: The future of promotional flyers. *International Journal of Retail and Distribution Management, 43*(6), 488–502.

Cristina Ziliani is Associate Professor of Marketing at the Department of Economics and Management, University of Parma, Italy. She is the author of several journal articles and books on loyalty programs and customer insight in retailing and the Scientific Director of the Loyalty Observatory (www.osservatoriofedelta.it). Her research interests are: retail, promotions, loyalty and Customer Relationship Management (CRM).

Marco Ieva is Postdoctoral Research Fellow in Marketing at the Department of Economics and Management, University of Parma, Italy. His research interests are: media effectiveness, retailing, loyalty marketing and customer experience.

Juan Carlos Gázquez-Abad is Associate Professor of Marketing at the Department of Economics and Business, Faculty of Business and Economics, Agrifood Campus of International Excellence ceiA3, University of Almería, Spain. He has been also visiting professor at the University of Ghent (Department of Marketing), Belgium. He serves as Associate Editor of the International Journal of Business Environment and belongs to the Advisory Board of European Retail Research. His research interests cover retailing—especially assortment issues and feature advertising—and consumer behavior. Professor Gázquez-Abad is the author of several books, and has contributed to several marketing journals and conference proceedings.

Ida D'Attoma is Senior Assistant Professor in Economics Statistics at the Department of Statistical Sciences, University of Bologna, Italy. She received her PhD in Statistical Methodology for Scientific Research from the University of Bologna. She is involved in scientific societies and committees. Since 2010, she is member of the American Evaluation Association and since 2016 she is member of the Italian Statistical Society. Her research mainly focuses on program evaluation methodology and micro data mining with applications in the area of policy evaluation. Special interest is devoted to the selection bias issue in observational studies and to the heterogeneity of effects.

A Framework for Omnichannel Differentiation Strategy. Integrating the Information Delivery and Product Fulfilment Requirements

Erne Suzila Kassim and Husnayati Hussin

Abstract Technology and innovation have the capability to change many aspects of business, for good and bad. With technology capabilities, customers are demanding better products and service delivery anytime, anywhere. Thus, companies and retailers are driven to a new model of business, omnichannel. However, delivering an omnichannel solution is a challenging effort. It requires unique strategies for implementation success. In this chapter, we present the experience of a card design and printing company in their journey to an omnichannel business. Two main questions are addressed: how does information delivery and product fulfilment fit the information-fulfilment matrix and what is the formula for omnichannel differentiation strategies. While the practices fit into the four components of the matrix, the major implementation focus is on the offline information-store pickup and online information-store pickup quadrants. In addition, the four major omnichannel tasks are managing a good customer relationship, aligning knowledge and technology to the current trend, retaining customer trust, and having a strict policy on security and data confidentiality. In essence, omnichannel requires a harmonious integration of people-technology-organization for its sustainability. Based on the case, we provide suggestions to guide organizations with similar plans, and the implications for the industry and body of knowledge.

E. S. Kassim (✉)
Faculty of Business Management, Centre for Applied Management Studies,
Universiti Teknologi MARA, Shah Alam, Malaysia
e-mail: ernekassim@puncakalam.uitm.edu.my

H. Hussin
Faculty of Information and Communications Technology, International Islamic University
Malaysia, Selangor, Malaysia

© Springer Nature Switzerland AG 2019
W. Piotrowicz, R. Cuthbertson (eds.), *Exploring Omnichannel Retailing*,
https://doi.org/10.1007/978-3-319-98273-1_11

1 Introduction

Ubiquitous technologies create huge potential for business success, but also push for changes in the business models employed. Today's focus for business success may be defined as the ability to connect to customers without barriers. Technologies allow this to happen and a new business model emerges—the omnichannel. Omnichannel is a concept that integrates channels for communication and transaction with customers. It is perceived as an evolution of a multichannel approach (Piotrowicz and Cuthbertson 2014). The interaction is via various interfaces such as the traditional store, social media, the web portal, sales agents, mobile applications, kiosks, and virtual images, all contributing to what makes omnichannel very fundamental to customer relationships. The role of social media enhances its importance. With social media, omnichannel is the realization of social business. Businesses that are able to identify omnichannel as an area of growth aligned with their own strategy and understanding of their customers are likely to be the winners.

With new technologies, new dimensions of customer decision making are being innovated. Customers are not considering solely the price and product quality when they make a decision to purchase. Relationship quality, service quality, and trust all influence their decision. As the aim of an omnichannel approach is to offer seamless relationships and services to customers, managing them well is crucial. Businesses must have the ability to adopt the knowledge-infused process of customer relationship management combining different elements, such as community, experience analytics, and customer data.

Although many omnichannel success stories revolve around fashions and gadgets, and documented by giant organizations, such as Disney and Starbucks, omnichannel is not limited to any specific industry. The key point here is for the business to understand how technologies could be harvested for achieving maximum business potential. Customers are becoming omnichannel in their thinking and behaviour (Bell et al. 2014). Therefore, having the right strategies on how to implement effective omnichannel is crucial. In order to succeed in omnichannel, businesses must understand two significant challenges: information delivery and product fulfilment deployment (Bell et al. 2014). The idea is to reduce frictions in every phase of the buying process through a "cost effective and narrative-enhancing way, information that removes initial uncertainties and barriers to purchase" and fulfilment options that allow customers to receive products and services in the most convenient and cost-effective ways (Bell et al. 2014, p. 45).

While current literature recognizes the need to integrate across multiple channels, Hansen and Sia (2015) assert that there is limited knowledge on how such integration can be accomplished in practice. Omnichannel is an emerging concept that requires more insights to be explored on discovering issues, challenges, and the success factors necessary to implement a profitable omnichannel solution.

This chapter aims to provide a better understanding of the topic by identifying and analysing the different strategies for implementing omnichannel by exploring the aspects of information delivery and product fulfilment.

Focusing on a card design and printing company in Malaysia, a case study was conducted. To accomplish the aim, we took three steps. First, we conducted a review of key literature on online retailing. Second, we used a case study to provide an in-depth understanding of one omnichannel implementation experience, and the strategies and operations for information delivery and product fulfilment. Third, we used the empirical findings to develop a framework for omnichannel implementation with respect to fulfilling different channels.

This chapter begins by explaining omnichannel retail and strategies from the literature. A review of Malaysian e-commerce development and omnichannel retailing are then presented. The next sections describe the methodology and a detailed discussion of the case study, including the findings. The paper ends by concluding on the implications for practice and future research areas.

2 Literature Review

This section first explores the evolution of omnichannel, defining the process and describing related models. As this chapter considers a case study of a Malaysian-based company, a description of e-commerce and omnichannel development in the local context is also provided.

2.1 Omnichannel Retail

The ability to shop anywhere, anytime, and to get instant feedback or historical reviews is important for customers in this digital era (Golombek 2013). Omnichannel retailing is the set of activities involved in selling merchandise or services through all channels, whereby the customer can trigger full channel interaction and/or the retailer controls full channel integration (Beck and Rygl 2015).

In addition to information delivery and product fulfilment strategies for successful omnichannel development (Bell et al. 2014), Brynjolfsson et al. (2013) offer several other tips for success depending on the product, the level of demand, and the type of consumers. These are (1) provide attractive pricing and curated content, (2) harness the power of data and analytics, (3) avoid direct price comparison (4) learn to sell niche products (5) emphasize product knowledge (6) establish switching costs and (7) embrace competition.

2.2 Information Delivery and Product Fulfilment

Omnichannel strategies could be considered from various perspectives, such as last mile fulfilment and omnichannel distribution in the supply chain (Hübner et al.

2016), as well as embracing channel partners and leveraging employees roles (Hansen and Sia 2015). While various approaches to development are offered, most emphasize general approaches, and do not specifically address the cross-channel specifications. However, Bell et al. (2014) suggested omnichannel success could be achieved by focusing on each individual cross-channel, which could be segmented into four quadrants of online/offline information and product pickup/delivery. The focus is on information delivery and product fulfilment.

The first quadrant is called traditional retail, with offline information and store pick-up product fulfilment, in which customers get direct access to product information via the physical access to products. It is specifically well-suited to retailing products that have significant "high-touch" elements or significant non-digital attributes. Product fulfilment is carried out via store pick-up. The second quadrant is described as the shopping and delivery hybrid. Customers can get access to product information via various channels, including online information, but products are to be picked up from the stores. This combination of online-information and pickup-fulfilment is most suited to products containing non-digital attributes and for consumers who have experiences with a brand. The third quadrant is the online retail plus showroom. As the name suggests, customers have direct access to product information from the showroom but they can place an order at any time and products will be delivered directly to them. This method relaxes some of the design constraints for the retailer's physical locations. The last quadrant is pure-play e-commerce, which allows customers to search for product information online and products will be delivered directly to them.

3   E-commerce and Emergence of Omnichannel in Malaysia

In Malaysia, e-commerce is well-accepted and related research focusing on both supplier and consumer studies is flourishing. Factors such as improved Internet access, high mobile penetration, and enhanced security promote e-commerce growth. A recent survey of consumer online shopping behaviour conducted by AEON for its e-marketplace project reveals 68% out of 3700 respondents were reported to engage in both online and offline shopping while only 7% participated in offline shopping only. The figures represent untapped markets and opportunities for e-commerce players to look for strategies in promoting online shopping. The top three categories of products are fashion & accessories, home & living, and health & beauty (eCommerce Milo 2016). The history of e-commerce development in Malaysia dates back to 1999 when Poslaju (National Postage and Courier) became the first company to launch a national e-commerce service. Then in 1999, Lelong.com launched their portal, followed by e-Bay Malaysia in 2004. However, e-commerce has only started taking off in Malaysia since 2011, which coincides with the group buying era. Big e-commerce players such as Rakuten, Zalora, and Lazada have dominated online shopping since 2012 alongside existing retailers, such as Tesco.

Government support is fundamental for online business growth. As such, the Malaysian government via the Malaysian Communication and Multimedia Commission (MCMC) is providing tax incentives for the development of e-commerce enabled websites to promote more local companies to sell online (MCMC 2012). The initiative has increased the number of online sellers, and according to the statistics from Companies Commission of Malaysia, in between 2012 and 2016, there were approximately 30,000 online businesses registered.

Omnichannel retailing in Malaysia has just started to grow. Though related literature on the local context is very limited, reports claim an incredible potential for an omnichannel approach due to the exploding presence of smartphones and social media connectivity. The Federation of Malaysian Manufacturers (FMM) has worked together with GS1, which is an international body that develops and promotes the GS1 standards of article numbering, bar coding and electronic communication worldwide. With the GS1 standard (GS1 Malaysia, 2013), there will be three benefits to omnichannel retailing, which are:

1. consistent product identification across all channels using Global Trade Item Numbers (GTINs)
2. enhanced accurate product data
3. better inventory management

One of Malaysia's first omnichannel retailing platform is Super Pharmacy Megastore, which specializes in healthcare, wellness and lifestyle. Utilizing the power of social media and personal networks, the company is transforming from a traditional brick and mortar single channel to multichannel, then cross-channel and now to omnichannel retailing. Collaborating with Alibaba Group, deploying the B-B-C and O-O application sales platform while maintaining the physical store, Super Megastore aims to reach and satisfy customers with products and service quality.

4   Research Design

In the attempt to understand how omnichannel integration can be accomplished, we decided to conduct a case study that could provide an in-depth understanding of an implementation strategy in pursuing a brick and click channel. Although case study research cannot offer grounds for establishing the reliability of any findings, it serves as an exploratory tool for investigating the 'how' question. Using the purposive sampling strategy, we first identified companies that have implemented an omnichannel strategy. Then we invited them to participate in the study. One of the traits that we looked for was responsiveness. Hence, based on the prompt response, one agreed to take part.

Data was collected by conducting semi-structured interviews and observing both the physical store and digital channels. The semi-structured interviews allowed for probing answers by asking more questions. Even though the aim was to obtain insights of the company's experience and best practices in deploying an omnichannel strategy, we started by asking general followed by specific questions. Krueger and Casey (2000) suggest using questions that can encourage participant involvement and questions should be focused. We also avoided using academic jargon as these terms may not be understood by business practitioners. The interview with the business owner and the company director lasted for more than an hour, generating a 13 page transcription report.

Using Atlas.ti application, the data was analysed by following the constant comparison method (Boeije 2002) that allows for discovering the concepts. There were four phases involved namely, exploration, specification, reduction and integration. Following Corbin and Strauss (2014) three coding processes of open, axial, and selective were adhered to in the exploration phase. The validation of the findings was achieved by obtaining the respondent's approval for the narrative summary. In addition, we also observed the web portal and the business-customer communication that took place in the social networking environment. As the aim of the study was to get an in-depth understanding of the omnichannel differentiation strategies from the business perspective, we did not take into consideration the views of the customers.

5 Findings and Discussion

This section provides a description of the company and the findings generated from the data. The discussion first emphasizes the general omnichannel strategic deployment based on the information delivery and product fulfilment needs. Then it continues with detailed discussion on different aspects that focus on customer management, knowledge, and technology alignment, customer trust, and data security and confidentiality.

5.1 Company Background

The company that served as the case for the study is kadkahwinku.com that sells event-related items, specifically for weddings. The products include cards, boxes, paper bags, gifts, canvas, and wedding stationery. The physical store is located in Sri Kembangan, a city which is very close to Kuala Lumpur, the capital of Malaysia. Customers can conduct transactions via the web portal of http://www.kadkahwinku.com, or via social media on Facebook (FB) facebook.com/kadkahwinkud.com, and Instagram (IG) instagram.com/kadkahwinku.com. Other channels of communication are through SMS (text messages), email, and mobile apps.

Kadkahwinku.com has been in operation since the year 2000. During the early years of operation, three outlets were set up at Danga Bay, which is in the southern part of the country, Kuala Lumpur, and Kajang. However, due to high operational costs, a decision was made to focus on only one physical store, but service a wider market by reaping the advantages of information and communication technologies.

During its initial setup, the information and communication technologies capabilities and infrastructure were quite limited. However, despite the limitations, the company has become one of the pioneers in championing an online business within the sector by having the dot com store. As the technology evolves, so does the company. Fulfilling the customers' needs is their priority. They are not only able to design a unique and distinctive card that signifies the customer's personality, but they are also able to capture the simplification of bringing the products and services via various channels.

Different channels are used to allow for seamless purchase, transaction, and communication. Navigating from one channel to another is supported by the use of technology. The online portal imitates the physical store where customers can browse not only the range of items, and they can obtain very detailed information about the products. Interestingly, a review for each product is also made available so that customers can get some idea of product acceptance. In addition, they are also able to pick add-ons, combo selection, and packaging through the shopping cart. Customers are also able to create their own wish list, account, and shop online. The order history is also generated for each customer. Moreover, should they need prompt reply on their queries, the social media of Facebook and Instagram can work as the communication channel. Both the Facebook and Instagram provide a link to the online store.

In addition, the online web portal and social media allows the company to reach customers abroad. However, they are limited to Malaysians or those who understand the national language since all information is written in the local languages. As there are customers from other regions of the world, such as Egypt, the United Kingdom, and Australia, and time differences matter, the company has structured the communication strategy to allow for almost real-time conversation with customers from diverse geographical areas. This is achieved by creating the working shift and schedules to reflect this reality.

5.2 The Omnichannel Strategic Deployment

In an omnichannel environment, information delivery and product fulfilment are fundamental requirements. Consistency and seamless channel switch are also necessary. Therefore, information delivery is channelled via various forms. For different customer segments across various geographical areas and different demographic cohorts, the Internet and social media are utilized for getting closer to the customers. Mapping this to the information-fulfilment omnichannel matrix by Bell et al. (2014), we found that the company's practices fall into all quadrants but with different weightings (Fig. 1).

Since customers' behaviours and decisions require different needs and preferences, the company believed maintaining the traditional retail channel was still significant. By retaining the traditional store, customers are able to feel, touch, see, sense, and even smell the various products they offer. Arranging a wedding can be a

	Traditional Retail	Offline Retail and Product Delivery
Offline	Physical showroom Main market segmentation: older generation Traits: physical inspection, important to see, feel, touch, sense and smell Increase in brand awareness Incur travel costs to consumers	Physical store visit Direct access to product information Incur waiting time and shipping costs Showroom must be appealing and sales agents must be accessible
INFORMATION DELIVERY Online	**Online Retail Plus Physical Store** Immediate access to purchased cards Provide flexibility to customers who are constrained by the time Constraint of uncertainties about card attributes especially to first-time customers	**Pure Click and Mortar** Fair degree of expectation certainty Well-suited to the new generations and repeat customers
	Pickup **PRODUCT FULFILMENT**	**Delivery**

Fig. 1 Information delivery-product fulfilment matrix of the card design and printing company (based on Bell et al. (2014))

tedious business, especially when it involves 1000 or 2000 invitations as could happen in Malaysia. Therefore, the physical store becomes a place of discussion, especially for high-end customers with big accounts. A wedding is a family affair in many cultures. For some Malay communities in Malaysia, the wedding invitation involves everybody in the family. The colours of the card, the theme, the wording, the style and fonts, the selection of the card materials, the size and all are the business of the family members. Therefore, it is common for the company to receive all three generations of a family, to come together to the store to discuss one single wedding card design. Once the design is approved, the delivery can be picked up by the customers. This type of traditional store and product pick up falls into the first quadrant of the matrix in Fig. 1.

There are also cases when the customers are more comfortable in selecting the design from an online portal, make the payment online, but pick up the cards from the store. This falls into the second quadrant of online information delivery and store pickup fulfilment (Fig. 1).

In addition, the business also allows for customers to select the items from the store and make the necessary payment either by cash or debit/credit card. However, the products will be delivered by postage or courier to the delivery address. This maps to the third quadrant of the matrix.

The final business operation of the fourth quadrant is when customers buy solely from the web portal, and the order is delivered to them via postage or courier. Comparing all four quadrants, the company claimed the first and the second type of information delivery and product fulfilment are highly preferred by customers.

In addition, the segmentation of the physical and virtual store that makes up the omnichannel functions can be explained by comparing the characteristics of each business process (Table 1).

Table 1 The Omnichannel business functions

Business process/ Function	Offline/Physical store	Online/Website/Mobile and Other social networking
Product information	Face-to-face interaction and communication between buyer and seller	Website info by product categories
Product selection	Face-to-face and personalized order	Shopping cart
Payment	Cash/credit card/online banking	Credit card/online banking
Product promotion	Catalogs and printed materials	Online banner
Data security	Personalized account and database management system DBMS	Personalized account and database management system (DBMS); account login
Customer service and relationship	Handling customers with patience and honesty	Handling customers via written text
Customers trust	Agreement, terms and condition	Terms and conditions as an expression of not hiding any issue

5.3 The Omnichannel Differentiation Strategy

As the main aim of an omnichannel approach is to provide the best services for the customers through cross-channels and technology is the backbone, based on the analysis, the company's implementation strategy thus focuses on people who are the customers and employees, as well as the technology. Specifically, their main foci are on customer relationship, knowledge and technology alignment, customer's trust, security, and data confidentiality. A detailed description of each aspect is provided in the following sub-sections.

5.4 Managing Customer Relationship

While traditional marketing and retailing focuses on location, the company strongly believes that the ability to manage customers is crucial for business survival and this is consistent with their understanding that business is about interaction. The wedding business requires the company to ensure that employees have specific attentive skills. This is because wedding and marriage is one of the important events in one's life. Therefore, customers could be emotional at any stage of the processes and each single detail matters, including the design of the wedding card. Hence, great patience is the key to winning customers. Specific examples were responding to customers' queries promptly and using nice and humble words even in a tense situation, especially if everyone in the family thinks his/her idea is the best. While there are channel differences in offline and online communication and information delivery, the principle that the customer relationship is fundamental to the business is upheld in both interactions.

Studies have concluded that telecommunication technology, such as social media and social networking, helps in establishing closer business-customer relationships. However, it requires 'smart' adoption as improper usage may kill a relationship. In a specific case, when WhatsApp was introduced and available, the company utilized it as a means to communicate with customers. However, by communicating via WhatsApp, the company noticed customers were highly demanding for prompt and real-time reply. Failure to respond on time caused the company to lose potential business. Therefore, they have shifted to private messages on Facebook (FB). With FB, customers could tolerate a slight delay in response. As the customers are worldwide, the company is ensuring a good communications system for servicing customers by providing working shifts and so communication is available 24/7.

In addition, the company has placed a very heavy emphasis on treating customers with appropriate manners and language, including body contact in a physical environment. The company ensures all team members are well trained, especially for handling customers' complaints. Personal mentoring is provided for new employees. Based on the interview material, the company shared their practices in dealing with customer complaints and dissatisfaction. When there are issues or complaints, the relevant member of staff will be advised and coached for better service management in the future.

5.5 Creating and Retaining Customers Trust

Ensuring the trust of customers is another fundamental requirement. Trust exists when customers feel safe not only during the online/offline transaction but also trust the products and communication. Trust is created by both tangible and human traits. The physical factors include building a trusted business image, and creating a functional and user-friendly online business. Trust is expressed through product commitment, reliable business processes, and ensuring customer satisfaction. At the same time, creating customer's trust through human traits requires the company to always exhibit responsiveness, honesty, and politeness, as well as placing the customer's interests as the top priority.

Studies have found customer trust increases when information systems that meet the expectation of the customers are deployed (Ha and Stoel 2009). Hence, the company is continually revisiting its position in e-commerce by upgrading the database system, hiring bloggers for promoting the business via social media, making professional videos for YouTube upload, and hiring professional photo editors for enhancing the card images on the website. As a result, customers are more confident when they see the business is in tune with online trends.

5.6 Knowledge and Technology Alignment

Since its establishment, being competitive in the industry has always been a main goal. With more demanding clients, the company is always searching for the best tools that allow for process optimization and improvement in offering lasting relations with the customers. As technologies keep evolving, they require investment not only in the facilities, but most importantly in knowledge know-how, emphasizing the need for employees to know the details of the business operations.

The story of the knowledge and technology alignment dated back to the early business set up. Back then, customers' acceptance of online banking for product purchase and payment was low. Similarly, the online channel of communication was limited. However, the company had and has a strong belief in what and how information technology could be used as an advantage. Therefore, the company ensures each single member of the employees is tech-savvy.

A specific example regards the payment system. Understanding that users have different preferences, the company adopted a mixed approach to payment and bill settlement, and the system is changed to align with new trends. They have had experience of using iPay88, an online payment service for South East Asia countries for credit card payment but not PayPal as the acceptance on the latter was very low. Then when the acceptance of online and mobile banking became high, they created another option for customers. For customers from neighbouring countries, the company provides a payment alternative with Money Express. As a result, the technology know-how enables a sustainable business.

5.7 Ensuring Tight Security and Confidentiality of Customer Data

In the business, customers' information is very important. Data security and confidentiality should not be compromised. When a customer makes an order, the information will be digitally recorded and protected by an authorized personal login. Similarly, for the online purchase, a customer needs to create his personalized account. His shopping cart is only visible to authorized staff. To ensure everything is secured, the company is highly selective in choosing trusted employees to manage the system. A number of layers of database security are implemented. Similarly, data synchronization is a top priority. When an online customer would like check her order physically or to conduct another purchase at the showroom, it can be done without any hassle. The new information will be updated. Similarly, when the offline customer would like to shop online, it can be handled seamlessly too. The ability to provide a highly secured system for omnichannel transactions enables the company to create customer confidence and loyalty, which becomes a factor of business sustainability.

5.8   Issues and Challenges

Although the company is able to synchronize across channels, there are two main issues that challenge business growth. One is the facilities and infrastructure support from government and the telecommunication provider. Cross-channel integration requires stable Internet and data connections. Therefore, the government and telecommunication providers must ensure connectivity is supported at all times. Second is the issue of intellectual property (IP). As there are plenty of card designs in various sizes, colors, themes, and purposes, it is very challenging to protect the designs. If they would like to register for IP, it should be done for each individual card and product. Therefore, the company is highly exposed to the danger of design imitation by competitors.

6   Conclusion

Technology and innovation has changed many aspects of human lives. Achieving omnichannel success requires a clear understanding of its purpose. Providing services to customers require attention to the details of both online and offline conduct. The Internet, mobile devices, and social media have revolutionized the customer experience by allowing customers to shop from anywhere at anytime. As such, challenges are placed on companies to look for strategies that allow them to integrate the different channels seamlessly. Figure 2 illustrates and summarizes the framework of key areas for omnichannel strategy and implementation for the case study company.

In an omnichannel environment, customer engagement is crucial. Similarly, it is very important to create a trusted environment for customer loyalty. More importantly, it requires a harmonious integration of people, technology, and organization for business sustainability.

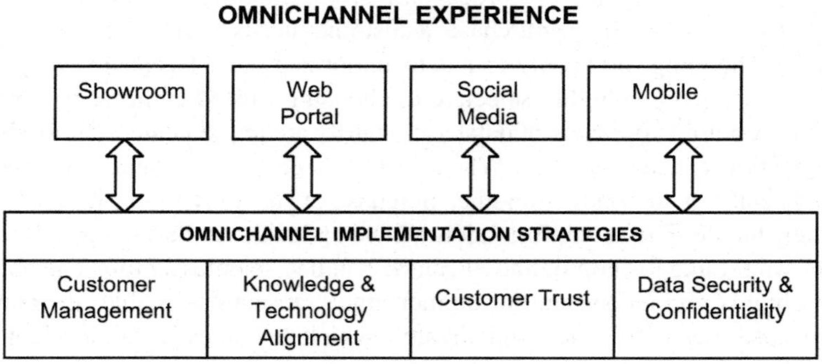

OMNICHANNEL EXPERIENCE

Showroom	Web Portal	Social Media	Mobile

OMNICHANNEL IMPLEMENTATION STRATEGIES

Customer Management	Knowledge & Technology Alignment	Customer Trust	Data Security & Confidentiality

Fig. 2 Framework of Omnichannel Strategy Implementation

In this chapter, we represent a case that highlights the journey of a card design and printing company in their omnichannel adoption. We show 'how' the omnichannel strategy is implemented by focusing on the information delivery and product fulfilment requirements. Our study offers insights on such issues. Research findings suggest, in the omnichannel environment, companies need to offer services in different ways according to each distribution channel. However, across channels, people, technology, and organization must blend together for seamless integration.

These result in the ability of the company to align different channels and become adaptive to change, while at the same time able to balance the harmonization of demanding customers. Good customer relationship practice creates chain effects where this becomes a source of word-of-mouth to the customers' family, circle of friends, and beyond. In particular, 24/7 online communication, being patient with customers, ensuring good manners, and the ability to handle different customers in different channels yields a fruitful outcome for the company.

The theoretical contribution of this case highlights the importance of linking information delivery and product fulfilment requirements in each channel. Our framework suggests that the roles of customer management, knowledge and technology alignment, customer trust, and data security and confidentiality all enhance the omnichannel experience. The framework serves as a basis for exploring more options in closer business-customer relationships via various technologies. Additionally, it could assist other businesses to understand the key issues in their plans to implement omnichannel developments.

However, despite the fact that the framework was developed based on an in-depth case study investigation, we did not assess the views of customers on the omnichannel experience. Thus, it offers a lot of potential for future research. Building on a qualitative framework, we suggest further studies could be designed to provide measurement for each concept within the framework and validation through quantitative studies. By exploring the issue in both qualitative and quantitative approaches, a more holistic understanding could be achieved on providing an effective strategy for omnichannel implementation.

Questions for Discussion and Review

1. Refer to the information delivery-product fulfilment matrix. Which channel do you prefer the most? Are there differences between product groups which you buy?
2. Discuss the roles of various information and communication technologies that could be used for omnichannel retail. What specific technologies are more appropriate for the fashion and retail industry, food and beverages and fast moving consumer goods?
3. If you were an entrepreneur, what specific omnichannel strategies would you adopt for different product groups?
4. One of the strategies implemented by the company in the case study is focusing on data security and confidentiality. How company can assure customer data protection?

5. How do you think omnichannel will shape the future of retailing?
6. How companies can build trust with customers? Are there differences between country cultures in this matter?
7. Cards are specific for the special events. How this product category differs from everyday shopping? How company should respond to customer needs in this category?
8. What are the problems and issues to serve international customers, located across the globe? How to solve such problems?
9. How social media such as Facebook and Instagram can be used to leverage position of the company?
10. Is the business model used by the case company possible to transfer to different countries and for different product category?

References

Beck, N., & Rygl, D. (2015). Categorization of multiple channel retailing in multi-, cross-, and omni-channel retailing for retailers and retailing. *Journal of Retailing and Consumer Services, 27*, 170–178.

Bell, D. R., Gallino, S., & Moreno, A. (2014). How to win in an omnichannel world. *MIT Sloan Management Review, 56*(1), 45.

Boeije, H. (2002). A purposeful approach to the constant comparative method in the analysis of qualitative interviews. *Quality and Quantity, 36*(4), 391–409.

Brynjolfsson, E., Hu, Y. J., & Rahman, M. S. (2013). Competing in the age of omnichannel retailing. *MIT Sloan Management Review, 54*(4), 23.

Corbin, J., & Strauss, A. (2014). *Basics of qualitative research: Techniques and procedures for developing grounded theory*. Thousand Oaks, CA: Sage.

eCommerce Milo. (2016). *Malaysian online shopping insights 2016 by Shoppu*. Retrieved from http://www.ecommercemilo.com/2016/03/malaysian-online-shopping-insights-2016-shoppu.html

Golombek, J. (2013). *Omni-channel: The future of retailing*. Working Paper, The Pennsylvania State University. Retrieved from http://www.personal.psu.edu/users/j/l/jlg5690/images/White Paper.pdf

GS1 Malaysia – Omni-Channel Industry – The Changing Retail Model. (2013). Retrieved from http://www.massa.net.my/gs1-malaysia/

Ha, S., & Stoel, L. (2009). Consumer e-shopping acceptance: Antecedents in a technology acceptance model. *Journal of Business Research, 62*(5), 565–571.

Hansen, R., & Sia, S. K. (2015). Hummel's digital transformation toward omnichannel retailing: Key lessons learned. *MIS Quarterly Executive, 14*(2), 51–66.

Hübner, A., Kuhn, H., & Wollenburg, J. (2016). Last mile fulfilment and distribution in omni-channel grocery retailing: A strategic planning framework. *International Journal of Retail and Distribution Management, 44*(3), 228–247.

Krueger, R. A., & Casey, M. A. (2000). *Focus groups: A practical guide for applied research* (3rd ed.). Thousands Oaks, CA: Sage.

Malaysian Communication and Multimedia Commission. (2012). *Guideline for the Annual Certi fication of E-Commerce Websites – Pursuant to Income Tax (Deduction for Cost of Developing Website) Rules 2003*. Retrieved from http://mcmc.gov.my/Sectors/Celco/Codes-Guidelines/Guidelines/Guidelines/Guideline-for-the-Annual-Certification-of-E-Commer.aspx

Piotrowicz, W., & Cuthbertson, R. (2014). Introduction to the special issue information technology in retail: Toward omnichannel retailing. *International Journal of Electronic Commerce, 18*(4), 5–16.

Erne Suzila Kassim is Senior Lecturer at the Faculty of Business and Management, Universiti Teknologi MARA, Malaysia. She received her Bachelor Degree from Indiana University in Bloomington, USA, majoring in Economics and Sociology. Upon her graduation, she worked as a Quality Engineer and was responsible for managing the Total Airport Management Solutions for the Kuala Lumpur International Airport (KLIA), Malaysia. She then studied for MSc in Information Technology and also a PhD in Information Technology, mainly specializing in digital innovations. She has been awarded with research grants for projects among others in the fields of e-learning, green IT, e-commerce and IT for micro-enterprises. She has written for numerous journal articles and conferences proceedings. Her research interests include social networking, business intelligence analytics for improving customer equity and big data for halal applications. Erne has experiences in leading and managing research and academic programs at the university, holding various positions as Head of Program, Research Coordinator, Internal Auditor and Head of Department.

Husnayati Hussin, Professor of Information Systems, Faculty of Information and Communications Technology, International Islamic University Malaysia. She received her PhD in Information Systems from the Loughborough University, UK and her MSc in Management Information Systems and BSc in Computer Science from Northern Illinois University, USA. Her current research interests include E-business, IT management, IT and small business, E-Government and ethical issues of IT. She has published articles in journals such as Journal of Strategic Information Systems, International Journal of Electronic Government Research, Campus-Wide Information Systems, Total Quality Management and Business Excellence and Business Process Management Journal.

Last Mile Framework for Omnichannel Retailing. Delivery from the Customer Perspective

Wojciech Piotrowicz and Richard Cuthbertson

Abstract The aim of this chapter is to explore the last mile delivery logistics in omnichannel grocery retailing. The *last mile framework for omnichannel retailing* was constructed by combining relevant academic literature with a review of the delivery options offered in an advanced online grocery market. Leading British retailers were investigated to understand their fulfilment and delivery methods from a customer point of view. The variables that have to be taken into account were extracted and then synthesized in the framework. The framework covers issues such as the delivery model (home delivery or Click and Collect), delivery points and their characteristics, as well as consideration of related issues, such as delivery windows, fees, and subscriptions. The framework can be used as a starting point for further academic studies, and can be applied by retailers considering their delivery options and design of logistics operations in multi- or omnichannel retailing.

1 Introduction

In omnichannel retailing, customers have the opportunity to freely select what, when, and how to buy (Hübner et al. 2016a). As omnichannel retailing grew, new models of distribution emerged (Hagberg et al. 2016b). These new logistics models are heavily supported by various technologies (Hagberg et al. 2016b), especially information technologies. However, new storage and delivery solutions, such as lockers or dedicated vans, have also been developed. E-commerce has already

W. Piotrowicz (✉)
Supply Chain Management and Social Responsibility, Department of Marketing, Hanken School of Economics, Helsinki, Finland

Oxford Institute of Retail Management, Saïd Business School, University of Oxford, Oxford, UK
e-mail: Wojciech.Piotrowicz@hanken.fi

R. Cuthbertson
Oxford Institute of Retail Management, Saïd Business School, University of Oxford, Oxford, UK

© Springer Nature Switzerland AG 2019
W. Piotrowicz, R. Cuthbertson (eds.), *Exploring Omnichannel Retailing*,
https://doi.org/10.1007/978-3-319-98273-1_12

changed logistics, moving towards small parcel sizes, frequent deliveries, and returns. Omnichannel management has also moved away from a silo mentality, where separate units, or even companies served brick & mortar and online customers. Moreover, the mobile revolution blurred the lines between store and online shopping (Piotrowicz and Cuthbertson 2014). However, building a complete omnichannel is not straightforward, as an omnichannel approach influences the whole company, thus changing from a multi- to an omnichannel approach requires restructuring and a move away from the silo structure (Picot-Coupey et al. 2016). There is a need to change structures, processes, and people. Logistic systems, delivery, and fulfilment practices are among the areas that need to be analysed to develop, test and employ new models, tools and techniques, looking for solutions that are not just modern and convenient for customers, but also profitable. Changes in the customer side of delivery might result in a complete redesign of the operations and the augmentation of new supply chain models optimised for omnichannel retailing.

This chapter is focused on the delivery models used in the grocery retail; home delivery as well as Click and Collect options are reviewed. However, this chapter is limited to the experience of leading UK grocery retailers, and is written from the customer point of view. Thus, data available to customers are analysed to identify aspects that should be considered in omnichannel grocery delivery.

More specifically this chapter explores the questions:

RQ1 What options are available to customers in receiving grocery shopping?
RQ2 What variables should be considered when planning an omnichannel grocery delivery system?

The chapter is structured as follows. Firstly, the academic literature on the topic is reviewed. This is followed by a presentation of findings from the customer perspective. The key section is the construction of a framework for online grocery delivery in omnichannel retailing. Finally, recommendations for academia and practice are drawn.

2 Omnichannel Grocery Retail Design

For omnichannel grocery retail development, an effective and efficient design for the logistical and distribution system is a must. Without this, profits from sales may be overwhelmed by the delivery costs. However, this is very challenging (Punakivi et al. 2001). Grocery retailing is still not the norm using an online channel. Its acceptance was much slower than expected (Huang and Oppewal 2006). This is partly related to the logistical challenges of providing satisfactory solutions. Delivery costs for the last mile are estimated to be at the level of 50% of total Supply Chain costs (Hübner et al. 2016b). However, failures to design delivery systems are common among companies (Boyer et al. 2009). Moreover, many attempts for online food retailing initiated in the early 2000s failed (Delfmann et al. 2011). Companies such as Webvan and Homegrocer were unable to stay in the market (Boyer and Hult

2005). Through learning such lessons, retailers are experimenting with different delivery models and technologies.

3 Main Delivery Models

The delivery to customer, or collection by the customer, is the last element of the whole delivery process. The earlier stages are: (1) order acceptance and (2) fulfilment, when an order is prepared for delivery (Boyer et al. 2009). Product distribution is composed of forward distribution to the store or customer, as well as backward distribution, if a product is returned (Hübner et al. 2016b). In omnichannel grocery retail, home delivery of online-ordered goods to the customer is one model. However, other less common models for home delivery exist. For example, goods may be ordered in the physical store and then delivered to the customer's home by the retailer. This may be appropriate where the goods are particularly bulky or the customer has difficulty transporting the products bought, such as an elderly person taking the bus home.

As omnichannel is an emerging concept, retailers are experimenting with different models and designs, which are also adjusted to local market conditions and customer needs. The first necessary condition for fulfilment is customer access to the internet, the web pages, and apps available for grocery shopping. However, these issues are outside the scope of this chapter, which focuses on supply rather than demand issues. The second critical aspect is the retailer's strategy and target customer. An omnichannel approach might not be suitable for all retailers and customers, for example discounters with a low-cost strategy.

There are differences between countries, with various models gaining popularity in different places (Hübner et al. 2016b).

The delivery models chosen are determined by issues such as:

- Availability of transport service providers (Visser et al. 2014)
- Delivery cost (Boyer et al. 2009)
- Delivery mode and picking operations (Delfmann et al. 2011)
- Design of the city transport networks (Morganti et al. 2014)
- Geographical scope of delivery, from local to international (Hübner et al. 2016b)
- Legal requirements for returns acceptance (Hübner et al. 2016b)
- Outlets density (Hübner et al. 2016b)
- Population density (Boyer et al. 2009; Hübner et al. 2016b)
- Privacy and security (Huang and Oppewal 2006)
- Product category (Delfmann et al. 2011)
- Restrictions set by local authorities, such as city delivery (Ducret 2014)
- Retailer abilities for coordination and process integration (Hübner et al. 2016b)
- Travel time to store and access by car (Hübner et al. 2016b)
- Primary purpose of customer journey (Huang and Oppewal 2006)

The delivery model should be aligned with local market conditions, such as location, population (demography, household size and distribution), as well as customer habits and preferences (working time, family life). There are different requirements for delivery to urban, suburban, and rural populations (Boyer et al. 2009). Moreover, low price marketing strategies need to be matched by low cost operations (Boyer and Hult 2005). In the omnichannel context (Hübner et al. 2016b), it is possible to distinguish between traditional deliveries to the store, home deliveries, and pick-up from store by the customer (Click and Collect). In addition, different models of Click and Collect are being tested, offering the ability to pick-up goods in different locations. The major delivery models, to home and pick-up, are overviewed in the following sections.

3.1 Home Delivery

Home delivery is common in countries such as the UK and the Netherlands (Hübner et al. 2016b). This is usually done by a van designed to transport ambient, chilled, and frozen goods. However, home delivery may also be done via insulated boxes to keep food at the required temperature (Punakivi et al. 2001). Home delivery can be *attended*, when someone is present at the moment of collection (Hübner et al. 2016a, b). It can also be *unattended*, when items are left without the presence of the customer (Hübner et al. 2016a, b). This is also referred to as *unsecured delivery*—where items are left by the front door or in another, more secure location, such as a garden shed (McKinnon and Tallam 2003). *Unattended delivery* is not possible under all conditions. There may be no place for leaving goods or it is simply not safe enough due to theft, perishability, or accidental damage (Hübner et al. 2016a, b). In unsecured home delivery there is also no proof that the goods have been received by a customer, which can result in customer claims (McKinnon and Tallam 2003).

However, there are also problems potentially arising with *attended home delivery*. This relates to a time when a customer, or other family member, is available at home, and so is likely to restrict both the customer and the retailer during the allotted timeslot. So potential customer absence and retailer delay should be reflected in the planning and selection of the delivery slots offered to avoid the delivery having to be re-scheduled or cancelled. *Unattended delivery* tends to eliminate such problems but is not always possible or secure enough; however leaving a delivery with neighbours may be a solution when this problem arises, and could still be classified as an unattended delivery (McKinnon and Tallam 2003).

An alternative to an *attended delivery* is to leave the order in a defined pick-up point near the customer's home or work place, such as an office or apartment reception, which is staffed during the day. In some solutions, goods can also be delivered to a *home reception box* or *communal reception box* designated specifically for online deliveries (McKinnon and Tallam 2003). Some *reception boxes* are designed specifically for grocery delivery—incorporating cooling systems to keep products fresh (Punakivi et al. 2001).

A combined model, when goods are left in a designated location and the customer has to collect items, can be classified as one of many types of Click and Collect delivery.

3.2 Click and Collect

Click and Collect is in fact a diverse concept and provides a whole family of solutions, as it might include various types of collection, from pick-up points, such as an independent local store, a drive-through fuel station, an automated collection point in a shopping centre, or some other designated location.

There are several Click and Collect (pick-up) classifications, and new models are under development so classifications might change over time.

Hübner et al. (2016a, b) separated to *in-store collection, attached* to the store, and *solitary* (independent to the retailer's location). Collection points can be also divided into *attended* (staffed) and *unattended* without a worker (McKinnon and Tallam 2003).

3.2.1 Click and Collect: In and Near the Store

An *in-store collection* point is located inside a store, such as at a reception desk. This option is relatively easy to create at low cost. At the beginning, it could be an existing customer service desk incorporating an additional collection service. However, there are limitations of this solution, such as the opening time needs to coincide with the store opening hours. This approach also requires customers to enter the store, usually after parking a car, so a convenient parking place is needed to be able to easily carry goods to the car (Delfmann et al. 2011). This approach may provide additional sales opportunities, as when the customer visits the store, they might also purchase additional goods or services during the visit. To address some of the weaknesses of in-store collection, *attached points* were developed, both *attended* (discussed here) and *unattended* (discussed as part of *automated collection points*).

An *attached collection point*, could be a dedicated *drive-through point* next to the retail store, thus there is no need to enter a store and carry goods from the store. The customer arrives by car, after getting to the *drive-through point* goods are loaded into the car and the customer drives away. Such *attached points* can be open at different times to the store. Another option of *attached points*, still located close to the store is *lockers—or automated collection points*.

3.2.2 Click and Collect: Automated Collection Points

According to Visser et al. (2014), collection (pick-up) points can be divided into *staffed* and *non-staffed,* such as lockers, which may also be referred to as *pick stations*. An *automated collection point (automated locker, automated pick-up points)* can be located close to a store, serving as an *attached delivery point* (Hübner et al. 2016a, b). An *automated point* has an advantage as it typically allows for a consolidated delivery to the stations from the warehouse or fulfilment centre, thus they are more cost efficient than non-consolidated solutions (Visser et al. 2014). There is also no need to plan routing according to delivery windows, as for the home delivery. Deliveries can be made several times per day to restack the point after items are taken within an agreed time. *Automated non-staffed points* also tend to have more flexible opening times than staffed points, and may operate constantly 24/7. Those points to be used for grocery delivery are usually designed with dedicated sections for ambient and frozen goods. Another option is to place the collection point in places which are easily available to customers but not close to the store, known as *solitary collection points*. Such places need good access, such as a railway or petrol station.

3.2.3   Click and Collect: Solitary Collection Points

Retailers and third parties may provide a network of *staffed solitary points*. Pick-up is common in countries, such as France, where several thousands of points for drive-through collection are available (Hübner et al. 2016a, b). Such points can be located in a range of places, such as kiosks, newsagents, stationary and book shops, florists, dry cleaning, and fuel stations (Morganti et al. 2014), or any other place that is easily accessible for customers, especially those that experience high footfall and long opening hours. The majority of such points are in small, local, independent stores and service businesses (Morganti et al. 2014).

A *solitary collection point* may also be a separate location, such as a *drive-through station* (also referred to as *click & drive*) which is located away from the retail store. *Solitary collection points* need more substantial investments than an attached point (Hübner et al. 2016a, b). Some solitary points can be attached to a *shadow warehouse* that serves as local fulfilment centre (Delfmann et al. 2011).

3.3   Postal, Courier and Other Transport Services

Transport providers have different abilities to deliver to certain places and delivery windows. They may be specialised in specific types of goods and packages and include couriers, postal services, parcel operators, and trucking companies (Visser et al. 2014). However, some of these operators may not be suitable for grocery shopping, due to requirements of temperature control or security. However, in some countries, postal transportation can be also used for frozen and perishable goods delivery, using a cooled box (Delfmann et al. 2011). Postal services and couriers can be used for both home delivery (attended and unattended) as well as for delivery to Click and Collect points—lockers and attended collection points. Postal services may have an advantage if they cover the majority of the population. For example, in Switzerland 95% of the population can be reached this way (Delfmann et al. 2011).

3.4   What Else to Consider for Delivery and Collection?

While in the previous section, delivery and collection modes were presented, this section now considers other issues, with a focus on two important aspects; *delivery charges* and *time*. In addition, some of the back *office operations* are highlighted, such as preparation for delivery, collection, or routing.

3.4.1   Delivery Charges

Fees can be charged for delivery to the home or another address. The impact of fees still needs to be understood better. Huang and Oppewal (2006) noted that the existence of fees is not the main factor for channel selection, but the level of fees plays a role in consumer decision making. For example, a fee of 5 GBP appears to have less impact than the time to travel to a store. However, Hübner et al. (2016a, b) conclude that customers are still reluctant to pay delivery fees, while Delfmann et al. (2011) indicate that 75% of German customers are willing to pay for home delivery. There are differences in attitude to fees and the sensitivity to the level of charges between countries and customer segments. The fees charged are not only used to cover some of the costs of delivery, but also as a tool to manage demand in delivery slots, for example higher fees are used to reduce delivery demand at peak times.

3.4.2   Delivery Time and Slots

Delivery time has several variables, firstly it is time *from order to delivery*, reflected in days, or even part of the day (same, next day, by noon),. This is defined as *velocity* by Hübner et al. (2016a, b). Secondly, the *time slot*, or *delivery window*, is the part of the day, from a certain to a certain hour, when the delivery should arrive.

The delivery time relates to distance and area (city, village, or remote location). In some cases, delivery might not be available at all due to a excessive distance from the store or warehouse to the customer or the collection point.

The delivery window depends on population density (Boyer et al. 2009). It is important to stress that according to research by Murfield et al. (2017), omnichannel customers are particularly focused on time as one of the quality aspects, so on-time delivery is critical for this group of customers. The most common timeslots for grocery products are 1 or 2 hours. The more specific and shorter the time slot, the harder it is to fulfil the promise (Boyer and Hult 2005). There is also the issue of how *flexible* is the choice of the timeslot for the customer. In some cases, the timeslot is pre-defined by the retailer, and delivery is possible only during certain hours of the day, which can differ between weekdays and weekends. As mentioned earlier, different fees can be applied to manage the demand for different timeslots. A lower fee motivates the customer to select a timeslot which fits the retailer better (Hübner et al. 2016a, b). Another limitation of the delivery slot could be at low traffic times only, avoiding traffic jams, or along pre-planned routes.

3.4.3 Back Office Operations

While this chapter is focused on the customer perspective, the following subsections briefly indicate some issues to be considered by retailers, as these back office operations, also referred to as back-end fulfilment (Hübner et al. 2016a, b) influence the choice of options available to customers. Influential back operations include preparation for delivery, picking, and route planning.

3.4.4 Preparation for Delivery: Consolidation

Before being posted or collected, there is usually some consolidation of the items purchased. In grocery retail, we observe several options (Huang and Oppewal 2006). Among preparation for delivery we can distinguish between:

- *Warehouse based model*—items are collected from the warehouse; it could be a central or regional warehouse
- *Store pick-up model*—this is not much different to asking someone to do shopping, giving the shopping list, a worker picks the required items from the store.
- *Supplier model*—here delivery is directly from the supplier, which may be justified when handling specific or niche items (bulky items or organic).
- *Fulfilment centre model*—all items are delivered to dedicated consolidation centre, where they are prepared for shipment.
- *Mixed model*—some items are collected in the shop by a worker, while others are from the warehouse or from a supplier.
- *Mixed model, shop oriented*—as above, with the majority of items from the shop.
- *Mixed model, warehouse oriented*—as above, with the majority delivered directly from the warehouse.

There are also differences in how items can be picked, from manual pick in store, to semi and fully automated in warehouses and fulfilment centres (Hübner et al. 2016a, b). The picking mode should be aligned with delivery mode (Delfmann et al. 2011). Dedicated fulfilment centres may be referred to as *Dark Stores* or *Home Shopping Centres*.

3.4.5 Route Planning

To plan the most suitable route, planning tools, which include routing algorithms, are used. Route planning includes path of travel, location, number of stops, and delivery timeslot. It is determined by aspects such as truck capacity, sales volume, and customer density (Boyer et al. 2009). Routing can be optimised using dedicated software and adjusted by data that reflect real-time driving conditions (traffic jams, weather, accidents, and roadworks).

4 Methodology

This particular study started from desk research. The academic papers relevant to the topic were identified via e-journal databases and a Google Scholar search. After identifying key papers, a citation analysis was performed. The assembled papers were manually analysed for relevance, then reviewed to extract the main variables used. The second stage of research included a review of the web pages of leading British retailers, identifying the delivery conditions available. These conditions were put into tables, analysed, and mapped against the variables identified in academic papers. This analysis enabled the identification of aspects that were not yet covered in the literature. As a result, a new, modified, framework was proposed—a framework that syntheses the findings. The retailers for analysis were selected according to the following criteria:

- Highest level of market share in the United Kingdom (UK)
- Network of brick and mortar stores
- Online grocery sales via web page
- Grocery app-based shopping for mobile devices, such as smartphones
- Use of social media for communication with customers
- Both home delivery and Click and Collect services are offered to customers

Under these conditions for analysis, the following British retailers were selected: Tesco, ASDA, Sainsbury's, and Waitrose.

5 British Experience: From Customer View-Point

This section presents some facts about grocery retail in the UK, with a focus on online and omnichannel. The different delivery models are then presented and analysed.

5.1 British Grocery Retail Market

Online grocery retailing in the UK is recognised as world leading (Delfmann et al. 2011). In the UK, online grocery sales were 82 Euro per capita, while just 2 € in Germany, and 23 € in Switzerland (Delfmann et al. 2011).

The grocery market in the UK is complex, with many competitors beyond the traditional big four grocers: Tesco, Sainsbury's, Asda (Walmart), and Morrisons, and their smaller competitors, such as Waitrose. Niche players exist by focusing on the supply of particular products to niche consumers, such as organics, for example Able & Cole, and Riverford, or wine to budget consumers, such as Aldi. A national pure online competitor has also been established in the shape of Ocado, while international competitors, such as Amazon also provide food products. Indeed, underneath the surface, the situation is further complicated through supply chain collaborations. For example, Ocado supply logistics services to Morrisons, while Waitrose supply product to Ocado, and Morrisons supply fresh product to Amazon. Moreover, the boundaries between online grocery retailing and non-food retailing are increasingly blurring.

5.2   Delivery Options

The basic requirement used to select retailers for the analysis was that they offered both home delivery and Click and Collect. Among the leading grocery retailers only one, Morrisons, did not offer Click and Collect at the time of the analysis, and so is not analysed further. However, there is a difference between companies. Some are smaller in home delivery and larger in Click and Collect, especially as approaches to Click and Collect vary, such as the use of automated lockers. Table 1 provides an overview of the delivery options available in the UK among top grocery retailers. It is worth noting that "Home delivery" may actually be to any address in the UK, so this could be to a holiday cottage or work place, as well as the home.

In-store pick-up is a standard option, as it does not require substantial investments, compared to other solutions. However, the remaining options differ in popularity. Drive-through stations are in use, both attached to the store, as well stand alone, but still on the retail premises, such as at a hypermarket fuel station.

Table 1 Overview of the delivery options available in the UK among top grocery retailers as at November 2015

	Leading UK retailers				
Delivery or collection mode	Tesco	Asda	Sainsbury's	Morrisons	Waitrose
Home delivery	Yes	Yes	Yes	Yes	Yes
Click and collect pick-up					
Staffed					
In-store	Yes	Yes	Yes		Yes
Drive-through stations, attached	Yes	Yes	Yes		
Mobile pick-up points, from the van, solitary	Yes	Yes	Yes		
Other businesses	Yes				
Automated, lockers					
Attached to stores		Yes			Yes
Solitary lockers	Trialled	Yes	Trialled		Yes

The biggest difference is in use of automated lockers, which are newer solutions and require significant investment. Lockers can be classified as *attached*, located near the store (Asda, Waitrose), as well as *unattached,* such as lockers placed by Waitrose at railway stations. Online shopping is open to customers who are over 18 years old, with a further restriction for alcohol. Registration also requires a credit or debit card as well as a default delivery address.

5.3 Home Delivery

Home delivery is already an established delivery model. It is available from all the retailers analysed. The UK-based discounters (Lidl and Asda) do not offer delivery services, except for high value niche products, such as wine. Waitrose is the only retailer among those analysed that offers home delivery of goods bought in the brick and mortar shop at the time of the analysis.

Coverage, Availability Coverage of home delivery depends on the store network and internal policies. For example, Tesco covers most of the UK residential addresses, but some, such as camp sites, might be excluded. Sainsbury's states that it covers 88% of the UK mainland and part of Northern Ireland. All retailers provide search facilities for service coverage. The customer just has to input a postcode on the webpage to find out if delivery is available in the selected area.

Delivery Days and Times Deliveries are available 7 days a week from morning to late evening. There are differences between companies. Some might offer the same delivery time at weekends and weekdays, while others have reduced hours during the weekends and holidays. Delivery times by Waitrose vary between branches, and can be found online.

Delivery Timeslot Length Timeslots also differ between retailers. The most common windows are 1 or 2 hour slots. So called "flexible" slots (Flexi Saver Slot) are offered by Tesco. The customer selects a 4 hour slot, and then is informed by a text message which exact hour of those 4, the delivery will be conducted. This allows reducing waiting time for a customer and flexibility for Tesco to plan routing.

Delivery Velocity Typically, a customer should select the delivery at least day in advance, up to a certain cut-off time. However, limited same day deliveries are offered by Tesco and Sainsbury. For same day deliveries, the earliest delivery slot is 6–7 pm (Sainsbury). Asda allows additional products to be added to the order at any time up to midnight the day before the delivery timeslot, while removing goods must be done by 5 pm the day before.

Basket Value There are different approaches to the minimum size basket, but by value is the most common. The cost varies from £60 at Waitrose, via £40 at Tesco, to £25 for Asda and Sainsbury's. However, this is related to delivery fees, conditions, and models. Missing goods that are not available in-store, as well as substitutions proposed by the store, are not considered when defining the basket value. Asda also pointed that it might use a different basket value depending upon the relevant store. The basket value can be calculated for grocery only or for a mix of grocery and non-grocery items, depending on the approach by a retailer. Different basket values are employed for subscription models, which are discussed later.

Delivery Fees Delivery fees are associated with the value of the basket. In general, the higher the basket value the cheaper the delivery, with free delivery in exchange for a higher basket value. For example, at the time of writing, Waitrose had the highest basket value, £60, for free delivery. Sainsbury set their minimum basket value at £25, however under £40 is charged at £7 for delivery (£9 for same day delivery), while over £100 basket value is free delivery on Monday–Thursday after 2 pm, including same day delivery. A minimum delivery fee charge is also defined by Tesco (Minimum Basket Charge) and is £4. Asda has a minimum delivery charge of £1 and the fee depends on the day of the week, with the cheapest delivery during afternoons in midweek.

Subscription Models: Basket Value, Time and Fees Subscriptions models provide an alternative to fees. There are choices between monthly, quarterly, half yearly, or annual payments. Such programmes are called *Delivery Saver* by Tesco or *Delivery Pass* by Asda and Sainsbury's. Subscription programmes offer a choice of delivery fees, days, and defined minimum basket value. All programmes have similar features. A customer pays a regular fee, in exchange for free delivery, though minimum basket values still apply. A customer can select between lower cost mid-week working day deliveries (Tuesday to Thursday) or, for a higher fee, the whole seven days a week. In a subscription-based model, the customer is entitled to one delivery per day during the days defined in the conditions. To promote such an approach, retailers allow free monthly trials, as well as comparing regular, fee based orders against a subscription, to illustrate the lower cost subscription. As an extra benefit, customers may have priority during a high demand period, such as Christmas delivery slots (Tesco and Sainsbury). At Tesco, subscription members also do not pay for the Click and Collect service. Customers can select different programmes, periods, and fees (Table 2).

Table 2 Subscription programme—fees and lengths available as at June 2017

Anytime (7 days per week)	Longest period available 12 months	6 months period	Shortest period available
Tesco	£72	£42	£8 for 1 month
Sainsbury	£60	£35	£20 for 3 months
Asda	£60	£36	£8 for 1 month
Midweek (Tuesday-Thursday)			
Tesco	£36	£21	£4 for 1 month
Sainsbury	£30	£18	£10 for 3 months
Asda	£24	–	–

Asda customers, on subscription fees, can select *Recurring Slots,* which means a regular weekly delivery, at the same time of the day. Orders in a *Recurring Slot* should be submitted two days before the delivery is scheduled. Sainsbury introduced *greener grocery* delivery, which means slots that are linked to already scheduled trips, so that the delivery is not a single dedicated trip, i.e. the address is on, or close by, to an already planned route.

Delivery Addresses Subscription plans allows delivery to different addresses. Customers can also add extra information, helpful for the delivery, for example, how to access the home, which door to enter, or that the doorbell does not work. A typical fee based delivery is to the specified address provided at the online checkout.

Packaging In the UK, the retailer is required to charge for plastic bags by law. Hence, customers have a choice to select delivery with or without bags.

Receiving Person All companies state that orders and registration for online shopping is for over 18s. This is also reflected in delivery policies. Items can be delivered to anyone over 18, but alcohol, will be delivered to customers over 25 years old only, who additionally might be asked to provide a document to confirm their age. All retailers have similar restrictions in place.

Absence of Customer If a customer is absent, or if there is no one over 18 years old, then typically a delivery would be taken back, information left for the customer, and a new delivery time would be arranged. Drivers also try to phone the customer. There may be a charge for a redelivery.

Leaving Goods Drivers can refuse to carry goods into the property when the delivery is perceived as unsafe, without a clear permit to enter the property, or a significantly long distance. In flats without a lift, items would be delivered to communal areas. For business addresses, typically the retailer delivers to the reception, not to individual offices or desks.

5.4   Click and Collect

Click and Collect is available for all the retailers under analysis. Customers can order online, and then collect from the selected location. Both Tesco and Asda have substantial experience in Click and Collect, as this option was introduced around 2010. In the case of Sainsbury's, it is a more recent offering (from 2015), with the acquisition of Argos adding to the opportunities.

Click and Collect locations can be searched online, by postcode as well as availability for selection when the order is placed. Similarly to home delivery, Click and Collect might not be available in certain areas. There are differences between types of Click and Collection points, with the most common at the retail store, with drive-through attached points as well as solitary points and lockers also in use. While in-store collection can be considered as an established solution, the rest continue to evolve.

In-store collection is available for all the retailers under analysis. Click and Collect points, located in store, serve not only for grocery, but also for other product categories.

Click and Collect: Attached Drive-Through Points Drive though points, attached, are located near the store, in the car park. Such locations might simply consist of a canvas roof over a dedicated parking space with appropriate signage. In other cases, it may be of light construction; a small, standalone building with an extended roof over the parking place, so that the customer can collect items from staff. This may also serve as a collection point for non-food products, as well as grocery products.

Click and Collect: Staffed Solitary Collection Points Those are points that allow collection, but are not located close to the supermarket, for example, Tesco *community collection points*. These are places where a Tesco delivery van arrives at certain slots and waits for customers. Such points can be located at car parks at schools, shopping centres, or hotels.

Click and Collect: Automated Collection Points This is not a standard offer, and retailers are still experimenting with this form of collection. Automated collection points, while not staffed, require technology investments, especially in the case of grocery, where certain temperatures may need to be maintained. Typically, each order is split into three locker compartments, each with different temperatures of storage.

Coverage, Availability As for home delivery, Click and Collect depends on the store and collection point network coverage. A customer is able to find which store offers Click and Collect, or where and what type of collection point is available by inputting their postcode on the webpage. The relevant stores and points available nearby are listed and shown on a map. The available points are visible before the order is placed, with the most suitable point selected, so that the customer knows where to collect goods. Finally, point locations are confirmed after the order is placed and again in the reminder forwarded to the customer regarding the collection time.

Collection Days and Times Details, such as the opening times are available online, as in-store collection is aligned with store opening times. As a result collection times vary by branch. There are legal restrictions on store working hours on Sundays, so in-store collection is limited as it is linked to the store opening times. As there are limits to sell alcohol, collection hours also reflect those.

Automated, and attached, collection points might have longer opening hours, for example Asda opened an automated collection point at *Haydock Petrol Station*, which can be used around the clock.

Collection Slot Orders are waiting in certain collection places at the selected time slot. Collection slots (windows) booked by a customer are 2 or 1 hour long. In the case of collection from a van parked at a predefined place (solitary collection point), a slot is the only choice, as the van would drive away after parking during the allotted collection time. If a customer is late at the collection point, then in most cases they can still collect the items after contacting the retailer.

Collection Velocity Increasingly, retailers allow both next and same day collection. The cut-off point for next day (from 8 am) delivery is the day before. Same day delivery depends upon the time of the order: for example, order by 9 am, collection from 12 noon; order by 1 pm, collection by 4 pm. (Tesco). Same day delivery is usually not available on Sundays.

Basket Value There is no minimum basket value for Click and Collect at Tesco, However, there are different fees for baskets over and under £40. At Waitrose, the minimum value is £40 for grocery products. £40 is also the cut-off point at Sainsbury's, over £40 collection is free, while under £40 there are fees added, but there is no minimum basket value.

Changes in the Order Customers can change their orders up to a defined time. For example, Tesco allows changes in next day orders by 11.45 pm the night before collection to add and remove products, while same day collections can be modified until 1 pm on the day of collection.

Click and Collect Fees Tesco introduced fees for Click and Collect. The fees depend upon the time between order and collection as well as the value of the basket. It may also differ between stores and collection slots. Next day collection is free for orders over £40 and for customers subscribed to the *Delivery Saver* programme, other customers have to pay at least £4 if the order is below £40. Same day delivery fees are from £2. Other retailers have similar variations, from free collection to limited charges. Subscription members (for home delivery) generally do not pay for next day Click and Collect.

Packaging Packaging arrangements are the same as for home delivery, as determined by national (British) legislation. So, a customer can select a free option without a bag, or pay for plastic bags, similar to home delivery or store shopping.

Customer Identification, Proof of Age There are different approaches amongst retailers, as well as between collection from staffed or automated collection points (lockers). In all cases, customers receive messages with a confirmation of the order and collection details. To collect items from a Tesco point customers should show a Clubcard or identity document (ID) with picture. Asda does not require documents, but customers have to answer a security question. For age-restricted goods, proof of age (ID) is needed. For example, Sainsbury's requires the booking confirmation as well as identification documents, such as a card with name of the person who ordered goods and ID with a picture (passport, driving licence or other documents listed on the webpage).

Automated lockers can be accessed by data sent to a customer device (phone or smartphone). For example, Waitrose sends a text message as well as email with a PIN number required to access a locker. Customers may also have to provide date of birth and payment card details. Asda for its automated collection point also uses a QR code, generated by an app scanned at the automated point.

Loading Shopping into the Car At staffed collection points, workers might help with loading and carrying the shopping. For example, Sainsbury's offers this option. At staffed drive-through collection points staff can pack items, so in fact the customer might stay in the car while the items are loaded by the staff.

6 Synthesis: Customer-Centric Last Mile Framework for Omnichannel Retailing

While the earlier section provides a snapshot of grocery retail, this section synthesises all the findings and links them with the literature. In this section, a last mile framework for omnichannel retailing is proposed (Fig. 1).

Firstly, the basic questions should be answered (Fig. 1). Each of the elements are dependent upon one another to some degree, thus all factors should be analysed and reanalysed as other variables change.

The **How** to deliver is related to the factor **Where** current and prospective customers are located, this is influenced by the store network and has an impact on the time required to deliver, **When** delivery is possible, while all the factors have an impact on delivery **Costs**, including delivery fees.

The key decision points included in the *last mile framework for omnichannel retailing* are now discussed in more detail.

HOW to deliver provides several options within a home delivery, and/or Click and Collect model. The available delivery and collection points must be considered. The ability to form partnerships or acquisitions of existing networks influences the options for a company, and as result for the customer. The creation of a network of in-store collection points, as well as providing home delivery are common first steps in omnichannel development for existing store-based retailers. Attached collection points, such as drive-through, as well as automated collection points require more

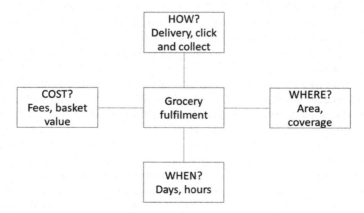

Fig. 1 Last mile framework for omnichannel retailing: key decision points

investment. Similarly, the establishment of solitary collection points, such as auto-mated points, for larger (drive-through), as well as smaller orders (railway stations) are relatively new in a grocery context, and require further analysis regarding the implications of the delivery models on the wider business. Solitary points, such as vans parked at certain times in certain places, look an easy option, but may be limited in reality.

WHERE to deliver is a basic issue. The delivery area, coverage and location of delivery and collection points are directly related to the store network and spatial location of customers. A dense store network should allow for easier Click and Collect for the customer. However, retailers can increase point density by cooperating with other businesses, which can be used as collection points, or retailers can invest in automated points. Home delivery generally requires a less dense network than Click and Collect, but is still influenced by the number and distribution of warehouses and/or stores, as well as the location of customers in relation to distribution points. The denser the customer network, the easier it is to justify introducing new delivery models. Thus we can expect growth of new delivery models in highly dense urban areas.

WHEN to deliver must be considered. Delivery days and times need to be set for each delivery channel, home delivery, as well as Click and Collect. This needs definition on which days the service is available, including weekends and national holidays. Which time slots are offered, from which to which hour. How service at weekends and during holidays differs from working days. How services differ between stores, which might have different working hours. Automated collection points can be considered to extend the time of operation. The time aspect is also related to the length of the delivery slots. The shorter the slot, the harder is to keep the promise of on-time delivery. The same is true for short lead times for Click and Collect, from placing an order until delivery or preparation. This could be critical as omnichannel customers are time sensitive and are expecting that a given promise will be fulfilled. Again, the higher density of the delivery and/or collection points, the easier it is to offer 1 hour slots and same day delivery. The issue of how early customers can place an order looks less problematic. However, as time to delivery increases there might be more desire to change the order. Thus there is also the challenge of defining a cut-off point for changing the order: adding, removing, or exchanging goods.

COST of the delivery is critical. Ideally, the delivery fee should generate profits but in practice this is rarely the case. Thus, issues such as fees, subscriptions, and the value of the shopping basket should be analysed. Fees must be considered together with customer loyalty and increased sales volumes via new channels. Free delivery may be acceptable for high basket values and/or high value customers. High fees might work as a barrier to use a service from a customer point of view. This may be especially true in the case of Click and Collect, where the customer has to spend time and effort to collect the ordered goods in any case.

As an alternative to individual delivery fees, subscription programmes may create regular income but may also encourage increased use for smaller baskets, as well as generate higher switching costs. Another issue is the use of dynamic pricing, where delivery fees vary for different slots and days, and so are used for capacity management and route planning. While midweek, and other low demand periods may be cheaper, there are also options to use pricing to group deliveries in one area or along a delivery route, reducing total costs and passing part of the cost reduction on to customers. Differentiation in delivery fees could be analysed depending on the area, reflecting delivery costs, influenced by travel time and distance.

There are also additional, but important issues to consider: such as communication with customers, customer identification, packaging and extra services offered. Communication with the customer is particularly important to run a smooth delivery system, as well as to deal with unexpected events. How should customers be reminded about the collection or delivery? Which communication channels and devices should be used and when? In some cases, a message may be used for customer identification at a collection point. There should be a clear procedure in place to assure that goods are passed to the right owner, not to mention the ability to fulfil all age restriction regulations. Packaging is a separate issue, such as what types of crates might be used, and the usage of plastic bags and relevant charges. It should be clearly defined what extra services are offered when goods are passed to the customer. In the case of a home order for example, what are the restrictions around carrying goods upstairs or to certain room. In the case of Click and Collect, what are the expectations regarding loading a car boot or carrying to the parking lot? To avoid misunderstanding, there is a need to clearly describe the process, so that the customer knows what to expect from staff. At the same time, staff should be trained to deliver the service at the defined level.

7 Dealing with Problems and Exceptions

As with all omnichannel development, there is a need to closely monitor processes and consider deviations from a pre-defined path. There should be procedures in place when things do not move in line with expectations, for example:

- customers misses a slot
- no adult is present at home during delivery
- customer has no identification document to confirm age
- smartphone of a customer is without battery power, so the customer cannot be identified in the usual way
- a redelivery is required
- a customer is too early or too late for a collection
- an item waits a long time for collection

Different scenarios should be analysed, responses defined, and communicated to both workers and customers. An exception, after being dealt with, should be added into the process description, so that staff members will be able to handle future similar issues arising or the system or process is redesigned.

The major differences between fulfilment modes can be broadly summarised in Table 3:

Table 3 Major relative differences between fulfilment modes for the retailer

How	Customer pick up		Customer receive at address	
	From store	From locker	Unattended	Attended
Locations	Few	→	Many	
Timing window (delivery slot)	Wide	→	→	Narrow
Dealing with exceptions or issues arising	Easy	→	→	Difficult
Cost of delivery	Low	→	→	High

8 Conclusions

Omnichannel retailing is increasing, and grocery is no exception. Home delivery and Click and Collect solutions in grocery retail will continue to develop. However, as mentioned earlier, omnichannel development is not a compulsory solution for all retailers. The decision about entering into an omnichannel strategy depends upon the overall retail strategy and target customers. This might change over time, as customers and technology changes. Thus, we can expect that not only traditional retailers will extend Click and Collect and other forms of online purchasing, but also that new online players will move into the market. We will witness experiments with different models, technologies, and automated collections. In the longer term, there may be hi-tech approaches, such as drones, self-driving cars, and robots, and also the crossover of new technology with traditional approaches, especially in emerging economies, where delivery models, may combine new and old, such as using mobile orders delivered by push bike. Shared economy models are also an option where the goods are delivered by people who are already shopping in a store or delivery by employees to others on their way home from a store or warehouse. In addition, while we can see situations today where goods are bought in a traditional shop then delivered to the home, this is not currently typical. However, in an ageing society, this could also become an expanding market. The relative sustainability, social, and environmental impact of new solutions should be also considered. There is space for innovation in fulfilment, creating new business models, developing new technologies, as well as rediscovering old ways of doing business in new, technology enabled forms.

8.1 Conclusions for Academia

This chapter discussed the last mile in omnichannel delivery, linking academic papers, and analysing existing practices. However, despite providing the *last mile framework for omnichannel retailing* which can be used for future research, this chapter, and the book as a whole, have also generated a multitude of questions, as many important issues are in flux, as online retailing and omnichannel development grows. The views of both retailer and customers need to be considered, as well as suppliers and third parties, including society and the environment. How are services perceived? What performance metrics are most effective in an omnichannel environment? How does each solution change performance? Which models are most suitable under what conditions? How do models differ across countries, regions, market segments, and product categories? As the topic is relatively new, there are plenty of research questions waiting to be solved, using different theoretical lenses and disciplines.

8.2 Conclusions for Practice

The findings of this chapter, and book, such as the decision points included in the *last mile framework for omnichannel retailing*, can be used by retailers and others on their journey into omnichannel development. Managers can use the findings to inform how to design their business systems and operations, as well as to consider potential costs and benefits. Meanwhile, as company learning, consumer behaviour, and new technology develops through both successes and failures, new delivery models will continue to emerge. This book provides a snapshot of the lessons for today, and suggests lessons for the future in omnichannel development.

8.2.1 Questions for Discussion and Review

1. Discuss the advantages and disadvantages of home delivery. Refer to your own experiences, as well as secondary data.
2. Automated lockers are the future of omnichannel grocery retail. Explain why you agree or disagree with this statement?
3. How can we divide different fulfilment models according to delivery, collection, and location?
4. Which model, fee, or subscription based service is better from a customer or retailer point of view?
5. What are the major issues that should be taken into consideration by retailers when designing a grocery delivery service?
6. On-time delivery is critical for omnichannel customers. What should be considered to assure that a promised delivery time is met?
7. Discuss the relationship between delivery fees and the value of a basket of goods. How can they be interlinked?
8. How can you plan to deal with exceptions and unexpected events in delivery processes?
9. How do grocery products differ from other product categories, such as fashion and furniture, from a delivery perspective?
10. If a store-based retailer would like to introduce a home delivery service, what should be examined before a decision is made?

References

Boyer, K. K., & Hult, G. T. M. (2005). Extending the supply chain: integrating operations and marketing in the online grocery industry. *Journal of Operations Management, 23*(6), 642–661.

Boyer, K. K., Prud'homme, A. M., & Chung, W. (2009). The last mile challenge: Evaluating the effects of customer density and delivery window patterns. *Journal of Business Logistics, 30*(1), 185–201.

Delfmann, et al. (2011). *Concepts, challenges and market potential for online food retailing in Germany*. No. 108. Working Paper, Department of Business Policy and Logistics, University of Cologne.

Ducret, R. (2014). Parcel deliveries and urban logistics: Changes and challenges in the courier express and parcel sector in Europe—The French case. *Research in Transportation Business and Management, 11*, 15–22.

Hagberg, J., Sundstrom, M., & Egels-Zandén, N. (2016). The digitalization of retailing: An exploratory framework. *International Journal of Retail and Distribution Management, 44*(7), 694–712.

Huang, Y., & Oppewal, H. (2006). Why consumers hesitate to shop online: An experimental choice analysis of grocery shopping and the role of delivery fees. *International Journal of Retail and Distribution Management, 34*(4/5), 334–353.

Hübner, A., Holzapfel, A., & Kuhn, H. (2016a). Distribution systems in omnichannel retailing. *Business Research, 9*(2), 255–296.

Hübner, A., Kuhn, H., & Wollenburg, J. (2016b). Last mile fulfilment and distribution in omnichannel grocery retailing: A strategic planning framework. *International Journal of Retail and Distribution Management, 44*(3), 228–247.

McKinnon, A. C., & Tallam, D. (2003). Unattended delivery to the home: An assessment of the security implications. *International Journal of Retail and Distribution Management, 31*(1), 30–41.

Morganti, E., Dablanc, L., & Fortin, F. (2014). Final deliveries for online shopping: The deployment of pickup point networks in urban and suburban areas. *Research in Transportation Business and Management, 11*, 23–31.

Murfield, M., et al. (2017). Investigating logistics service quality in omnichannel retailing. *International Journal of Physical Distribution and Logistics Management, 47*(4), 263–296.

Picot-Coupey, K., Huré, E., & Piveteau, L. (2016). Channel design to enrich customers' shopping experiences: Synchronizing clicks with bricks in an omnichannel perspective–the Direct Optic case. *International Journal of Retail and Distribution Management, 44*(3), 336–368.

Piotrowicz, W., & Cuthbertson, R. (2014). Introduction to the special issue information technology in retail: Toward omnichannel retailing. *International Journal of Electronic Commerce, 18*(4), 5–16.

Punakivi, M., Yrjölä, H., & Holmström, J. (2001). Solving the last mile issue: reception box or delivery box? *International Journal of Physical Distribution and Logistics Management, 31*(6), 427–439.

Visser, J., Nemoto, T., & Browne, M. (2014). Home delivery and the impacts on urban freight transport: A review. *Procedia-Social and Behavioural Sciences, 125*, 15–27.

Wojciech Piotrowicz (PhD Brunel, MA Gdańsk, PGDipLATHE Oxon) is Associate Professor in Sustainable Supply Chains and Social Responsibility, at Hanken School of Economics and HUMLOG Institute, Helsinki, Finland. In addition he is an International Research Fellow at the University of Oxford, Saïd Business School and is a member of Wolfson College, Oxford. His research is related to information systems, logistics, supply chain management, performance measurement and evaluation, with a focus on transitional countries and retail contexts. Wojciech has considerable experience as a member of large international research projects within both the public and private sectors, working with organisations such as Intel, BAE Systems, the European Commission and the Polish government. He is recipient of Outstanding and Highly Commended paper awards from the Emerald Literati Network for Excellence.

Richard Cuthbertson is a Senior Research Fellow and Research Director at the Oxford Institute of Retail Management at Saïd Business School, University of Oxford and Vice-Principal of Green Templeton College, University of Oxford. His research interest lies in understanding and assessing the challenges of the increasingly digital world on retail, particularly through technology innovation and the use of customer data. His work is international in scope, looking at how retail practice and policy are developing in countries like India and China, and he regularly acts as a consultant to retailers and governments. He is author of over 100 published articles and has worked with many companies, including Tesco, Sainsbury's, P&G, Casino, T-Mobile, BP, Abbey, IBM, KPMG and BCG. Richard is a ex-Board member of the Charity Retail Association. He was awarded the Emerald Literati Network Award for Excellence (twice) and the Pegasus Prize for eBusiness Future Insights (2006).

Printed by Printforce, the Netherlands